Mammals of the Pacific States

California, Oregon, and Washington

Lloyd G. Ingles

Stanford University Press, Stanford, California

This book was originally published in 1947 as *Mammals of California*.
A revised edition, *Mammals of California and Its Coastal Waters*,
was published in 1954. The present edition, which for the first time
extends the coverage of the book to Washington and Oregon,
was first published in 1965.

Stanford University Press
Stanford, California
Copyright © 1947, 1954, 1965 by the Board of Trustees
of the Leland Stanford Junior University;
"An Artificial Key to the Skulls (except Cetacea), " in Chapter 4,
copyright 1949 by Lloyd Glenn Ingles
Printed in the United States of America
Cloth ISBN 0-8047-0298-5
Paper ISBN 0-8047-1843-1
Original printing 1965

Last figure below indicates year of this printing:
99 98 97 96 95 94 93 92 91 90

To all my helpers:
Students, colleagues, and friends

Preface

This book, like its two previous editions, has been written for all persons who wish to study mammals, particularly those species that are now found wild in California, Oregon, and Washington. It is not intended to be a treatise, but rather a book that can be used in college classes dealing with mammals and as a reference for the layman or field worker who not only needs to know the correct names of Western mammals, but also wishes to learn something about their interesting adaptations and ways of life.

Many years of teaching zoological science have convinced me that students must study *mammals* if they are to understand and appreciate the biological concepts and principles as they apply to modern mammalogy. This book is an aid in the classification of mammals, their geological history, their range and distribution, their habitats in the biotic communities, and their status in the ecosystems they inhabit.

The writer is convinced that species, not subspecies or races, are the units that should be emphasized with beginning students. Here only such well-known animals as deer will be considered subspecifically. The genera names will be those used by Walker (1964). The species names, except for more recently suggested changes, will be those used by Miller and Kellogg (1955).

Because the book is intended mostly for beginners in mammalogy, it is assumed that the reader will have had general zoology and will be familiar with certain general terms and principles. For persons unfamiliar with the use of the traditional type of key there are drawings showing external features of all the species in the three states. These drawings are accompanied by brief descriptions of each mammal. Photographs, made by the writer except as credited otherwise, serve as supplements in identification. They were made to show as many of the external features as possible while the animals were wild or held as temporary captives. Range maps are included for most groups. These are a valuable aid in the identification of most species because they represent the known *present* range.

The game departments of all three states and many mammalogists have given valuable aid and advice in the construction of these maps. The keys were checked with students in several college and university classes in the three states over a period of three years. Many modifications were suggested and accepted as a result of these trial runs. Finally, the range maps and keys were tested by the writer during two summers (1962 and 1963) in field work carefully planned for that purpose.

The group discussions of certain taxa often include current or relatively recent researches emphasizing physiological and behavioral adaptations, with the hope of stimulating the reader to investigate further in the cited references or to initiate similar studies of his own.

It must be emphasized that no part of this book is considered definitive, and when used as a textbook it should be supplemented by lectures, laboratory exercises, and selected readings. It is hoped that it will serve as a tool—as a stimulant for further study by those who use it for a better understanding of mammals and particularly their conservation.

Conservation has been defined as the wise use of natural resources. Conservation practice, then, implies intelligent action and, where any vertebrate animal is involved, should first be preceded by a planned search for knowledge about its niche, its position in the ecosystem, and the peculiarities of its population.

There is a great need for interested people to do these kinds of investigation, but there is an even greater need for adequately prepared teachers and camp and club leaders, especially among young people, to disseminate the truth about predators and their prey in order to dispel erroneous information and even folktales about some of our most valuable but little-known animals. There must then be others who, understanding these natural biological relationships in an ecosystem or population, must strive for laws to protect mammals for the national good and not merely for the misguided, selfish, and often misinformed pressure groups.

Laboratory biologists have used certain mammals in their study of physiology, experimental medicine, and comparative psychology. One might expect that these detailed studies would have resulted in a better understanding of mammals as a class, as compared with fishes, amphibians, reptiles, or birds. Such, however, has not been the case, and knowledge of great numbers of wild species has scarcely been advanced at all by such studies. Unfortunately, too many laboratory biologists have had a tendency to apply their findings on the white rat or guinea pig to mammals in general. Biologists without field knowledge about mammals might well be expected to make such mistakes.

It is regrettable that many scientists are being *trained* today in depth in their fields but are not being *educated*, in that they lack the necessary foundational breadth to support their specialized training. Only by studying a mammal in its total environment can its peculiar anatomy, physiology, and behavior be understood and fully appreciated. A study of the habits and ecology alone can give information regarding the normal modes of life of the various species. This kind of study can prevent the many oversimplifications and immature generalizations about mammals. Biology is the study of organisms, and biologists must be concerned not only with molecular and cellular biology, with organs and systems, but also with whole individuals, their populations, and the ecosystems involving many species.

The atomic age will doubtless see many changes in the study of mammals. Studies of fallout radiation suggest many new problems in mammalogy. It has been demonstrated that certain isotopes that fell on a pasture hundreds of miles from the site of bomb explosions have been concentrated and have showed up in the milk of cows feeding on the vegetation. This can also happen when deer feed on such energized vegetation and are then eaten by man or carnivores. Likewise, meadow mice and grasshoppers that concentrate an isotope in their bodies may, when eaten, pass it on for further concentration in the bodies of foxes, skunks, and other carnivorous mammals. The effects of such doses of radiation on wild mammals are yet to be studied. However, it is well known that radiation may greatly increase chromosomal aberrations and gene mutations, which may result in inviable gametes and varying degrees of sterility. This could conceivably reduce a population of a species in time, and it certainly could produce a greater variety of phenotypes, which might speed up evolution. Since most changes in genes have been shown to be deleterious under natural conditions, however, it is doubtful if the species would immediately profit from such an increased mutation rate.

Perhaps more serious are the pernicious pathological effects of radiation on an animal's body when relatively large amounts of it are received. Certainly more research is needed on these aspects of the effects of radiation on all kinds of organisms.

A marked decrease, or increase, in the population of many mammals, especially in carnivorous species, could upset the ecological relationship of an entire biotic community. The subtle effects of radiation on populations of mammals may not be evident until several generations have acquired the genetic aberrations and mutations.

These are but a few of today's problems in mammalogy that challenge the eager investigator.

Finally, there is another reason why we study mammals. Interested people simply found it fun to investigate these furred and hairy creatures. These scientifically minded people for the most part had no thought about how significant their work might be to agriculture, to forestry, or to health. Their sole interest was to enjoy the thrills of discovery of new truths about nature, and by so doing, they created a stockpile of data from which the more practical principles of conservation and control could be effected.

Many people have helped in one capacity or another. To them I am very grateful. Besides Mrs. Elizabeth Ingles, who helped with the field work and criticized the manuscript, there are others whose interest and efforts must be given the highest recognition possible. Mrs. Winona Toffoli did all the new drawings and helped allocate them in the manuscript. Assistance has been received from many people in the Northwest: from Washington, Dr. Murray Johnson of Tacoma and Mr. F. H. Armstrong of Naches; from Oregon, Mr. Alex Walker and Mr. William Wick of Tillamook, Mr. Will

Koogler of Reedsport, Mr. Eugene Kridler and Mr. John Scharff of the Malheur Wild Life Reserve, Mr. Roy Albrights of Dayton, Dr. Kenneth M. Walker of Monmouth, and Mr. Chester E. Kebbe, Mr. Willard E. Nelson, and Dr. George Fisler of Portland.

Those living in California who have been especially helpful are Mr. and Mrs. Arvil Parker of Courtland, Dr. Dallas Sutton of Chico, Dr. George Bartholomew of Los Angeles, Dr. Robert Orr of San Francisco, Dr. Thomas C. Poulter of Palo Alto, Dr. Richard E. MacMillen of Claremont, Dr. Aryan Roest of San Luis Obispo, Dr. Velma Vance of Los Angeles, Dr. Harold J. Severaid of Sacramento, Mr. Robert Bell and Mr. Norman Cleaver of Bodie, Mr. Keith Murray of Berkeley, Dr. Charles A. McLaughlin of Los Angeles, Dr. Galen Clothier of Cotati, Mr. Harold Williams of Santa Barbara, Mrs. Rita Middleton of Long Beach, Dr. John Goodman of Redlands, Mr. Harry N. Coulombe of Los Angeles, Miss Ann Hopping of Fresno, and Mrs. Diane Fouts of Fresno.

L.G.I.

Contents

Part I. General Accounts of Mammals

1. Mammals and Mammalogy

Mammals are hairy or furry creatures that are widely distributed over the earth. Man himself is a mammal, and since time far before recorded history he has depended on various kinds of mammals for food, for clothing, and for carrying heavy loads. Although use of the mammal as a beast of burden has virtually ceased in the United States in the last 25 years, it is still used to do the heavy work over most of the world. Mammals are important as a source of food and clothing, as carriers of disease, in sport and recreation, and as major participants in biotic communities that more subtly affect the ways of living of all peoples.

Mammalogy is the zoological science dealing with the study of mammals. Formerly it was concerned almost entirely with *systematics* or *taxonomy*, but more recently it has tended toward the functional or physiological point of view. Today, the study of mammals deals directly with such fields as adaptive morphology, adaptive physiology, populations, genetics, and ecology, and these may cross several taxonomic categories.

The recent emphasis on different levels in biology from the molecular upward is mostly applicable to mammals at or above the level of the whole organism. While much work is indeed only conducted on the molecular and cellular levels and on organs of mammals, most of mammalogy today is concerned with life histories, adaptations, populations, and the relatively unknown parts that mammals play in ecosystems (see p. 28).

This book assumes a basic knowledge of elementary zoology. The chapters in the first part are concerned with briefly introducing the reader to other concepts and zoological information as they apply to mammals, particularly on the Pacific Coast. Briefly covered are morphology, classification, ecology, and geology, with suggestions on how to study mammals. Although it is true that mammalogy is today largely concerned with descriptive data, more and more mathematical formulas and models based on descriptive and experimental data are encountered in publications based on field work, as the science becomes more quantitative. The serious student should prepare himself mathematically to understand these investigations and to carry them out himself.

The second part of this book is somewhat traditional in its organization of the taxonomic groups. However desirable it may be to understand biological principles and concepts as they apply to mammals, a student certainly must also be well grounded in classification and anatomy. The primary purpose of this book is to familiarize the reader with mammals, particularly as they are represented in the Pacific States—California, Oregon, and Washington. The chapters in this part of the book include not only the keys, drawings, photographs, and brief descriptions of the mammals of the particular orders represented in the Pacific States, but also general accounts of some of their representatives as they illustrate various biological principles and concepts. In some cases, these accounts point out the direction of current research. Again, as in the first part, these chapters are introductory and are intended to stimulate the interest of the student to read further and to investigate for himself.

Distinguishing Characteristics

Body Temperature. Mammals are a successful class in the animal kingdom, probably in large part because they are "warm-blooded" or homoiothermal (endothermal). Besides having hair, mammals also nourish their young with milk. The mammals and birds differ from other classes of vertebrates, which are "cold-blooded" or poikilothermal (ectothermal). The body temperature of an active mammal or bird does not usually vary with changes in temperature in the external environment as does the body temperature of a frog or snake. The body temperature of an active mammal averages a little less than 100° F. and may not vary over 0.5° F. throughout a 24-hour period (Lyman, 1963). The mammal is cooled by evaporating water and warmed by increasing metabolism. Homoiothermy is apparently controlled by the hypothalamus of the brain. All mammals when active except the monotremes (duckbills and spiny anteaters) and edentates (tree sloths, armadillos, and anteaters) have remarkably even temperatures.

Scattered among the various other orders are species that can allow their temperature to drop, with an accompanying decrease in metabolism. This condition allows the animals to sink into a *torpor,* in which the body temperature may be far below its temperature when active. This period of torpor is most frequently known as *hibernation.* The term means "to pass the winter" and is not wholly appropriate, since certain mammals become torpid during summer or autumn (*estivation*), whereas others (certain pocket mice) may become torpid only during periods of inclement weather, and still other mammals (bats) may experience a period of dormancy during the day (*diurnation*). The place used by animals during periods of dormancy is their *hibernaculum.*

Some mammals become very obese before becoming torpid (marmots and ground squirrels), others make food caches in their dens, on which they occasionally feed after a brief arousal (chipmunks). The onset of these periods of *hypothermy* and torpor does not always seem to be dependent on the *ambient temperature* (temperature of the surrounding air), since it may occur anywhere when the environmental temperature is between 32° and 86° F. (Bartholomew and Cade, 1957).

The picture of an animal about to experience hypothermy varies with the species. Generally speaking, the animal becomes lethargic. It coils up to form (as nearly as possible) a sphere (which offers the least surface per volume). Its heart rate may be reduced to 2 or 3 beats per minute, although the blood pressure may remain quite high. The respiratory rate may be reduced to perhaps less than one breath per minute. The temperature of the animal may be within a degree or two of the temperature of the nest, as long as that temperature remains above 32° F. Death occurs if the animal's temperature drops below freezing. The metabolic rate is greatly reduced. Arousal may require only minutes or a few hours. It usually is accompanied by violent shivering before the active condition is obtained and the high metabolic rate is resumed.

Lyman (1963) believes that hibernation is a controlled process which has been developed through evolution to permit the animal to escape periods of stress and unfavorable environmental conditions. It has been developed independently in several different groups, though it does not occur in certain orders, such as the artiodactyls and the carnivores. It is a way of life that certain modern mammals have evolved which enables them to adapt to more niches (see p. 27) in a greater range of environments by conserving energy, usually during times of food shortage or inclement weather conditions.

Limb Modifications. Mammals have become adapted in the course of evolution to living in nearly all kinds of environments. The most striking adaptations are concerned with the different means of locomotion.

Mammals that live mostly on the ground are *ambulatory* (walking) or *cursorial* (running). They may be *plantigrade* if they walk or run with the heel on the surface, such as men, shrews, or bears; they are *digitigrade* if they run on their toes, as do rabbits, bobcats, and coyotes; others run on the tips of their toes and are *unguligrade,* such as deer.

The mammals that live in trees are referred to as *arboreal.* They usually have long toes terminating in sharp claws, as in squirrels; they may also have a grasping hand or foot, as in monkeys, or they may have merely a soft pad under the foot, as in the African hyrax, which enables the animal to climb nearly vertical trees far above the ground. Some arboreal mammals are also *glissant* or *volant* and are able to glide considerable distances from tree to tree, like the flying squirrel or the colugo of the Philippine Islands.

Bats are the only mammals with the capacity for *true flight.* The forelimb of a bat has been modified by the greatly elongated fingers, with thin webs between the digits and connecting them with the hind limbs and the tail.

The burrowing or *fossorial* mammals show remarkable modifications of the forefeet for digging. The broad hand of a mole or the long claws of a pocket gopher are found duplicated on other continents in other fossorial mammals that are only distantly related to our own burrowing species. This phenomenon is called parallel or *convergent evolution*.

The limbs of truly *aquatic* mammals have undergone tremendous modifications. In the seals and their relatives the limbs have assumed the shape of paddles; in the whales the forelimbs are flippers, and only internal vestiges remain of the posterior girdle and its limbs. Except for the whales, mammals have the digits terminated with horny covering called *claws*, *nails*, or *hoofs*. Claws terminate the tip of the digit and are curved and pointed. Nails are at the end on the dorsal side of the digit and are usually flat. Hoofs surround the blunt end of the digit and are not curved or acutely pointed.

Teeth. The teeth of mammals usually indicate the type of food that constitutes their main diet. Except for the baleen whales, anteaters, and pangolins, all adult mammals have teeth. There are usually two sets of teeth (*diphyodont*): the *milk teeth* and the *permanent teeth*. The milk teeth of the pinnipeds have degenerated to such an extent that only a single set of teeth appear (*monophyodont*).

The tooth of a mammal is an ectodermal structure. Its bulk is largely *dentine*, which is composed mostly of calcium phosphate. The interior mass of the tooth is the pulp cavity, containing nerves and small blood vessels. Covering the outside of the dentine is usually a thin, hard calcareous layer of *enamel*. A layer of cement covers the root of the tooth and sometimes also the various folds or re-entrant angles of the crown (fig. 42).

The front teeth are *incisors* followed by a single pointed *canine*, then the *premolars*, and finally the *molars*, each with two or more roots. The molars are not normally shed, but the premolars are deciduous.

The primitive dental formula for placental mammals is considered to be 3-1-4-3/3-1-4-3 $\times$ 2 = 44. This formula is applicable only to the permanent dentition. In other words, on each side of each jaw of a primitive placental mammal there were three *incisors*, one *canine*, four *premolars*, and three *molars*, making a total of 44 teeth (fig. 7). In the course of their evolution most mammals have changed from this primitive number to fewer teeth, although some of the toothed whales have far exceeded it. The dental formulas of the genera of mammals occurring in the Pacific States are of great value as an aid in identifying skulls of mammals (p. 484).

Rodents and lagomorphs have large chisel-shaped ever-growing incisors, which are sharpened as the animal rubs the cutting edges together. The tusks of an elephant are the enormously enlarged second incisor teeth.

Canine teeth are lacking in rodents and lagomorphs and on the upper jaws of most hoofed mammals. They may grow to 20 inches or more in length in the walruses. Most mammals use the canines in fighting and tearing flesh; hence, these teeth are best developed in the carnivores. The lower canine of many artiodactyls has become shaped like an incisor (*incisiform*) and lies close to the third or outside incisor. The 9-foot-long spiral tusk projecting ahead of a narwhale is the left upper canine tooth.

Some mammals, such as the pinnipeds, have molars and premolars that resemble each other, although in most mammals they are differently shaped. The molar usually has a more complicated crown and more roots. Most flesh-eating mammals, like many of the fissiped carnivores, have the fourth upper premolar (Pm⁴) and the first lower molar (M₁) developed into scissor-like shearing teeth (*carnassials*) for cutting flesh. These are known also as *sectorial* teeth.

Some mammals, such as man and pigs, have cusped (*bunodont*) low-crowned molars. The deer has the cusps changed into crescents (*seleno-dont*). The cow also has selenodont molars but they are high-crowned (*hypsodont selenodont*).

The *lophodont* molar is a tooth with transverse ridges with low places between them. The extinct mastodon had low-crowned teeth of this type (*bunodont lophodont*). Modern elephants, however, have high-crowned molars with laminations running across them (*hypsodont lophodont*).

The crowns of the molar teeth of mammals have had an interesting evolutionary history as they have evolved from their simplified reptilian progenitors. There are various theories concerned with the evolution of mammalian molars, but perhaps the best known and most widely accepted of these is the *tribosphenic* molar theory, proposed almost a century ago by the famous paleontologist Edward D. Cope and elaborated on by Henry Fairfield Osborn and William K. Gregory. It is also known as the Cope-Osborn-Gregory theory of molar development. Much of the knowledge of the evolution of mammals through geologic time has been based upon changes that various groups have made from this tribosphenic condition. The primitive pantotheres that lived in Jurassic times have been assigned as possible ancestors of both the marsupial (pouched) mammals and the placental mammals of modern times because of the construction of their molar teeth.

The tribosphenic theory holds that three cones or cusps on a molar of some ancestral reptile were moved out of their original straight line to form *trigons* (upper jaw) and *trigonids* (lower jaw) (fig. 1). These cusps or cones from anterior to posterior are the *paracone, protocone,* and *metacone* on the teeth of the upper jaw, and the *paraconid, protoconid,* and *meta-conid* on the teeth of the lower jaw. According to the theory, the protocone moved out of line lingually, or the paracone and the metacone moved out of line labially, to produce the *trigon* of a molar on the upper jaw. The movement on the lower jaw was just the reverse, to produce a *trigonid* that would shear with the upper trigon (fig. 1). This tribosphenic molar thus provided a base from which the molars of all living mammals (except the Monotremata) have been evolved. The original three cones or cusps have been supplemented by many smaller cones (*conules* and *styles*), a *hypo-cone* (which may not be homologous in the different groups), ridges, and crests, which are sometimes called *lophs* or *lophids*. The cusps in the various groups of mammals have become specialized in response to the action

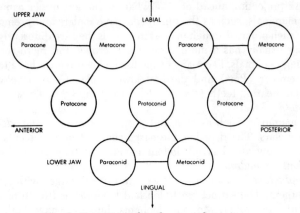

Fig. 1. Primitive tribosphenic molar pattern.

of natural selection on genetically based variations, resulting in teeth adapted to perform certain functions better than could be expected by the primitive trigons and trigonids. The success of the various mammals in eating different kinds of foods and then in occupying a variety of habitats has been largely attributed to the evolution of their teeth.

One example of such specialization is found in the harvest mice (*Reithrodontomys*), which feed on a great variety of seeds, fruits, and green vegetation (fig. 2). The features on the molars of other cricetid mice may be compared with the diagram of the molars of harvest mice or deer mice (figs. 3, 35).

Reproduction, Development, Maturity, and Longevity. Mammals nourish their young while they are developing within their bodies. Exceptions are the egg-laying monotreme mammals of the Australian region.

The young of the *metatherian* or *pouched mammals* are born, after a short period of gestation, as immature "larval" animals that usually immediately find their way into the mother's pouch, where they attach themselves to the teats and finish their development.

The breeding season of *eutherian* or *placental mammals* may extend throughout the year or be limited to a few weeks. During *oestrus,* the period of sexual heat, or shortly thereafter, the female is bred by *copulation* with the male. The ova are *fertilized* by the spermatozoa, and the *implantation* of the fertilized ova into the wall of the uterus takes place. The *placenta* develops from both the embryo's fetal membranes and the mother's uterus, and through the placenta nourishment and oxygen pass from the mother's bloodstream to the embryo. Waste products from the embryo's bloodstream pass into the bloodstream of the mother, from which they are eliminated. After a period of *gestation,* the young are born (*parturition*). The young are then nursed by the mother through her mammary glands, which secrete milk which is sucked through the *nipples* of the teats.

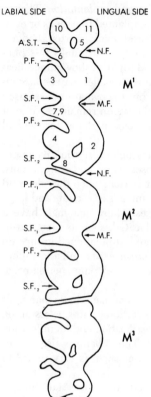

LABIAL SIDE   LINGUAL SIDE

A.S.T.
P.F.,
S.F.,
P.F.,
S.F.,
P.F.,

N.F.
M.F.
N.F.

M¹

1. Protocone
2. Hypocone
3. Paracone
4. Metacone
5. Anteroloph
6. Anterior cingulum
7. Mesostyle
8. Post cingulum
9. Mesoloph
10. Anterior external conule
11. Anterior internal conule

A.S.T. Anterior secondary fold
P.F., First primary fold
S.F., First secondary fold
P.F., Second primary fold
S.F., Second secondary fold
M.F. Major fold
N.F. Minor fold

M²

S.F.,
P.F.,
S.F.,

M.F.

M³

Fig. 2. Diagram of the crown pattern of the right upper molars of a harvest mouse (*Reithrodontomys*) (modified after Hooper, 1952).

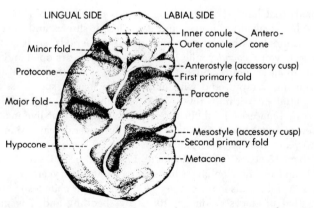

LINGUAL SIDE   LABIAL SIDE

Minor fold

Protocone

Major fold

Hypocone

Inner conule ⟩ Antero-
Outer conule ⟩ cone
Anterostyle (accessory cusp)
First primary fold
Paracone
Mesostyle (accessory cusp)
Second primary fold
Metacone

Fig. 3. First left upper molar M¹ of *Peromyscus maniculatus*.

Some eutherian mammals have a period of *delayed implantation*. That is, after the ovum is fertilized, it does not become implanted for weeks or even months after breeding has taken place. The weasel, mink, marten, badger, and the pinnipeds have such a delayed implantation. In minks this phenomenon is associated with the length of day. Many bats show a modification of the ordinary type of reproduction in that the females may be *inseminated* with spermatozoa in the fall of the year, but the ova are not released from the ovary until the spring. All this time the sperm remain capable of reproduction in the female's reproductive system, perhaps for several months.

The position of the testes varies in different mammals. In primitive mammals the testes are abdominal, as they are in insectivores and chiropterans. In others they are abdominal until the breeding season, when they descend into a *scrotum* outside the body cavity. Such mammals as rodents and lagomorphs have a temporary descent of the testes. Many mammals have a scrotum in which the testes are permanently located, such as man, carnivores, and artiodactyls. When the testes in these last-mentioned groups do not descend, a condition known as *cryptorchidism* exists and the higher body temperatures in the body cavity affect the developing spermatozoa, frequently causing sterility.

Another structure in the reproductive apparatus of many male mammals is the *os penis* or *baculum*. This bone, found in certain groups, is assuming a position of considerable importance in the classification and identification of various difficult species (figs. 137, 146, 159). The *os penis* is also of considerable importance in age determination and, as such, is very useful in wildlife management work.

The breeding season for many mammals is restricted to a certain time of the year. This normally corresponds to a season when food is most abundant. Light and length of day are factors that seem to be important, frequently through hormonal control, in the breeding season of many mammals.

Animals that have short gestation periods usually have *altricial* young that are born naked, with eyes and ears closed; shrews and mice are examples. Animals with relatively long gestation periods, such as the hare and deer, have *precocial* young that have eyes and ears open and are able to move about soon after birth (figs. 84, 248). Growth in most mammals while nursing is rapid, and with many of the smaller species sexual maturity is attained within a few weeks. Certain meadow mice (*Microtus*) attain sexual maturity in about three weeks. Species that live many years, however, may not become sexually mature for several years. Man requires 12 to 15 years, the Sumatran rhinoceros about 20 years, and the Indian elephant about 15 years. (*Traité Zoologie*, **17**, Part 1, p. 766, says 13–14 years for male and female elephants; unusual cases at eight years.)

Molts. As mammals mature, the coat of fur or hair changes in an orderly process that produces distinct patterns by shedding and new growth at least once a year. These patterns are peculiar to the species concerned.

The fur of a nestling young is usually replaced by the *juvenal pelage*, which is frequently different in color and texture from that of the *subadult* and *adult* pelages which follow. Mammals that have two or more molts per year may have an entirely different appearance in the different pelages (figs. 93, 94). The winter pelage of a mammal may have long *guard hairs* and thick *underfur* compared with its summer pelage, in which mostly coarse guard hairs may be present.

Several mammals in summer pelage have grayish or *agouti* hairs, banded with different color patterns. They may shed this pelage to become pure white in winter. Such changes appear to be genetically based but respond to the environment differently in the different groups of mammals. Hall (1951) reports that long-tailed weasels (*Mustela frenata*) from a population that normally is white in winter will continue to turn white in winter when moved to a region where this species does not change its color. Weasels from populations that do not change to white in winter, when moved into regions where the native population does change to a white pelage, still retain their brown color. Long eras and periods of geologic time by selection and evolution seem to have fixed this character genetically so firmly that moving to a different environment does not change it. There are other mammals, however, such as collared lemmings (*Dicrostomyx groenlandicus*) from Greenland, which lose their capacity to change to a white pelage after a year or more in a milder climate.

A remarkable case of evolution in action with selection on the pelage of lagomorphs is reported for the varying hare (*Lepus timidus*) of northern Europe. A couple of these hares were introduced into the Faroe Islands about 1854. This pair and their offspring turned white for several years even though there was no snow present. They were very conspicuous in the dark landscape and were an easy mark for predators. Twenty years later only half of the population was white in winter. Thirty years later about one-fourth of the population became white, and when a study was made in 1930 none of the hares had changed to white in winter. Apparently natural selection had eliminated the gene that brings about white pelage in these hares in winter in less than three-quarters of a century.

The longevity of mammals ranges from that of the dusky shrew (*Sorex obscurus*), which seldom lives beyond 16 months, to man, whose life span sometimes exceeds 100 years. Deer mice usually live less than seven years, a coyote less than 15 years, a giraffe about 28 years, and a hippopotamus about 50 years. Elephants seldom if ever reach 70 years of age, but a small bat may live 20 years.

Classification of Mammals

All objects must be designated with a name if we are to speak, study, or write about them intelligently. Mammals are no exception. The science of classifying and arranging animals is known as *taxonomy* or *systematics*. The taxonomic mammalogist is concerned with classifying and naming mammals by arranging them in groups (orders, families, genera, and species) mostly on the basis of their morphological characteristics. The basic principles with which the taxonomist in mammalogy works have been described by Simpson (1945).

The class Mammalia includes three subclasses: Prototheria, which includes only the egg-laying mammals of the order Monotremata; Allotheria, which includes only extinct orders, the Multituberculata, and possibly the Triconodonta; and Theria, which includes all other extinct and living orders. The living therian mammals are further subdivided into two infraclasses: Metatheria includes but one order, the pouched mammals, the Marsupialia; Eutheria includes all the remaining 16 placental orders of mammals.

The placental orders are frequently grouped into four *cohorts*, as follows: Unguiculata (with nails or claws)—Insectivora, Dermoptera, Chiroptera, Primates, Edentata, and Pholidota; Glires (gnawing mammals)—Rodentia and Lagomorpha; Mutica—whales; and Ferungulata (carnivores and hoofed mammals)—Carnivora, Tubulidentata, Proboscidea, Hyracoidea, Sirenia, Perissodactyla, and Artiodactyla.

The class Mammalia includes 18 living and 16 fossil orders, each of which is composed of families, which in turn are made up of genera (singular is genus); and the genera are composed of *species*, which are the *kinds* of animals. Although species are the units, they are sometimes further divided into *subspecies*, which are merely geographic variations or races of the species. Beginning students should be concerned with the species of animals, especially with learning the name. As a rule, only advanced students of animal distribution or speciation find the names of the subspecies useful.

About 10,000 species of mammals are described in the scientific literature, and each one is given a *scientific name*. There are about 3,500 living species that belong to 1,000 genera (Walker, 1964). There are at present 233 recognized species of mammals, nearly all living in a wild state, along the coast and within the boundaries of the Pacific States.

The scientific name of an animal includes the name of the *genus*, beginning with a capital letter, followed by the uncapitalized *species* name. The scientific name is italicized or underlined. The "International Rules for Zoological Nomenclature" provides that a particular species will have *one and only one* scientific name anywhere in the world. Thus, *Homo sapiens* is the name for man and is recognized throughout the civilized world. The *common* names vary from country to country, or even from one locality to the next, especially if there are language differences. In the Pacific States *Felis concolor* is called by the common name "mountain lion," in Arizona it is called "cat," in Florida it is called "cougar," and in Mexico "el puma." These common names all refer to the same species. In order to be understood, the serious zoology student will learn not only the scientific name but one or more common names for each species of mammal in his vicinity, and he will become thoroughly familiar with their classification. The classification and the check list of all the Pacific States mammals are shown on p. 473. A brief description of the 18 living orders of mammals follows.

Order **Monotremata**. These mammals are similar to birds in that they have a bill-like rostrum covered with a hard, rubbery layer of skin; they lay eggs and possess a *cloaca*. The cloaca is a large chamber formed by the ends of the intestine, the excretory system, and the reproductive system. Monotremes have cervical ribs, such as are possessed by certain reptiles, coracoid bones, and certain features about the shoulder girdle which show an indelible stamp of their ancient reptilian ancestry. Both sexes have epipubic bones above and outside the pubis. Although no fossil remains have been found to trace their ancient ancestral evolution, they show little in common with other mammals, and hence their origin is assumed to have been from reptilian stocks in the Age of Reptiles, but perhaps independent (*polyphyletic*) of the origin of other mammals (fig. 10). The duck-billed platypus (*Ornithorhynchus anatinus*) and species of the spiny anteater (*Tachyglossus*) live in the Australian region and are representatives of the order. These are the most primitive of all living mammals although specialized in certain ways.

Order **Marsupialia**. The mammals of this order are primitive in structure but are not hatched from eggs. There is usually no placental attachment, however, and since the young develop from practically yolkless eggs, they are born at an early stage of development and are reminiscent of the embryonic stages of placental mammals. The bandicoots (Peramelidae) are the only marsupials with a fairly complete placental attachment. The rest are born in a very undeveloped state, and then usually finish their development in a pouch on the abdomen of the female, called a *marsupium*. The mammary glands are located in the pouch. The immature young become attached to the nipples, which swell up within their mouths; thus the young remain more or less permanently attached to the teat for days or even weeks after their birth. Some people actually believe that the marsupial young are developed and born on the teats! The milk is not sucked by the young animal but is forced into its mouth by the contraction of muscles around the mammary gland. During this time the trachea of the young is connected directly across the pharyngeal cavity with the internal opening of the nose, thus preventing strangulation. It is weeks before the immature young are able to shift for themselves. Most species of marsupials live in the Australian region and include the kangaroos, wombats, phalangers, koalas, bandicoots, and possums. Three skeletal peculiarities of the order are the epipubic or marsupial bones, a characteristic also of the monotremes; the nasal bones, which are almost always wider behind than anteriorly; and the inturned angular process of the jaw. The last upper premolar is the only milk tooth lost in marsupials. The order is extremely old and extends back into the Age of Reptiles (fig. 10). Long before man appeared on the earth, some of the marsupials had attained the bulk of rhinoceroses, but the changing environment was unfavorable, and they became extinct long ago.

The order is frequently divided into two groups, including five living superfamilies: Didelphoidea are opossums; Dasyuroidea include the Tasmanian wolf and pouched mice; Perameloidea include the bandicoots;

Caenolestoidea include the opossum rats of South America; and Phalangeroidea include the phalangers, koalas, and kangaroos. One group of these superfamilies has only one pair of lower incisors on each side of the jaw and is called the *diprotodonts*. In this group of animals the second and third hind toes are small and are so closely grown together as to appear as one toe with a double claw. This peculiar characteristic is also found in certain of the bandicoots, which belong in the next group. The "double toe" serves as a combing device, but may have evolved as an aid in climbing. Included in the diprotodonts are the kangaroos, wombats, honey possums, and phalangers. The other group, the *polyprotodonts,* has several lower incisors. This group includes the bandicoots, banded anteaters, pouched "mice," and the American opossums.

Some marsupials may have the pouch directed downward or backward instead of upward or forward. In others it may be rudimentary or even absent. It is never present in the males.

Studies of comparative anatomy, many on North American fossils, indicate the superfamily Didelphoidea to be most primitive. The earliest didelphoids gave rise to all other marsupials. All of the living representatives in the Americas except the opossum rat belong in this superfamily.

There is but one species found in the Pacific States, the common opossum (*Didelphis marsupialis*), which has been successfully introduced from the eastern part of the United States. Sometimes the little murine opossums (*Marmosa* sp.) come to the United States in clusters of bananas from Central and South America, but they have never become established here. Some marsupials are quite generalized feeders, but others are extremely specialized and feed only on a particular kind of plant. The koala, for example, eats the leaves of a certain kind of eucalyptus tree. In Australia the order Marsupialia has had little competition with larger animals of the more specialized orders for millions of years. There are, for example, marsupials that feed and hop about like jackrabbits, others that glide like flying squirrels, others that burrow in the ground like moles, and still others that hunt and eat their prey, using the tactics of wolverines. In fact, they occupy ecological niches which in other parts of the world are filled by mammals representing several orders. Thus, the Marsupialia in Australia represent a good example of *adaptive radiation,* which implies that the different species of animals have become adapted to live in different kinds of environments. Their appearance and behavior have been modified to such an extent that they may be hardly recognizable as belonging to the same group.

Order **Insectivora.** This order, like all of those that follow, is placental in its development. There are many scientists who regard the ancient Insectivora as ancestral to all modern placental orders (fig. 10). Representatives of this order are found in North America, Africa, Europe, and Asia, but not in Australia, and they seem to have invaded South America less than 30,000 years ago. The species are for the most part small with long, pointed noses, with five toes armed with claws, and with conical points on the molar teeth. They range in size from a rabbit down to a shrew, the smallest of known

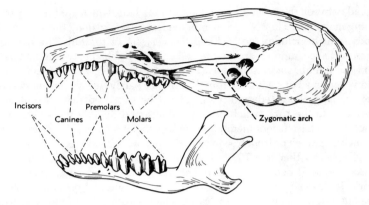

Fig. 4. Side view of the skull of a broad-handed mole (Insectivora), showing teeth.

mammals. Some tiny shrews weigh scarcely more than a dime. Many of the species have what is considered to be the primitive number of teeth in placental mammals (see p. 6). Their testes are mostly abdominal and there is a tendency to suppress the milk teeth as in other ancient orders (Marsupialia, Edentata, and Cetacea).

There are five superfamilies of the order Insectivora with living representatives. Only one of these, the Soricoidea, which includes the moles and shrews, is indigenous to North America proper and to the Pacific States. However, in Cuba and Haiti is found the rabbit-sized solenodon, which belongs to the superfamily Tenrecoidea. The tenrecs are mostly native to Madagascar and are interesting in that they have the primitive tribosphenic or tritubercular-type molars from which the complicated molars of other orders are thought to have developed. The spiny hedgehogs of Europe, Asia, and Africa, and the naked-tailed gymnures of the Malay Peninsula belong in the Erinaceoidea. Two other superfamilies are found in Africa: the Macroscelidoidea, or elephant shrews, which resemble miniature kangaroos, with large ears, long snouts, and strong hind legs; and the Chrysochloridea, or golden moles, which are fossorial, are blind, have no visible tail, and, like our moles, have large auditory bullae, which probably enable them to detect vibrations in the earth.

In the Pacific States the order includes the species of moles *Scapanus,* the shrew mole *Neurotrichus gibbsii,* and species of three genera of shrews, *Sorex, Microsorex,* and *Notiosorex.* They mostly feed on arthropods and annelids, but the moles sometimes feed on bulbs and roots. Some shrews include seeds in their diet.

Order **Dermoptera.** These arboreal cat-sized mammals are the so-called "flying lemurs" of the Philippines, Borneo, Sumatra, and southeastern Asia. A better name for them, however, is "colugo," for they do not really fly and they certainly are not lemurs. Some zoologists believe them to be transitional between the arboreal mammals and the bats, which are the only truly flying mammals. They have a membrane from the jaw along the sides of the body, which includes the legs and the very tip of the tail. The hands of these strange mammals are lengthened and are webbed between the fingers and the thumb, suggesting an early stage in the evolution of a bat's wing. However, in a bat's wing the thumb is free or partly free and the fingers are very greatly elongated, and it should not be supposed that the colugo is ancestral to the bats, which probably developed directly from insectivore ancestors. This efficient membrane enables the animal to glide swiftly from branch to branch or from tree to tree. From a height of 35 feet one was seen to glide to another tree 70 yards away. The colugo feeds on green leaves, buds, and seed pods. It has a voluminous stomach and long, coiled intestines. Its lower incisors resemble small combs mounted on narrow stems; the outer upper incisors and the canines have two roots, a unique feature of the mammal. It moves along the underside of branches similar to the manner in which a sloth travels in the tropical forests of the New World.

Order **Chiroptera.** This is the second largest order of mammals, and its members are the only ones that have the ability to fly.

The wing of a bat consists of a membrane that stretches between the fingers (but not the thumb) and the hind legs, and may include more or less of the tail. The hind limbs of bats have undergone a reversal process that lets the knees bend backward instead of forward as in other mammals. This gives greater support to the interfemoral membranes in flight.

The suborder Megachiroptera is composed of the fruit-eating flying foxes of the south Pacific regions, Asia, and Africa. All of the New World bats belong to the suborder Microchiroptera, which feed on insects, small fishes, fruits, nectar of flowers, and the blood of vertebrates. The vampire bats (*Desmodus* and *Diphylla*) of tropical America are the *only truly parasitic mammals.* They are known to be important carriers of rabies to livestock and man in Mexico and most of the rest of Latin America.

So far as is known, all of the bats in the Pacific States are insect-eating, the possible exception being the long-tongued bat (*Choeronycteris mexicana*), which is a tropical species that rarely comes as far north as San Diego, California. It probably feeds on fruits and the nectar of night-blooming plants. All bats roost head down during the day, in caves, buildings, and even on the foliage of trees. Ages before man appeared on the earth, bats were already coursing their ways through the air, feeding on insects very much as they do now. They seem to have developed directly from the primitive insectivores that lived in the trees. The arboreal life doubtless favored and preserved the mutations that produced longer fingers and larger membranes which made jumping and gliding from limb to limb or from tree to tree easier and safer. The colugos and the flying squirrels probably represent analogous stages in the evolution of flight today, though neither was ancestral to the bats. As the wings became perfected, the bats left the trees and invaded the air. Inasmuch as the air was already occupied by the birds, many of which also fed on insects, it seems likely that those bats that fed in late evening or at night had less competition and were more successful; finally, by mutation and selection, the whole order became largely nocturnal and insect- or fruit-eating. Bats are among the most interesting of all mammals.

Order **Primates.** This is the order to which man belongs. The various species are characterized by having thumbs opposable to the other digits, by having nails instead of claws on some of the fingers or toes, and by having the orbits almost or entirely walled off from the temple region by bone. In tropical Mexico and Central and South America the monkeys usually have prehensile tails and the marmosets do not. Both generally have a wide septum between the nostrils, which are directed more or less outward. They do not have ischial callosities or cheek pouches inside the mouth, but do possess three premolars on each side, both above and below. In Africa and Asia the monkeys, on the other hand, do not have prehensile tails, and, for the most part, the septum between the downwardly directed nostrils is narrow. The Old World monkeys frequently have ischial callosities, occasionally cheek pouches, and have only two premolars on each half of the jaws. Because of the differences between their nostrils, the New World primates (except man) are frequently called platyrrhines (flat-nosed) and those of the Old World are catarrhines (down-nosed).

Included in the order also are the baboons, mandrills, lemurs, tarsiers, aye-ayes, lorises, and the tail-less great apes, all natives of the Old World. The apes include the gibbons, orangutans, chimpanzees, and gorillas and are man's nearest living relatives.

Order **Edentata.** These mammals lack teeth or have simple ones without a covering of enamel. The incisors are entirely absent as a rule. The various species feed largely on leaves, insects, and other arthropods. The testes are abdominal, a primitive characteristic. The skin of some species is covered with horny plates; that of others has bony scutes embedded in it. They have accessory zygapophyses in the lumbar vertebrae and sometimes also in other vertebrae. They are usually provided with powerful claws on the front feet and much smaller ones on the hind feet. The order is essentially one that lives only in tropical America, although the nine-banded armadillo (*Dasypus novemcinctus*) ranges north into Arkansas, and Pleistocene remains of three large species of ground sloths have been found in the La Brea Tar Pits in Los Angeles and in some places in Oregon. The order includes armadillos, sloths, and anteaters.

Order **Pholidota** (sometimes called **Nomarthra**). These strange reptile-like creatures are natives of Asia and Africa. They are popularly known as scaly anteaters or pangolins. Some species grow up to six feet long. In the African species the head is covered with small scales, but the neck, legs, back, and all of the tail are covered with large overlapping scales. When attacked, the animal rolls up into a ball, with the sharp-edged scales opening to form an effective protection. If its adversary should stick its snout or toes between the scales, the pangolin quickly extends its body or tail, thus closing the scales and cutting the attacker.

There are five toes on each foot. Those on the front feet are provided with long sharp claws with which it digs burrows and tears into insects' nests. The eyes are small and there are no protruding ears and no teeth. There is a long sticky tongue. The animal walks about at night on its hind legs, using the tail as a brace. When it uses the forefeet in walking, its claws are turned in and its knuckles are placed on the ground. Practically nothing is known about a pangolin's life history.

The genus *Manis* lives in Asia, and the single African species belongs to the genus *Smutsia*, although Simpson (1945) places them both in *Manis*.

Order **Lagomorpha.** This order was formerly included with the Rodentia, but it differs in a number of characteristics. The lagomorphs have four upper incisor teeth, two small ones behind the two larger ones (fig. 5). They, too, have no canine teeth and a long diastema between the incisors and the cheek teeth. Except for the last molar, the crowns of the cheek teeth have a transverse enamel plate (lophodont-like). Like those of the rodents, the incisors of lagomorphs continue to grow throughout life, but, unlike those of rodents, these teeth have enamel also on the posterior surfaces. The family Leporidae has large supraorbital processes (fig. 5). Most of the species have long ears and short tails and hop instead of walking or running. They are strictly herbivorous. Hares have precocial young (fig. 84), but rabbits, cottontails, and pikas have altricial young. The order is represented in the Pacific States by hares, cottontails, brush rabbits, pigmy rabbits, and pikas.

Order **Rodentia.** This is the largest of the orders of mammals and comprises more than half of all of the living mammalian species. When it originated in Eocene time, the archaic order Multituberculata began to dis-

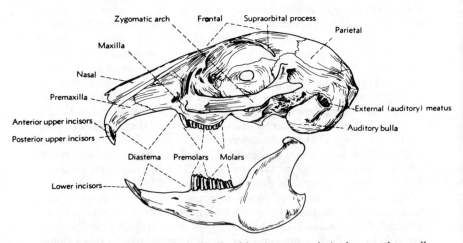

Fig. 5. Side view of the skull of a brush rabbit (Lagomorpha), showing the small upper incisor teeth behind the larger ones and some of the bones of the skull.

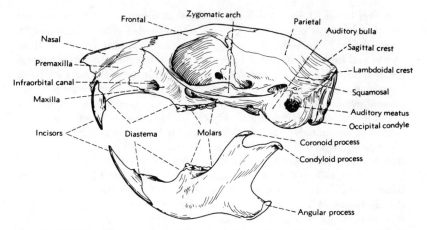

Fig. 6. Side view of the skull of a Douglas squirrel (Rodentia), showing teeth and bones of the skull.

appear, suggesting a similarity of niches (fig. 10). Today rodents are world-wide in distribution; even Australia, which is often thought of as harboring only monotremes and marsupials, has over 50 native species. They have two upper and two lower incisor teeth, each with enamel only on the front sides. The incisor teeth are separated from the first cheek teeth (premolars and molars) by a long space or *diastema* (fig. 6), there being no canine teeth. The incisors continue to grow through the life of the animal. Another characteristic of the order is the manner in which the mandible can be moved backward and forward (*propalinal*) into chewing and gnawing positions. Most rodents are plant eaters, but some of them will occasionally feed on the flesh of vertebrates, insects, or eggs.

The group is very important economically and medically in the West. Here the order includes the Old World rats and mice, cricetine and microtine rats and mice, marmots, beavers, and porcupines.

There are three well-defined suborders of rodents. The skull features of each (shown in figs. 12, 31, 32) are squirrel-like (Sciuromorpha), mouse-like or ratlike (Myomorpha), and porcupine-like (Hystricomorpha). The guinea pig (*Cavia*), chinchilla (*Chinchilla*), nutria (*Myocastor*), and many other Central and South American rodents belong in the last suborder. The infraorbital opening is small and oval and is located on the lower half of the *rostrum* in the Sciuromorpha (figs. 6, 12). The Myomorpha have this opening extending onto the upper half of the rostrum (fig. 32). It is usually wider at the top than at the bottom and smaller in area than the *foramen magnum*. The opening in the Hystricomorpha is usually much larger than the *foramen magnum* (fig. 31).

Order **Cetacea** (whales, dolphins, and porpoises). The mammals of the order Cetacea are mostly marine, and some species are the largest animals that ever lived. All have forelimbs modified as flippers, which are without functional nails or claws. The powerful tail, provided with a horizontal fin (the "flukes"), immediately distinguishes the cetaceans from the large sharks and fishes, all of which have vertical tail fins. Most cetaceans retain rudimentary hind limbs concealed in the ventral body wall. Certain whales have many more bones in the fingers and have many more teeth than are present even in the most primitive mammals. Hair is generally limited to a few stiff bristles on the muzzle and lower jaw. Serving the same function as hair in other animals is the thick layer of fat beneath the skin, known as blubber, for which these large mammals have been hunted for centuries. The single newborn young may be one-third the length of the mother, and is nourished with milk from two mammary glands located in grooves posteriorly on the ventral surface. The nostrils are represented by a single or double blowhole located well back on the top of the head. The complex stomach comprises at least four chambers.

The term "whale" is usually applied to those cetaceans over 15 or 20 feet long, and the smaller ones are called dolphins and porpoises. The distinction between a dolphin and a porpoise is somewhat confused. Some scientists apply the term "porpoise" to the blunt-nosed little cetaceans having triangular dorsal fins and blunt spade-shaped teeth, and use "dolphin" for those having definite beaks, recurved dorsal fins, and sharp pointed teeth.

The toothed cetaceans comprise the suborder Odontoceti and include the porpoises, dolphins, killer whales, and sperm whales. Their jaws are provided with one or more teeth, but there is no preceding set of milk teeth. They usually feed on fishes and squids. The killer whales also attack aquatic birds, seals, and other cetaceans. Toothed cetaceans have but one blowhole.

The whales of the suborder Mysticeti may have milk teeth as fetuses, but they never have functional teeth as adults. Instead they have baleen or whalebone hanging from the roof of the mouth. This baleen may be comparable to the transverse ridges found in the roof of the mouth in many other mammals. When the tongue forces the water out through these plates of baleen, the food is retained. The chief food items of most species are small shrimplike crustaceans (euphausiids) known as krill. Baleen whales have two blowholes. The rorquals are those baleen whales having dorsal fins, pleats, or grooves on the underside, and flippers that are shorter than the head.

Cetaceans never come ashore except by accident. They are very old geologically and their origin is near the base of the trunk of the mammalian tree. There are seven families of cetaceans that frequent our coastal waters. Of the Mysticeti, the Balaenidae have no furrows on the throat, the Eschrichtidae have two or three throat furrows, and the Balaenopteridae have many deep longitudinal furrows on the throat. The four remaining families are all Odontoceti or toothed whales. The Delphinidae are those with functional teeth on both jaws, the Ziphiidae have one or two pairs of functional teeth in the mandible, the Physeteridae (including the formerly recognized family Kogiidae) have nine to 30 pairs of teeth in the mandible. (See p. 310 for the species in these families that are found in the eastern Pacific Ocean.)

Order **Carnivora.** The carnivores, or flesh eaters, include a great assemblage of eutherian mammals, such as the dogs, cats, weasels, civets, hyenas, bears, seals, and walruses. It must not be assumed, however, that all of the species in this order are flesh eaters. There are many that are omnivorous, like most bears, and some species, like the giant panda, are largely vegetarians. There are also mammals in other orders that are carnivorous in their food habits.

Carnivores have curved claws on their toes. Their canine teeth are longer than the incisors and are adapted for seizing and holding their prey (see fig. 7).

The skeletons of carnivores have several interesting features. Although they have specialized away from the primitive types by nearly losing the collarbones (or clavicles), they have nevertheless retained the radius and ulna and tibia and fibula as separate bones. Thus these bones are primitive and are not fused as they are in many other orders, including even some species of present-day insectivores. On the underside of the skull there are two deep trenches—the glenoid fossae (fig. 28), in which the two half-cylinder-like condyles of the jaw articulate. Thus the jaws of carnivores can move only in an up-and-down motion and cannot be rotated as is frequently seen in other mammals.

There are two well-defined suborders, the Fissipedia, which are largely terrestrial, and the Pinnipedia, which are mostly marine. The fissiped carnivores usually never have the appendages modified into a paddle or flipper. The toes of most kinds have no webs between them, and they are adapted for use on land. A nearly constant feature also is the presence of three pairs of incisor teeth both above and below in each side of the head. The pinni-

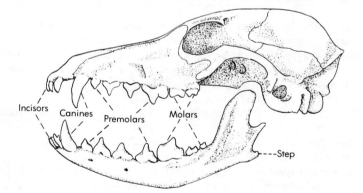

Fig. 7. Side view of the skull of a gray fox (Carnivora), showing teeth.

peds have molars and premolars of about the same shape, whereas those of the fissiped carnivores are differently shaped in the same animal for shearing flesh or for grinding. The milk set of teeth is well developed.

The suborder Fissipedia includes seven rather well-defined families:

The Canidae include flesh-eating wolves, dogs, foxes, and their relatives, some of which have the primitive placental dentition (see p. 6). The fourth upper premolar (Pm^4) and the lower molar (M_1) are sectorial and oppose one another as shearing or carnassial teeth used in cutting flesh. The upper-cheek tooth row is strongly bent outward in the family at the junction of the molars and the premolars. The species are digitigrade and their claws are nonretractile. All have long, bushy tails.

The Ursidae, or bears, are large plantigrade mammals with nonretractile claws. Their cheek teeth form a nearly straight line and are not carnassial or sectorial in the species living in the Pacific States, but are bunodont molars with flat crowns for crushing the food of their omnivorous diet. Bears have short tails.

The Procyonidae include raccoons, ringtails, coatis, kinkajous, and olingos. They have plantigrade feet with five toes terminated with nonretractile claws. They are omnivorous and possess bunodont nonsectorial teeth. Their tails are often ringed and in some species are prehensile.

The Mustelidae include weasels, minks, martens, fishers, wolverines, river otters, sea otters, badgers, and skunks. There are five toes on each foot, which may be plantigrade or digitigrade. The claws are nonretractile. The teeth are typically sectorial with well-developed carnassials. In most species there are well-developed anal musk glands. Their tails are bushy and vary in length.

The Viverridae include civets, genets, mongooses, and their relatives. None of the species lives in the Pacific States. Some have sectorial teeth; others are more of the bunodont type. The feet are more digitigrade than plantigrade, with five toes on each foot. The claws are semiretractile. Musk glands are usually present. The tail is of variable length and is usually bushy.

The Hyaenidae include hyenas and the aardwolves of Asia and Africa. Hyenas have powerful jaws and teeth adapted for crushing bones in order to obtain marrow. The carnassials are highly developed. The aardwolves have weak dentition and feed on termites, ants, and other insects. There are four toes on each of the digitigrade feet. The claws are not retractile. These animals have bushy tails.

The Felidae include the many kinds of cats, all of which have rounded heads with short muzzles. They have five toes on the forefeet and four on the hind feet. The claws are retractile. The cats are digitigrade. The teeth are reduced to 28 or 30 in these carnivorous mammals and represent the most extreme specialization of sectorial development. Cats usually have tails covered with short hair, which are not bushy.

The suborder Pinnipedia is sometimes considered a separate order of mammals. Most zoologists, however, agree that this group, which includes the seals, eared seals, and walruses, is specialized for aquatic life and should be considered a suborder. These animals show some similarities to the bears, especially in structure of the skull. The pinnipeds feed mostly on fish, molluscans, and crustaceans.

They differ from the fissiped carnivores (with toes) in having all five of the digits enclosed in a web to form a flipper. Although the forefeet and hind feet are greatly elongated, most of the appendages above the wrist or ankle are enclosed in the integument of the body proper. Unlike other carnivores, the pinnipeds have the toes of the hind limb that correspond to the big toe and little toe stronger and generally longer than the other three toes. The molars and premolars are all similar. The milk teeth are rudimentary and are sometimes shed before birth.

The suborder has three well-defined families. The Otariidae, or eared seals, have tiny external ears and hind feet that can be turned forward under the body like those of other carnivores. Each of the toes ends in an elongated flap of skin resembling the finger of an empty glove, which extends well beyond the claw. The sea lions and fur seals belong in this family.

The Odobenidae, or walruses, are similar to eared seals in that they can direct their hind limbs forward under the body, but they have no external ears. The most characteristic feature of these large Arctic mammals, however, is the pair of canine tusks that protrude down from the upper jaw, some of which are nearly two feet long. The cheek teeth have low blunt crowns adapted for crushing molluscan food. Old walruses lose most of their hair but have a thick layer of blubber.

The Phocidae include true seals and elephant seals. They cannot bring their hind limbs up under their bodies and they have no external ears. The "thumb" of the front flipper is always longer than the other digits. All digits have well-developed claws at the ends, and they generally lack the flaps of skin found on the eared seals. Unlike the other families, the soles of their feet are covered with hair. The members of this family have thus departed further from the land-living carnivores than those of the other two families, and are therefore considered to be more specialized.

Order **Tubulidentata.** The aardvarks or antbears are African mammals which are long-snouted, big-eared, piglike creatures that live largely on ants and termites. They are about five feet long and may weigh as much as 100 pounds. They have four toes on each front foot and five on the back ones, all armed with powerful claws used to tear apart insects' nests and to dig deep burrows. There are no canine or incisor teeth, and the molars and premolars are composed of nearly microscopic solid columns. These teeth are peculiar also in that they are made up of tiny tubes of vasodentine which radiate from the central part of each tooth. The animal uses its long sticky tongue to extricate insects from tubes and passages. It is nocturnal and is an extraordinarily active burrower. Its fatty flesh is prized by the natives, and the animal is frequently dug out with great pains. Very little is known about the life history of this interesting animal. The order has two species, both belonging to the genus *Orycteropus*.

Order **Proboscidea.** These very large, nearly hairless mammals have the nose and the upper part of the lip greatly elongated as an extremely prehensile trunk or snout. The joints of the legs have limited articulation, and each digit on each leg is covered with a heavy nail. In living species the second upper incisors are greatly elongated, especially in the males, to form ivory tusks. The tusks of a large African elephant may weigh more than 170 pounds each. The molar teeth are the hypsodont-lophodont type. The short jaws cannot accommodate all of the molar teeth in position at one time, hence new ones move forward into place as the older teeth are worn away. Normally there is but one molar exposed on each half-jaw at one time. The mammary glands are pectoral and the testes are abdominal. A large skull filled with long tubular air cavities provides attachments for the huge muscles necessary to support the heavy tusks and trunk. The cerebellum is entirely uncovered, which suggests primitiveness, but the cerebrum is well convoluted. The mammals of this order are plant feeders.

The Proboscidea is a dying order, for today only two of the 300 species of elephants remain. The animals of the Indian species, which have four nails on the hind foot, are frequently used as beasts of burden, and are the species most often seen in zoos. The animals of the African species, which have five nails on the hind foot, and very large ears, are said to be less easily controlled and are less often seen away from their native habitat. The African elephant is the largest land-living mammal, often standing over nine feet high at the shoulders and weighing up to seven tons.

Order **Hyracoidea.** These are the true conies or hyraxes of Africa and Syria. They are practically tail-less, and each toe, except the innermost of the hind feet, has a strong flattened nail. The inner toes of the back feet have a strong claw used in gripping sideways. There are four toes on the forefeet and three on the back feet, as in the tapir. On the soles of the feet are thick pads that undoubtedly aid in clinging to the surfaces of smooth stones and tree trunks. The animals are about the size of a marmot or mountain beaver. There is one pair of upper incisors, triangular in cross section in the males and rounded in the females. There are two pairs of lower incisors, and a diastema between them and the cheek teeth. The cheek teeth resemble those of a rhinoceros. They have canines only in the milk dentition, as do certain hoofed animals. Blood serum tests in England indicate a closer relationship with the elephants than with any other order of mammals. They are plant feeders and live in colonies. Some live in trees and others inhabit rocky places, especially cliffs. There are in Africa three genera and several species.

Order **Sirenia.** These are entirely aquatic mammals. Many parts of their anatomy are similar to those of the large elephants, but the anterior limbs are modified as flippers for swimming. The external hind limbs are lacking and there is a broad flat tail. Because of the anatomical similarities with the probocideans, and because the fossil representatives of both orders are even more similar, some zoologists consider the sirenians to be elephants adapted to life in the water. The nostrils are provided with valves and are located on the upper part of the muzzle, which in certain species is divided and has stiff bristles that aid in browsing. Sirenians are entirely herbivorous. The stomach is complex, similar to that of the cud chewers. They are similar to the whales in that they have an obliquely placed diaphragm and several pairs of molars. The manner in which the molar teeth replace one another as they are worn out, however, is like the elephant. The pectorally situated mammary glands also represent a similarity to the elephants. Their bones are massive and heavy. The manatees (*Trichechus* sp.) have but six cervical vertebrae, and have divided upper lips. They are found in the southeastern United States, Mexico, and Central and South America.

The dugongs (*Dugong* sp.) are Asiatic, African, and Australian species. Their upper lip is not split. The mermaid stories are thought to have originated when sailors saw mother dugongs stand upright in the water to nurse their young. However, such stories of beings that were half human and half fish were current in Europe long before there was any knowledge about dugongs.

Near the Bering Straits are found the remains of the Steller sea cows (*Hydrodamalis stelleri*), slaughtered to extinction by the Russian trappers and traders in 1768. The teeth of this animal had almost entirely disappeared and horny plates and pads had replaced them. It was a large mammal, attaining a length of nearly 25 feet, and was exceedingly bulky. The naturalist Steller, who had studied them off Bering and Copper islands in the north Pacific Ocean, wrote a paper suggesting that these great animals could be used as food by explorers. Within 30 years after its original discovery, the explorers had killed the last one of these interesting mammals. Its food was large seaweeds.

In the Miocene formations along Monocline Ridge in western Fresno County, California, are frequently found the shiny black teeth of *Desmostylus,* an ancient marine sea cow. Other remains have been found in Oregon.

Order **Perissodactyla.** These are hoofed mammals in which the plane of symmetry passes through the middle or dominant toe on each foot. The brachydont to hypsodont molars are lophodont, which facilitates the grinding of plant foods such as grasses, which contain large amounts of silica. There are three important types of living representatives of the order: the tapirs and the rhinoceroses (Ceratomorpha), and the horselike animals (Hippomorpha). Tapirs are found in the tropical forests of Latin America and in Asia. They have a more or less prehensile proboscis about a foot long. Rhinoceroses live in Africa and southern Asia. They have one or two horns that appear to be composed of an agglomeration of hairlike structures but are actually laminated filaments which lack the cuticle of true hairs. Although horses disappeared from the Western Hemisphere long before the white man came, the Spanish reintroduced them.

Wild horses and wild burros that originated from domestic stock occur in a few places in the Pacific States. Perhaps those most easily seen are found in Death Valley and the surrounding mountains.

Order **Artiodactyla.** These are hoofed mammals, frequently of large size, in which the plane of symmetry passes between the two major toes on each foot. They can be divided into two major groups: the hippopotamus and piglike forms (Suina), and those that chew cud (Ruminantia), such as the chevrotains, deer, giraffes, antelopes, cattle, sheep, and goats. The former group of animals all have simple stomachs, with canines frequently elongated into tusks. They also have bunodont molars. Animals of the latter group have selenodont molars, and rarely possess any upper incisors. These swallow their food rapidly when grazing but regurgitate it as cud, to be more thoroughly masticated at leisure when out of reach of predators. Associated with cud-chewing is a complicated stomach, consisting of a *rumen, reticulum, omasum,* and *abomasum.* The food is swallowed into the rumen. There it is acted upon by a rich flora of anaerobic bacteria that hydrolyze cellulose and other carbohydrates of plants. There is no digestive enzyme in this part of the stomach. It is from the rumen that food is regurgitated into the mouth. Most of the cud chewers have either *antlers,* which are usually present only on the males and are generally shed annually, or permanent *horns,* which are usually not shed and may occur on both sexes. All are plant feeders, but the pigs and their relatives eat a considerable amount of animal food such as insects and snakes. The order is represented in the Pacific States by the white-tailed deer, mule deer, elk, moose, woodland caribou, pronghorn, mountain sheep, mountain goat, and wild pig. Small bands of feral Old World sheep and goats also occur locally, where they have escaped or have been introduced intentionally.

2. Ecology

There may be a wealth of material and knowledge about the molecular and cellular aspects of a particular mammal, or about the structure and physiology of its organs and systems, but an animal is really never known until it has been studied in relation to its total environment. This is *ecology,* or environmental biology. The manner in which different species react to their environments is the product of evolution on their anatomy, physiology, and behavior over long periods of time. Each species of mammal has developed genetically based peculiarities so that it performs a given function in its habitat. The place of an animal in its habitat or its role in a particular community is its *ecological niche.* The niche includes the responses the animal makes to temperature, humidity, snow, water, soil, wind, sunlight, food, predators, and disease. No two species have identical niches, although closely related species may overlap considerably. When the competition between two species with similar niches becomes too great, one will eventually displace the other (Gause's principle).

The habitat of a mammal thus contains many factors to which it must be tolerant (Shelford's Law). There may be too little or too much of certain factors to allow the mammal to live in a particular habitat. Some mammals are so dependent upon one factor of their habitat that they disappear entirely when this factor is removed or modified too much. The distribution of an animal will be controlled by that environmental factor for which it has the narrowest range of adaptability or control (Liebig's Law of the Minimum). The Audubon cottontail, for example, depends on the presence of wild blackberry brambles in the Sacramento Valley of California to protect it from its many enemies. Where these patches of berries are burned or cleared away as a part of irrigation practice to make arable land, the cottontails have entirely disappeared. Other mammals, however, may benefit when their native environment is modified, and their numbers actually may be greatly increased. As an example, the Brazilian free-tailed bat (*Tadarida brasiliensis*) has undoubtedly increased in numbers since man began to erect buildings that provided it with shelter. Rarely now are these bats found (in California) in their native caves. Nearly all of them live in buildings. The population of pocket gophers (*Thomomys*) has undoubtedly been increased many times in cultivated areas where man has greatly augmented the number of edible plants. They have increased also in over-grazed areas where certain herbs are encouraged to grow that are avidly eaten by the little rodents.

The concept of the *ecosystem* is essential for the beginning student who desires to do serious field work on mammals. It is the largest functional unit in ecology and includes the interactions between all the organisms and the abiotic environment (Odum, 1953). A lake or a mountain meadow is an example of an ecosystem. The flow of energy through the food chains within an ecosystem is of interest to the field mammologist. A *food chain* is the transfer of energy through a series of organisms at different *trophic levels*. As an example, the grass–meadow mouse–weasel–horned owl is a food chain.

The radiant energy from the sun falls on the grass of a meadow, where by photosynthesis about 1 to 5 per cent of it is "captured" and retained as latent chemical energy in molecules of food. This is the *autotropic* compo-nent of the ecosystem. The herbivores and carnivores make up the food chains of the meadow, which include many kinds of insects, meadow mice, mule deer, shrews, weasels, and mountain lions. They constitute the *hetero-tropic component*. The meadow mice and insects, feeding on vegetation, are the first level of this component. Golley (1960) found that meadow mice consume only about 2 per cent of the energy available to them. Insects use about 10 to 20 per cent of the energy stored in ingested food molecules. A large mammal such as a deer requires less energy per gram of weight for its maintenance than smaller mammals. Much of the energy of smaller ani-mals, with shorter life span, goes into reproduction, whereas the larger mammal expends its energy mostly on its maintenance.

The weasel represents the next trophic level. It eats about a third of the meadow mice in a meadow. Most of the energy in a weasel goes into its maintenance and very little is stored in its tissue. Shrews, with their high metabolic rate and small size, obtain energy from insects or from spiders, which are predators on insects. The mountain lion preys on the deer for much of its energy, which it uses for maintenance. Many square miles of browse and grass are required to support enough deer to keep one lion alive.

Thus radiant energy from the sun is changed by photosynthesis into chemical energy in food, which, when eaten by an animal, changes into other molecules in its body, according to the *first law of thermodynamics*. However, as energy flows through the different trophic levels of an eco-system, more of it becomes degraded into heat at each trophic level, ac-cording to the *second law of thermodynamics*. It then becomes obvious that more energy is available to those species that feed closer to the base of the pyramid. Thus, more men can live on plant food growing on a given area than can live on animals that eat the plant food that grows on the area.

The status of most mammals in an ecosystem is poorly known. Roughly speaking, the reduction in energy from sunlight to the plant is about 100 to one, and each step in a food chain has a factor of about 10 (Odum, 1953). This means that, if 2,000 calories of light energy are absorbed by the green plants on a square meter, only about 20 calories would be available as food in the plants. The herbivores that eat the plants would reconstitute about 2.0 calories, and the carnivores that eat the herbivores would have only 0.20 calorie of the original energy. It is evident that, after a few links in the food chain, the food would be reduced to a point where only a few mammals could be supported if they had to get all their energy at the end of a food chain.

Many mammals are very important to other organisms in an ecosystem. The beaver builds dams across streams, which raise the water table under meadows, which in turn produce more willows and more grass, resulting in more deer and more lions; or more insects, more spiders, and more shrews; or more meadow mice and more weasels. If the beaver is removed, the constitution of the ecosystem obviously changes profoundly. Thus, in an ecosystem the factors of the physical environment greatly influence the mode of life and the kind of living creatures on an area. They, in turn, change the physical environment and influence each other's mode of living, as is shown by the beaver.

An understanding of population dynamics is important to the person who studies the ecology of mammals. A *population* may be defined as a group of mammals of the same species living on an area at a particular time. Populations are subject to a complex of factors constantly acting to change their sizes and compositions. Probably no single factor ever causes the rise or decline of a population. Students who wish to learn about such phenomena as equilibria, growth, declines, oscillations, cycles, mechanisms, and forces as these apply to populations are referred to other sources and their bibliographies (Davis and Golley, 1963).

One would expect that as a result of the long process of evolution mechanisms must have developed in individuals of certain species to prevent over-utilization and destruction of their environment. Most frequently failure of the food supply, enemies, disease, or other environmental causes are given as the *only* controls on populations. Recently it has been shown that in certain rodents, lagomorphs, and deer there is a "feedback" system, dependent upon *adrenocorticotrophic hormone*, that regulates population growth quite as well without destruction of the habitat.

According to Christian (1961), the sociophysiological effects are quite independent of environmental factors in determining population size. The sociophysiological effects resulting from increasing the numbers of individuals in a population act through the nervous system to stimulate the release of ACTH (adrenocorticotrophic hormone), which causes the adrenal gland to secrete its hormones. These raise the level of homeostasis (i.e., produce stronger reactions to stimuli) and prepare the individual animal for the stresses that come as a result of living in close proximity to other individuals. These same hormones, however, also reduce reproductive capacity. The number of implanted embryos that are absorbed, for instance, may be only one in 10,000 in mice living in a population of low density. The number undergoing absorption may increase to one in ten in high-density populations (Davis and Golley, 1963). Furthermore, the increase in activity of the adrenal cortex may also inhibit the production of certain

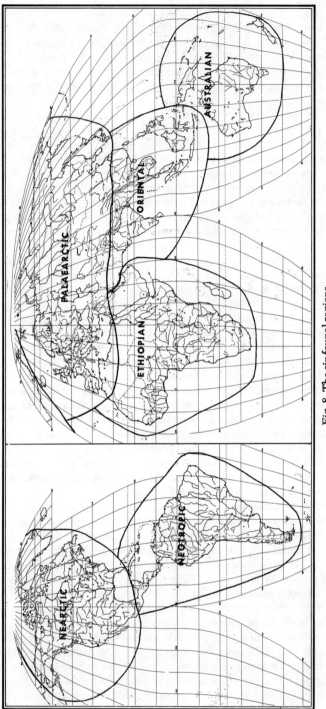

Fig. 8. The six faunal regions.

antibodies and thus make the animals living in high-density populations much more susceptible to disease and death. Hence such populations are self-regulatory and may be so quite independently of external environmental factors. Because the evolution of a species is most likely to depend on reproduction of dominant or well-adjusted individuals, the selective process would seem to be operating in the direction of increasing the importance of behavioral adaptation (Christian, 1961). It would appear that such means of population regulation may represent an advance over those of populations that depend on environmental factors as a means of control. Regulation is achieved by "internal" operation before a population gets too large and overeats its food supply. Hence endocrine regulation would tend to reduce the great oscillations in populations and thus conserve energy that would otherwise be lost to the species through premature death. Other species are known to regulate their population size by their peculiar behavior patterns, especially as these relate to territoriality (Errington, 1963).

There are various methods of estimating population size, but probably the best known is the Lincoln Index. This method involves sampling a population on an area by live-trapping, marking, and releasing. Then the same area is retrapped for the same length of time, and the number of "repeats" in the second trapping is noted. These data are then substituted in the formula

$$x = \frac{an}{r},$$

where
  x = the number of animals in the population on the area,
  a = the number of individuals caught the first time,
  n = the total number of individuals caught the second time,
  r = the number of individuals that repeated or were taken in both the first and second trapping periods.
In other words, $x/a : n/r$.

This formula is very useful for the person working on population problems involving such factors as fertility, mortality, predation, and emigration.

Biogeography

Why do mammals live where they do? This story of the origin and dispersal of the various taxa extends back to Jurassic times. Only the general principles, with a few examples as they relate to the fauna of the Pacific States, can be given here. The student should supplement these statements on zoogeography with more detailed information by such authorities as W. H. Burt (1958), P. J. Darlington, Jr. (1957), and G. G. Simpson (1953).

After many decades of study it is generally agreed that there are six distinct faunal regions in the world (fig. 8). The Nearctic includes North America north of southern Mexico. The Neotropic includes South America north to southern Mexico. The Australian includes Australia and the adjacent islands. The Oriental includes Asia roughly south of 30° N. latitude. The Ethiopian includes Africa and Madagascar roughly south of 30° N. latitude. The Palaearctic includes Eurasia and the part of Africa that lies roughly north of 30° N. latitude.

Within each faunal region certain general principles cause subdivision into smaller faunal areas sometimes referred to as *terrestrial communities*. In the Northern Hemisphere these terrestrial communities, from north to south, are *tundra and ice, taiga, temperate deciduous forest, Mediterranean scrub forest, grassland, desert,* and *tropical rain forest.* These are represented in the Pacific States by all but the temperate deciduous forest and the tropical rain forest. The tundra and ice community is found only on the tops of the highest mountains. The taiga is the coniferous forest belt that extends along the Sierra Nevada Mountains, along the northwestern California coast and over most of Oregon and Washington. The grasslands occur in the central valley of California and in eastern Washington. The Mediterranean scrub forest is represented in California along the coast south of Fort Ross. The desert extends up from Mexico through southern and eastern California nearly into Washington. These terrestrial communities are subdivided again to make up the plant communities and life zones (pp. 33–39).

From the equator northward the principal factors determining these terrestrial communities are temperature, solar radiation, and precipitation.

The main factor concerned with east-west gradients is the amount of precipitation an area receives as a result of its position with respect to mountain ranges and prevailing winds. Thus, the west slopes of the Cascade Range, the Coast Range, and the Sierra Nevada Mountains have heavy coniferous forests. The humid air from the Pacific Ocean moves over them as prevailing westerly winds, but drops most of its moisture before descending to the east slopes, to the deserts in California, large sagebrush areas in Oregon, and grasslands in Washington.

Besides the horizontal north-south and east-west gradients in the Pacific States, there is the vertical gradient in the mountains. This too is related to temperature, precipitation, and solar radiation and closely parallels the north-south gradient. In fact, as a person ascends the mountains, he experiences climatic changes similar to those he would experience if he traveled north.

Climatic conditions and flora determine the kind of animals a terrestrial community has.

The life zones and plant communities (pp. 33–39) all result from action of the horizontal and vertical gradients. Keeping these zoogeographical principles in mind, one can easily understand how the vegetation and mammalian fauna change as one goes north, or east, or into the mountains. One can also understand how certain boreal species, like the wolverine and pika, are found far south in California but only in the high mountains, or how species inhabiting the Sonoran deserts of Mexico, like certain pocket mice and kangaroo rats, can extend hundreds of miles north in California into the deserts that lie to the east of the Sierra Nevada range.

Life Zones

Familiarity with life zones, plant communities, and habitats is the first step in beginning field biological studies. Life zones were first conceived by C. Hart Merriam at the beginning of the twentieth century as he observed the bands of vegetation around San Francisco Peak, north of Flagstaff, Arizona. According to Dr. Merriam, the northward (or, on a mountain, upward) distribution of terrestrial organisms is primarily dependent upon the total of the positive temperatures for the growth season, and the southward (or lower) distribution depends upon the mean temperature for the hottest part of the season. Thus, theoretically there would be different bands of vegetation (and different animals inhabiting them) across North America from south to north, or from low to high, called *life zones*.

Merriam's Life Zone concept has been severely criticized by many ecologists, and today it is largely being replaced by "plant communities" or "plant zones." However, so much Western literature concerned with mammals uses the concept that it is necessary to understand and recognize various life zones. This concept has the advantage of applying to the whole area of the three Pacific States, whereas the "plant communities" of California are not quite the same as the "plant zones" of Oregon and Washington. Uniformity in naming the plant communities or plant zones of the whole area is highly desirable but cannot at this time be achieved. Care must be taken not to confuse "plant zone" with "life zone."

Life zones range from the Lower Sonoran, occupying the lower altitudes, successively through the Upper Sonoran, the Transition, the Canadian, and the Hudsonian to the Alpine-Arctic Life Zone, in which lie the tops of the highest mountains. Life zones generally lie above one another at successively cooler temperature belts. However, latitude as well as altitude is a determinant. Although the dominant plants of any zone differ in various parts of the three states, the most satisfactory way to learn the life zones is by learning the plants that typify them. Thus, if a person finds himself among blue oaks and digger pines, he will know he is in the Upper Sonoran Life Zone. Some of the plant indicators for the life zones in the Pacific States are listed below.

Lower Sonoran Life Zone: arrowweed, agave, palo-verde, yucca, sycamore, valley oak, Fremont cottonwood, and many kinds of cacti.

Upper Sonoran Life Zone: buckbrush, redbud, yerba santa, most manzanitas, blue oak, mesa oak, interior live oak, scrub oak, flat-top buckwheat, chamise, grease wood, salt brush, rabbit brush, digger pine, and sagebrush. Some botanists, however, place sagebrush in the "dry Transition Life Zone."

Transition Life Zone: yellow pine, sugar pine, Douglas fir, white fir, incense cedar, western red cedar, mountain mahogany, Oregon maple, black oak, tan oak, Sitka spruce, redwood, and Port Orford cedar.

Canadian Life Zone: red fir, lodgepole pine, silver pine, western hemlock, spruce, and Jeffrey pine.

Hudsonian Life Zone: mountain hemlock, alpine fir, Alaska cedar, whitebarked pine, and Sierra juniper.

Alpine-Arctic Life Zone: This zone lies above the timber line on the highest mountains. Its plant life consists of certain grasses and other herbaceous plants, such as steer's head, *Trisetum*, dwarf willows, and red and white heathers.

Just as a particular species of plant is found in a particular life zone, so a species of mammal may be limited in its zonal distribution (fig. 113). Many mammals, indeed, are specific to a single life zone; for example, the roundtailed ground squirrel, *Citellus tereticaudus*, is only in the Lower Sonoran Life Zone, while other species may occur in two or more life zones. The Mount Lyell shrew (*Sorex lyelli*) is found in both the Hudsonian and the Canadian life zones, and the deer mouse (*Peromyscus maniculatus*) is found in all the life zones.

A newer and much more accurate classification used widely in biological field work involves the use of plant communities and plant zones. The scheme used in this book for California will follow that suggested by Munz and Keck (1949, 1950), and for Oregon and Washington by Daubenmire (1952). It is possible that future work will show these plant communities and plant zones to be nearly identical with the *biotic communities*. These are here conceived as assemblages of plants and animals that function as units ecologically, in that *all of the requirements of all the organisms*, such as food, shelter, temperature, moisture, and soil, are met within the community. In order to understand the ecological position of a mammal in such a community, one must know something about the general structure and development of the biotic community itself.

It is supposed that communities had their beginning either in water or from the rocks that originally formed the earth's crust. As the lakes filled up, or as the rocks crumbled away to make the soil, successive stages of plants and animals lived on the area until finally one stage arrived which is the present *climax community*. The climax community is determined by climate (temperature, humidity, rainfall, winds, etc.), and by *edaphic* factors (soil, salinity, ground water, etc.). In order to understand *succession* in a community, let us see how it operates today in a shallow moraine lake in the Red Fir Forest.

In the water of the lake are many tiny plant and animal organisms that depend on one another for their living; these supply the food for larger forms. Around the shore are certain plants that float. Still closer to the bank are others that grow in the water, and on the bank itself are willows, creek dogwood, and other species that need water about their roots. Back still farther are the red firs, which cover the hills. As the lake fills up, the species of plants and animals that require standing water disappear, and those that need wet soil take their place. As the floating and emergent plants give way to the willows, grasses, and sedges, the water shrew disappears and the mountain beaver and mountain meadow mouse come to the wet meadow. Finally, as the meadow itself builds up with more and more soil, the water-loving willows, grasses, and sedges disappear and the red firs start growing on the area that was once a lake. With the willows, grasses, and sedges go the mountain beavers and the mountain meadow mice, and with the red firs come the Douglas squirrels and the porcupines. The mountain beavers, the mountain meadow mice, the willows, and the sedges are *successional species*, but the Douglas squirrels, the porcupines, and the red firs are *climax species* and are here to stay. Should the climax community be destroyed by fire or lumbering, or should it be killed by an artificial lake, the community would ultimately return to climax as long as the climate remains the same in the region.

As might be expected in a region with such varied topography as the Western states, altitudinal differences are more important in determining the climate, and consequently the vegetation, than differences in latitude.

Plant Communities of California

1. Coastal Strand. Sandy beaches and dunes along the entire coast, with low or prostrate plants. Some representative plants are *Artemisia pycnocephala, Franseria bipinnatifida,* and *Lathyrus littoralis.*

2. Coastal Salt Marsh. Salt marshes along the coast, with such plants as *Salicornia virginica, Suaeda californica, and Distichlis spicata.*

3. Freshwater Marsh. Marshes of interior valleys and river bottoms from sea level up to about 500 feet. Typical plants: *Scirpus olneyi, Typha latifolia,* and *Carex senta.*

4. Northern Coastal Scrub. The narrow strip of low plants that grow between the Coastal Strand and the Redwood Forest from Oregon south to Point Sur, Monterey County. Typical plants: *Baccharis pilularis, Mimulus aurantiacus,* and *Castilleja latifolia.* There are often large areas of grass in the community.

5. Coastal Sage Scrub. Plants that grow on the dry, rocky slopes of the south Coast Ranges below the Chaparral Community (mostly below 3,000 feet). Typical plants: *Artemisia californica, Salvia apiana, Eriogonum fasciculatum, Rhus integrifolia,* and *Encelia californica.*

6. Sagebrush Scrub. Largely silvery gray shrubs, mostly east of the Sierra Nevada and San Bernardino Mountains up to 7,500 feet. Typical plants: *Artemisia tridentata, Chrysothamnus* spp., *Atriplex confertifolia,* and *Purshia tridentata.*

7. Shadscale Scrub. Plants generally less than two feet high, found on mesas and flats up to 6,000 feet in the Mojave Desert and Owens Valley, etc. Typical plants: *Atriplex confertifolia, Grayia spinosa,* and *Kochia californica.*

8. Creosote Bush Scrub. Widely spaced shrubs up to ten feet high,

usually below 3,500 feet in the deserts. Typical plants: *Larrea divaricata, Franseria dumosa, Dalea* spp., and *Opuntia* spp.

9. Alkali Sink. Low gray or fleshy holophytes, found on poorly drained flats in the Great Central Valley and in the dry desert regions. Typical plants: *Atriplex* spp., *Sarcobatus vermiculatus, Allenrolfea occidentalis,* and *Suaeda torreyana.*

10. North Coastal Coniferous Forest. Outer north Coast Ranges from Mendocino County northward. Up to 110 inches of rainfall, with dense fogs; trees 150–200 feet or more. Typical plants: *Tsuga heterophylla, Pseudotsuga taxifolia, Abies grandis,* and *Acer circinatum.*

11. Closed-cone Pine Forest. The interrupted forest from Mendocino plains southward near the immediate coast to Santa Barbara County, from near sea level to 1,200 feet. Northward it is on the seaward side of the redwoods in barren soils. Typical plants: *Pinus muricata, Pinus contorta, Pinus radiata,* and *Cupressus macrocarpa.*

12. Redwood Forest. From central Monterey County north to Oregon on the seaward slope of the Coast Ranges. Typical plants: *Sequoia sempervirens, Pseudotsuga taxifolia,* and *Myrica californica.*

13. Douglas Fir Forest. Scattered remnants from Sonoma and Marin counties northward, mostly east of the Redwood Forest; up to 4,500 feet; trees up to 200 feet, often in pure stands of *Pseudotsuga.*

14. Yellow Pine Forest. Along the northern Coast Ranges, across northern California, and down the Sierra Nevada into southern California. Typical plants: *Pinus ponderosa, Pinus lambertiana, Libocedrus decurrens, Abies concolor, Pseudotsuga taxifolia,* and *Quercus kelloggii.*

15. Red Fir Forest. Above the Yellow Pine Forest in the higher mountains of the state. Typical plants: *Abies magnifica, Pinus murrayana, Pinus monticola, Pinus jeffreyi, Castanopsis sempervirens, Ceanothus cordulatus,* and *Populus tremuloides.*

16. Lodgepole Forest. Northern California and along the high Sierra Nevada. In Fresno County, from 8,500 to 10,000 feet. Sometimes in open forests with extensive meadows. Typical plants: *Pinus murrayana, Tsuga mertensiana, Potentilla breweri,* and *Castilleja culbertsonii.*

17. Subalpine Forest. On the highest mountains, up to 11,000 feet. Known also as *Krummholz,* they may be prostrate or up to 40 feet high. Typical plants: *Pinus albicaulis, Pinus balfouriana, Pinus flexilis, Pinus murrayana, Tsuga mertensiana,* and *Eriogonum incanum.*

18. Mixed Evergreen Forest. Along the inner edge of the Redwood Forest and on higher hills within the northern Coast Ranges, but also as far south as the Santa Cruz Mountains and the northern side of the Santa Lucia Mountains. Typical plants: *Lithocarpus densiflora, Arbutus menziesii, Umbellularia californica, Castanopsis chrysophylla,* and *Quercus chrysolepis.*

19. Northern Oak Woodland. Inland from the Redwood Forest, from Napa County and Yolla Bolly Mountains north; ascending to 3,000–5,000 feet; trees, 25–75 feet, in rather open woodland. Typical plants: *Quercus garryana, Quercus kelloggii, Quercus chrysolepis, Quercus wislizenii, Acer macrophyllum,* and *Aesculus californica.*

20. Southern Oak Woodland. South from Los Angeles County. In the interior valleys up to 5,000 feet. Typical plants: *Quercus agrifolia, Juglans californica,* and *Rhus integrifolia.*

21. Foothill Woodland. In the foothill and valley borders up to 3,000 feet along the inner Coast Ranges and western Sierra Nevada. Extends south as far as Los Angeles County. Typical plants: *Pinus sabiniana, Aesculus californica, Quercus douglasii,* and *Ceanothus cuneatus.*

22. Chaparral. South from Shasta County on the dry slopes and ridges of the Coast Ranges and below the Yellow Pine Forest on the western slopes of the Sierra Nevada Mountains. Typical plants: *Adenostoma fasciculatum, Heteromeles arbutifolia, Quercus dumosa, Cercocarpus betuloides, Yucca whipplei, Fremontia californica, Ceanothus* spp., and *Arctostaphylos* spp.

23. Coastal Prairie. Open hill grasslands, glades, or bald hills on the west slopes of the outer and middle Coast Ranges from Mendocino and Trinity counties northward and on scattered meadows south to San Francisco Bay, mostly below 4,000 feet; bunch grasses with various flowering herbs. Typical plants: *Festuca idahoensis, Danthonia californica,* and *Calamagrostis nutkaensis.*

24. Valley Grassland. On the floors of the Great Central Valley and such smaller valleys as the Salinas, San Benito, and Antelope, up to 4,000 feet in the southern mountains and along the southern coast. Originally plants were perennial grasses, such as *Stipa pulchra, Poa scabrella,* and now species of *Bromus, Festuca,* and *Avena.*

25. Alpine Fell-fields. Almost entirely perennial herbs. Lies above timber line on the highest mountains. Typical plants: *Carex helleri, Carex breweri, Festuca ovina, Poa rupicola,* and *Eriogonum ovalifolium.*

26. Northern Juniper Woodland. From southern Mono County north along the eastern Sierra Nevada slope to Oregon. Typical plants: *Juniperus occidentalis, Pinus jeffreyi, Pinus monophylla,* and *Artemisia tridentata.*

27. Pinyon-Juniper Woodland. Along the eastern Sierra Nevada and White-Inyo ranges southward through the higher desert ranges, between the Yellow Pine Forest and the Joshua Tree Woodland or Sagebrush Scrub. Typical plants: *Pinus monophylla, Juniperus californica,* or *Juniperus osteosperma,* and *Purshia glandulosa.*

28. Joshua Tree Woodland. On well-drained mesas and slopes up to 4,000 feet, from Owens Valley, Inyo County, to the Colorado Desert. Typical plants: *Yucca brevifolia, Juniperus californica* or *Juniperus osteosperma, Salazaria mexicana,* and *Eriogonum fasciculatum.*

Plant Zones of Washington and Oregon

1. Alpine tundra. Usually above 7,000 feet elevation on the highest peaks. Typical plants: *Silene acaulis, Lupinus lyallii, Saxifraga tolmiei,* and *Salix nivalis.*

2. *Tsuga mertensiana,* mountain hemlock. This heterogeneous zone forms a belt along the Cascades and Olympics and into the Siskiyou Moun-

tains. Typical plants: *Tsuga mertensiana, Abies lasiocarpa, Pinus albicaulus, Rhododendron albiflorum,* and *Menziesia ferruginea.*

3. *Picea engelmanni,* Engelmann spruce. From 5,500 to 8,000 feet in elevation in the Blue, Wallowa, Baker, and western Selkirk ranges; also in the Okanogan highlands. Typical plants: *Picea engelmanni, Pinus monticola* (seral), *Pseudotsuga taxifolia* (seral), *Acer glabrum, Alnus tenuifolia, Arctostaphylos nevadensis,* and *Vaccinium scoparium.*

4. *Thuja plicata,* canoe cedar. West of the Cascades below the Okanogan highland mountain hemlock zone from sea level up to 4,000 feet elevation. Other climatic climax dominants are *Tsuga heterophylla, Abies grandis, Abies amabilis,* and *Chamaecyparis lawsoniana.* Perhaps the commonest tree is the *Pseudotsuga menziesii,* but it is thought to represent a seral, or developmental, stage.

5. *Pseudotsuga menziesii,* Douglas fir. On the eastern slopes of the Olympics, the Coast Ranges, the Cascades, and the Blue Mountains just above the *Pinus ponderosa* belt. Most of southwestern Oregon except the highest and lowest belong in this zone. In some places *Pinus lambertiana* and *Libocedrus decurrens* are the dominant trees.

6. *Pinus ponderosa,* yellow pine. Widely over central and eastern Oregon and Washington east of the Cascades, where there is enough moisture. Groves of *Populus tremuloides* occur in moist places. Also associated with it are *Purshia tridentata, Arctostaphylos patula,* and *Ceanothus velutina.*

7. *Pinus cembroides,* Parry pine. Scattered stands in the southeastern quarter of Oregon. Chiefly represented by *Juniperus occidentalis,* which grows where there are 10–15 inches of precipitation annually. Typical plants: *Artemisia tridentata, Purshia tridentata,* and *Chrysothamnus viscidiflorus.*

8. *Quercus gambellii,* Gambel oak. Only a few small regions, typically near the tops of ridges in southeastern Oregon. Typical plants: *Cercocarpus betuloides* and *Cercocarpus ledifolius.* One of the largest stands is in Malheur County on Mahogany Mountain.

9. *Quercus wislizenii,* interior live oak. Includes all the rest of the oak woodlands in Oregon, especially in the southwest.

10. *Artemisia tridentata,* sagebrush. The most extensive and continuous vegetation type in Oregon where the rainfall is 10 inches or less per annum.

11. *Agropyron spicatum,* bunch wheat grass. Eastern portions of both states where rainfall is 12–20 inches per annum. Many other species of grasses are also present. Most of the zone is farmed.

The occurrence of most of the species of mammals in these plant communities and plant zones is a fertile field for future students of mammalogy and one that promises to become very important, because the key to intelligent control and successful habitat management of wildlife lies in the accumulation of data, which are for the most part still ungathered. Doubtless a few mammals will be found that live in only one community. Many more will appear to live equally well in three or more communities, like the Douglas squirrel in the Redwood Forest, Yellow Pine Forest, Red Fir Forest, Lodgepole Forest, and Mixed Evergreen Forest. Some species will always be found to occupy successional stages, and others only the final or climax community. Some species will doubtless live as *ecotone* species, at the edge or at the borders of the plant communities or plant zones.

When the communities occupied by species of mammals are known, they are given in the brief accounts accompanying the pictorial keys. Also included are the much more complete data on life zones, although reference to biotic communities tends to have more meaning and to be more precise. Compare, for example, the two classifications for the Canadian elk: "meadows of the Redwood Forest" is far more precise than "meadows of the Transition Zone."

Habitats

The plant community and the plant zone may be further subdivided into *habitats*, or the places where the animals actually live. Habitats are usually determined by the type of soil, slope, water, wind, sunshine, and other local features. By genetic variation and selection, mammals have been adapted to live in thousands of different habitats. Bogs, sand dunes, swamps, cliffs, and rock slides are a few examples in the Pacific States. The distribution of a species can usually be most accurately defined by its habitat. For example, the pika (*Ochotona princeps*) might be assigned to the Alpine Fell-fields, or Alpine Zone, but it occurs mostly where there are large rock slides or talus slopes, which constitute its proper habitat.

Many species, such as the ubiquitous deer mouse (*Peromyscus maniculatus*), are found living equally well in several communities and zones. Most mammals, however, have one habitat to which they seem better adapted and in which they are found in greater numbers.

The smallest ecological division in space is the habitat, which must not be confused with *niche* (see p. 27). As previously stated, the niche is the position the animal occupies or the role it plays in its habitat. The vagrant shrew (*Sorex vagrans*) lives in the Red Fir Community in the willow-scirpus habitat along with the long-tailed meadow mouse (*Microtus longicaudus*). The two animals have entirely different *niches*. The shrew lives under the thick cover of sedges on the marshy ground, along with the meadow mouse, but it feeds largely on animal food, whereas the meadow mouse takes mostly plant food. Both species are adapted in structure and behavior patterns to obtain their proper food. Two species could, then, never occupy the same niche, but many species could be in the same habitat. Although the niche is the smallest definable ecological unit, the habitat gives the greatest help in describing the distribution of a species.

Other concepts that are useful in studying mammals are those of *home range* and *territory*. Whereas range is used in describing the area covered by a species or subspecies, *home range* applies to an individual animal's travels about its establishment or nest in carrying out its normal activities that center about mating, caring for the young, and food getting. Such an area must be large enough so that the requirements of a particular niche of the male, female, and young will be supplied. Thus, the home range of an animal may be variable in size, depending on its habitat, season, sex, and age.

Territoriality is exhibited by some mammals. That part of the home range that is defended against other individuals of the same species is the *territory* of an animal. Wood rats (*Neotoma*) defend their nests against others of the same species, and it is probable that many other small mammals do likewise; hence the nest and its immediate vicinity may be considered a small territory (Wynne-Edwards, 1964).

Territory and home range behavior have been developed by evolution, and benefit the species by keeping the population spread out. This not only assures sufficient food for the occupant but protects the species from heavy predation and diseases spread by contact. Errington (1963) stated that mammals that limit their populations by well-developed home ranges and territories have predation limited for the most part to the young, crippled, and diseased—the expendable parts of the population. Predators rarely reduce such populations; they take only the excess individuals that never find adequate home ranges. Such populations are remarkably stable regardless of an excess of predators. Species having weak or little territoriality, however, often show violent fluctuations in numbers as their populations are reduced by predation, disease, emigration, or malnutrition. Overpopulation often follows the removal of predators, and the individuals then frequently die of disease, malnutrition, or starvation. Such appears to have been the case of the mule deer on the Kaibab Plateau, Arizona, after the mountain lions were removed.

Many methods of studying the home ranges of mammals involve live trapping, marking, releasing, and retrapping. Some of these methods are described by Hayne (1949), Stickel (1954), and Burt (1940, 1943).

3. Mammals in Geologic History

Study of fossil remains indicates that the great reptiles which dominated the sea, land, and air for over 100 million years during the Mesozoic Era suddenly died off with the beginning of the Cenozoic Era (fig. 9). This Age of Mammals began nearly 80 million years ago. The first mammals appeared, however, far back in the Jurassic Period of the Mesozoic Era. They had apparently evolved from certain mammal-like reptiles called *theriodonts* and, following them, the *ictidosaurs*. Just when these reptiles with mammalian characteristics became mammals is difficult to ascertain. Various lines of the mammal-like reptiles might have developed into mammals. Hence, mammals may have had a *polyphyletic* origin, and not a single, or *monophyletic*, beginning, as is generally assumed.

Whatever their origin, it is certain that small mammals belonging to four extinct orders were living at the time of the dinosaurs in the Jurassic Period. These were the Triconodonta, Symmetrodonta, Multituberculata, and Pantotheria (fig. 10). Thus, throughout the aeons of Mesozoic time, while the "saurs" were the rulers of *all* environments, there were even then small beasts that probably had hair on their bodies. Some doubtless laid eggs, but others must have produced young from eggs that developed within their own bodies. Some of these early mammals doubtless even nourished their unborn young through a placenta and, after the young were born, with milk. Already these hairy creatures, like some of the mammal-like reptiles before them, had developed peculiarities of anatomy that enabled them to maintain a more constant body temperature, thus permitting them to remain active on cold days, when their gigantic contemporaries became chilled and sluggish, and making for survival when it was hot. The thermal control mechanism led to greater adaptability in the Class Mammalia than in the Class Reptilia.

Thus, changed earth and climatic conditions spelled doom for the highly specialized saurians, and the long reign of the dinosaurs and their kin terminated with the Cretaceous Period.

In the Cenozoic Era, which began at the close of the Cretaceous Period, the more adaptable mammals soon became masters of the new environ-

ERAS	PERIODS	EPOCHS	EVENTS
Cenozoic Age of Mammals	Quaternary	Recent	Modern man
		Pleistocene	Primitive man
	Tertiary	Pliocene	Mammals decline
		Miocene	Mammals at maximum; modern carnivores
		Oligocene	Higher mammals
		Eocene	Archaic mammals disappear; modern mammals appear
		Paleocene	Archaic placentals
Mesozoic Age of Reptiles	Cretaceous		Marsupials, Insectivores, Great Reptiles
	Jurassic		First toothed birds; first mammals
	Triassic		

Fig. 9. The geologic time chart.

ment, which also contained some of the more generalized reptiles and other animals and plants.

One notable group of mammals which made the transition was the multi-tuberculates. These interesting creatures of unknown ancestry, although not the oldest of the mammals, had their origin far back in the Jurassic Period (fig. 10). Throughout the rest of the Age of Reptiles and all through the long Paleocene Epoch, they appeared to have occupied ecological niches similar to those of the rodents of today. The long incisors were somewhat rodent-like, but the molars had two or three rows of little tubercles or bumps, from which the order gets its name.

Another group that appears to have originated independently from the primitive reptiles is the monotremes, or egg-laying mammals (fig. 10). The two genera living today are primitive in many respects but very specialized in others. No other mammalian group seems to have originated from them, although some authorities believe that they may be considered altered marsupials.

Among the other groups of Jurassic mammals, one, at least, seems potentially capable of having been the progenitor of other modern mammals (except monotremes). This group was known as the pantotheres (fig. 10); the surfaces of each molar tooth show three cusps, or the asymmetrical trigonid condition similar to that found in later groups. This molar pattern changed into the *tribosphenic* molars, which developed around three basic cusps arranged as reversed triangles on opposing teeth (fig. 1). The teeth of the pantotheres were like those of opossums (Marsupialia) and ancient insectivores, but much simpler. Hence, the pantotheres could be considered ancestral to the Marsupialia and ancient Insectivora, even though the pantotheres themselves did not survive the Age of Reptiles.

In any case, when the Cenozoic Era began, there were two main groups of mammals with a promising future, those with pouches (Marsupialia) and those with placentas (Eutheria), and *from the latter group developed all of the later orders*. First, however, these ancient insectivore-like animals gave rise to many fossil groups as well. The taeniodonts had long, gnawing canine teeth, heavy claws, and other specializations that led them to early extinction without giving rise to any modern order. Two other archaic groups were the creodonts and the condylarths, which were both at first omnivorous. The creodonts became more and more carrion eaters and then carnivorous, while the condylarths became more and more herbivorous. Modern carnivores arose from the old creodonts, and modern herbivores apparently descended from the condylarths, but possibly not from the North American representatives.

About the beginning of the Eocene Epoch both Europe and North America were invaded by hordes of mammals, apparently from Asia, that belonged to a number of modern orders. These mammals had evolved beyond the archaic types, and most of the old North American creodonts and condylarths readily succumbed and passed to extinction, although the hyaenodont creodonts persisted until the Oligocene Epoch. Those in South America, however, lived on, because that continent had become isolated by the submergence of parts of Central America after those archaic groups had become established there and before the great invasion of modern orders had reached North America. Hence, the later mammals of South America originated from the old types that were there (and formerly elsewhere), while most, but not all, of the later mammals of North America came from new stocks that came in from Asia. Special attention should be called to two groups that seem to have developed in South America, but not from its archaic stocks. They are the primates and the rodents. Primates are known to have been in that continent since the Miocene Epoch, but how they got there is a mystery. Whether they came from an early Eocene tarsier type known in North America and went into South America before the continent became isolated, or whether they developed from kinds that made a "crossing from Africa" is not known. The rodents had a similar history in South America. The metropolis of the rodent suborder, Hystricomorpha, is in South America with a minor center in Africa. The only representative of this suborder in North America is the porcupine, which appar-

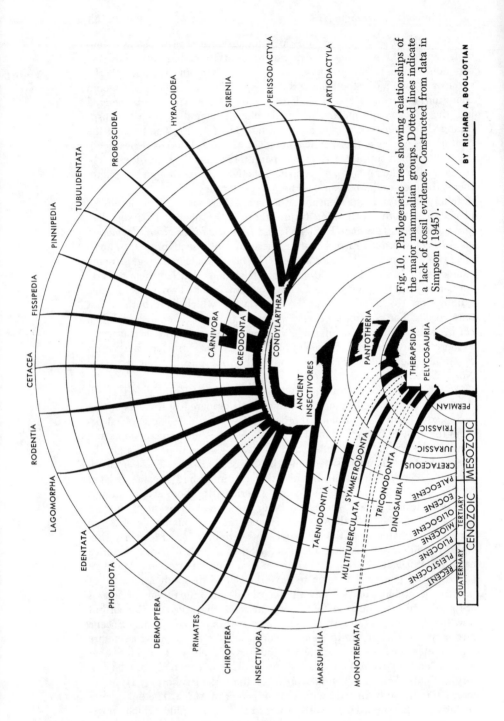

Fig. 10. Phylogenetic tree showing relationships of the major mammalian groups. Dotted lines indicate a lack of fossil evidence. Constructed from data in Simpson (1945).

BY RICHARD A. BOOLOOTIAN

ently came in from South America as a Pleistocene invader. How the original rodent stocks got to South America is, like the origin of the primates there, an unsolved question.

From the primitive insectivores somewhere in Asia perhaps also came the tree shrew, a little tarsier-like primate, and other primates including man himself, although the latter did not appear in North America until late Pleistocene times.

Perhaps nowhere in North America does the past history of mammalian life unfold so clearly as in the John Day formation of north-central Oregon. The oldest mammalian fossil remains in Oregon are near the crossing on the John Day River called the Clarnos bridge; these fossils are referable to the Eocene. The most abundant remains of fossil mammals come from the John Day Oligocene and Miocene formations. These include many carnivores such as the saber-toothed cats, and dogs, and herbivores like the horses, rhinoceroses, camels, and pigs. Many rodents and rabbits and even the opossum are present. There are many creatures, such as the oreodonts, in these fossil beds quite unlike anything living today. Beautiful examples of three-toed horses and horned rhinoceroses have been found.

The Mascall Beds of Oregon are separated from the John Day by basaltic lavas. They contain more highly developed types of horses (i.e., capable of grazing instead of browsing), a hornless deer, and a camel.

Another formation in the John Day region known as the Rattlesnake is referable to Pliocene time. Here are found still more advanced types of mammals. The grazing horses in these strata apparently had only one functional toe, the others being greatly reduced in size. The rhinoceroses were among the last found in North America. Large camels and mastodons were common. Among the smaller mammals were cats, mustelids, coyotes, bear-like dogs and a species of bear.

Pliocene species of mammals are also found in numbers in the San Francisco Bay region in California. These include not only many genera that today occupy the region but such creatures as the elephant-like mastodons, three-toed horses, camels, hyaenoid dogs, rhinoceroses, and a hornless antilocaprid about the size of a sheep. The Pleistocene deposits found in this part of California include many present-day genera and mammoths, camels, true horses (*Equus*), and a very peculiar antilocaprid with four long horns (*Tetrameryx*).

All evidence points to the fact that the climate in the John Day region was temperate and wet, not semiarid, as it is today. Most of these fossils were in lake basins or along the borders of freshwater lakes. Where lineages can be traced, these fossil remains clearly show definite evidence of evolutionary changes which permitted the mammalian species to adapt to the climatic change from wet to arid, and from warm to cold.

The mammalian deposits in the Pacific States, along with those from other Western states, show clearly three salient features: (1) the indigenous development of several families from Paleocene to Pleistocene times, (2) immigrations from Asia at various times throughout the Cenozoic Era,

Fig. 11. The Rancho La Brea Tar Pits perhaps 100,000 years ago, as conceived by the artist, H. Wayne Trimm. In the foreground a ground sloth (*Paramylodon harlani*) is attacked by a saber-tooth (*Smilodon californicus*). Across the pool a large dead emperor mammoth (*Archidiskodon imperator*) is sinking in the tar as a couple of dire wolves (*Aenocyon dirus*) prepare for a feast. In the background at the right are two Western horses (*Equus occidentalis*). Flying and waiting about the pool are the striking condor-like vultures (*Teratornis merriami*). All of this Pleistocene life was within what is now the City of Los Angeles.

and (3) a great period of dying-off of many species during the Pleistocene Epoch. Thus we arrive at present-day, or Recent, fauna.

Now let us consider some Western mammals as they were more recently, say a few thousand to 300,000 years ago, in the later part of the Pleistocene Epoch. The descendants of types like the small four-toed eohippus (*Hyracotherium*) of Eocene times had long ago developed through the three-toed stages represented in the John Day formations to become the one-toed horse. The tapir-size *Moeritherium* and its relatives had through their descendants developed into the huge mammoths and mastodons. The seaways that had dissected Central America at different times and places had disappeared, and the land bridge to the south was re-established. Already many kinds of North American cats, peccaries, horses, tapirs, mastodons, and camel-like animals had gone to South America, and South America's own archaic species were rapidly dying out. A few like the anteaters, sloths, and armadillos survived, however, and some, like the ground sloths, had moved in reverse—coming all the way north to California and Oregon. In both North and South America the indigenous horses and mastodons soon died out.

The famous Rancho La Brea Pits in Hancock Park, Los Angeles, was a cemetery for these later Pleistocene mammals for thousands of years (fig. 11). These pits of sticky tar were formed by petroleum oozing slowly to the surface of the earth, and were as effective in catching and holding a mammoth as flypaper catches and holds a fly. The struggling herbivores attracted the carnivores, which were in turn trapped. All of their bones gradually sank and were preserved to the finest detail by the tar itself. Today, through the pioneer work of John C. Merriam, and later of Chester Stock and his associates of the California Institute of Technology, more than 180 kinds of California Pleistocene animals and plants are known to science from these tar pits alone.

The topography of the landscape about La Brea Pits during the last part of the Pleistocene age was doubtless very similar to what was there when the white men first came. It was perhaps open rolling country on which grew an interior type of rather arid vegetation; largely grass-covered but interspersed with copses of trees and brush. The climate was perhaps as equable as it is today, with possibly more rain. This was an ideal environment for the ancient giant bison, which had recently come to North America from Asia, Western horses, grazing ground sloths, Columbian mammoths, camels, dire wolves, and great saber-toothed cats. These and many other interesting species were the inhabitants along what is now Wilshire Boulevard in Los Angeles perhaps a hundred thousand years ago! Then the Age of Mammals was as dominant in North America as it is in Africa today.

As one reviews these successions of dominant faunas through geologic time, as one considers the fact that the dominance of the mammals is waning, one can speculate about the present dominant position of that supermammal—man. Will his day too pass, and after him, what?

4. The Study of Mammals

What is it? This is probably the first question a person will ask about any animal new to him. The correct name is very important, especially for one who expects to study mammals seriously. One of the most important things to learn, then, is how to identify a mammal.

With some animals, such as birds, the correct identification is relatively easy and can nearly always be made on the basis of such externally observed features as markings, color, song, call, silhouette, and manner of flight. These features can readily be described or figured, and many bird students can identify certain birds while still several yards away or out of sight in the green foliage. The identification of many species of small mammals, however, can seldom be accomplished "out of the hand," and frequently the skull and teeth give all-important clues. Mammals are largely nocturnal, and, although more mammals than birds inhabit most regions, they are rarely seen. For purposes of study, it is often necessary to hold them captive for controlled observation or make them up as study skins.

Although many animals in the wild state are difficult to identify, some can be recognized easily. Others can be identified readily to the genus (e.g., *Thomomys,* pocket gopher) or to the family (e.g., *Ursidae,* bear), which leads to the correct source for the specific name.

Identification

Use of Measurements and Color in Identification. Even when the mammal to be identified is at hand, there are several things a person must know before he can proceed with identification. Most important are measurements, the making and recording of which are described in the Appendix (see p. 448). *Known* measurements of adult animals are given in the keys and accounts, which are of limited help in identifying a mammal that is not fully grown. Further, measurements of adult animals vary greatly from one part of their range to another.

Color is widely used in the keys and in the accounts of the species in this book. It too has limitations, frequently differing in juveniles and adults, in individuals from different parts of the range, and even with the different annual molts of the same animal. Unfortunately there are no color charts which the student can use to compare the color of a mammal's pelage. Such terms as "buffy," "mummy brown," "fuscous," "dusky gray," and "rufous" are widely used in the literature of mammals, yet the visual images of colors indicated by these terms differ. The dictionary definition helps. So does checking the color of *known* specimens against descriptions using the term. For example, the dorsal color of the house mouse (*Mus musculus*) is *buffy brown*. If a specimen at hand is *known* to be a house mouse, then the color *buffy brown* is learned.

Use of Range Maps in Identification. Range maps of most native mammals of the Pacific States, except the whales (Cetacea), are placed near the species accounts. These small maps show the range of the species as it is *now*, not what *it used to be*. Range maps have their limitations. Not only does their small size make location difficult, but they become out of date.

After a specimen or an observed mammal has been identified tentatively by means of the keys, drawings, or photographs, its place of capture or observation should be located on the range map. If it falls within its known range, the tentative identification is *probably* correct. If, however, other species of the genus are also found at the same place (that is, are sympatric), then the next step is to resort once again to the keys, drawings, descriptions, and photographs for the group for further clues that will help separate the species from the other species. Although the range map may be a valuable aid in the final identification of a species, it should always be used in conjunction with the keys, drawings, photographs, and descriptions. Maps of the three Pacific States are provided inside the book covers.

Although the known range of a mammal may cover a given area, the actual distribution of the species may be limited to certain habitats within a biotic community or life zone. The pigmy rabbit, for example, ranges throughout the eastern parts of Oregon and California. It is very limited in its distribution, however, and is found only within its range where the individual sagebrush plants are growing close together. The pika ranges along the Sierra Nevada and Cascade mountains above timberline but only where there are habitats of loose rocks under which it can hide.

These factors of external peculiarities, measurements and colors, range maps, zones, biotic communities, and habitats have been incorporated in this book and are designed especially to aid in the identification and study of the species of mammals occupying the Pacific States.

Advanced Study Methods. When a prolonged study is desired, it may be necessary to keep the animal for a time in captivity. The account given should help in feeding and caring for the captive.

It may be desirable to make the specimen up into a study skin or simply to preserve its baculum. Many research problems, especially those involving classification, life history, ecology, and population studies, even of an elementary nature, involve making study skins from different localities or at different seasons. Methods for making bacula preparations are presented in Appendix A (pp. 457–58).

Extraordinarily sophisticated techniques are being used in ecological studies. Radio isotopes of various elements contained in metal bands have been attached to the legs, tail, or ears, or have been inserted in capsules under the skin of living moles, meadow mice, and other small mammals. With the aid of a scintillation counter attached to a long pole, the movements of the animals can then be followed in the deep grass or, when gamma rays are used, even under a few inches of earth. This new method greatly facilitates the study of behavior and home ranges without the necessity of catching and releasing the marked animal more than once. Even modern electronic equipment is being employed. Tiny radio sending sets energized by the sun attached to the horns of the bighorn sheep or even on a collar around the necks of smaller mammals are suggested as a modern means of keeping track of these elusive mammals and learning more about their movements and home ranges.

The general group and specific accounts here included should help one to acquire a concept of the role a particular mammal occupies in nature. These accounts are designed to help students understand mammals by presenting information which should result in more intelligent conservation and control. Many erroneous statements and beliefs are current, and fallacies regarding the life histories of mammals are commonly accepted as fact. Only by careful study can the real facts be determined. Some forms actually beneficial to man are not infrequently accused of being detrimental, and vice versa. For example, a pocket gopher in a vineyard is a nuisance and should be eliminated. A pocket gopher in the high mountain meadows is beneficial, since it digs underground burrows that soak up runoff water and thereby conserve it.

How to Use the Keys. The most important means of identifying a mammal is to use a key. In this book there are two kinds of keys, the "conventional key" and the new "pictorial key," in which the species are represented by drawings to show the principal external diagnostic features. Both kinds of keys are scattered throughout the book; associated with them are brief descriptions or accounts accompanying each mammal pictured.

Perhaps the best way to identify a mammal that is entirely unknown would be to start with the general key, p. 51, or if only a skull is at hand, to use the skull key on p. 51. These are the conventional type of key. Read carefully what is written under 1A and 1B and decide which the specimen fits better. If this leads to another number at the right of the page, then go to the A and B parts of that number, and continue until a *name is reached* or the reader is referred to another key.

However, if the animal is known to be some species of ground squirrel or kangaroo rat, the general key may be ignored and the appropriate key to complete its identification should be located in the text. When the animal has been tentatively identified, the photographs, drawings, brief descriptions, and range maps should be consulted for confirmation. The species description which the animal in question *most closely* fits is likely to be the *correct one,* even if it does not seem to fit the photograph, drawing, or brief description in *all* of the features. If no range maps are included for the group, then the animal may be compared directly with the pictures and the brief descriptions. Not all species are included in the photographs.

After the correct species name has been learned, a naturalist may wish to know to which geographic race the animal should be assigned. To get this information, it is perhaps best to secure expert advice or to send the specimen to one of the fine museums where there is a large series of specimens from different localities and where a specialist in a certain genus or family is available.

General Key to the Orders

1A. No more than three upper incisors on each side; no epipubic bones; no pouch in the female 2
1B. Upper incisors five on each side; epipubic bones present; females with pouch (Marsupialia). Lowlands in the western half of all three states. *Didelphis marsupialis*, common opossum. P. 76, fig. 52.
2A. Forelimb not modified for flying 3
2B. Forelimb modified for flying (bats, Chiroptera). See key, p. 114.
3A. Hind limbs present 4
3B. Hind legs absent externally (whales, Cetacea). See p. 310.
4A. Feet with claws 5
4B. Feet with hoofs. See key, p. 413.
5A. Canines present 6
5B. Canines absent 7
6A. Canines smaller than incisors (moles and shrews, Insectivora). See keys, pp. 82, 97.
6B. Canines longer than incisors (flesh-eating, Carnivora). See keys, pp. 335, 395.
7A. With two upper incisors (mice, rats, squirrels, etc., Rodentia). See key, p. 153.
7B. With four upper incisors (two smaller ones behind the large outer ones) (rabbits, hares, pikas, Lagomorpha). See key, p. 136.

An Artificial Generic Key to the Skulls (except Cetacea)

Note: When counting teeth which are out of their sockets, recall that the incisors and canines leave one hole (alveolus); each of the cheek teeth leave two or more holes. The young and very old animals may not have the dental formula given here; in very old animals the cusps may also be worn away.

1A. *No canines*; with a long diastema between upper incisors and cheek teeth; skull length less than 150 mm.; orbit not enclosed posteriorly by a junction of the postorbital process of the frontal bone and the zygomatic arch (fig. 12); rodent or rabbit-like animals 54
1B. *With or without canines*; when canines are absent, the skull is more than 150 mm. in length; diastema, if any, is usually shorter than the canine; the orbit may be enclosed in a bony case (fig. 13) 2
2A. Fewer than 50 teeth; fewer than five incisors on each side of upper jaw 3
2B. 50 teeth (may be fewer in young animals); five incisors on each side of upper jaw; small brain case; 5-1-3-4/4-1-3-4. Order Marsupialia.
    Didelphis, common opossum.

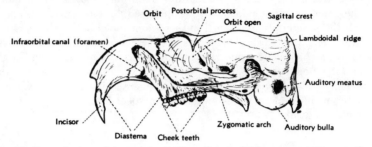

Fig. 12. Lateral view of the cranium of a yellow-bellied marmot (*Marmota flavi-ventris*) showing orbit open posteriorly and other features. It is a representative of the rodent Suborder Sciuromorpha.

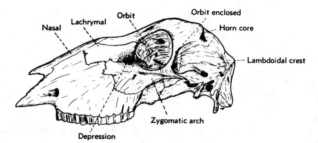

Fig. 13. Lateral view of the cranium of a female domestic sheep (*Ovis aries*) showing the lachrymal bone in contact with the nasal bone.

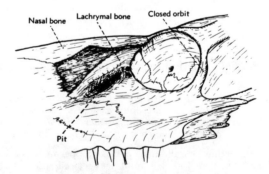

Fig. 14. Lateral view of a part of the cranium of the mule deer (*Odocoileus hemionus*) showing the large lachrymal pit and the lachrymal bone not contacting the nasal bone.

3A. Skulls with orbit enclosed posteriorly by the postorbital process of the frontal bone uniting with zygomatic arch (except some pigs, which have orbit not entirely enclosed but which have very prominent lateral lambdoidal crests). Orders Primates, Artiodactyla, and Perissodactyla (fig. 13)   4

3B. Skulls with the orbit opening posteriorly (not enclosed by the union of a postorbital process of the frontal with the zygomatic arch (fig. 12)   .   16

4A. Orbits facing forward; rostrum very short, making face nearly vertical; 2-1-2-3/2-1-2-3. Order Primates.

     Homo, man.

4B. Orbits on the sides of the skull facing more or less laterally; rostrum elongated (not vertical)   5

5A. Without prominent lateral lambdoidal ridge; cheek teeth selenodont or lophodont (fig. 15); canines, if present, shorter than upper incisors   .   6

5B. Large skull with very prominent lateral lambdoidal ridge; canines longer than incisors; canines turned outward and somewhat triangular in cross section; cheek teeth bunodont (fig. 16); orbit *may or may not* be enclosed by a postorbital process posteriorly. (Note: Last two molars may not have come through the bone in young animals.) 3-1-4-3/3-1-4-3. Order Artiodactyla.

     Sus, domestic and feral pigs.

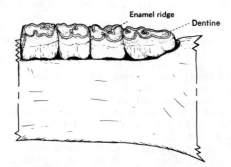

Fig. 15. Showing the high-crowned selenodont-type teeth of the domestic horse (*Equus caballus*) with enamel ridges.

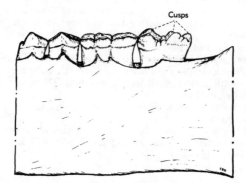

Fig. 16. Showing the low-crowned bunodont-type teeth of a domestic pig (*Sus scrofa*) with cusps.

6A. Large skull with *upper incisors present*; face very long; cheek teeth are the hypsodont-lophodont or hypsodont-selenodont type (fig. 15). (Note: canines may or may not be present.) 3-1-4-3/3-1-3-3. Order Perissodactyla.

　　　Equus, horse, mule, burro.

6B. Large skull with *upper incisors absent*; face long; cheek teeth are of the hypsodont-selenodont type (fig. 15) 7

7A. Large skull with short horn core one-half to four inches long on frontal bone directly above the orbits and directed forward in both sexes; horn sheaths are formed from what appears to be agglutinated hair, with one fork (forward) in males and no fork in females. 0-0-3-3/4-0-3-3.* Order Artiodactyla.

　　　Antilocapra, pronghorn.

7B. Large skull with the horn core or bony antlers (if present) directed backward, arising near the top of skull but not immediately above the orbits. Order Artiodactyla (except Suidae and Antilocapridae) 8

8A. Lachrymal bone (fig. 13) in contact with nasal bone; horns may be in both sexes; horn sheaths made of horny substance. Bovidae 9

8B. Lachrymal bone (fig. 14) not in contact with nasal bone; antlers normally only in males but sometimes in females also (*Rangifer*). Cervidae . 13

9A. Cheek teeth row more than 110 mm. in length; skull length more than 350 mm. 12

9B. Cheek teeth row less than 110 mm. in length; skull length less than 350 mm. 10

10A. Horns not black; larger than six inches in circumference at the base 11

10B. Horns black, saber-like, less than six inches in circumference at the base; 0-0-3-3/3-1-3-3.

　　　Oreamnos, mountain goat.

11A. With a well-defined pit or depression on the lachrymal bone; six cheek teeth on each side of lower jaw; 0-0-3-3/3-1-3-3.

　　　Ovis, native and domestic sheep.

11B. With only a slight pit or depression in front of the orbit; with seven cheek teeth on each side of lower jaw; 0-0-3-3/3-1-4-3.

　　　Capra, domestic goat.

12A. Large skull with premaxillary bone extending to the nasal bone; when viewed from directly above the skull, the anterior part of the zygomatic arch *is not obscured* by the frontal bone; horn core *with* a conspicuous boss (knoblike swelling at the base), 0-0-3-3/3-1-3-3. Bovidae.

　　　Bos, domestic cattle.

12B. Large skull with premaxillary bone not extending to the nasal bone; when viewed from directly above, the anterior part of the zygomatic arch *is obscured* by the laterally projecting frontal bone; horn core *without* a conspicuous boss; 0-0-3-3/3-1-3-3. Bovidae.

　　　Bison, American bison.

13A. Antlers more or less palmate in both sexes, or with a skull over 500 mm. 14

13B. Antlers cylindrical, never palmate, skull less than 500 mm. in length 15

14A. Both sexes with antlers, skull length less than 500 mm.; 0-0-3-3/3-1-3-3.

　　　Rangifer, caribou.

14B. Males only with antlers, skull over 500 mm. in length; 0-0-3-3/3-1-3-3.

　　　Alces, moose.

15A. Brow and bez tines present (p. 426); upper canines present; upper cheek teeth row more than 110 mm. in length; 0-1-3-3/3-1-3-3.

　　　Cervus, wapiti or elk.

---

* The outside lower "incisor" tooth is actually considered a canine, in which case the formula would be 0-0-3-3/3-1-3-3 for all native Artiodactyla except *Cervus,* which is 0-1-3-3/3-1-3-3.

Fig. 17. Ventral view of the rostrum of the Trowbridge shrew (*Sorex trowbridgii*) showing the incisors arranged longitudinally. (Some zoologists consider the canine tooth, shown here, in shrews to be a premolar.)

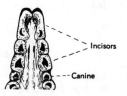

15B. Brow and bez tines absent; upper canines absent; upper cheek teeth row less than 110 mm. in length; 0-0-3-3/3-1-3-3.
    Odocoileus, deer.

16A. Incisor teeth (except the first two large ones) run longitudinally down the skull instead of transversely (fig. 17); canines about the same size or smaller than the unicuspid incisors; slender zygomatic arch or none. Order Insectivora 17

16B. Incisor teeth slightly arched, or set transversely across the skull (figs. 18, 27) 21

17A. With a slender zygomatic arch; upper larger anterior incisors, not chestnut-brown-colored, project down at right angles to the skull. Talpidae . 18

17B. Without a zygomatic arch; teeth frequently tipped with chestnut brown color. Soricidae 19

18A. Total length of upper tooth row over 12 mm.; palate slightly prolonged behind the level of the last molars; 3-1-4-3/3-1-4-3.
    Scapanus, moles.

18B. Total length of upper tooth row less than 12 mm.; palate ending with the level of the last molars; 3-1-2-3/3-1-2-3.
    Neurotrichus, shrew-mole.

19A. Three unicuspid teeth on each side of upper jaw, behind the large anterior bilobed incisors; 3-1-1-3/2-0-1-3. Sometimes written 3-1-1-3/1-1-1-3.
    Notiosorex, gray shrew.

19B. Five unicuspid teeth (only three may be visible from lateral view) on each side of upper jaw, behind the large anterior bilobed incisors (fig. 19); 3-1-3-3/1-1-1-3 20

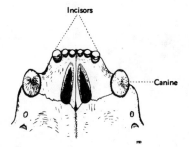

Fig. 18. The incisors are arranged horizontally across the cranium in a mountain lion (*Felis concolor*).

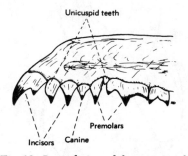

Fig. 19. Lateral view of the rostrum of the Trowbridge shrew (*Sorex trowbridgii*). (Some zoologists consider the canine tooth, shown here, to be a premolar.)

20A. Five unicuspid teeth *visible* when viewed laterally (fig. 19); condylobasal length 14.2–24 mm.
      Sorex, shrews.
20B. Three unicuspid teeth *visible* when viewed laterally (all five visible from ventral view); condylobasal length 13–16 mm.; 3-1-3-3/1-1-1-3.
      Microsorex, pigmy shrew.
21A. Skull length more than 33 mm. (Carnivora and Pinnipedia)   .   .   . 33
21B. Skull length less than 33 mm. (Chiroptera)   22
22A. Premaxillary bones united anteriorly without a space between the two middle incisors (fig. 20) 23
22B. Premaxillary bone separated anteriorly with a space between the two middle incisors (fig. 21) 25
23A. With two upper incisors on each half of jaw   24

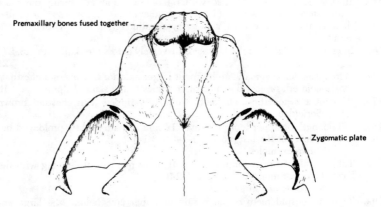

Fig. 20. Anterior end of the cranium of a mountain lion (*Felis concolor*) showing the fused premaxillary bones and wide zygomatic plate.

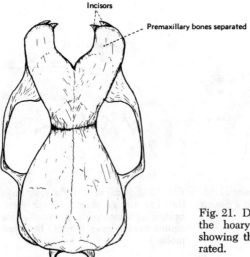

Fig. 21. Dorsal view of the cranium of the hoary bat (*Lasiurus cinereus*) showing the premaxillary bones separated.

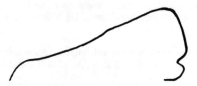

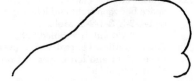

Fig. 22. Profile of the cranium of the silvery-haired bat (*Lasionycteris noctivagans*) showing the low forehead.

Fig. 23. Profile of the cranium of the long-eared or lump-nosed bat (*Plecotus townsendii*) showing high forehead.

23B. With one upper incisor on each half of jaw; 1-1-2-3/2-1-2-3 or 1-1-1-3/2-1-2-3. Molossidae.
     Eumops, mastiff bat.
24A. Skull length about 22 mm.; 2-1-2-3/2-1-3-3. Phyllostomatidae.
     Macrotus, California leaf-nosed bat.
24B. Skull length about 29 mm.; 2-1-2-3/0-1-3-3.
     Choeronycteris, long-tongued bat.
25A. With three premolar and three molar teeth on each side of upper jaw (six cheek teeth in all on each side); skull length 12–17 mm.; broad U-shaped anterior emargination of the palate; 2-1-3-3/3-1-3-3. Vespertilionidae.
     Myotis, mouse-eared bat.
25B. With fewer than three premolars on each side of upper jaw (fewer than six upper cheek teeth) 26
26A. With three premolars and three molars on each side of lower jaw (six lower cheek teeth on each side) 27
26B. With fewer than three premolars on each side of lower jaw (fewer than six lower cheek teeth on each side) 28
27A. Dorsal outline of skull (lateral view) is nearly straight (fig. 22); length about 16 mm.; a distinct concavity between the lachrymal bone and the anterior nare; 2-1-2-3/3-1-3-3. Vespertilionidae.
     Lasionycteris, silvery-haired bat.
27B. Dorsal outline of skull (lateral view) is distinctly oval (fig. 23); length about 15–17 mm.; breadth less than one-third length; 2-1-2-3/3-1-3-3. Vespertilionidae.
     Plecotus, lump-nosed bat.
28A. With eight teeth in each half of upper jaw 29
28B. With fewer than eight teeth in each half of upper jaw 30
29A. Skull length about 11 mm.; dorsal outline (lateral view) is nearly straight; 2-1-2-3/3-1-2-3. Vespertilionidae.
     Pipistrellus, Western pipistrelle.
29B. Skull length about 21 mm.; dorsal outline with a distinct bulge of the forehead; 2-1-2-3/3-1-2-3. Vespertilionidae.
     Euderma, spotted bat.
30A. Premolars 1/2 (4/5 cheek teeth); skull usually more than 18 mm. in length
     31
30B. Premolars 2/2 (5/5 cheek teeth); skull usually less than 18 mm. in length
     (*Tadarida molossa* may be slightly longer) 32
31A. Two upper incisors on each half of jaw; dorsal outline of skull (lateral view) is nearly straight; space between each pair of upper incisors is about 2 mm.; 2-1-1-3/3-1-2-3. Vespertilionidae.
     Eptesicus, big brown bat.
31B. One upper incisor on each half of jaw; dorsal outline of skull (lateral view) is distinctly oval; space between incisors is about 1 mm.; 1-1-1-3/2-1-2-3. Vespertilionidae.
     Antrozous, pallid bat.

32A. Dorsal outline (lateral view) shows a distinct angle down over the nose; space between right and left upper incisors less than 3 mm.; 1-1-2-3/2-1-2-3 or 1-1-2-3/3-1-2-3. Molossidae.
      Tadarida, free-tailed bat.
32B. Dorsal outline (lateral view) over the nose is a smooth curve; space between right and left upper incisors is greater than 3 mm.; 1-1-2-3/3-1-2-3. Vespertilionidae.
      Lasiurus (hairy-tailed bat), hoary and red bats.
33A. Some of the cheek teeth sectorial (flesh-cutting) (fig. 24); or all of the cheek teeth with flat human-like crowns; never fewer than three incisors on each half of lower jaws (except in sea otter, which has only two). Suborder Fissipedia   34
33B. Cheek teeth all peglike with single conical crowns (fig. 25), or each with three cusps or lobes in a line; never more than two incisors below on each half of jaw. Suborder Pinnipedia   49
34A. Zygomatic width (fig. 26) more than 140 mm., with 42 teeth (may be fewer in older specimens); crowns of cheek teeth are low and human-like (bunodont); 3-1-4-2/3-1-4-3. Ursidae.
      Euarctos and *Ursus,* bears.
34B. Zygomatic width less than 140 mm., or, if more, with fewer than 32 teeth   35
35A. With ten teeth on each half of upper jaw   36

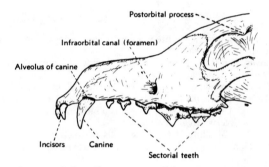

Fig. 24. Lateral view of the anterior part of the cranium of a coyote (*Canis latrans*) showing the sectorial cheek teeth.

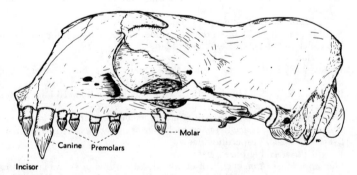

Fig. 25. Lateral view of the cranium of the Steller sea lion (*Eumetopias jubata*). Note the peglike molars and premolars.

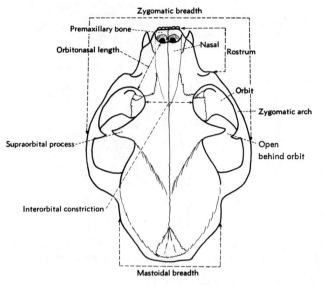

Fig. 26. Dorsal view of the skull of a house cat (*Felis domestica*) showing common measurements.

35B. With fewer than ten teeth on each half of upper jaw 40
36A. Upper tooth row length less than 55 mm. 37
36B. Upper tooth row length more than 55 mm. Canidae 38
37A. With palate extending posteriorly beyond the last molar by a distance as great as the length of the posterior three cheek teeth; 3-1-4-2/3-1-4-2. Procyonidae.
  Procyon, raccoon.
37B. With palate extending posteriorly beyond the level of the last molar by about the length of the last cheek tooth; 3-1-4-2/3-1-4-2.
  Bassariscus, ring-tailed cat.
38A. Upper tooth row length more than 90 mm. (fig. 28) (except small breeds of dogs); postorbital process thick and convexed on the dorsal surface; 3-1-4-2/3-1-4-3.
  Canis, wolf, coyote, dog.
38B. Upper tooth row length less than 90 mm.; postorbital process thin and concaved on the dorsal surface 39
39A. With temporal ridges nearly parallel or V-shaped to form a sagittal crest posteriorly; mandible without a notch or "step" below the angular process; 3-1-4-2/3-1-4-3.
  Vulpes, red fox and kit fox.
39B. With temporal ridges U-shaped; mandible with a distinct notch or "step" below the angular process (fig. 7); 3-1-4-2/3-1-4-3.
  Urocyon, gray fox and island fox.
40A. Upper molar (last cheek tooth or M^1) small, much less than half the size of the last premolar (fig. 28), with a total of 30 teeth or fewer. Felidae 41
40B. Upper molar at least half the size of the last upper premolar; a total of 32 teeth or more. Mustelidae 42
41A. With two upper premolars (three cheek teeth); 3-1-2-1/3-1-2-1.
  Lynx, bobcat and Canadian lynx.

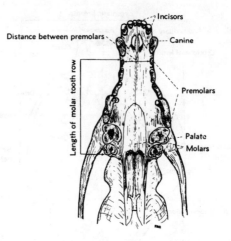

Fig. 27. Ventral view of the cranium of a coyote (*Canis latrans*) showing the limits of the measurements used in distinguishing coyote from dog skulls.

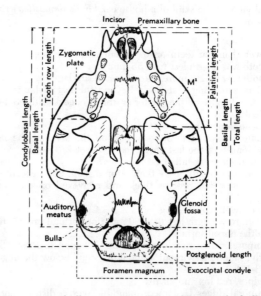

Fig. 28. Some common skull measurements on a house cat's skull (*Felis domestica*). Note that total length always extends from extreme anterior to extreme posterior.

41B. With three upper premolars (four cheek teeth); the orbit is generally open posteriorly (fig. 26), but it may be closed by the supraorbital (postorbital) process uniting with the zygomatic arch; 3-1-3-1/3-1-2-1.

    Felis, mountain lion and domestic cat.

42A. With nine teeth in each half of upper jaw 43

42B. With eight teeth in each half of upper jaw 45

43A. Total length of skull more than 140 mm.; sagittal crest extending 10 mm. or more posteriorly behind the lambdoidal ridge; 3-1-4-1/3-1-4-2.

    Gulo, wolverine .

43B. Total length of skull less than 140 mm.; sagittal crest not extending posteriorly beyond the lambdoidal ridge 44

44A. Greatest width of the skull across the auditory bullae (mastoid breadth) more than 60 mm. (fig. 28); diameter of the infraorbital foramen greater than the alveolus of the canine (fig. 24); M^1 wider than long, rhomboid-shaped; 3-1-4-1/3-1-3-2.

    Lutra, river otter.

44B. Greatest width of the skull across the auditory bullae (mastoid breadth) less than 60 mm.; diameter of infraorbital foramen less than the diameter of the alveolus of the canine; M^1 about two-thirds as long as wide; 3-1-4-1/3-1-4-2.

    Martes, marten and fisher.

45A. Total length of skull over 100 mm. 46

45B. Total length of skull less than 100 mm. 47

46A. Two lower incisors on each half of the mandible; all cheek teeth with part of crowns flat; M^1 oval, wider than long and widest at midwidth; 3-1-3-1/2-1-3-2.

    Enhydra, sea otter.

46B. Three lower incisors on each half of the mandible; crown of M^1 (last tooth) on upper jaw is triangular and is longer than it is wide; 3-1-3-1/3-1-3-2.

    Taxidea, badger.

47A. The anterior-posterior diameter of the inner half of last upper tooth (M^1) *less* than the anterior-posterior diameter of its outer half (fig. 29); palate extending only to the level of the posterior edge of M^1. Subfamily Mephitinae. 48

47B. The anterior-posterior diameter of the inner half of last upper tooth (M^1) *greater* than the anterior-posterior diameter of its outer half (fig. 30); palate extending behind the last molar (M^1) farther than the distance of the anterior-posterior diameter of the M^1; M^1 about half as long as wide; 3-1-3-1/3-1-3-2.

    Mustela; weasel, ermine, mink.

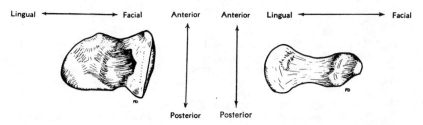

Lingual ←——————→ Facial   Anterior   Anterior   Lingual ←——————→ Facial

Posterior   Posterior

Fig. 29. Last upper molar (M^1) of a striped skunk (*Mephitis mephitis*) showing the inner (lingual) half as less than the width of the outer (facial) half.

Fig. 30. Last upper left tooth (M^1) of a long-tailed weasel (*Mustela frenata*) showing the inner (lingual) half as wide, or wider, and larger than the outer (facial) half.

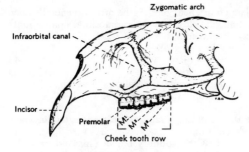

Fig. 31. Lateral view of the anterior part of the cranium of the porcupine (*Erethizon dorsatum*), a representative of the rodent Suborder Hystricomorpha.

48A. Total length of skull less than 56 mm.; length of upper M¹ (last tooth) is less than 7 mm.; 3-1-3-1/3-1-3-2.
     Spilogale, spotted skunk.
48B. Total length of skull more than 56 mm.; length of the upper M¹ (last tooth) is greater than 7 mm.; 3-1-3-1/3-1-3-2.
     Mephitis, striped skunk.
49A. No distinct postorbital process on frontal bone; upper incisors pointed. Phocidae 50
49B. A distinct postorbital process on the frontal bone; upper incisors transversely notched on the crown. Otariidae 51
50A. Skull length less than 300 mm., with molariform (cheek) teeth (except Pm¹) large, double-rooted, and 3-lobed; 3-1-4-1/2-1-4-1.
     Phoca, harbor seal.
50B. Skull length more than 300 mm., with molariform teeth small, single-rooted, not lobed; 2-1-4-1/1-1-4-1.
     Mirounga, northern elephant seal.
51A. Occipital (lambdoidal) and sagittal crests small and not prominent (under 10 mm. high) 52
51B. Occipital and sagittal crests very prominent (30–50 mm. high in males); molar (last tooth) and premolars not separated by a space as wide as a premolar; 3-1-4-1/2-1-4-1.
     Zalophus, California sea lion.
52A. Space between the premolars and molar not as wide as a premolar . 53
52B. Space between the premolars and molar (last tooth) as wide as a premolar; sagittal and occipital crests not strongly developed (under 23 mm. high) in males; 3-1-4-1/2-1-4-1.
     Eumetopias, Steller sea lion.
53A. With five (rarely six) molariform (cheek) teeth on each half of upper jaw; sides of palate not parallel between Pm¹ and Pm³; 3-1-4-2/2-1-4-1 or 3-1-4-1/2-1-4-1.
     Callorhinus, northern fur seal.
53B. With six molariform teeth on each half of upper jaw; sides of palate parallel between Pm¹ and Pm³; 3-1-4-2/2-1-4-1.
     Arctocephalus, southern fur seal.
54A. With four upper incisor teeth (two small ones behind the two large outer incisors). Order Lagomorpha 81
54B. With two upper incisor teeth. Order Rodentia 55
55A. Anterior opening of the infraorbital canal or foramen (fig. 12) smaller in area than the foramen magnum 56
55B. Anterior opening of the infraorbital canal (foramen) (fig. 31) larger in area than the foramen magnum; nasals extending far posterior to the premaxillary bones; front side of incisor is red or yellow; 1-0-1-3/1-0-1-3. Suborder Hystricomorpha.
     Erethizon, porcupine.

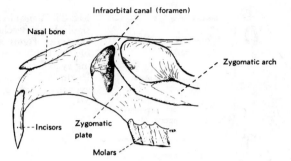

Fig. 32. Lateral view of the anterior part of the cranium of the deer mouse (*Peromyscus maniculatus*), a representative of the Suborder Myomorpha.

56A. Anterior opening of the infraorbital canal (foramen) low on the zygomatic plate, or with an opening low and more anteriorly on the rostrum (fig. 12); its greatest diameter is generally less than the width across the base of the two upper incisors. Suborder Sciuromorpha 57

56B. Anterior opening of the infraorbital canal extends high up on the rostrum along the inside of the zygomatic plate (fig. 32); its greatest diameter is generally more than the width of the two upper incisors. Suborder Myomorpha 68

57A. Without a postorbital process on the frontal bone (sometimes a bump is present) 63

57B. With a postorbital (supraorbital) process on the frontal bone (fig. 12). Sciuridae 58

58A. Length less than 75 mm.; skull usually not concaved or noticeably depressed between the ends of the nasals and the crown . . . 59

58B. Length more than 75 mm.; skull clearly concaved or depressed between the ends of the nasals and the crown; usually with a distinct sagittal crest posteriorly (fig. 12); 1-0-2-3/1-0-1-3.
Marmota, marmot.

59A. Zygomatic arches clearly bulging outward at mid-length and flattened from side to side; total length 38–42 mm.; 1-0-2-3/1-0-1-3.
Glaucomys, northern flying squirrel.

59B. Zygomatic arches nearly parallel, or converging toward the rostrum (fig. 33) 60

60A. Zygomatic arches almost or clearly straight and parallel at mid-length with the longitudinal axis of the skull; zygomatic arches flattened more from side to side than dorsoventrally (fig. 98) 61

60B. Zygomatic arches not parallel but converging at mid-length toward the end of the rostrum (fig. 33) 62

61A. Less than 63 mm. total length; 1-0-1-3/1-0-1-3.
Tamiasciurus, Douglas squirrel.

61B. More than 63 mm. total length; 1-0-1-3/1-0-1-3 or 1-0-2-3/1-0-1-3.
Sciurus, tree squirrels.

62A. Notch in the zygomatic plate (fig. 33) of the maxillary bone is opposite the M¹; anterior part of the zygomatic arch flattened dorsoventrally (fig. 98); anterior-posterior diameter of the upper incisor alveolus is less than one and a half times its transverse diameter; 1-0-2-3/1-0-1-3.
Citellus, Otospermophilus, Callospermophilus, Ammospermophilus; ground squirrels.

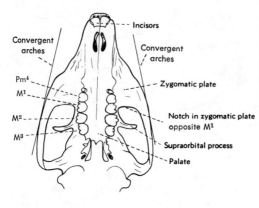

Fig. 33. Ventral view of the skull of the Beechey ground squirrel (*Otospermophilus beecheyi*) showing converging zygomatic arches at mid-length and the notch in the zygomatic arch opposite the M¹.

62ʙ. Notch in the zygomatic plate (fig. 33) of the maxillary bone is opposite Pm⁴ (fourth tooth from the back), or at least extends forward to the level of its posterior border; anterior-posterior diameter of an incisor (at posterior edge of the alveolus) is about twice its transverse diameter; 1-0-2-3/1-0-1-3.
　　　Eutamias, chipmunks.
63ᴀ. Less than 50 mm. in length 65
63ʙ. More than 50 mm. in length 64
64ᴀ. Less than 80 mm. in length, triangular-shaped, width across auditory meatus (ears) equal to zygomatic width; palate extending behind the last molar by a distance about equal to the crown length of that molar; five cheek teeth on each half of upper jaw; the molars have cups on the grinding surfaces; 1-0-2-3/1-0-1-3.
　　　Aplodontia, mountain beaver.
64ʙ. More than 80 mm. in length; except for a slender median projection, the palate extends only to the posterior edge of the last molar; four cheek teeth on each half of upper jaw; 1-0-1-3/1-0-1-3.
　　　Castor, beaver.
65ᴀ. Mastoid breadth less than the zygomatic breadth (fig. 26); zygomatic arch strong, usually more than 1 mm. thick; outer face of incisors with faint groove near inner edge; 1-0-1-3/1-0-1-3. Geomyidae.
　　　Thomomys, pocket gophers.
65ʙ. Mastoid breadth about equal to, or more than, the zygomatic breadth (fig. 26); zygomatic arch weak, less than 1 mm. thick; strongly grooved upper incisors. Heteromyidae 66
66ᴀ. Greatest breadth of skull more than 16 mm.; auditory bullae extending laterally more than 1 mm. beyond the width of the zygomatic arch (fig. 34) 67
66ʙ. Greatest breadth of skull less than 16 mm.; auditory bullae scarcely as wide as the zygomatic arches; crowns of M¹ and M² are U-shaped; 1-0-1-3/1-0-1-3.
　　　Perognathus, pocket mice.
67ᴀ. Greatest breadth of the skull (across the bullae) more than 20 mm.; outer edges of cheek teeth simple, no folds; 1-0-1-3/1-0-1-3.
　　　Dipodomys, kangaroo rats.
67ʙ. Greatest breadth of the skull (across the bullae) less than 20 mm.; 1-0-1-3/1-0-1-3.
　　　Microdipodops, kangaroo mice.
68ᴀ. Upper incisors distinctly grooved longitudinally (fig. 160) . . . 69
68ʙ. Upper incisors not grooved longitudinally 70

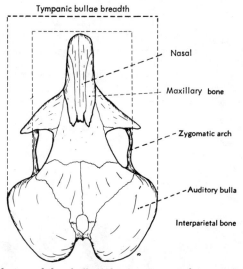

Tympanic bullae breadth

Nasal

Maxillary bone

Zygomatic arch

Auditory bulla

Interparietal bone

Fig. 34. Dorsal view of the skull of the San Joaquin kangaroo rat (*Dipodomys nitratoides*).

69A. With four upper cheek teeth (rarely three) on each half of jaw; infraorbital canal as large as or larger than the rest of the zygomatic plate; skull length 21–26 mm.; 1-0-1-3/1-0-0-3. Zapodidae.
    Zapus, jumping mice.

69B. With three upper cheek teeth on each half of jaw; infraorbital canal not larger than the zygomatic plate; skull length 19–22 mm.; 1-0-0-3/1-0-0-3. Cricetidae (in part).
    Reithrodontomys, harvest mice.

70A. With two or three rows of little cusps running down the crowns of each cheek tooth row (figs. 35–36); crowns are not flat but are generally covered with enamel and do not usually show the dentine; if dentine does show, it is then not enclosed in triangles 71

70B. Without rows of cusps on crowns; crowns flat with little triangles or "puddles" filled with dentine and surrounded by enamel, or with S-shaped ridges on the crowns (figs. 41–44, 46, 49) 74

71A. With two rows of cusps running down the crowns of the tooth row (fig. 35). Cricetidae (in part) 72

71B. With three rows of cusps running down the crowns of the tooth row. Muridae (figs. 36, 37) 73

72A. Palate scarcely extending beyond the posterior side of the last molar; coronoid process (fig. 38) of the mandible not higher than the condyloid process; third molar crown nearly half as large as the second molar; anterocone of M^1 broadly transverse and not distinctly in the outer row of cusps (fig. 3); 1-0-0-3/1-0-0-3.
    Peromyscus, deer mice.

72B. Palate extending beyond the posterior side of the last molar by a distance at least equal to the width of the molar; coronoid process of the mandible is higher than the condyloid process and is directed backward; third molar crown about one-third or less the size of the second molar; anterocone of M^1 is cone-shaped and is clearly in the outer row of cusps; 1-0-0-3/1-0-0-3.
    Onychomys, grasshopper mice.

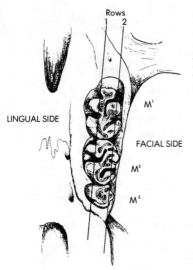

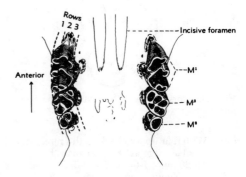

Rows
1 2

LINGUAL SIDE

FACIAL SIDE

M¹

M²

M³

Fig. 35. Crown view of upper left molars of the deer mouse (*Peromyscus maniculatus*) showing two rows of cusps.

Rows
1 2 3

Anterior

Incisive foramen

M¹

M²

M³

Fig. 36. Crown view of the upper molars of the house mouse (*Mus musculus*) showing three rows of tubercles.

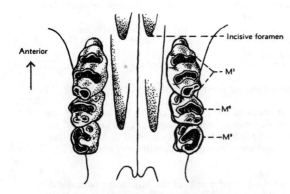

Anterior

Incisive foramen

M¹

M²

M³

Fig. 37. Crown view of the upper molars of the black rat (*Rattus rattus*) showing the shape of the three longitudinal rows of cusps.

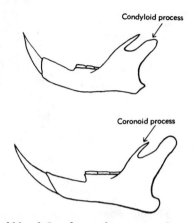

Fig. 38. (*Top*) Mandible of *Onychomys leucogaster* showing the coronoid process higher than the condyloid process. (*Bottom*) Mandible of *Peromyscus maniculatus* showing the coronoid process lower than the condyloid process.

73A. Incisive foramen extending posteriorly to about the level of the middle of the first molar; skull length less than 30 mm.; M^1 (first cheek tooth) length is greater than combined length of M^2 and M^3; (fig. 36); 1-0-0-3/1-0-0-3.
    Mus, introduced house mouse.

73B. Incisive foramen extending posteriorly to about the level of the anterior edge of the first molar; with definite supraorbital ridges; skull length more than 30 mm.; crown length of M^1 (first cheek tooth) is about equal to or less than the rest of the cheek teeth row (fig. 37); 1-0-0-3/1-0-0-3.
    Rattus, introduced Norway and black rats.

74A. Length usually more than 37 mm. 75
74B. Length usually less than 37 mm. Subfamily Microtinae (in part) . . 77
75A. Length less than 55 mm. 76
75B. Length more than 55 mm.; cheek tooth row more than 10 mm.; palate ending in an arrow-shaped process; 1-0-0-3/1-0-0-3. Cricetidae; subfamily Microtinae.
    Ondatra, muskrat.

76A. With a notch that is longer than it is wide, when viewed dorsally, where the zygomatic arch joins the skull anteriorly (fig. 39); palate ending behind the last molar; with S-shaped ridges on the crowns of the molars (fig. 41); spinous process projecting forward from the upper end of the zygomatic plate; 1-0-0-3/1-0-0-3. Cricetidae.
    Sigmodon, hispid cotton rat.

76B. With a notch that is about as wide as it is long, when viewed dorsally, where zygomatic arch joins the skull anteriorly (fig. 40); with supraorbital ridges; palate ending about the level of the middle of the last molar; crowns of teeth with dentine surrounded by enamel (figs. 49, 50); incisive foramen longer than cheek tooth row; 1-0-0-3/1-0-0-3. Cricetidae.
    Neotoma, wood rat.

77A. Upper M^3 with four projections on the lingual side (figs. 42, 45) or with four transverse elements (fig. 48) 78
77B. Upper M^3 with two or three projections on the lingual side (figs. 46, 47) 80

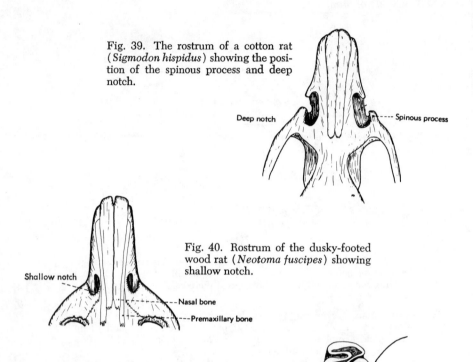

Fig. 39. The rostrum of a cotton rat (*Sigmodon hispidus*) showing the position of the spinous process and deep notch.

Deep notch

Spinous process

Shallow notch

Fig. 40. Rostrum of the dusky-footed wood rat (*Neotoma fuscipes*) showing shallow notch.

Nasal bone

Premaxillary bone

Lingual

Facial

Fig. 41. Crown of the upper left molars of the cotton rat (*Sigmodon hispidus*) showing S-shaped or Σ-shaped patterns.

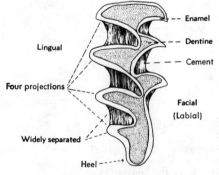

Enamel

Dentine

Cement

Lingual

Four projections

Facial (Labial)

Widely separated

Heel

Fig. 42. Crown of the last left upper molar (M^3) of the California meadow mouse (*Microtus californicus*).

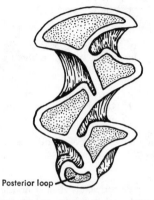

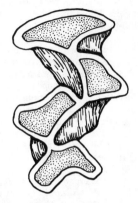

Fig. 43. Crown of the second left upper molar (M²) of the meadow mouse (*Microtus pennsylvanicus*) showing five loops.

Fig. 44. Crown of the second left upper molar (M²) of the long-tailed meadow mouse (*Microtus longicaudus*) showing four loops.

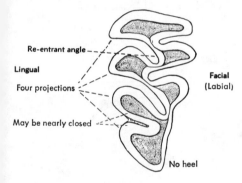

Fig. 45. Crown of the last upper left molar (M³) of the Western red-backed mouse (*Clethrionomys occidentalis*).

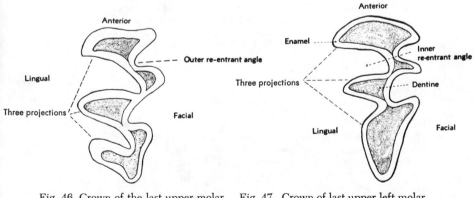

Fig. 46. Crown of the last upper molar (M³) of the heather vole (*Phenacomys intermedius*).

Fig. 47. Crown of last upper left molar (M³) of the sagebrush vole (*Lagurus curtatus*).

78A. Upper M³ with four projections on the lingual side 79
78B. Upper M³ with four transverse elements (fig. 48) on the crown; 1-0-0-3/ 1-0-0-3.

     Synaptomys, bog vole.

79A. Last two projections on lingual side of M³ may be closely appressed (fig. 45), re-entrant angle between them usually deeper than wide; without a "heel" projecting posteriorly on the M³; 1-0-0-3/1-0-0-3.

     Clethrionomys, red-backed mice.

79B. Last two projections on lingual side of M³ wide open, re-entrant angle between them usually wider than deep (fig. 42); with a "heel" projecting posteriorly on the M³; 1-0-0-3/1-0-0-3.

     Microtus, meadow mice.

80A. Upper M³ with both re-entrant angles on the lingual side noticeably deeper than those on the facial side (fig. 46); cheek teeth with tiny roots; 1-0-0-3/ 1-0-0-3.

     Phenacomys, phenacomys and red tree mice.

80B. Upper M³ with only one of the re-entrant angles noticeably deeper on the lingual side than those on the facial side (fig. 47); 1-0-0-3/1-0-0-3.

     Lagurus, sagebrush vole.

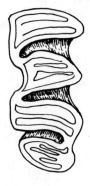

Fig. 48. Crown of last upper left molar (M³) of the bog vole (*Synaptomys borealis*).

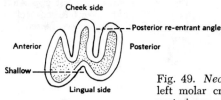

Fig. 49. *Neotoma lepida.* Last upper left molar crown (M³) showing the posterior re-entrant angles on the cheek side (upper right) as straight, the one on the lingual side as shallow.

Fig. 50. *Neotoma fuscipes.* Last upper left molar crown (M³) showing the posterior re-entrant angle on the cheek side (upper right) as bent, the one on the lingual side (lower) as deep.

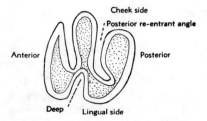

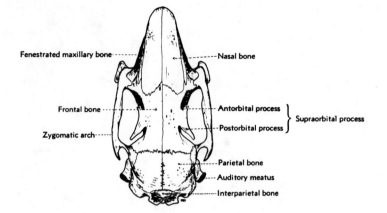

Fig. 51. Dorsal view of the skull of an Audubon cottontail (*Sylvilagus auduæ bonii*).

81A.   With large supraorbital processes on the frontal bones (fig. 51); six cheek teeth on each side of upper jaw; sides of rostrum (maxillary bones) conspicuously fenestrated ("lace-work," fig. 51). Leporidae 82
81B.   Without a supraorbital process on the frontal bone; five cheek teeth on each side of the upper jaw; sides of rostrum (maxillary bones) not conspicuously fenestrated; 2-0-3-2/1-0-2-3. Ochotonidae.
     Ochotona, pika.
82A.   Interparietal bone never distinct (in adults) from parietals; upper cheek tooth row usually more than 13 mm.; 2-0-3-3/1-0-2-3.
     Lepus, black- and white-tailed hares, snowshoe hares.
82B.   Interparietal bone separated by distinct sutures (in adults) from the parietals (fig. 51); upper cheek tooth row between 10 and 13 mm. long; 2-0-3-3/ 1-0-2-3.
     Sylvilagus, cottontails and rabbit.

Part II. Accounts of the Species

5. Order Marsupialia

The order Marsupialia owes its name to the pouch, or *marsupium*, in which the young finish their development. It is located on the lower abdomen of the females of most of the species. Other characteristics that separate this interesting metatherian group from the other mammals of North America will be briefly described.

The marsupials have much smaller brains than eutherian mammals of the same size and there is no *corpus callosum* connecting the two cerebral hemispheres. The uterus is double throughout and there is no chorioallantois-type placenta in the marsupials. The young are born in a very undeveloped embryonic state. The marsupials share with the egg-laying mammals (Monotremata) fully developed epipubic bones regardless of whether they are male or female, or whether they have a pouch or not. No eutherian mammal has these bones. The teeth of marsupials are mostly monophyodont; only one of the cheek teeth (Pm^4) is shed, and it is believed to be replaced by the first upper molar (M^1). There are thus three premolars and four molars in the final set, which is just the reverse of the condition found in primitive eutherian mammals.

The marsupials were worldwide in their distribution during the late Cretaceous and early Tertiary times. Today they are largely limited to the New World and to the Australian region. A polyphyletic origin of mammals is possible in which various groups of mammal-like reptiles separately gave rise to separate groups of mammals. However, most zoologists and paleontologists agree that the fossil and anatomical evidences are sufficient to predict a monophyletic origin of the Monotremata, Marsupialia, and early Insectivora, although the common ancestry may have been well back into Mesozoic time. The fossil evidence indicates there were didelphoid-type marsupials associated with the ancient insectivores of the late Cretaceous Period. Some of these ultimately grew to the size of rhinoceroses in early Tertiary times.

The order Marsupialia consists of five living superfamilies: Didelphoidea, in North America; Dasyuroidea, Perameloidea, and Phalangeroidea, in the Australian region; and Caenolestoidea, in South America.

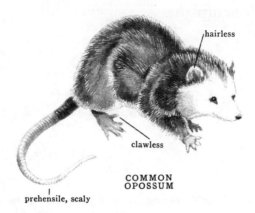

hairless

clawless

**COMMON
OPOSSUM**

|
prehensile, scaly

Common opossum (*Didelphis marsupialis*). 5-1-3-4/4-1-3-4. Length 730–850 mm., about 32 inches; tail scaly, round, prehensile, 240–320 mm.; *hind foot 60–79 mm., with inner toe clawless and diverging widely away from the other toes*; ear membranous, about 40 mm. (crown); skull 116–27 mm.; five incisors on each half of the upper jaw; blackish or grayish, often with nearly black ears and feet. Introduced, but now ranging widely at low elevation in all three states. Fig. 52, Map. 1.

Family **Didelphidae** (Opossums)

The name of this polyprotodont family comes from the fact that the two uteri remain separate and do not fuse together along their lower extremities, as is true of the eutherian mammals (monodelphids). The group includes the most primitive of the marsupialians and ranges back through time to the Age of the Dinosaurs (Cretaceous Period). Some of the skeletons of the marsupials that lived 80 million years ago are found only in the New World. They are represented today by such interesting species as the mouse possums (*Marmosa*), which are pouchless; in Mexico and Central America they are often found in bunches of bananas. The common opossum ranges all the way from Argentina to the United States, where it is the only native marsupial.

Common Opossum (*Didelphis marsupialis*), fig. 52

The common opossum is the only living native mammal in the United States that belongs to the ancient order Marsupialia. Although it is not native to the Pacific Coast, it has been widely introduced and now occupies all but the coldest and driest parts of all three states. It is a cat-sized primitive mammal, with woolly fur overlaid with long guard hairs, a long snout, naked ears, pentadactyl feet, and a long scaly prehensile tail. Like most other marsupials, the opossum has epipubic bones and the female has a pouch, or marsupium, on the lower abdomen. The skull has a very high sagittal crest and the brain cavity is exceedingly small in relation to the size of the skull when compared with that of a fox or raccoon. The tympanic bulla is poorly developed, the middle ear being protected by a downward-projecting process of the alisphenoid bone. The polyprotodont-type dentition includes 50 teeth, which readily distinguishes the skull from that of any other native mammal in the country.

The opossum has no chorioallantois-type placenta as do all other mammals in the Pacific States. Like the embryos of eutherian mammals, however, those of an opossum are covered with fetal membranes. The amnion contains amniotic fluid, and on the outside the chorion functions by making intimate contact with the wall of the uterus, thereby enabling the embryos to be fed by securing nourishment from the mother, even though no true placenta forms for extended nourishment. Wastes are also excreted by way of the chorionic blood vessels across to the blood vessels of the uterus.

Twelve to 13 days after the eggs are fertilized, the female licks her pouch constantly, apparently as a result of stimulation by a hormone. The licking is extended to the cloacal opening, where the young, the amniotic fluid, and the fetal membranes begin to emerge. Without the licking and other aid from the mother in freeing the young animals from the fetal membranes,

Fig. 52. Common opossum (*Didelphis marsupialis*).

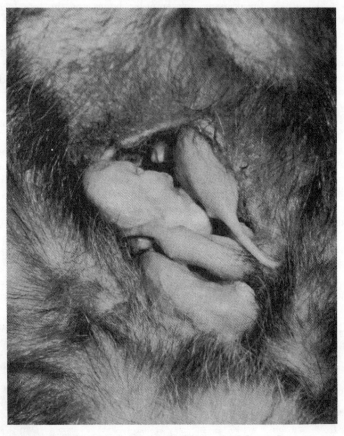

Fig. 53. Young opossums in the pouch of the mother.

the young ones have been observed to drown in their own amniotic fluid. When parturition begins, the mother sits with the cloacal opening directed forward and upward. Contraction of abdominal and uterine muscles forces the embryonic young out of the opening. At birth the young ones average about 1 centimeter in length and weigh about 0.39 gram. Some fall to the ground and are lost. Those that are to live must crawl upward through the abdominal hairs under their own power into the marsupium, where they will finish their development (fig. 53). There are normally 13 teats in the pouch. Hence those in a litter in excess of the number of teats are doomed to starvation.

After being freed by the mother from the liquid and the afterbirth, the young opossums move their forelimbs in such a manner that they can move only upward—which leads to the pouch. Once in the pouch, the young one finds an available nipple and takes it in its mouth. The end of the nipple may enlarge, which aids the young animal in holding onto its source of nourishment; however, it can and does find the nipple again, if it is removed.

The epiglottis of the young opossum is high and projects well up toward the back part of the nasal cavity. This arrangement allows normal breathing while feeding. Twenty days after birth a young animal may weigh about 4 grams, or ten times what it did when it entered the pouch. After 90–100 days the young opossums are weaned and leave the mother.

The young females may breed after they are six months old. The males become sexually mature after they are eight months old. The breeding season extends from the middle of January to the middle of October. Two litters of five to ten young are not infrequent for each female each season. The large litters and the frequency with which they come are factors that help the species to maintain itself successfully.

Opossums are unsociable with their kind and are mostly nocturnal. Their dens are in a hollow tree or rock pile, under buildings, or the dry burrows made by other animals. The nest is frequently lined with dry grass and leaves that have been transported by means of the animal's prehensile tail.

The common opossum is almost completely omnivorous. Fruits, eggs, young birds, and the helpless young of small mammals are on its menu. The opossum is often hunted by those who relish its flesh when served with sweet potatoes.

A curious behavior trait is the feigning of death by an opossum when it is attacked or threatened. This "playing possum" serves the species well, for many animals survive severe attacks when left as dead. Electroencephalograph records taken before, during, and after feigning death reveal that the opossum is not in an involuntary cataleptic state induced by physiological changes caused by the attack ("Science and the Citizen," 1964).

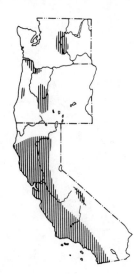

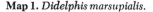

Map 1. *Didelphis marsupialis.*

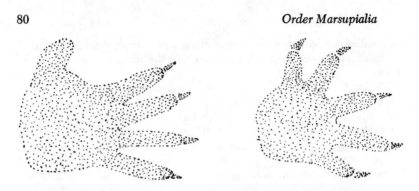

Fig. 54. Track of an opossum; nearly actual size.

The peculiar track (fig. 54) and droppings (see Appendix B) of the opossum are readily distinguishable from those of other similar-sized mammals.

Opossums have found the climate and habitats of northwestern Oregon especially to their liking and have increased and spread since their introduction there in 1939. They were introduced into northeastern Oregon in about 1912. The presence of opossums in Owens Valley, California, is reported but not verified. The animals have been reported also from Chelan County in central Washington (Map 1).

6. Order Insectivora

The Insectivora constitute the oldest living order of placental unguiculate mammals. Representatives are found on all the continents except Australia. The insectivores are for the most part small; none is over 50 centimeters (two feet) in length and some may weigh as little as 2.2 grams. Hence this order includes the smallest mammals. Although striking specializations are present in some species, all betray their ancient primitiveness by such characteristics as a long snout, pentadactyl plantigrade feet with toes terminated in claws, tuberculate molars, well-developed clavicles, smooth cerebral hemispheres, a bicornate uterus, abdominal testes, a ringlike tympanum that may be free from the cranium, and other features. The canines are small and may resemble the incisors or the premolars. The zygomatic arch is weak and may be entirely lacking.

The species of insectivores that live on the Pacific Coast are nearly all inhabitants of damp, moist places. However, the gray shrew and the Merriam shrew may be found under quite arid conditions.

The insectivores are mostly carnivorous; those of the Pacific Coast feed chiefly on arthropods, although some plant food is eaten. Because of their bizarre anatomical structure and odd behavior patterns and the small size of some of them, insectivores have a particular interest for the zoologist. Two families, the shrews (Soricidae) and the moles (Talpidae), are represented on the Pacific Coast.

Fig. 55. Vagrant shrew
(*Sorex vagrans*).

Fig. 56. Dusky shrew
(*Sorex obscurus*).

KEY TO THE SHREWS (Soricidae)

External ears present. Skulls are necessary for the best use of this key.

In identifying any of the 15 shrews found in the Pacific States, greater care must be taken than with any other group of mammals. Because of their small size, errors in measurements are likely to result in improper keying.

The skull and teeth are more important in identifying shrews than are external features. Familiarization with the position of the *foramen magnum* in the occiput (figs. 59, 60), the condylobasal length (fig. 28), and the dental formulas of each of the species generally will be required to use the key and the brief descriptions. Shrews tentatively identified with this key should be checked by expert mammalogists associated with museums. (See skull measurements in figs. 26 and 28.)

1A. Tail more than a third of the total length; five unicuspid teeth between the front bicuspid incisors and the large premolars on each side of the upper jaw (though only three or four may be seen from a lateral view) (figs. 61, 62); one lower incisor on each side 2

1B. Tail about a third of the total length; three upper unicuspid teeth between the front bicuspid incisors and the large premolars on each side of the upper jaw; two lower incisors on each side; gray dorsally; 3-1-1-3/2-0-1-3.* Usually arid regions of southern and eastern California.
Notiosorex crawfordi, gray shrew, p. 91.

2A. Tail usually 60 per cent or more of head and body length; 4 at least of the unicuspid teeth (upper jaw) clearly visible in lateral view; *Sorex,* 3-1-3-3/1-1-1-3 3

2B. Tail 50–60 per cent of head and body length; very small third and fifth unicuspid teeth may not be visible in lateral view (fig. 63); grayish brown; 3-1-3-3/1-1-1-3. Dry pine woods in northeastern Washington; very rare.
Microsorex hoyi, pigmy shrew, p. 91.

3A. In continental California, Oregon, and Washington 4

3B. Restricted to Santa Catalina Island, California; bicolored tail; condylobasal length 17.6 mm.
Sorex willetti, Santa Catalina shrew, p. 87.

4A. Hind foot usually more than 18 mm.; toes and sides of hind foot edged with a comblike fringe of stiff hairs directed downward (sometimes inconspicuous); living in or near water 5

4B. Hind foot usually less than 18 mm.; toes and sides of feet without a comblike fringe of stiff hairs 6

5A. Upper parts dark brown or black, may be very little lighter ventrally; tail nearly unicolored; condylobasal length 21–24 mm. Marshes and damp ravines in the humid Transition and Canadian life zones; north from San Francisco Bay and in western Oregon and Washington.
Sorex bendirii, marsh shrew, p. 87.

5B. Upper parts blackish or brownish, with gray to brownish underparts; tail sharply bicolored; conspicuous hairs on sides of hind foot; condylobasal length 18–21 mm. Cold mountain streams chiefly in the Canadian and Hudsonian life zones of central California to Canada.
Sorex palustris, water shrew, p. 85 and fig. 57.

6A. Third unicuspid (unworn) as large as or larger than the fourth . . 7

6B. Third unicuspid (unworn) smaller than the fourth (figs. 61, 62) . . 10

7A. Condylobasal length greater than 14.6 mm. 8

* Sometimes written 3-1-1-3/1-1-1-3.

7B. Condylobasal length 14.6 mm. or less; brownish; tail bicolored. In the Blue Mountains along willow-fringed streams and marshes in the eastern parts of Oregon and Washington.
' *Sorex preblei,* Malheur shrew (rare), p. 87.

8A. Not in central Sierra Nevada of California 9

8B. In California, central high Sierra Nevada in grass and under willows; brownish; condylobasal length 15.2–15.4 mm.; tail bicolored.
Sorex lyelli, Mount Lyell shrew, p. 87.

9A. Maxillary breadth 4.6 mm. or less; tan to yellowish brown dorsally; gray underparts. Washington.
Sorex cinereus, masked shrew, p. 89.

9B. Maxillary breadth more than 4.6 mm.; grayish dorsally; whitish underparts. Arid regions of eastern California, eastern Oregon, and the Columbian Plateau east of Ellensburg, Washington.
Sorex merriami, Merriam shrew (rare), p. 91.

10A. Tail unicolored or weakly bicolored, usually less than 80 per cent of the head and body length; cinnamon, gray, or brown dorsally; never black 11

10B. Tail sharply bicolored and usually over 80 per cent of the head and body length; black, dark gray, or dark brown dorsally and very little lighter ventrally. Under litter in coniferous forests in the mountains and coastal regions of California and western half of Oregon and Washington.
Sorex trowbridgii, Trowbridge shrew, p. 91.

11A. Foramen magnum extending about halfway to the top of the skull (fig. 59). Around Ashland, Oregon, or in California 14

11B. Foramen magnum not extending halfway to the top of the skull (fig. 60). Widely distributed in all three states 12

12A. Total length usually less than 130 mm.; hind foot less than 16 mm.; skull about 16–18 mm. long 13

12B. Total length usually more than 130 mm.; hind foot more than 16 mm.; cinnamon all over; skull about 21–23 mm. long. Northwestern California and southwestern Oregon, especially in reduced forests.
Sorex pacificus, Pacific shrew, p. 85, fig. 58.

13A. Total length usually less than 110 mm.; tail usually less than 46 mm.; interorbital width usually less than 3.3 mm.; brain case flat (fig. 62).
Sorex vagrans, vagrant shrew, p. 85, fig. 55.

13B. Total length usually more than 110 mm.; tail usually more than 46 mm.; interorbital width 3.3 mm. or more; brain case high (fig. 61).
Sorex obscurus, dusky shrew, p. 85, fig. 56.

14A. Restricted to California 15

14B. Restricted to region around Ashland, Oregon at base of the Siskiyou Mountains; tail about 55 per cent of the head and body length; condylobasal length 15.8 mm. or less; palatal length 6 mm. or less.
Sorex trigonirostris, Ashland shrew, p. 89.

15A. Condylobasal length more than 15.8 mm. West of Sierra Nevada crest and south from Napa County, California 16

15B. Condylobasal length less than 15.8 mm.; tail bicolored. Under rocks and logs in canyon bottoms in eastern California in the Upper Sonoran Life Zone.
Sorex tenellus, Inyo shrew, p. 87.

16A. Never blackish; palate more than 6.7 mm. Not on Grizzly Island; streams and brush-covered hillsides of the Sonoran and Transition life zones of California.
Sorex ornatus, ornate shrew, p. 89.

16B. Nearly black all over; palate less than 6.7 mm. On Grizzly Island and nearby tidal marshes, Solano County, California. (Rudd, 1955, suggests that this species may be only a subspecies of *S. ornatus.*)
Sorex sinuosus, Suisun shrew, p. 89.

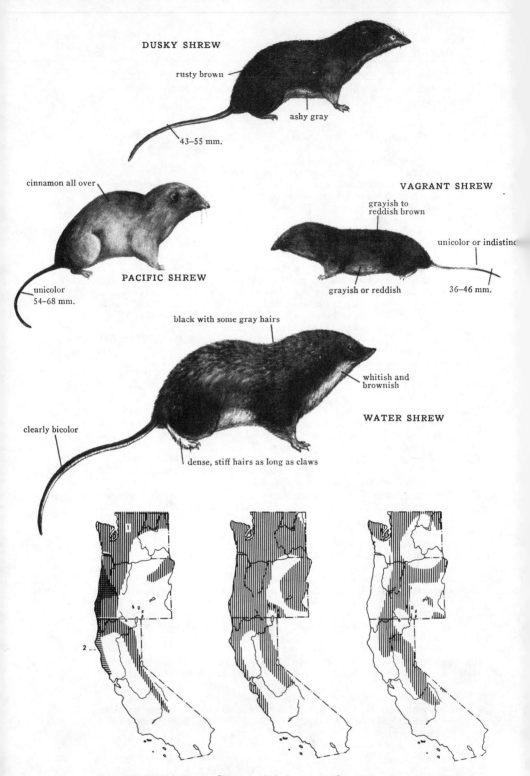

DUSKY SHREW

rusty brown

ashy gray

43–55 mm.

cinnamon all over

VAGRANT SHREW

grayish to
reddish brown

unicolor or indistinct

PACIFIC SHREW

unicolor
54–68 mm.

grayish or reddish

36–46 mm.

black with some gray hairs

whitish and
brownish

WATER SHREW

clearly bicolor

dense, stiff hairs as long as claws

Map 2, left. (1) *Sorex obscurus*, (2) *Sorex pacificus.* **Map 3, center.** *Sorex vagrans.* **Map 4, right.** *Sorex palustris.*

Sorex Dental Formula 3-1-3-3/1-1-1-3

Dusky shrew (*Sorex obscurus*). Length 105–25 mm.; tail 43–55 mm.; hind foot 11–14 mm.; condylobasal length 16.4–19.1 mm.; *foramen magnum* low in the occiput (fig. 60); fourth unicuspid larger than the third; interorbital width 3.3 mm. or more; *skull profile with high brain case* (fig. 61); tail unicolored or indistinctly bicolored (i.e., gradually grading from the dark dorsal side to the lighter underside); upper parts are rusty or reddish brown, underparts are brownish gray; widely distributed over the forested areas in all three states near streams, chiefly in the Canadian Life Zone. (This species is considered to be a race of *Sorex vagrans* by Findley, 1955.) Fig. 56, Map 2.

Pacific shrew (*Sorex pacificus*). Length 129–60 mm.; tail unicolored, 54–68 mm.; hind foot 15–19 mm.; condylobasal length 20–22 mm.; *foramen magnum* low in the occiput (fig. 60); *skull profile flat* (fig. 62); upper parts cinnamon brown; underparts light cinnamon; humid coastal region of western Oregon and northwestern California, under decaying logs in the spruce and redwood forests. Transition Life Zone. (This species is considered to be a race of *Sorex vagrans* by Findley, 1955.) Fig. 58, Map 2.

Vagrant shrew (*Sorex vagrans*). Length 100–110 mm.; tail 36–46 mm.; hind foot 11–13 mm.; condylobasal length 16–17 mm.; *foramen magnum* low in the occiput (fig. 60); fourth unicuspid larger than the third; interorbital width 3.3 mm. or less; *skull profile flat* (fig. 62); upper parts (summer) brown, underparts gray tinged with brownish; tail unicolored or indistinctly bicolored (i.e., gradually grading from the dark dorsal side to the lighter ventral side). Widely distributed in Washington, Oregon, and the forested regions of California, in the Transition and Canadian life zones. Fig. 55, Map 3.

Water shrew (*Sorex palustris*). Length 139–63 mm.; tail 63–83 mm.; tail bicolored, about 70–105 per cent of body length; hind foot 18–22 mm.; condylobasal length 18.8–21.5 mm.; fourth unicuspid larger than the third; hind feet have a conspicuous fringe of hairs along the sides and toes; "frosted" with gray-tipped hairs dorsally, underparts whitish tinged with brown. Chiefly Canadian and Hudsonian life zones, in or along small, swift, cold streams and lakes in all three states. Fig. 57, Map 4.

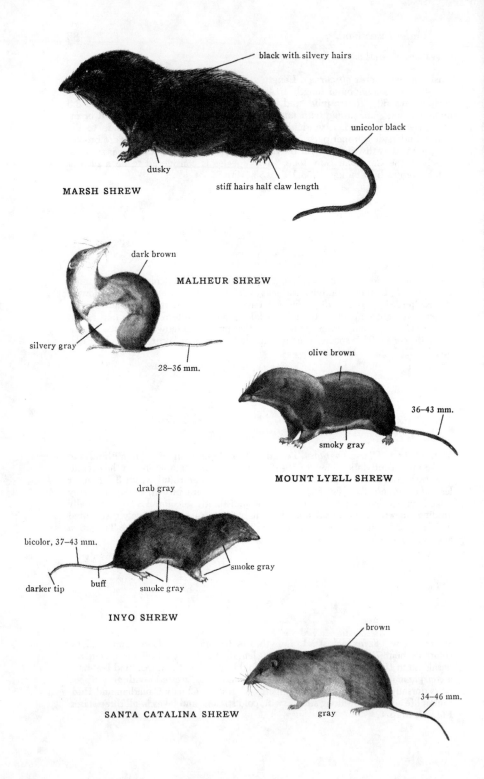

black with silvery hairs

unicolor black

dusky

stiff hairs half claw length

MARSH SHREW

dark brown

MALHEUR SHREW

silvery gray

28–36 mm.

olive brown

36–43 mm.

smoky gray

MOUNT LYELL SHREW

drab gray

bicolor, 37–43 mm.

smoke gray

darker tip

buff

smoke gray

INYO SHREW

brown

34–46 mm.

SANTA CATALINA SHREW

gray

Marsh shrew (*Sorex bendirii*). Length 145–74 mm.; tail unicolored, 61–80 mm.; hind foot 18–22 mm.; condylobasal length 20.8–23.8 mm.; hind feet with a weak fringe of inconspicuous hairs about half as long as the claws; black or sooty brown dorsally, frequently "frosted" with silver-tipped hairs; underparts very little lighter than upper parts. Swamps, marshes, damp ravines, and under logs in damp woods in the Transition and Canadian life zones of northwestern California and the western third of Oregon and Washington. Map 5.

Malheur shrew (*Sorex preblei*). Length 77–95 mm.; tail 28–36 mm.; upper parts dark brownish gray, underparts silvery gray; tail about 60 per cent of body length; hind foot 10–11 mm.; condylobasal length 14.0–14.6 mm.; fourth unicuspid tooth about equal to or smaller than the third; foramen magnum low in the occiput (fig. 60). Along willow-fringed creeks and marshes in the Upper Sonoran and Transition zones in eastern Oregon. Map 5.

Mount Lyell shrew (*Sorex lyelli*). Length 100–103 mm.; tail 36–43 mm.; hind foot 11–12 mm.; condylobasal length 15.0–15.4 mm.; fourth unicuspid tooth is equal to or smaller than the third; first and second unicuspid teeth distinctly larger than the third and fourth; foramen magnum low in the occiput (fig. 60); drab or olive brown on upper parts, smoke gray on underparts; maxillary breadth about 4 mm. Rare; in grass or under stream-side willows in the central Sierra Nevada within or near Yosemite National Park. Map 5.

Inyo shrew (*Sorex tenellus*). Length 85–116 mm.; tail 36–43 mm., about 70 per cent of body length; hind foot 9–13 mm.; condylobasal length 15–15.2 mm.; foraman magnum high in the occiput (fig. 59); fourth unicuspid larger than the third; first and second unicuspids noticeably larger than the third and fourth; dorsally dark gray with pale smoky gray underparts. Under boulders and logs in canyon bottoms in shaded places in the Sagebrush Scrub, Upper Sonoran Life Zone of eastern California. Rare. Map 5.

Santa Catalina shrew (*Sorex willetti*). Length 104 mm.; tail 34–46 mm.; tail bicolored, about 50 per cent of body length; hind foot 12 mm.; brown upper parts, gray underparts; condylobasal length 17.6 mm.; foramen magnum high in the occiput (fig. 59). Rare; Avalon Canyon, Santa Catalina Island, California. Map 5.

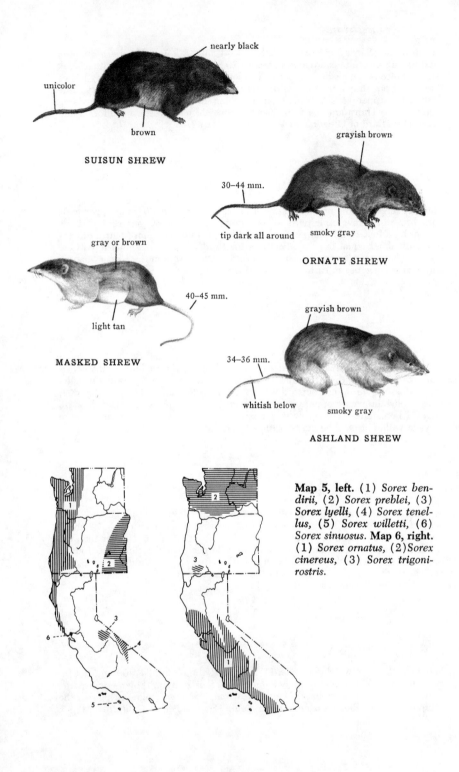

nearly black

unicolor

brown

SUISUN SHREW

grayish brown

30–44 mm.

tip dark all around   smoky gray

ORNATE SHREW

gray or brown

light tan

40–45 mm.

MASKED SHREW

grayish brown

34–36 mm.

whitish below   smoky gray

ASHLAND SHREW

Map 5, left. (1) *Sorex bendirii,* (2) *Sorex preblei,* (3) *Sorex lyelli,* (4) *Sorex tenellus,* (5) *Sorex willetti,* (6) *Sorex sinuosus.* **Map 6, right.** (1) *Sorex ornatus,* (2) *Sorex cinereus,* (3) *Sorex trigonirostris.*

Suisun shrew (*Sorex sinuosus*). Length 95–105 mm.; tail 37–41 mm.; tail uni-colored, about 60 per cent of body length; hind foot 12 mm.; condylobasal length 16.4 mm.; foramen magnum high in the occiput (fig. 59); nearly black all over; known only from the tidal marshes around Grizzly Island, Solano County, California. *Note*: Recent findings indicate that this species may ultimately be considered a subspecies of *Sorex ornatus* (Rudd, 1955). Map 5.

Ornate shrew (*Sorex ornatus*). Length 86–110 mm.; tail 30–44 mm., 55–65 per cent of body length; hind foot 10–14 mm.; condylobasal length 16–17 mm.; foramen magnum high in the occiput (fig. 59); fourth unicuspid larger than the third; first and second unicuspid teeth noticeably larger than the third and fourth; sooty brown or grayish brown dorsally, smoky gray on underparts. Along streams and brush-covered hillsides in the Valley Grassland, Foothill Woodland, and Yellow Pine Forest of the Sonoran and Transition zones in the southern two-thirds of California. *Note*: Recent work suggests that this species with its sub-species and *Sorex sinuosus* might all be arranged as subspecies of *Sorex vagrans* (Rudd, 1955). Fig. 55, Map 6.

Masked shrew (*Sorex cinereus*). Length 77–110 mm.; tail 31–45 mm.; hind foot 10–13 mm.; condylobasal length 14.5–16.0 mm.; fourth unicuspid tooth equal to or smaller than the third; maxillary breadth about 3.8 mm.; foramen magnum low in the occiput (fig. 60); grayish, brownish, or tan, with lighter underparts. Rare; Washington in humid coastal areas and in mountainous regions. Map 6.

Ashland shrew (*Sorex trigonirostris*). Length 95–106 mm.; tail 34–36 mm.; tail about 55 per cent of body length; hind foot 12–14 mm.; condylobasal length 15.6 mm.; grayish brown dorsally, smoky gray ventrally (summer); fourth unicuspid larger than the third and both smaller than the first and second; foramen magnum high in the occiput (fig. 59). North base of Siskiyou Mountains of southwestern Oregon up to 3,500 feet elevation. *Note*: This apparently disjunct population may ultimately be shown to be a race of *Sorex ornatus*. Map 6.

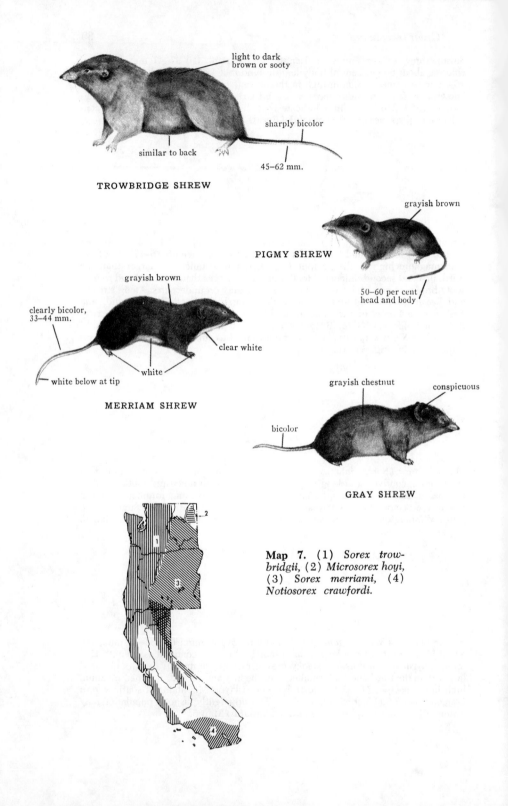

light to dark
brown or sooty

sharply bicolor

similar to back

45–62 mm.

TROWBRIDGE SHREW

grayish brown

PIGMY SHREW

50–60 per cent
head and body

grayish brown

clearly bicolor,
33–44 mm.

clear white

white

white below at tip

MERRIAM SHREW

grayish chestnut

conspicuous

bicolor

GRAY SHREW

Map 7. (1) *Sorex trow-bridgii,* (2) *Microsorex hoyi,* (3) *Sorex merriami,* (4) *Notiosorex crawfordi.*

Trowbridge shrew (*Sorex trowbridgii*). Length 101–32 mm.; tail 45–62 mm.; *tail usually sharply bicolored,* about 80–95 per cent of body length; hind foot 12–15 mm.; condylobasal length 16.4–18.8 mm.; fourth unicuspid tooth larger than the third; upper unicuspids weakly pigmented, but never pigmented to the cingulum; dark gray, brown, or blackish dorsally, underparts very little lighter. In litter of the forest floor, woodland canyons, and meadows, frequently far from water in the Redwood, Douglas Fir, and Yellow Pine forests of the Transition Life Zone in the northern two-thirds of California and the western halves of Washington and Oregon. Map 7.

Pigmy shrew (*Microsorex hoyi*). Dental Formula 3-1-3-3/1-1-1-3. Length 82–89 mm.; tail 27–31 mm.; tail 50–60 per cent of body length; hind foot 9 mm.; condylobasal length 13–15.8 mm.; weight 2.2 to 3.8 grams; third unicuspid is disk-shaped and compressed longitudinally (fig. 63); upper parts sepia to reddish brown, underparts more gray in summer. Pine forests of northeastern Washington, under rotting logs, avoiding excessively wet conditions. Map 7.

Merriam shrew (*Sorex merriami*). Length 88–108 mm.; tail 33–44 mm.; tail 55–65 per cent of body length; hind foot 11–13 mm.; condylobasal length 15.8–17.0 mm.; upper parts light brownish gray, underparts, including feet and under-surface of tail, white; fourth unicuspid smaller than or equal to the third; foramen magnum low in the occiput (fig. 60). Most frequently found in bunch grass in the arid regions of Sagebrush Scrub and Pinyon-Juniper in Upper Sonoran and lower Transition life zones in the eastern parts of California, Oregon, and Washington. Rare. Map 7.

Gray shrew (*Notiosorex crawfordi*). Dental Formula 3-1-1-3/2-0-1-3. Length 80–92 mm.; tail 22–31 mm.; tail 45–52 per cent of body length; hind foot 10–11.5 mm.; condylobasal length 16–17 mm.; only three upper unicuspid teeth on each side; ears project conspicuously out of fur; juvenile pelage is light silver gray, adults are lead gray with a brownish wash dorsally; underparts pale gray; lateral skin glands conspicuous. Rare; mostly in arid Sagebrush Scrub and Coastal Sage Scrub in the Sonoran life zones of southern California. Map 7.

Fig. 57. Water shrew (*Sorex palustris*).

Fig. 58. Pacific shrew (*Sorex pacificus*).

Family **Soricidae** (Shrews)

This family comprises the most primitive species of living placental mammals. Shrews are found over the entire world except Australia, most of South America, and in the polar regions.

Although shrews are diurnal and nocturnal, they are rarely seen, even though in many places they are the most common species of mammal. Shrews, like moles, have long pointed noses and pentadactyl plantigrade feet. They have small functional eyes and clearly visible external ears. The well-developed tail is scaly, with very short hairs.

The ringlike tympanic bone is not solidified to the skull and there are no zygomatic arches. There are two articulations for each side of the jaw. The incisors of *Sorex* are unlike those of any other mammal. Those on the lower jaw are reduced to one on each side and project almost straight forward; the inner or foremost incisor of the three on each of the upper jaws is very large and sickle-shaped, with a large basal bump or projection (fig. 63). The molars are behind the large bicuspid incisors, unicuspid incisors, canines, and premolars. They have a W-shaped or *dilambdodont* pattern on the crowns. Other important features that aid in identification are the relative height of the foramen magnum in the occiput (figs. 59, 60) and the height of the forehead (figs. 61, 62).

Very little is known about the food of the Western shrews. They are known, however, to feed on adult insects and their larvae and pupae, some of which are detrimental to man's interest. It seems likely that these little mammals may ultimately prove to be of much greater importance, especially in the ecology and welfare of forests, than is now attributed to them.

It has also been shown that as homoiothermal animals become smaller, their metabolic rate rises (Pearson, 1953). The Sonoma race of the vagrant shrew (*Sorex vagrans sonomae*) weighs about 10 grams and consumes a little over 5 cc. of oxygen per gram per hour. The still smaller Trowbridge shrew weighs about 7 grams and consumes about 7 cc. of oxygen per gram per hour. The tiny masked shrew (*Sorex cinereus*) weighs only 4 grams and needs about 11 cc. of oxygen per gram per hour. Hence it has been calculated that a shrew weighing less than about 2 grams would require an infinite amount of oxygen and could never eat enough! This is the lower limit of size in mammals.

Shrews then are the smallest mammals, and as such their chief problems are concerned with heat conservation because of heat loss and the high metabolic rate. A small body has a relatively larger surface area per unit of volume than a larger body. Mathematically it can be demonstrated that the surface of a body increases with the square of a linear dimension, while its volume increases with the cube. Hence smaller bodies have proportion-

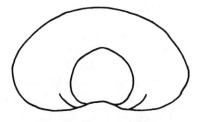 

Fig. 59. Foramen magnum high in the occiput, as in *Sorex ornatus, S. tenellus, S. sinuosus, S. willetti,* and *S. trigonirostris.*

Fig. 60. Foramen magnum low in the occiput, as in *Sorex cinereus, S. lyelli, S. obscurus, S. pacificus, S. preblei, S. merriami,* and *S. vagrans.*

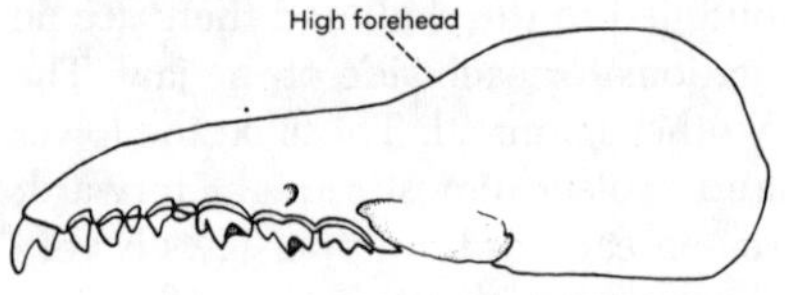

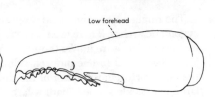

Fig. 61. Cranium profile of the dusky shrew (*Sorex obscurus*).

Fig. 62. Cranium profile of the vagrant shrew (*Sorex vagrans*).

ately more surface from which heat loss occurs. Shrews do not hibernate, although they frequently live in cold regions where small arthropods, which constitute their chief food, may be inactive for months. Because the metabolic rate of a shrew is very high and because it loses heat rapidly from the surface of its small body, the shrew is continually faced with problems of getting enough food to keep itself warm and alive, frequently in subzero air temperatures. How enough food is obtained throughout the long winter months in the high mountains of the Pacific States is still unknown.

The adaptations that shrews have made both in structure and behavior to their peculiar habitats are among the most fascinating in the class Mammalia and will be described for two species of the Pacific States.

The water shrew (*Sorex palustris*) and the dusky shrew (*Sorex obscurus*, fig. 56) illustrate the manner in which these tiny creatures live as a result of structural and behavior adaptations, respectively.

Hikers and fishermen in high country occasionally see a small animal resembling a large whirligig beetle gyrating about on the smooth surface of a lake or plunging into a turbulent mountain stream. This is the water shrew, a mouse-sized creature that is almost black above and white below. From below, the lighter underparts resemble the shining surface of the water to a big trout that might use the shrew as food as it floats at the surface. From above, the shrew's dark upper parts serve admirably to make the active little mammal inconspicuous to a mink or a bird of prey that looks down on it against the dark depths of a pool. The fur of the water shrew is so thick that the cold water cannot get directly to the warm body as it swims about beneath the surface. Because of the trapped air, the shrew resembles a great silver bubble as it moves rapidly about under the water. It must work hard to reach the bottom of a pool because of the buoyancy

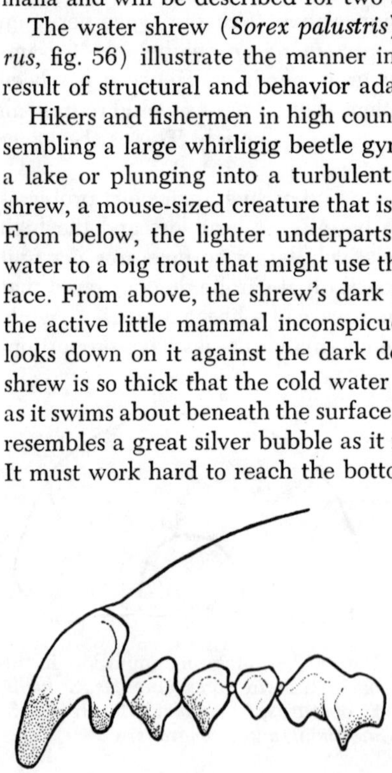

Fig. 63. Upper tooth row of the pigmy shrew (*Microsorex hoyi*) showing minute teeth between the second and third unicuspid teeth, and the third unicuspid and the premolar. It shows also the large basal projection (cusp) on the first upper incisor.

of the trapped air. When the leg action ceases, the animal bobs back to the surface and shakes itself. It is then apparently quite dry.

The hind feet of a water shrew, not noticeably different from those of other shrews when on land, have fringes of stiff thick hairs along the sides, which can be spread under water to make an effective propelling organ. The water shrew has been observed to trap large bubbles of air under the feet and to run or skate across the open surface of the water. The fimbriated feet aid in obtaining aquatic prey.

Radiating out from the continuously wiggling snout are long delicate vibrissae. Experiments indicate that the sense of sight is relatively unimportant and that the water shrew covers its home range by whiskering its way about until it has memorized every detail of stick, stone, and root so well that it can run or swim at full speed with its eyes shut. Some sense organ enables the shrew to follow a swimming tadpole, minnow, or water insect. The high metabolic rate necessary to maintain a constant temperature in the cold water means that the animal must consume an amount of food equal to its own weight each day. Although the water shrew does not hibernate, it manages to acquire nourishment even when ice covers the ponds and streams and the air temperature goes below zero. It has a 1.5-hour rhythm, in which 30 minutes are active and 60 minutes are inactive. There are also two major peaks of activity each 24 hours. One occurs about an hour before sunrise and one between sunset and midnight (Sorenson, 1962).

The water shrew lives about a year and a half. It makes its nest of dry moss (a good insulator) and produces about six young in a litter. There may be more than one litter a year.

Nature has endowed the dusky shrew with remarkable behavior patterns. This species comes in a variety of races, which differ in size and color. The dusky shrew (*Sorex obscurus*) is a resident of the wet swamps of the high Sierra Nevada. Unlike the Trowbridge shrew (*Sorex trowbridgii*), which inhabits the dry litter of the forest floor, the dusky shrew rarely is found more than a few yards away from water in summer. Its habitat is wet soggy meadows overgrown thickly with willows and tall sedges. Here it lays out its home range, which may vary from 40 to 250 feet across its longest diameter to include an average of about 4,000 square feet. Although the dusky shrew is a notoriously solitary animal and may fight viciously when it meets another of its kind, its home range may broadly overlap that of its surrounding neighbors. Eleven dusky shrews had their home ranges on 0.7 acre one summer at Huntington Lake, California (Ingles, 1963). As winter approached and food presumably became harder to find, one by one the shrews disappeared. When spring came, only two were left, but their home ranges broadly overlapped and covered nearly the whole area.

The dusky shrew has only one winter in its life, but it must be a rugged one. Daily it must search for food equal to its own weight (5–7 grams) in order to maintain life. It includes in its diet insects, arachnids, snails, and earthworms. Nothing is known of how enough of this quiescent prey is obtained in winter, under as much as 15 feet of snow, to provide the great amount of necessary energy for this small nonhibernating mammal with a high metabolic rate. Experimental studies indicate that there is a "built-in" behavior pattern of rhythmic activity that enables the shrew to acquire its food with a minimum amount of effort in summer. Presumably there is a similar device that serves it in winter. Its high metabolic rate and small size mean that the shrew must eat every two or three hours. There are three times each day when its activity is far greater than at other times (Ingles, 1960a). One peak of activity comes in the morning, when flying insects, water insects, and arachnids resume their diurnal activity and crawl up the grasses and sedges to warm up. In the afternoon, when it is warmest and the arachnids and insects are most active, and therefore hardest to catch, the shrew is least active. When the sun sets and the wet-wood termites emerge and fly, another peak of activity begins. The shrew catches and eats five or six termites. Then it incapacitates 50 to 60 more for future use. Some shrews have a poison in the saliva that partially immobilizes the prey; whether this is true of the dusky shrew is not known. Another period of activity occurs during the coldest hours of early morning, after the spiders and insects have crawled down the willows and sedges into the protecting duff. At this time the arthropods are cold, nearly inactive, and most easily obtained. Many more termites, which have now dropped their wings and are slowly crawling about looking for new nest sites, are captured.

Thus the daily behavior pattern of these shrews in summer is rhythmic and seems to correlate closely with the time of day or night when arthropod food is most available. When the dusky shrew is kept in captivity for several weeks, it still exhibits these rhythms of activity, even with food available at all times. This indicates that its pattern of behavior is genetically based and is the result of ages of selection, which have fitted the animal to its environment. The inherent behavior patterns of the dusky shrew seem to be just as important as are the peculiar structural adaptations of the water shrew. Both are the products of evolution: natural selection acting on genetic variability over very long periods of time.

The vagrant shrew (*Sorex vagrans*, fig. 55), like the dusky shrew, seldom lives beyond 18 months. It may breed twice each year, although one litter born in the spring seems to be the rule. The litter varies from two to nine young, with four to six being the normal size. The young weigh only about half a gram at birth but gain weight rapidly while in the nest. Until they are a month old, the litter huddles together in a furry ball, which conserves heat in the tiny bodies. When they disperse, the young shrews weigh 5 or 6 grams, but they do not attain their full weight of 7 to 8 grams until they are mature—which usually is in the spring about a year after they are born. The gestation period in the vagrant shrew is unknown, but it appears to be about two to three weeks in *Sorex araneus*, a European shrew of similar size.

The Pacific shrew (*Sorex pacificus,* fig. 58) is cinnamon-colored and larger than the brownish-gray vagrant shrew. Both are frequently trapped under the same redwood logs in northwestern California.

The Trowbridge shrew (*Sorex trowbridgii*) adults of the Sierra Nevada are nearly always gray because they seldom live long enough to acquire the dark brown pelage of the second summer. Rarely do these shrews live beyond 18 months. There are frequently two or three pregnancies following the birth of the first litter. These occur in quick succession. The diet includes considerable plant material. This shrew eats the seeds of the Douglas fir and may be a serious pest in the reforestation of this important tree in the Pacific States.

The gray shrew (*Notiosorex crawfordi*) lives under arid conditions and feeds on insects on which the exoskeleton can be opened. It apparently needs no water other than that obtained with its food (Hoffmeister and Goodpaster, 1962).

The masked shrew (*Sorex cinereus*) is believed to have a gestation period of about 18 days (Jackson, 1961). The young are born blind and hairless, in a litter of four to ten, and weigh about 0.1 gram. Ten days later they are half adult size and are fully furred. Twenty days after birth the young are independent. There is an occasional report of a masked shrew dying suddenly from "shock," for no apparent cause. Such deaths should be carefully investigated; hypoglycemia may be the explanation.

Owls, Steller jays, and trout are known to prey on shrews. Other predators seem to avoid them.

KEY TO MOLES AND SHREW-MOLES (Talpidae)

No external ears. See Maps 8–10.

1A. Total length more than 130 mm.; hind foot more than 18 mm.; 44 teeth   2

1B. Total length less than 130 mm.; hind foot less than 18 mm.; short hairy tail; 36 teeth. Coastal region north from Monterey County, California.
Neurotrichus gibbsii, shrew-mole. Fig. 67.

2A. Total length less than 195 mm.; hind foot 24 mm. or less 3

2B. Total length more than 195 mm.; hind foot more than 24 mm.; skull over 40 mm. long; blackish brown to nearly black. Coastal, extreme northwestern part of California and western third of Oregon and Washington.
Scapanus townsendii, Townsend mole. Fig. 64.

3A. Tail not flesh-colored, nearly covered with silvery coarse hairs; drab gray or coppery brown fur; hind foot 18–24 mm.; unicuspid teeth not evenly spaced and usually somewhat crowded. South-central Oregon except the south-central part, and most of California except southeastern deserts.
Scapanus latimanus, broad-handed mole. Fig. 66.

3B. Tail flesh-colored, sparsely haired; purplish black, blackish gray or very dark brown fur; hind foot 19–23 mm.; unicuspid teeth evenly spaced and not crowded. Coastal, extreme northwestern portion of California, through western Oregon and Washington; the Cascade Mountains of Washington, east along river valleys; northern Oregon into southeastern Washington.
Scapanus orarius, coast mole. Fig. 65.

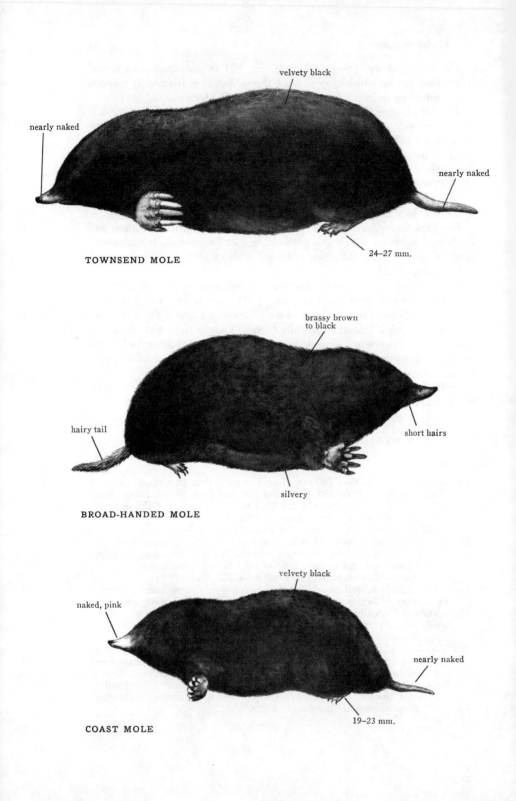

TOWNSEND MOLE

velvety black

nearly naked

nearly naked

24–27 mm.

BROAD-HANDED MOLE

brassy brown to black

hairy tail

short hairs

silvery

COAST MOLE

velvety black

naked, pink

nearly naked

19–23 mm.

Scapanus Dental Formula 3-1-4-3/3-1-4-3

Townsend mole (*Scapanus townsendii*). Length 195–237 mm.; tail 34–51 mm.; hind foot 24–28 mm.; skull length 41–44.6 mm.; fur blackish brown to purplish black with a metallic luster, some are brownish with gray markings; tail and snout nearly naked. Food: arthropods, annelids, and some vegetable matter. Young: litter of three (usually), born in March. Chiefly nocturnal; in meadows and fields, and on lawns in the Redwood, Douglas Fir, and Yellow Pine forests of the Transition Life Zone in extreme northwestern California and the western third of Oregon and Washington. Fig. 64, Map 8.

Broad-handed mole (*Scapanus latimanus*). Length 132–90 mm.; tail nearly covered with silvery hair to the tip, 21–45 mm.; hind foot 18–25 mm.; skull length 29.0–37.5 mm.; fur dark gray to coppery brown, appears silvery when smoothed; short hairs extend almost to the end of the snout; unicuspid teeth frequently crowded against each other and unevenly spaced. Soft soil in valleys and mountain meadows in several biotic communities from the Lower Sonoran to the Hudsonian life zones; throughout California except desert regions, also the central valleys to south-central Oregon. Fig. 66, Map 8.

Coast mole (*Scapanus orarius*). Length 147–75 mm.; tail 31–43 mm.; hind foot 19–23 mm.; skull length 33–39 mm.; purplish black fur lead-colored at base; tail and snout nearly naked; unicuspid teeth evenly spaced and not crowded. Food: arthropods, annelids, and perhaps some vegetable matter. Young: litters of four in March or April. Chiefly in deciduous woods in the Redwood, Douglas Fir, Yellow Pine, spruce and hemlock forests in the Transition Life Zone of extreme northwestern California, western and northern Oregon, and the western half of Washington. Fig. 65, Map 9.

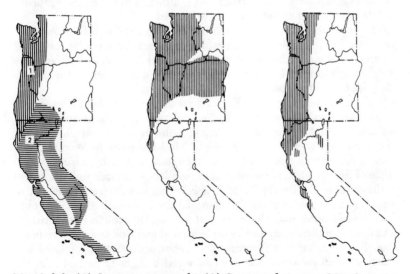

Map 8, left. (1) *Scapanus townsendii*, (2) *Scapanus latimanus*. **Map 9, center.** *Scapanus orarius*. **Map 10, right.** *Neurotrichus gibbsii*.

silvery hairs

black

scaly, hairy

SHREW-MOLE

Shrew-mole (*Neurotrichus gibbsii*). Dental Formula 3-1-2-3/3-1-2-3. Length 103–26 mm.; tail 32–43 mm.; hind foot 14–18 mm.; skull length 21–24.2 mm.; zygomatic arch present; fur gray to blackish iridescent; tail scaly with bristly hairs. Food: small arthropods, annelids, and some vegetable matter. Young: litters of one to four young, February to November. Subsurface runways usually near streams in Redwood, Douglas Fir, and Yellow Pine forests of the Transition Life Zone in northwestern California and western Oregon and Washington, including the eastern slopes of the Cascade Mountains. Fig. 67, Map 10.

Family **Talpidae** (Moles and Shrew-Moles)

Moles range over the Northern Hemisphere in Europe, Asia, and North America. True moles, of which the Western genus *Scapanus* is representative, are soft-furred, long-snouted fossorial mammals that are rarely seen on the surface of the ground (figs. 64–66). Members of this family possess a weak zygomatic arch and a bulla that is attached to the cranium; the dilambdodont crowns of the teeth are W-shaped.

It seems reasonable to assume that moles have developed from ancestral mammals that resembled very large shrews, which lived on the surface of the ground. Some of the modifications (fossorial adaptations) wrought by evolution to change a large shrewlike animal to a mole, fitted to live practically all of its life underground, will be discussed.

Nothing in the entire field of zoology is more fascinating than the way environment modifies the anatomy and behavior patterns of animals that live underground. More remarkable still is the manner in which distantly related mammals with similar modes of life have come to resemble each other in appearance and action, even though separated by oceans. An example of this principle of convergent or parallel evolution is well illustrated by the moles of the Pacific States. These belong to a different family (Talpidae) than the golden moles (Chrysochloridae) of South Africa, and even to a different order than the marsupial moles (Marsupialia) of Australia. Yet all three of these animals live underground and look and act very much alike. Such similarity in structure and behavior in distantly related and widely disjunct mammals has been achieved by ages of natural selection acting on the genetic variability of these unrelated fossorial mammals.

Fig. 64. Townsend mole (*Scapanus townsendii*).

Fig. 65. Coast mole (*Scapanus orarius*).

Fig. 66. Broad-handed mole (*Scapanus latimanus*).

Fig. 67. Gibbs shrew-mole (*Neurotrichus gibbsii*).

The cylindrical body of a mole, tapered at one end to a sensitive snout and at the other to an equally sensitive tail, is equipped to run either way in its tunnel with a minimum of friction. The soft velvety fur, to which dirt will not cling, is capable of lying forward almost as well as the hair on other mammals lies backward.

Living in continuous darkness has made eyes not only useless to a mole but even detrimental, so far as getting dirt in them is concerned. Hence selective pressure against the eye has resulted in a reduced organ with all of its parts present but crowded together so that it is unable to function.

External ears, designed for picking up sound waves in the air, have disappeared in moles. Since sound waves are conducted through the soil much more readily than in air, the mole in its tunnel probably "hears" with its whole body. Protruding external ears would also tend to hinder the mole as it moves through its tunnel. A broad-handed mole that was kept in a terrarium was observed to dig rapidly up through the earth unerringly to the place where an earthworm was wiggling on the surface. Apparently the vibrations caused by the worm were conducted through the soil and detected readily.

Moles appear to be neckless because the pectoral girdle over the ages has moved closer to the head. This change of position makes the digging forefeet stronger as the creature "swims" through the soil. The elements of the forelimb have been greatly shortened, as compared with terrestrial mammals. The strong hand seems to protrude directly from the body, and its palm cannot be turned flat against the ground as in other insectivores (fig. 64). The sternum, which is strongly keeled, provides firm attachments for the powerful pectoral muscles, which operate the short spadelike front feet. The anterior part of the body moves up and down between the vertically placed scopulae as the animal makes its familiar molehill.

The pelvic girdle too has been greatly modified. The hind feet must "dig in" to keep the animal anchored in place as it raises the earth above its head or moves its load upward with its wide forefeet. Hence the pelvic girdle must be firmly fastened to the vertebral column. All the sacral vertebrae are solidly fused to each other and to the ilium for rigidity, and by means of the ilium to the pubic bones as well. Thus the greatly narrowed, solidly attached pelvic girdle not only gives great support for the hind limbs but enables the hipless mole to turn around readily in its burrow. Such a narrow pelvis allows no room for the passage of the young at birth. However, the urogenital and alimentary tracts both lie ventrally completely outside of the pubic bones. The pubic bones remain separate, with the space between occupied by ligaments. So relatively large young are born, with large pectoral, shoulder, and nuchal muscles.

Moles are active the year round. Both the Townsend mole and the coast mole are detrimental to the dairy interests of northwestern Oregon, where their large earth mounds foul the machinery used to cut hay (fig. 68). According to Wick (1962), one mole may make from 200 to 500 "hills" during the rainy season, from October to April. Moles can best be controlled by using the diamond or scissor-type traps.

The diet of the Townsend mole is 80 per cent earthworms, the rest consisting of roots, seeds, and other plant material. Although it is a solitary animal and will quickly drive another mole out of its burrow, it nevertheless may use certain "highways," usually under fence rows, to get to different areas (Wick, 1962). As many as 20 to 30 moles have been trapped in these common pathways.

The coast mole is sometimes locally referred to as the "red-footed mole"

Fig. 68. Mole hill made by the coast mole (*Scapanus orarius*).

because of the color of its hind feet. This mole is not limited to forested areas and is sometimes found in pure population in grassy meadows where the soil is heavy with organic matter.

Molehills can be distinguished from those made by pocket gophers, since they are often cloddy with no evidence of a plugged hole; the pocket gopher hill is composed of fine soil with a plugged hole near one side of the mound (figs. 68, 131).

Breeding in western Oregon extends from late February into March. Three young are usually born from March to May. The young reach adult size in two months (Wick, 1962).

7. Order Chiroptera

The order Chiroptera (bats) includes the only mammals capable of true flight. The long bones of the hand have been modified into a wing (fig. 69). The hind limbs are rotated so the knees bend backward instead of forward as they do in other mammals. All North American bats belong to the suborder Microchiroptera. Those of the Pacific States belong in three families: the Phyllostomatidae, with a cutaneous nose leaf on top of the rostrum; the Vespertilionidae, with lips and muzzle simple and with the tail enclosed in a wide interfemoral membrane; and the Molossidae, with the tail extending posteriorly to the short interfemoral membrane.

The vampire bats of Mexico, Central America, and South America that feed on blood are the only true parasitic mammals. The order is related to the Insectivora, from which it was evolved. All of the bats of the Pacific States are insectivorous except two species that are rarely found in southern California, which may also eat nectar and fruit. Most bats are nocturnal. Except in the colder regions, bats are nearly universally distributed over the world, but they are most numerous in the tropics.

The morphological adaptations of bats for flight are unique, and easily distinguish them from other mammals. The nearly hairless but sensitive membrane is spread between the greatly elongated fingers of the hand-wing, between the wings and the hind legs, and in many species between the hind legs to include more or less of the tail. The legs bend forward, and the uropatagium (the membrane between the legs including the tail) forms a "basket" (fig. 74). The muscles and bones of the shoulder girdle are much more developed than those of the pelvis. The sternum is keeled as it is in birds (though to a lesser extent) to accommodate the large flight muscles. Quite in contrast to these specializations for flight, the teeth of the species of bats in the Western states have remained largely primitive, with a W-shaped outer ridge or ectoloph.

Although bats are mostly nocturnal, their eyes are small, and they do not rely to any extent on vision for orientation. The ears are usually well developed, with a fleshy tragus at the opening.

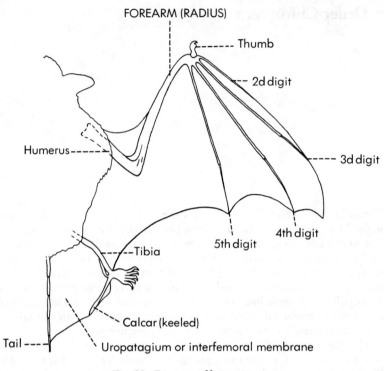

FOREARM (RADIUS)

Thumb

2d digit

Humerus

3d digit

4th digit

5th digit

Tibia

Calcar (keeled)

Tail

Uropatagium or interfemoral membrane

Fig. 69. Diagram of bat anatomy.

Bats have interesting physiological adaptations for the conservation of energy, which is extremely important to an animal that uses much energy in flight. At high altitudes and in latitudes where flying insects are active only in the early evening hours and are nearly completely absent during the long winter months, bats must adjust their lives accordingly. Such adjustments are, of course, genetically based, and are "perfected" by natural selection over long ages of time. Some bats meet these unfavorable conditions by migrating to more favorable regions during the winter; others undergo hypothermia and become dormant. Many bats apparently migrate out of their summer range when the temperature drops too low to support adequate insect food. The pallid bat (fig. 78), for instance, in the San Joaquin Valley of California in summer has a day roost and a night roost. The latter is used as a stopping place while it feeds on large insects such as the wingless Jerusalem cricket (*Stenopelmatus longispinus*). Sometimes a dozen bats feed at a night roost, where they are scarcely or never seen during the day. When the temperature at sunset falls below 50° F., about the first part of November, these bats never appear at the night roosts and are gone until late March or early April, when the weather becomes warm again (Ball,

1963). When the pallid bat is kept in a room below 50° F., it may lose up to 27 per cent of its weight over a period of five months (Orr, 1954).

Observations indicate that tree-dwelling species, such as the silvery-haired bat (*Lasionycteris noctivagans*) (fig. 75), the red bat (*Lasiurus borealis*), and the hoary bat (*Lasiurus cinereus*) (fig. 77), migrate and thus probably avoid cold weather.

Although certain bats that undergo hypothermy may be considered to have an inadequate thermoregulatory mechanism as compared with most other mammals, it nevertheless serves them well in conserving energy. Some bats lose up to one-third their weight during hibernation. During the

Myotis thysanodes, 16.6–17.0 mm.

Myotis yumanensis, 13.4–14.2 mm.

Myotis californicus, 12.4–14.2 mm.

Myotis evotis, 15.0–16.0 mm.

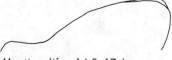
Myotis velifer, 14.0–17.6 mm.

Myotis keenii, 14.0–15.0 mm.

Myotis occultus, 14.2–16.0 mm.

Myotis subulatus, 13.9–14.7 mm.

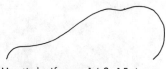
Myotis lucifugus, 14.2–15.4 mm.

Myotis volans, 13.7–14.2 mm.

Fig. 70. Profiles of the crania of *Myotis* with their total lengths.

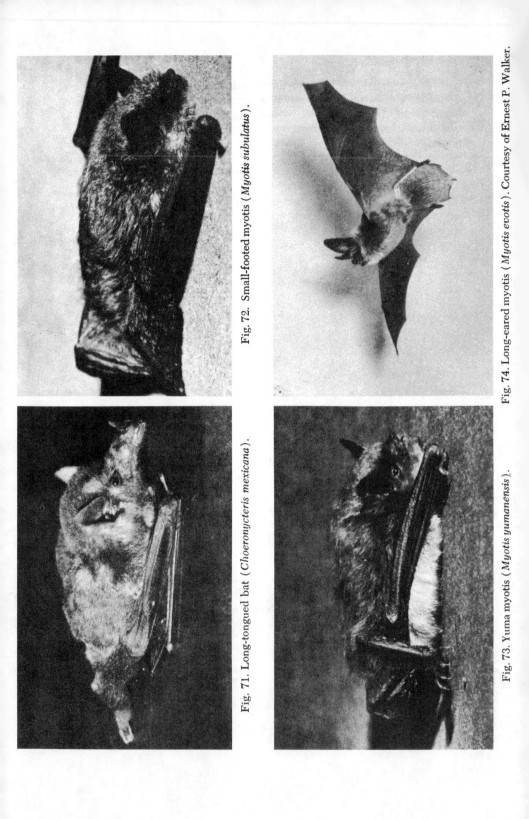

Fig. 71. Long-tongued bat (*Choeronycteris mexicana*).

Fig. 72. Small-footed myotis (*Myotis subulatus*).

Fig. 73. Yuma myotis (*Myotis yumanensis*).

Fig. 74. Long-eared myotis (*Myotis evotis*). Courtesy of Ernest P. Walker.

orderly process of a bat's waking, the whole body shivers violently, and heat is released until the active body temperature is attained. The hypothalamus of the brain seems to be the animal's thermostat, which, through the sympathetic nervous system, adjusts blood flow, heart rate, and breathing. What mechanism causes the partial inactivation of the bat's hypothalamus to bring about hypothermy remains for future investigation.

Some bats have a daytime resting temperature approximating that of the ambient temperature (diurnation). Thus they may reduce their metabolic processes and conserve energy while they sleep. This phenomenon is known to occur also in hummingbirds and is suggested in certain squirrels.

The aerial night life of a bat has placed a premium on peculiar specializations of structure and behavior. It has long been known that a bat can fly in total darkness and not bump into objects even though it has poor nocturnal vision. In the eighteenth century an Italian named Spallanzani showed that bats can avoid obstacles in total darkness, but what was not understood until recently was that part of Spallanzani's experiment showing that they *do* fly into objects if their ears are covered. Chiefly through the studies of Griffin (1950) and later workers, it is now known that bats orient themselves by means of *echolocation*. While flying, the bat utters a series of high-frequency sounds, which strike nearby objects and are echoed back. The human ear rarely can hear sounds of more than 20,000 cycles per second. Therefore, it cannot hear the ultrasonic squeaks of bats in flight, which may be of the order of 20,000 to 130,000 cycles per second. The bats' lower-frequency squeaks are not concerned with echolocation. An object over 0.18 mm. in diameter can be detected and avoided by a bat flying in total darkness (Griffin, 1959). As a bat approaches an object, it speeds up the number of sounds and may utter from 30 to 50 or more cries per second. Each cry may last only 1/500 second, with its beginning more highly pitched than the end. Thus the echo a bat hears of very near objects will be more highly pitched than the sound it hears at the instant of uttering. Some zoologists claim there are small muscles in the ears of bats which close the passages to the ears while the sound is being emitted but which open immediately after to hear only the echo. Experiments show that bats may detect objects and turn as close as six inches from them. Some bats seem to be able to "beam" the supersonic tones through their nostrils and thus have a precise judgment of the distance from nearby objects. Since a bat with its ears plugged will run into objects while flying in the dark, it is not known what part is played in the reception of these high-pitched echoes by the different sizes and shapes of bats' ears, the tragus, the noseleaf, and other extraordinary skin structures on the face.

Echolocation by bats is still such a recent discovery that much remains to be learned about it. It is, however, much more than a warning system against collisions. Griffin (1958) states that they use their echolocation system to hunt insects, so it must be very sharp and precise, which has been proved by laboratory experiments. There are many problems yet to be solved for a future mammalogist with knowledge of the physics of sound.

Fig. 75. Silvery-haired bat (*Lasionycteris noctivagans*).

Fig. 76. Western pipistrelle (*Pipistrellus hesperus*).

Fig. 77. Hoary bat (*Lasiurus cinereus*).

Fig. 78. Pallid bat (*Antrozous pallidus*)

Practically all the bats in the Pacific States are insectivorous; they capture and eat most of their insect prey while flying. Two species of the family Phyllostomatidae, which is common in Mexico, are rarely found in southern California; these two species, as already stated, may include fruit and nectar in their diet.

Reproductive behavior has not been studied in most of our bats. Some of the aspects of reproduction are closely related to the phenomenon of hibernation.

Pearson *et al.* (1952) made a model study on the lump-nosed bat (*Plecotus townsendii*) (fig. 79) in California. They found that during the spring and summer the adult males are usually solitary. The testes of the male are small during the winter, but they begin to enlarge in the spring and reach maximum size in September. The spermatozoa are stored in the epididymides, which bulge, thus readily distinguishing an adult male from a young male. Such spermatozoa are fertile for six months. Spermatozoa stored in the uterus in the fall are active for at least 76 days afterward. Usually copulation occurs in the winter roosting place, mostly perhaps while the female is torpid. Before the end of November all the females are inseminated. The Graafian follicle begins to enlarge in autumn and remains practically the same size throughout the winter. Ovulation may occur while the female is still at the winter roost or after she leaves in the spring. The gestation period is variable, lasting between 56 and 100 days, depending on the temperature of the female, which in turn depends on ambient temperature and whether she roosts in a cluster of bats, where it is warmer. The females segregate themselves in warm dark places to give birth. One young a year is born, which weighs about 2.5 grams. Young bats are able to fly when three weeks old, but they continue to nurse for several weeks longer. When the parent feeds, the young are left in the "nursery." The lump-nosed bat needs more than 300 acres to forage over. The population of a region seems to be determined by suitable roosting sites near a sufficient food supply.

Mating of the pallid bat may occur as early as October. A captive that was known to mate in December gave birth five months later, showing that in this instance later winter or early spring insemination was not necessary for fertilization (Orr, 1954). The gestation period of this bat is estimated to be about nine weeks. The young bats are born breech first and the female eats the placenta. The young are nearly naked at birth and their eyes do not open until about the tenth day. They may begin to fly at the seventh week.

The red bat (*Lasiurus borealis*) may have as many as four young, all of which cling to her fur as she hunts for food. Their combined weight may exceed that of the mother.

Except for man, bats have few enemies. Owls and snakes eat a few, and large trout catch some as they drink from lakes or pools while skimming over the water. Bats may live 20 years or more.

Fig. 79. Lump-nosed bat (*Plecotus townsendii*).

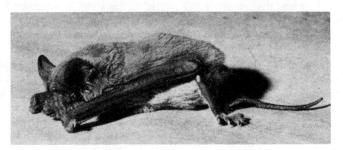

Fig. 80. Brazilian free-tailed bat (*Tadarida brasiliensis*).

Bats have been accused of carrying bedbugs and other insects detrimental to man, but the insects known to be parasitic to bats seem specific
to them and do not attack human beings. Much more serious, however, is
a bat's ability to carry rabies to other animals, including human beings.
Investigations show that bats belonging to the genera *Myotis* and *Tadarida*
may carry rabies without even exhibiting symptoms of the awesome disease themselves. There is now considerable evidence based on actual cases
of human rabies, as well as experiments based on keeping various carnivores in bat caves, indicating that a person need not even be bitten by an
infected bat to acquire rabies. Perhaps a tiny drop of urine from an infected
bat falling on an abraded bit of skin, or even the cave air itself, may be

infective. Caution must therefore be observed in working with bats. A number of species of bats from California have been investigated for the rabies virus, and the following have sometimes been found to be infected: *Tadarida brasiliensis, Myotis californicus, Myotis evotis, Lasiurus cinereus, Lasionycteris noctivagans, Antrozous pallidus, Pipistrellus hesperus,* and *Macrotus californicus.*

Three families of bats are known to frequent the Pacific States. The Phyllostomatidae, or leaf-nosed bats, are represented by two species in southern California, though rare. Both species are characterized by a projection of skin on the top of the snout, appearing like the horn of a rhinoceros. These tropical species are well represented in Mexico and Central America.

The so-called evening bats belong to the family Vespertilionidae, which is represented in the Pacific States by 19 species. All have tails almost entirely enclosed by the interfemoral membrane and tragi before their ear openings that are straight or nearly so.

The free-tailed bats belong to the family Molossidae; they have half or more of the tail extending free beyond the interfemoral membrane. Four species are found in the Pacific States.

The 25 species of bats occurring in the Pacific States may be tentatively identified by using the pictorial key or the conventional key and the brief descriptions which follow. The range maps should be checked for each species identified to ascertain if the specimen was observed or taken within the known range of the animal; if not, there may be an error in identification.

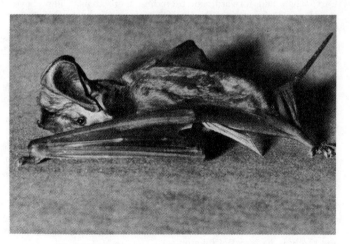

Fig. 81. Western mastiff bat (*Eumops perotis*).

KEY TO THE BATS (Chiroptera)

See fig. 69 for orientation

1A. With a fleshy nose-leaf projecting from the dorsal surface of the nose (resembling a rhinoceros horn) (Phyllostomatidae) 24
1B. Without a nose-leaf 2
2A. Tail projecting behind the interfemoral membrane for at least one-third the tail length (Molossidae) 3
2B. Tail nearly all enclosed within the interfemoral membrane (fig. 69) (Vespertilionidae) 6
3A. Total length less than 140 mm.; forearm less than 67 mm. . . . 4
3B. Total length more than 140 mm.; forearm 67–78 mm.; no space between the upper incisors (incisors contiguous); 1-1-2-3/2-1-2-3. Southern half of California.
　　Eumops perotis, western mastiff bat, p. 131, fig. 81.
4A. Ears connected across forehead; forearm more than 44 mm. . . . 5
4B. Ears not connected; forearm 44 mm. or less; 1-1-2-3/3-1-2-3. Common at low elevations but up to 4,000 feet in southwestern Oregon and all over California.
　　Tadarida brasiliensis, Brazilian free-tailed bat, p. 131, fig. 80.
5A. Forearm 58–64 mm.; ear (notch) 26–31 mm.; 1-1-2-3/2-1-2-3. Rare at low elevations in southern California.
　　Tadarida molossa (formerly *Tadarida macrotis*), big free-tailed bat, p. 131.
5B. Forearm 44–51 mm.; ear 19–23 mm.; 1-1-2-3/2-1-2-3. Rare at low elevations in southern California.
　　Tadarida femorosacca, pocketed free-tailed bat, p. 131.
6A. With six cheek teeth behind the canine on each side of the upper and lower jaws; tragus slender, pointed; dark brown, yellowish or buffy; 2-1-3-3/3-1-3-3 (*Myotis*) 7
6B. With fewer than six cheek teeth on each side of the upper jaw . . 16
7A. Ears, when laid forward, not extending more than 4 mm. beyond the muzzle; posterior edge of the interfemoral membrane naked, or with scattered single hairs, or with only a few scattered bunches of hairs . . 10
7B. Ears, when laid forward, extending 4 mm. or more beyond the muzzle; posterior edge of interfemoral membrane sometimes with many short hairs, which may be difficult to see 8
8A. Ears less than 19 mm. (from notch posterior to tragus) 9
8B. Ears 19–23 mm. (from notch posterior to tragus); light to dark brown dorsally; a few (easily overlooked) stiff hairs along the free border of the interfemoral membrane; forearm 35–41 mm.; tibia 16–17.5 mm.; skull 15–16.3 mm. (fig. 70). Forested areas throughout all three states.
　　Myotis evotis, long-eared myotis, p. 123, fig. 74.
9A. Forearm less than 40 mm.; ear (from notch) 14–18 mm.; glossy brown to dark brown dorsally; sometimes with scattered inconspicuous bristles along the free border of the interfemoral membrane; skull 14–15 mm. (fig. 70). Western Washington and Oregon.
　　Myotis keenii, Keen myotis, p. 121
9B. Forearm 40–46 mm.; tibia about 17.6 mm.; ear (from notch) 12–18.5 mm.; conspicuous clusters of short stiff hairs along the border of the interfemoral membrane; skull 16.6–17 mm. (fig. 70). Throughout California, Oregon, and rarely in eastern Washington.
　　Myotis thysanodes, fringed myotis, p. 119.

10A. Fur (except scattered hairs) not extending to elbow or knee on underside of wing, or, if thus covered with fur, with forearm less than 36 mm. . 11

10B. Fur extending to knee and elbow on underside of wing; forearm 35.5–42 mm.; tibia 16–19 mm.; hind foot 8 mm.; skull 13.7–14.2 mm. (fig. 70). Throughout California, Oregon, and Washington.
  Myotis volans, hairy-winged myotis, p. 121.

11A. Foot, not including calcar, 5–8 mm. and less than half the length of the tibia (about 40–45 per cent of its length); calcar keeled (fig. 69); forearm 30–34 mm. 12

11B. Foot, not including calcar, 7–12 mm. and more than half the tibia length (usually 48–60 per cent of its length); calcar not keeled; forearm 32–40 mm. 13

12A. Face brown; fur dorsally reddish brown, frequently with palest portion centrally on the hairs; forearm 30–33.2 mm.; tibia 12.5–15 mm.; forehead sharply rising from the short rostrum, skull 12.4–14.2 mm. (fig. 70). Throughout all three states up into the Transition Zone.
  Myotis californicus, California myotis, p. 121.

12B. Ears and face black (darkest fur is on the face); yellowish fur; forearm 30.8–33.2 mm.; tibia 12.3–13 mm.; forehead gradually rising from the rostrum, skull 13.9–14.7 mm. (fig. 70); calcar keeled; third metacarpal usually shorter than the forearm; fur dark at base, palest on the tips. Upper Sonoran and Transition zones throughout California. South of San Francisco Bay and in the eastern half of northern California, Oregon, and Washington.
  Myotis subulatus, small-footed myotis, p. 121, fig. 72.

13A. Skull more than 14 mm. in length 14

13B. Skull 13.4–14.2 mm.; with a high brain case arising from a short rostrum (fig. 70); forearm 34–37 mm.; tibia 13.5–16 mm. Throughout all three states in the Sonoran life zones.
  Myotis yumanensis, Yuma myotis, p. 123, fig. 73.

14A. Only near the Colorado River in California; skull with sagittal crests well defined 15

14B. Not along the Colorado River; forearm, 36–40 mm.; tibia 15–16.4 mm.; skull with moderately short rostrum (fig. 70); without sagittal crest; fur with a glossy sheen.
  Myotis lucifugus, little brown myotis, p. 119.

15A. Pelage, dull sepia; forehead moderate, rostrum short; tibia 15–17 mm.; forearm 40–47 mm.; skull 14–17.6 mm. (fig. 70).
  Myotis velifer, cave myotis, p. 119.

15B. Pelage, glossy tawny; forehead low, rostrum long; tibia 13.7–14 mm.; forearm 35–36.4 mm.; skull 14.2–16 mm. (fig. 70).
  Myotis occultus, Arizona myotis, p. 123.

16A. Forearm more than 35 mm. 17

16B. Forearm less than 35 mm.; five cheek teeth on each side of both jaws; yellowish gray, smoke gray, or whitish gray; face, ears, and membranes blackish; tragus blunt, with tip bent forward; 2-1-2-3/3-1-2-3. Southern two-thirds of California, eastern half of Oregon, and southeastern part of Washington.
  Pipistrellus hesperus, western pipistrelle, p. 127, fig. 76.

17A. Without three white spots dorsally; with more or fewer than 34 teeth . 18

17B. Blackish with three white spots dorsally; with 34 teeth, 2-1-2-3/3-1-2-3; ear 39–47 mm.; forearm 48–52 mm. Rare in southern and eastern California.
  Euderma maculata, spotted bat, p. 129.

18A. Dorsally usually not bright red or rich brown (but may be yellowish red) and without a combination of four upper cheek teeth and two upper incisors at each side 19

18B. Dorsally bright red or rich brown with black ears, wings, and interfemoral membrane; interfemoral membrane not covered with fur dorsally, and with a combination of four upper cheek teeth and two upper incisors on each side; 2-1-1-3/3-1-2-3; ears when laid forward rarely reaching nostrils. Throughout all three states in Sonoran and Transition zones.
   Eptesicus fuscus, big brown bat, p. 127.

19A. Ears when laid forward reaching far beyond the nose 20

19B. Ears when laid forward scarcely reaching to the end of the nose . . 21

20A. Forearm 39–45 mm.; with two conspicuous glandular lumps on the rostrum; ears 28–32 mm.; 2-1-2-3/3-1-3-3. Throughout all three states in Sonoran and Transition zones.
   Plecotus townsendii (formerly *Corynorhinus*), lump-nosed bat, p. 129, fig. 79.

20B. Forearm 45–52 mm.; no glandular lumps on rostrum; dull light yellow or light brown dorsally; membranes and ears slightly darker than dorsal fur; 1-1-1-3/2-1-2-3. Throughout most of the Sonoran Zone in all three states.
   Antrozous pallidus, pallid bat, p. 129, fig. 78.

21A. Chocolate brown, reddish brown, dark brown, reddish yellow, hoary gray, buffy white, or black with brown or silver-tipped fur dorsally . . 22

21B. Brick or rusty red, frequently with frosted yellowish fur; interfemoral membrane completely furred dorsally; forearm 37–43 mm.; 1-1-2-3/3-1-2-3. Roosting in trees throughout most of California.
   Lasiurus borealis, red bat, p. 125.

22A. Forearm usually less than 47 mm. 23

22B. Forearm usually more than 47 mm.; hoary yellowish gray or brown with white-tipped hairs; interfemoral membrane furred dorsally; 1-1-2-3/3-1-2-3. Roosting in trees throughout all three states.
   Lasiurus cinereus, hoary bat, p. 125, fig. 77.

23A. Length usually more than 110 mm.; dark brown, reddish yellow to buffy white; 1-1-1-3/3-1-2-3. Colorado desert, at Palm Springs in southern California. Rare.
   Lasiurus ega (formerly *Dasypterus*), western yellow bat, p. 125.

23B. Length usually less than 110 mm.; light brown or silver-tipped chocolate or blackish brown ventrally; inner upper incisor bicuspid; 2-1-2-3/3-1-3-3. Usually in forests of the Sierra Nevada and the northern half of California, from Monterey and Fresno counties north to include all of Oregon and Washington.
   Lasionycteris noctivagans, silvery-haired bat, p. 127, fig. 75.

24A. Ears when laid forward reaching far beyond nostrils; length usually more than 90 mm.; 2-1-2-3/2-1-3-3. Rare in low deserts in southern California.
   Macrotus californicus, California leaf-nosed bat, p. 117.

24B. Ears when laid forward never reaching to nostrils; length usually less than 90 mm.; very long snout; 2-1-2-3/0-1-3-3. Rare in southern California.
   Choeronycteris mexicana, long-tongued bat, p. 117, fig. 71.

Family **Phyllostomatidae** (Leaf-nosed Bats)

Tropical and subtropical; cutaneous nasal outgrowths; third finger with three bony phalanges; premaxillae fused; well-developed molars; two species in Pacific States.

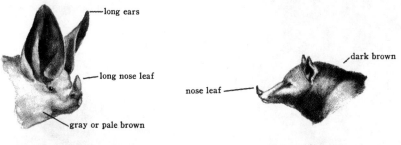

CALIFORNIA LEAF-NOSED BAT　　　　**LONG-TONGUED BAT**

California leaf-nosed bat (*Macrotus californicus*). Dental Formula 2-1-2-3/ 2-1-3-3. Length 84–103 mm.; forearm 49–57 mm.; *ear reaching well beyond the tip of the muzzle* when laid forward; tragus, smooth and acute, and about one-half the ear length; *vertical leaf-like projection on the nose*; drab pallid brown or gray; skull 22–24 mm.; 34 teeth, with upper incisors filling all the space in front of the canines. Riverside County and perhaps Los Angeles County, California, and south in the hottest part of the Lower Sonoran Life Zone. Map 11.

Long-tongued bat (*Choeronycteris mexicana*). Dental Formula 2-1-2-3/0-1-3-3. Length 77–86 mm.; forearm 43–45 mm.; *vertical leaf-like projection on the nose; ear not reaching the tip of the very long muzzle when laid forward*; skull 30–30.5 mm.; nectar feeder. San Diego region in California, in the Sonoran life zones. Fig. 71, Map 12.

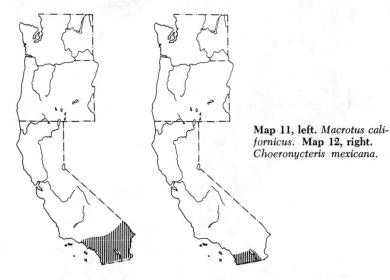

Map 11, left. *Macrotus californicus.* **Map 12, right.** *Choeronycteris mexicana.*

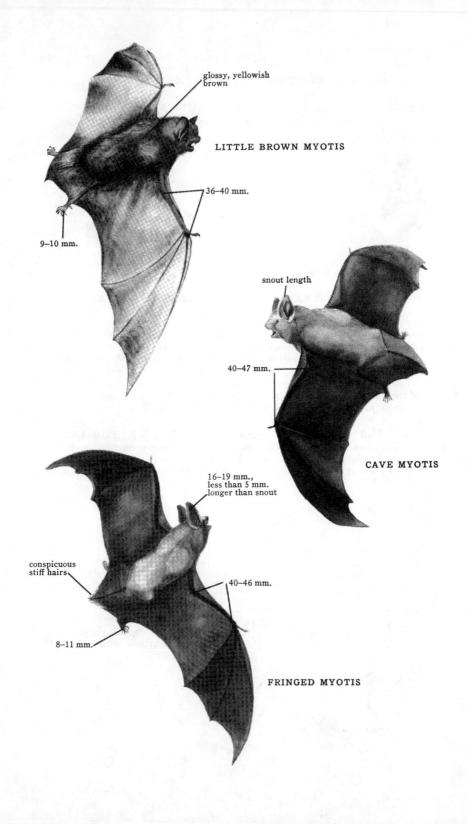

glossy, yellowish brown

LITTLE BROWN MYOTIS

36–40 mm.

9–10 mm.

snout length

40–47 mm.

CAVE MYOTIS

16–19 mm., less than 5 mm. longer than snout

conspicuous stiff hairs

40–46 mm.

8–11 mm.

FRINGED MYOTIS

Family **Vespertilionidae** (Evening Bats)

Muzzle and lips without cutaneous outgrowths; ears usually separate; tragus straight or slightly curved; tail long, nearly or entirely enclosed in the interfemoral membrane; third finger with two bony phalanges; bony palate conspicuously "notched" anteriorly; 19 species in the Pacific States.

Myotis Dental Formula 2-1-3-3/3-1-3-3; *see fig. 69 for orientation*

Little brown myotis (*Myotis lucifugus*). Length 79–93 mm.; forearm 36–40 mm.; *hair yellowish brown with glossy or burnished tips*; light buff beneath; dorsal hairs about 8 mm.; ear (notch) 14–15 mm., not extending beyond nose when laid forward; third finger longer than the fourth; *calcar not keeled* (fig. 69); *skull 14.2–15.4 mm., with moderate forehead and long rostrum* (fig. 70), *skull without a sagittal crest; foot relatively large*, 9–10 mm.; tibia 15–16.5 mm.; 38 teeth. Canadian and Hudsonian life zones of all three states. Map 13.

Cave myotis (*Myotis velifer*). Length 90–105 mm.; forearm 40–47 mm.; *ears (notch) usually reach only to the tip of the nose*; outer border of the interfemoral membrane is naked; *wing membrane arises from the bases of the toes of the hind foot*; hind foot is over one-half the length of the tibia; calcar not keeled; dull sepia or dull brown; *skull 14–17.6 mm.* (fig. 70); high forehead, short rostrum, sagittal crest present; 38 teeth. Chiefly desert dwellers along the Colorado River in southeastern California. Map 13.

Fringed myotis (*Myotis thysanodes*). Length 80–95 mm.; tail 37–42 mm.; forearm 40–46 mm.; foot 8–11 mm.; ear (notch) 16–19 mm., *extends less than 5 mm. beyond the nostrils when laid forward; drab yellowish brown; outer border of the interfemoral membrane conspicuously covered with tufts of stiff hairs*; wing membrane goes to base of the toes; *skull 16.6–17 mm.* high, similar to *M. californicus*, but with longer rostrum and lower occipital region (fig. 70); 38 teeth. In the Upper Sonoran Life Zone in open woods of California, Oregon, and eastern Washington. Map. 14.

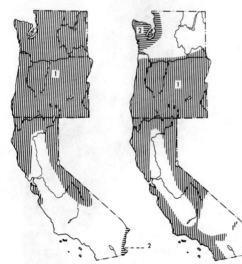

Map 13, left. (1) *Myotis lucifugus*, (2) *Myotis velifer*. **Map 14, right.** (1) *Myotis thysanodes*, (2) *Myotis keenii*.

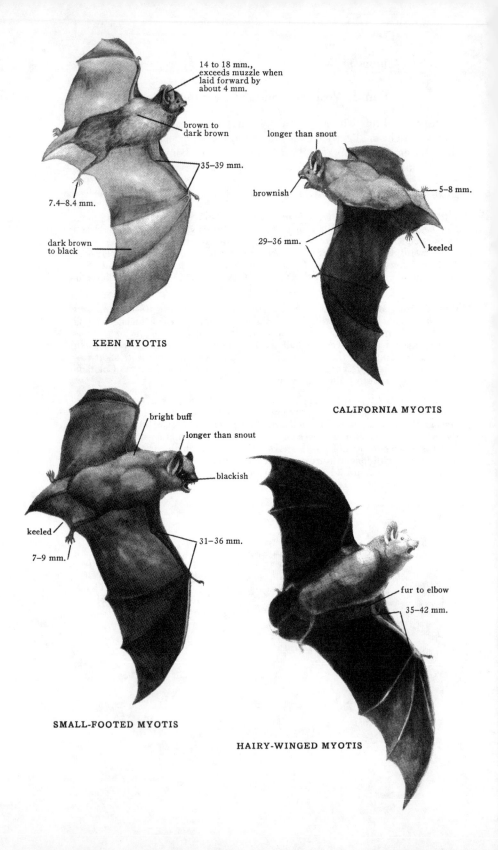

14 to 18 mm., exceeds muzzle when laid forward by about 4 mm.

brown to dark brown

35–39 mm.

7.4–8.4 mm.

dark brown to black

KEEN MYOTIS

longer than snout

brownish

29–36 mm.

5–8 mm.

keeled

CALIFORNIA MYOTIS

bright buff

longer than snout

blackish

keeled

31–36 mm.

7–9 mm.

SMALL-FOOTED MYOTIS

fur to elbow

35–42 mm.

HAIRY-WINGED MYOTIS

Keen myotis (*Myotis keenii*). Length 87–89 mm.; forearm 35–39 mm.; hind foot 7.4–8.4 mm.; brown to dark brown glossy fur; membranes dark brown to black; ear (notch) about 13 mm. and reaches 4 mm. beyond nostril when bent forward; *skull 14–15 mm.*; high forehead, short rostrum (fig. 70); 38 teeth; calcar not keeled. This species is considered to be conspecific with *Myotis evotis* by some mammalogists. Areas of western Washington and Oregon. Map 14.

California myotis (*Myotis californicus*). Length 74–85 mm.; forearm 29–36 mm.; tail 36–42 mm.; ear (notch) 11–14.5 mm., and extends beyond nostrils 1–4 mm. when laid forward; *ears and membranes dark,* contrasting with bright tawny brown dorsal fur with dark gray at base of hairs; *face not entirely blackish; foot relatively small,* 5–7 mm., less than one-holf tibia length; calcar distinctly keeled; *skull 12.4–14.2 mm.,* high forehead and short rostrum (fig. 70); 38 teeth. Living in all except the highest life zones in all three states. Map 15.

Small-footed myotis (*Myotis subulatus*). Length 75–88 mm.; forearm 31–36 mm.; ears barely reaching beyond nose when laid forward; *ears and membranes black;* contrasting with the bright buff or golden brown of the back; *face blackish; foot relatively small,* 7–9 mm., which is less than one-half tibia length; third and fourth finger about equal in length, calcar long and keeled (fig. 69); *skull 13.9–14.7 mm., low forehead, profile appears nearly flat* (fig. 70); 38 teeth. Arid uplands in Upper Sonoran and Transition life zones of California, and in eastern Oregon and Washington. Fig. 72, Map 16.

Hairy-winged myotis (*Myotis volans*). Length 87–103 mm.; forearm 35.5–42 mm.; tail 37–49 mm.; tibia 16.5–19 mm.; calcar distinctly keeled (fig. 69); *ears short, barely reaching nostril when bent forward; underarm and membrane covered with fur down to the elbow and knee;* yellowish cinnamon to dark brown above, membranes and ears blackish; *skull 13.7–14.2 mm.,* brain case and forehead fairly high, with short rostrum (fig. 70); 38 teeth. In open forest in the Upper Sonoran and Transition life zones in all three states. Map 17.

Map 15, left. *Myotis californicus.* **Map 16, center.** *Myotis subulatus.* **Map 17, right.** *Myotis volans.*

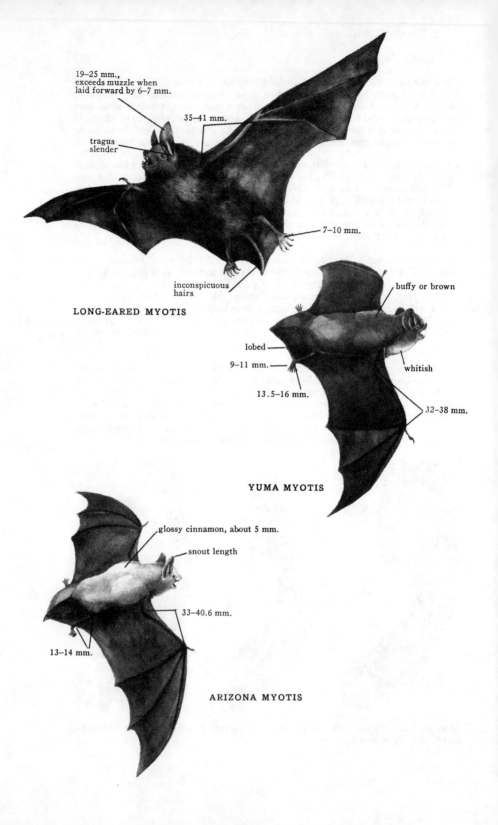

19–25 mm., exceeds muzzle when laid forward by 6–7 mm.

35–41 mm.

tragus slender

7–10 mm.

inconspicuous hairs

LONG-EARED MYOTIS

buffy or brown

lobed

9–11 mm.

13.5–16 mm.

whitish

32–38 mm.

YUMA MYOTIS

glossy cinnamon, about 5 mm.

snout length

33–40.6 mm.

13–14 mm.

ARIZONA MYOTIS

Long-eared myotis (*Myotis evotis*). Length 75–97 mm.; forearm 35.7–41 mm.; foot 7–10 mm.; ear (notch) 19–25 mm., *reaching 5–10 mm. beyond the nose when laid forward; dark to light golden brown fur; membranes and ears black; skull 15–16 mm.*, low forehead, long rostrum (fig. 70); 38 teeth; fringe of inconspicuous hairs at the edge of the interfemoral membrane. Mostly in woods in the Upper Sonoran, Transition, and Canadian life zones in all three states. Fig. 74, Map 18.

Yuma myotis (*Myotis yumanensis*). Length 73–91 mm.; forearm 32–38 mm.; tibia 13–16 mm.; foot 9–11 mm.; fur on back is buffy and belly whitish, *not shiny or burnished;* membranes and ears pale brownish; ear (notch) 13–15 mm., reaching nostril when laid forward; *skull 13.4–14.2 mm., forehead steep, high without sagittal crest;* rostrum short (fig. 70); 38 teeth; foot relatively large, 9–11 mm.; *a lobe at end of unkeeled calcar.* Chiefly open woods, the subboreal zones in all three states. Fig. 73, Map 19.

Arizona myotis (*Myotis occultus*). Length 85–90 mm.; forearm 33–40.6 mm.; hind foot 9–10.5 mm., over one-half tibia length; ear (notch), 11–15 mm.; *cinnamon or yellowish, with glossy sheen* on the back; hairs on back, about 5 mm.; *skull 14.2–16 mm.*, low forehead, long rostrum (fig. 70); with a pronounced sagittal crest; 38 teeth. Along the Colorado River in the Lower Sonoran Life Zone in southeastern California. Map 20.

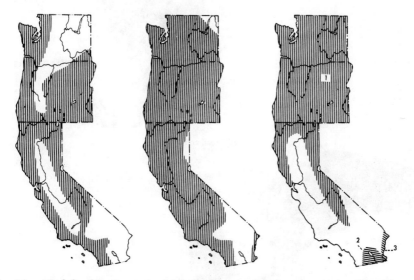

Map 18, left. *Myotis evotis.* **Map 19, center.** *Myotis yumanensis.* **Map 20, right.** (1) *Lasionycteris noctivagans,* (2) *Lasiurus ega,* (3) *Myotis occultus.*

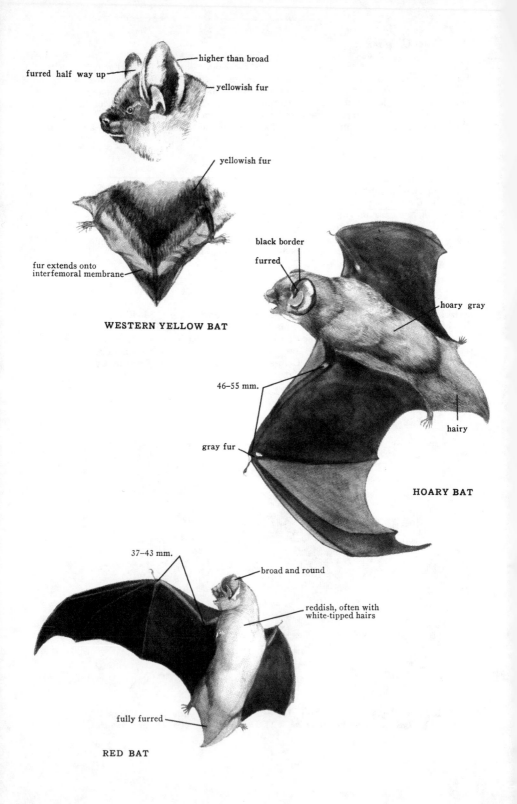

furred half way up

higher than broad

yellowish fur

yellowish fur

fur extends onto
interfemoral membrane

WESTERN YELLOW BAT

black border

furred

hoary gray

46–55 mm.

gray fur

hairy

HOARY BAT

37–43 mm.

broad and round

reddish, often with
white-tipped hairs

fully furred

RED BAT

Lasiurus Dental Formula 1-1-2-3/3-1-2-3 or 1-1-1-3/3-1-2-3

Western yellow bat (*Lasiurus ega,* formerly *Dasypterus ega*). Length 109–15 mm.; forearm 44–47 mm.; *yellowish brown fur,* which extends onto the basal parts of the wings and interfemoral membrane, and *halfway up the outside of the ear; ear considerably higher than broad, tapering to a tip,* and barely reaching the end of the nose when laid forward; 30 teeth. Lower Sonoran Life Zone in the Colorado Desert near Palm Springs, California. Map 20.

Hoary bat (*Lasiurus cinereus*). Length 128–46 mm.; *dorsal surface of the interfemoral membrane hairy;* long soft fur is yellowish gray or *yellowish brown tipped with white;* forearm 46–55 mm.; ears rounded, partially furred, with black naked rims; white patches of fur at the wrist and elbow on the dorsal surface; skull 16.9–18.5 mm.; 32 teeth. Roosts in the foliage of trees. Spends winter along the coast south from San Francisco. In April some move inland and north, at least to Port Angeles and Wenatchee, Washington, in the Sonoran, Transition, and Canadian life zones. Fig. 77, Map 21.

Red bat (*Lasiurus borealis*). Length 91–111 mm.; *dorsal surface of the interfemoral membrane hairy; body brick or rufous red with white-tipped hairs;* ears broad and rounded; forearm 37–44 mm.; skull 12–13.1 mm.; 32 teeth; tail vertebrate, longer than the forearm. Roosts in the foliage of trees. Displays migratory habit by spending the winter along the coast; some move inland in summer, where the sexes separate zonally. Most of California (no records for Oregon and Washington), Sonoran and Transition life zones. Map 22.

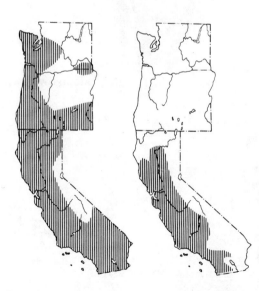

Map 21, left. *Lasiurus cinereus.* **Map 22, right.** *Lasiurus borealis.*

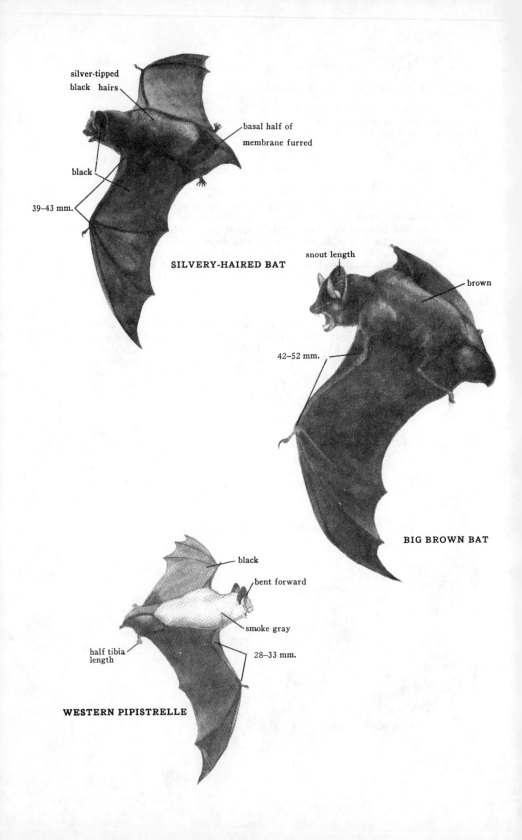

silver-tipped
black hairs

basal half of
membrane furred

black

39–43 mm.

SILVERY-HAIRED BAT

snout length

brown

42–52 mm.

BIG BROWN BAT

black

bent forward

smoke gray

half tibia
length

28–33 mm.

WESTERN PIPISTRELLE

Silvery-haired bat (*Lasionycteris noctivagans*). Dental Formula 2-1-2-3/3-1-3-3. Length 92–107 mm.; forearm 39–43 mm.; *hairs with blackish or chocolate brownish bases, usually tipped with silver; basal half of the interfemoral membrane furred;* ear barely or scarcely reaches nostril when bent forward; skull 15.5–16.5 mm.; 36 teeth. Roosts in the foliage of trees. North from Monterey and Fresno counties, California, in all three states in the Transition Life Zone chiefly. Fig. 75, Map 20.

Big brown bat (*Eptesicus fuscus*). Dental Formula 2-1-1-3/3-1-2-3. Length 107–22 mm.; forearm 42–52 mm.; *long glossy fur, bright brown; membranes, feet, ears, and nose blackish;* ears short, barely reach the end of the snout when laid forward; skull 18.8–19.4 mm.; 32 teeth; known to hibernate for months. In the Upper Sonoran and Transition life zones of all three states. Map 23.

Western pipistrelle (*Pipistrellus hesperus*). Dental Formula 2-1-2-3/3-1-2-3. Length 60–86 mm.; forearm 28–33 mm.; *ears, feet, nose, and membranes blackish,* contrasting with the *buffy gray or smoke gray coloration* on the back and the whitish on the belly; foot less than half as long as the tibia; *the tragus is bent forward;* skull 11.3–12.3 mm.; palate extending far behind the molars; 34 teeth. Chiefly in the Sonoran Life Zone, especially in the deserts of all three states. Fig. 76, Map 24.

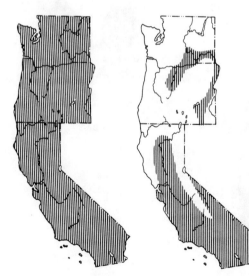

Map 23, left. *Eptesicus fuscus.* **Map 24, right.** *Pipistrellus hesperus.*

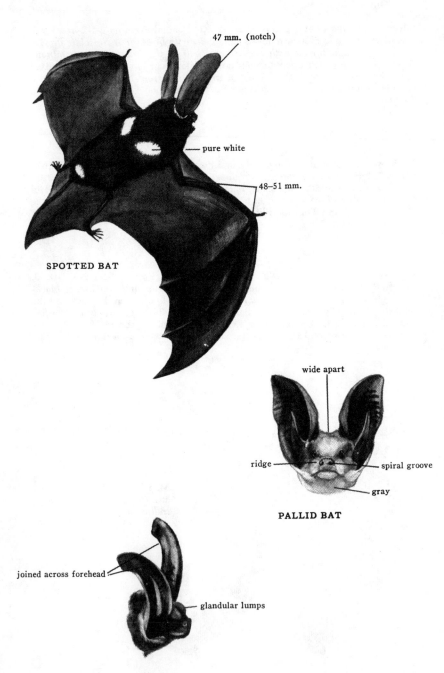

47 mm. (notch)

pure white

48–51 mm.

SPOTTED BAT

wide apart

ridge — — spiral groove

gray

PALLID BAT

joined across forehead

glandular lumps

LUMP-NOSED BAT

Spotted bat (*Euderma maculata*). Dental Formula 2-1-2-3/3-1-2-3. Length 107–15 mm.; forearm 48–51 mm.; *back is blackish with three white patches*; ears very large, 39–47 mm. from notch, about three-quarters the length of the forearms; skull 18.8–19 mm.; 34 teeth. Rare; in the Sonoran and Transition life zones in eastern California and possibly eastern Oregon. Map 25.

Pallid bat (*Antrozous pallidus*). Dental Formula 1-1-1-3/2-1-2-3. Length 114–35 mm.; forearm 48–60 mm.; *ears wide apart and reaching far beyond the muzzle when laid forward*; each nostril *under a horseshoe-shaped ridge at the end of a spiral groove*; tragus with wavy edge; *drab gray to buffy yellow*; ears and membranes dark brown; skull 19–24 mm.; 28 teeth; known to feed on Jerusalem crickets; often abundant in the Sonoran life zones of all three states. Fig. 78, Map 26.

Lump-nosed bat (*Plecotus townsendii*, formerly *Corynorhinus rafinesquii*). Dental Formula 2-1-2-3/3-1-3-3. Length 89–108 mm.; forearm 39–44 mm.; grayish brown; *ears very long, about three-quarters the length of the forearms, and joined across the forehead; large glandular lumps between the nostrils and eyes*; skull 15.5–17.4 mm.; 36 teeth. Sonoran life zones throughout all three states. (Some zoologists refer this bat to the genus *Corynorhinus*.) Fig. 79, Map 27.

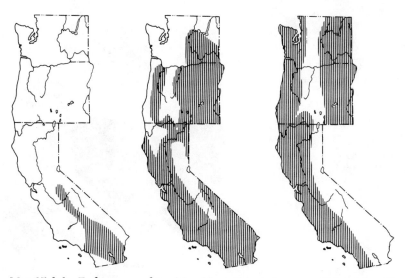

Map 25, left. *Euderma maculata.* **Map 26, center.** *Antrozous pallidus.* **Map 27, right.** *Plecotus townsendii.*

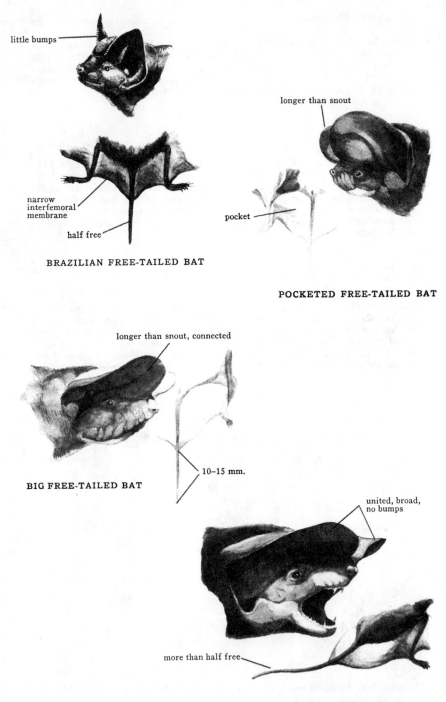

little bumps

narrow
interfemoral
membrane

half free

BRAZILIAN FREE-TAILED BAT

longer than snout

pocket

POCKETED FREE-TAILED BAT

longer than snout, connected

10–15 mm.

BIG FREE-TAILED BAT

united, broad,
no bumps

more than half free

WESTERN MASTIFF BAT

Family **Molossidae** (Free-tailed Bats)

Ears sometimes joined near the base; tail extending usually half or more of its length beyond the membrane; third phalange of third finger is cartilaginous except at base; four species in the Pacific States.

Tadarida Dental Formula 1-1-2-3/2-1-2-3 or 1-1-2-3/3-1-2-3

Brazilian free-tailed bat (*Tadarida brasiliensis*, formerly *T. mexicana*). Length 90–104 mm.; forearm 36–46 mm.; *tail about half free from the interfemoral membrane; ears usually not connected at the base and not reaching to the end of the nose when laid forward;* without a distinct bump between the nostril and eye; *ear with little bumps on front edge;* sooty or reddish brown; skull 14–18 mm.; males have longer canine teeth than females; 32 teeth with upper incisors converging at the tips. Shasta, Sonoma, and Mono counties and south, chiefly in the Sonoran life zones in California but also in southwestern Oregon. Fig. 80, Map 28.

Pocketed free-tailed bat (*Tadarida femorosacca*). Length 98–118 mm.; forearm 44.8–51 mm.; *free part of tail about 5 mm. longer than the part enclosed in the interfemoral membrane; pockets in the membrane by the femurs;* ear 21–24 mm. from notch, apparently connected and bearing small bumps on anterior surfaces; dull brown; skull 18.2–19.4 mm.; 30 teeth. Lower. Sonoran Life Zone in the Colorado Desert of California. Map 29.

Big free-tailed bat (*Tadarida molossa*). Length 125–32 mm.; forearm 58–64 mm.; *ears extending beyond the muzzle when laid forward and always connected at the base; free part of the tail 10–15 mm. longer than the part in the interfemoral membrane;* ears with wartlike bodies on the anterior edges; brown with whitish base on hairs; skull 22.4–24 mm.; 30 teeth, upper incisors parallel. Probably Upper Sonoran Life Zone in southern California. Map 30.

Western mastiff bat (*Eumops perotis*). Dental Formula 1-1-2-3/2-1-2-3. Length 157–84 mm.; forearm 73–80 mm.; *tail projecting far beyond interfemoral membrane; ears large, united above nostrils and projecting forward;* membranes and fur sooty brown; skull 30–33 mm.; 30 teeth, with upper incisors diverging at the tips. Uncommon; Alameda, San Benito, and Mariposa counties and south in the arid and semiarid lowlands, in the Lower Sonoran Life Zone in California. Fig. 81, Map 31.

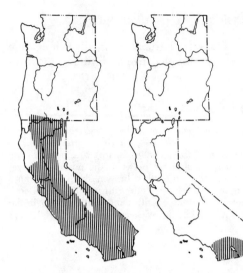

Map 28, left. *Tadarida brasiliensis.* **Map 29, right.** *Tadarida femorosacca.*

Map 30, left. *Tadarida molossa.* **Map 31, right.** *Eumops perotis.*

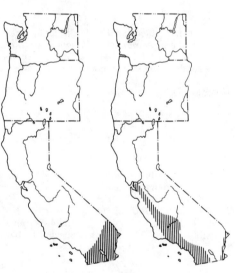

8. Order Lagomorpha

There are two families belonging to this order in the Pacific States. The Ochotonidae includes one species, the pika (*Ochotona princeps*). The Leporidae includes three genera. These are *Sylvilagus*, the cottontails and rabbits, with five species; *Lepus*, the hares, with three species; and *Oryctolagus cuniculus*, a domesticated European species of rabbit that long ago became feral on some of the San Juan Islands, Washington, and on the Farallon Islands, California, where it is very numerous and is a pest even to the extent of undermining houses with its burrows.

Considerable confusion exists in the use of vernacular names for species belonging to this order in the Pacific States. The pika is often erroneously referred to as a cony, a name first applied to species belonging to the Old World order Hyracoidea since Biblical times. The hares belong to the genus *Lepus*, but they are often referred to as "snowshoe rabbits" or "jackrabbits." The young of hares are precocial, and are born with eyes open and fully furred (Fig. 84).

The cottontails, brush rabbits, and pigmy rabbits (*Sylvilagus*) are much more like the Old World rabbits (*Oryctolagus*) in that they have naked, *altricial* young that are born with eyes closed. The fur-lined nest may be a shallow depression or even a spherical cavity dug by the female just below the surface of the ground.

Lagomorphs not greatly different from the species living today were in existence during the Eocene Epoch. The order is numerous today, as it has been in past ages, probably because of the great reproductive capacity and remarkable adaptibility of most of the species.

There are three zoological generalizations applicable to homoiothermal animals that are well illustrated by rabbits and hares of the Pacific States. These are Bergmann's, Allen's, and Gloger's rules. The first, in effect, states that the same or related species tend to be larger in colder regions. Allen's rule holds that such external features as ears, tails, and legs tend to become shorter in the colder regions. Gloger's rule infers that a race of a species living in humid regions is darker in color than one living under more arid conditions. The first two generalizations may be related to the surface-volume principle, which in turn is related to heat generation and loss. All mammals give off approximately the same amount of heat per unit of sur-

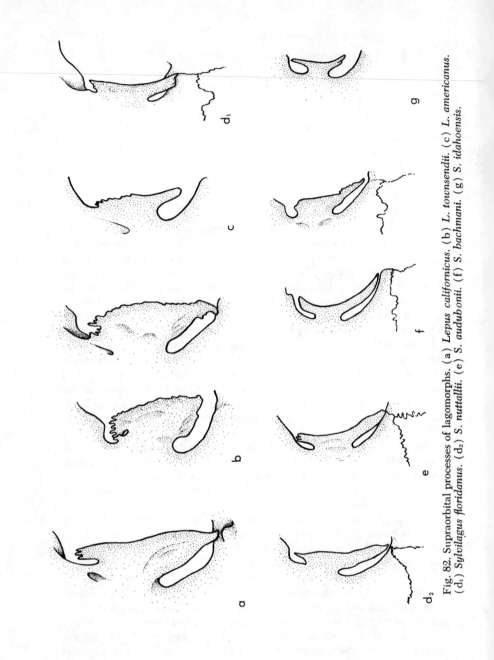

Fig. 82. Supraorbital processes of lagomorphs. (a) *Lepus californicus*. (b) *L. townsendii*. (c) *L. americanus*. (d₁) *Sylvilagus floridanus*. (d₂) *S. nuttallii*. (e) *S. audubonii*. (f) *S. bachmani*. (g) *S. idahoensis*.

face. Because the surface of an object increases as the square of the linear dimension, and the volume increases as the cube, it follows that larger animals of the same kind will lose less heat in relation to their weight than smaller ones and will therefore be better adapted to live in cold regions. It seems doubtful to some zoologists, however, that the relatively smaller surface of the larger mammal would give enough reduction of heat loss to be very significant. According to some ecologists, the animals' adaptation to the colder climates probably depends more on their insulation, vascularization, and tolerance of cold by the tissues (Kendeigh, 1961). Longer appendages such as ears, legs, and tails should lose heat more rapidly because of their greater surface, and, hence, animals with shorter ears, legs, and tails should be better adapted to cold regions. Evolution apparently *has favored* larger animals with relatively shorter ears, legs, and tails in colder regions.

There may, however, be other explanations for longer and shorter appendages. Brush rabbits (*Sylvilagus bachmani*) that live in the hot areas in the Lower California inland do indeed have longer ears than the same species living along the cool humid northern California coast. Sound, however, does not carry as well in hot, dry air as it does in cool, humid air, so perhaps the Mexican brush rabbit has developed longer ears in order to hear its enemies before they come too close and not because of the excess heat.

Gloger's rule may be illustrated with the black-tailed hare (*Lepus californicus*). Along the humid Pacific coast it is much darker than the same species in the arid Death Valley of California. Low humidity, however, is probably *not a direct factor* in producing paler coloration in the desert lagomorphs and rodents. Humidity may play an indirect role in dètermining the pale or dark pelage of an animal. Plant growth is more luxuriant and soil humus is darker in regions of high humidity. Less humidity brings about lighter soils and less dense vegetation. The genetic variation of animals that live in these two contrasting environments (i.e., dark and light) will be selected in one direction or the other, and the animals will become adapted to the place where they live without humidity directly affecting the darkness or lightness of their pelage.

Whatever the cause of the difference in size, shape, appendage lengths, and color, these lagomorphs illustrate these rules in their distribution from the far north toward the equator.

The Arctic hare (*Lepus arcticus*) of the far north is 26 to 27 inches long and weighs about 12 pounds. Its close relative, the white-tailed hare, in eastern parts of California, Oregon, and Washington, measures 23 to 25 inches and weighs up to ten pounds. The ears of the Arctic hare are only about three inches long, but those of the white-tailed hare (figs. 93, 94) are about 4.5 inches in length. The best way to express the relative ear lengths of hares living in different regions is to give them as percentages of total length. The Arctic hare's ears are about 12 per cent of its total length. The snowshoe hare, which ranges from northern Canada to the Sierra Nevada to central California, has ears about 13 to 14 per cent of its total length. The white-tailed hare, which lives farther south, in the mountains and eastern parts of the Pacific States, has ears about 18 per cent of its length. The black-tailed hare (fig. 92), which ranges still farther south, has ears about 19.3 per cent of its length in Washington and about 20.7 per cent in California. Still farther south, in Mexico, the antelope hare (*Lepus alleni*) has ears about 23.7 per cent of its length. One might expect the individuals of such a species living at high elevations, as in high latitudes, to be larger, with relatively shorter legs, ears, and tails than the population at lower levels. However, there are no studies as yet of the same or closely related species of mammals (or birds) living at different elevations or life zones in western mountains.

It may well be that such differences will not be found as one goes from lower life zones to higher ones on mountains. Perhaps the relatively short distance from one life zone to another on a mountain would make for too rapid a gene flow from one population to another, so that differences in morphology between high and low latitudes would not occur.

The European rabbits were introduced on the Farallon Islands almost a century ago. These rabbits reach a population peak of about 1,000 in the spring, when food is plentiful. As the dry season approaches and food becomes scarce, fighting and disease reduce the population to about 300 in the fall. A survey in 1960 showed that 16 per cent of these rabbits had blood type D, 26 per cent had F, and 58 per cent had the hybrid DF. A year later 15 per cent of the population had D, 24 per cent F, and 61 per cent DF, showing remarkable similarity to the previous year. The hybrids (DF) were significantly more plentiful than the 50 per cent to be expected, indicating that this blood type has an as yet unknown advantage.

KEY TO THE PIKAS, COTTONTAILS, RABBITS, AND HARES (Lagomorpha)

The animals belonging to this order have tails shorter than the hind foot. Except for the pika, which has nearly circular ears, they have noticeably long ears. The usual form of locomotion is by hopping. All have two small upper incisors behind the two large outer ones. The dental formula is 2-0-3-3/1-0-2-3, except for the pika, which is 2-0-3-2/1-0-2-3 or 2-0-2-3/1-0-2-3.

Identification of the various species of cottontails (*Sylvilagus*) is difficult, and it is frequently necessary to utilize skull differences, especially the supraorbital process (Fig. 82) and the size of the tympanic bullae.

1A. Not on the San Juan Islands, Washington, or the Farallon Islands, California   2
1B. On the San Juan Islands and the Farallon Islands. Hind foot 92–112 mm. Introduced from Europe, now feral.
     Oryctolagus cuniculus, domestic rabbit, p. 141 (no range map).
2A. Ears at least twice as long as wide; hind legs much longer than the forelegs; skull with supraorbital processes   3
2B. Ears round or ovate; hind legs scarcely longer than the forelegs; skull without supraorbital processes. Talus slopes in the Transition, Canadian, Hudsonian, and Alpine-Arctic life zones but also at lower elevations in northeastern California and southeastern Oregon.
     Ochotona princeps, pika, p. 139, fig. 85.

hind feet   forefeet

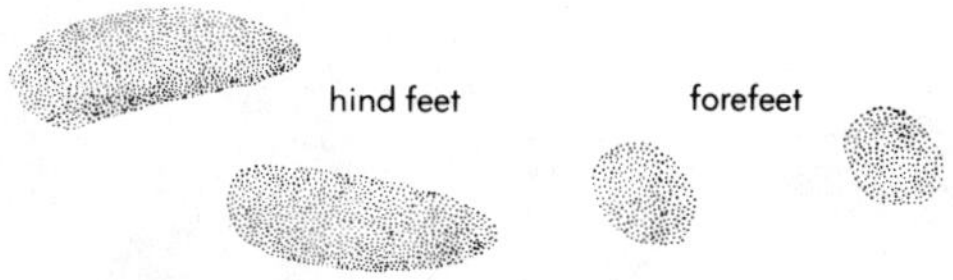

Fig. 83. Tracks of black-tailed hare.

3A. Hind foot more than 105 mm.; interparietals fused with parietals . 8
3B. Hind foot less than 105 mm.; interparietals not fused with parietals . 4
4A. Ear from notch more than 60 mm. 5
4B. Ear from notch less than 60 mm.; hind foot 58–72 mm. Thick sagebrush in
     northeastern California and in eastern Oregon and Washington.
          Sylvilagus idahoensis, pigmy rabbit, p. 143, fig. 91.
5A. Hairs on underside mostly white with some lead color at the bases; ears
     with dark tips; hind foot longer than 75 mm. 6
5B. Hairs on underside mostly lead-colored, with short white tips; ears uni-
     formly colored without darker tips; hind foot 65–80 mm.; posterior part of
     the bow-shaped supraorbital process touching skull only at tip if at all (fig.
     82). Chiefly in Upper Sonoran Life Zone in western Oregon and in Cali-
     fornia west of the Sierra Nevada crest.
          Sylvilagus bachmani, brush rabbit, p. 143, fig. 88.
6A. Rump more gray than brown 7
6B. Rump more brown than gray; dorsally pinkish-cinnamon brown mixed with
     black; posterior part of supraorbital process frequently notched and fused
     with cranium (fig. 82). Introduced into several counties in Washington.
          Sylvilagus floridanus, eastern cottontail, p. 143, fig. 89.
7A. Hairs on the distal part of the inside of the ear sparse and only about 2 mm.
     in length; rump gray and black, lightly washed with brown; supraorbital
     process not extending to the parietal bones, with prominently upturned
     edge, and antorbital blunt or notched (fig. 82). Lowlands in relatively
     open country in California.
          Sylvilagus audubonii, Audubon cottontail, p. 141, fig. 87.
7B. Hairs on the distal part of the inside of the ear thick and about 5 mm.
     long; rump gray and black; anterior part of supraorbital process comes to
     a point (fig. 82). Woods and sagebrush hills of northeastern California and
     in Washington and Oregon east of the Cascade crest.
          Sylvilagus nuttallii, Nuttall cottontail, p. 141, fig. 90.
8A. Ear more than 80 mm. (from notch) 9
8B. Ear less than 80 mm. (from notch); dark brown or dusky gray dorsally
     (may be white in winter in and east of the Cascades and Sierra Nevada);
     hind feet over 100 mm., mostly white with dark brown soles. Wooded areas
     in Transition, Canadian, and Hudsonian life zones of Washington, Oregon,
     and the northern half of eastern California.
          Lepus americanus, snowshoe hare, p. 139, fig. 95.
9A. Hind feet usually less than 145 mm.; dorsal black stripe on the brownish
     tail extends onto the rump; dorsally grayish at all seasons. Sonoran and
     Transition life zones from central Washington over most of Oregon and
     California.
          Lepus californicus, black-tailed hare, p. 139, fig. 92.
9B. Hind feet usually more than 145 mm.; tail all white or sometimes with
     dusky dorsal stripe that does not extend onto the rump; dorsally grayish
     brown in summer, but may be white in winter in parts of its range. Bunch-
     grass or sagebrush in hilly country of Sonoran to Hudsonian life zones in the
     eastern half of Washington and Oregon and in northeastern California.
          Lepus townsendii, white-tailed hare, p. 141, figs. 93, 94.

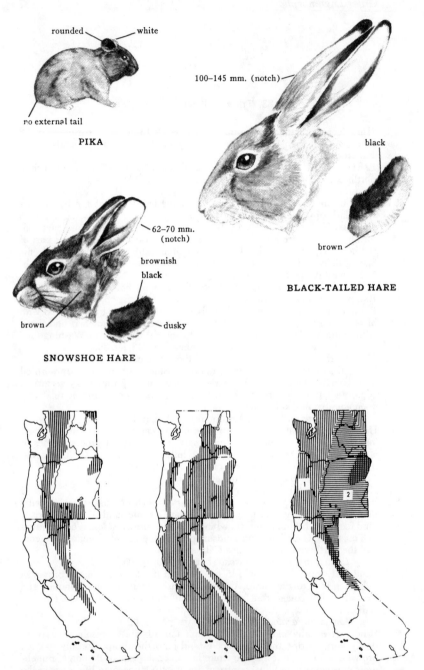

rounded — white

no external tail

PIKA

100–145 mm. (notch)

black

brown

BLACK-TAILED HARE

62–70 mm. (notch)

brownish black

brown

dusky

SNOWSHOE HARE

Map 32, left. *Ochotona princeps.* **Map 33, center.** *Lepus californicus.* **Map 34, right.** (1) *Lepus americanus,* (2) *Lepus townsendii.*

Pika (*Ochotona princeps*). Length 165–215 mm., or average about seven inches; no visible tail; hind foot 25–35 mm.; *ears round, much shorter than the head, with white edges; no external tail;* grayish buff to dark brown (one annual molt); no supraorbital process, as in rabbit's skull (fig. 82) on the frontal bone; skull 40–45 mm. Talus rocks north of Mount Whitney, Tulare County, in the Sierra Nevada, and in the Modoc Lava Beds of California and southwestern Oregon, hence across Oregon and Washington in the high Cascade Moutains; in the Sierra Nevada, mostly in the Alpine Fell-fields; Hudsonian and Alpine-Arctic life zones. P. 144, fig. 85, Map 32.

Black-tailed hare (*Lepus californicus*). Length 465–630 mm., average about 22 inches; tail 50–112 mm.; hind foot 112–45 mm.; *ear from notch 100–145 mm.,* with blackish tips; grayish dorsally and nearly white beneath (possibly two annual molts); *upper side of tail black, running up onto the rump, buffy gray below; outer edge of supraorbital process usually curves inward and postorbital process width is usually much less than half its length, with only two to four crenulations on narrow end, with tips nearly always touching the skull* (fig. 82); skull 66–77.4 mm. basilar length; interparietal bone fused with surrounding bones (not with distinct sutures as in fig. 51). Found in practically all communities except those of the higher mountains in the Sonoran and Transition life zones of California, Oregon, and south-central Washington. (Often incorrectly referred to as "jackrabbit.") P. 147, fig. 92, Map 33.

Snowshoe hare (*Lepus americanus*). Length 365–520 mm., average about 15 inches; tail 25–45 mm.; hind foot large and hairy, 112–50 mm.; *ear from notch 62–70 mm.;* brown in summer, white in winter (two or possibly three annual molts); *tail in summer brownish black above and dusky beneath; antorbital process small or lacking, with postorbital process not touching the skull* (fig. 82); skull 53–56.6 mm. basilar length; interparietal bone fused with surrounding bones (not with well-defined sutures as in fig. 51). Thickets of firs and riparian growths in the fir, lodgepole pine, spruce, and hemlock forests; chiefly in the Transition and Canadian life zones in northeastern California and over most of Oregon and Washington. P. 145, fig. 95, Map 34.

95–122 mm. (notch)

gray

white

dusky

WHITE-TAILED HARE

white in winter,
grayish brown in summer

dark-tipped

densely haired

54–64 mm.
(notch)

pure white to
roots of hairs

88–100 mm.

NUTTALL COTTONTAIL

dark-tipped

short, sparse hairs

65–80 mm.
notch)

brown and black

60–100 mm.

variously colored

92–112 mm.

DOMESTIC RABBIT

pure white to roots of hairs

75–100 mm.

AUDUBON COTTONTAIL

White-tailed hare (*Lepus townsendii*). Length 565–650 mm., average about 24 inches; tail 66–112 mm.; hind foot 145–80 mm.; *ear from notch 95–122 mm.*; grayish brown in summer, frequently white in winter (at least two annual molts in northern parts of range); tail always white but sometimes with a dull dorsal stripe *not reaching* the rump; outer edge of supraorbital process usually curves outward, heavy, with many crenulations and points; *width of the postorbital process at least half its length* (fig. 82); skull, basilar length, 67–75 mm.; interparietal bone fused with surrounding bones (not with distinct sutures as in fig. 51). Sagebrush areas and open spaces in higher communities in the Upper Sonoran and Transition life zones of northeastern California and eastern two-thirds of Oregon and Washington. P. 144, figs. 93, 94, Map 34.

Nuttall cottontail (*Sylvilagus nuttallii*). Length 350–90 mm., average about 14 inches; tail 44–50 mm.; hind foot 88–100 mm.; *ear from notch 54–64 mm. and densely haired on inner surface*; grayish brown dorsally and white ventrally; *tail hairs pure white to the roots; vibrissae black with some entirely white hairs*; feet densely covered with long hairs; supraorbital process strongly bowed inward, *antorbital process has a single point* and is less than half the length of the postorbital process, which is generally free from the cranium at least near its base (fig. 82); skull 46–51.7 mm. basilar length; interparietal bone with distinct sutures (fig. 51). Northern Juniper Woodland and Pinyon-Juniper Woodland and in sagebrush areas in the Upper Sonoran and Transition life zones in the eastern parts of all three states. P. 148, fig. 90, Map 35.

Audubon cottontail (*Sylvilagus audubonii*). Length 340–434 mm., average about 15 inches; tail 45–75 mm.; hind foot 75–100 mm.; *ear from notch 65–80 mm. and sparsely covered with short hairs all over*; mixed brown and blackish hairs dorsally and whitish beneath; *tail hairs white to roots; vibrissae always black but sometimes white-tipped*; edge of supraorbital process strongly curved upward, antorbital process less than half the length of the postorbital process, *antorbital process blunt or has many points*, entire supraorbital process sometimes closely fused to the cranium (fig. 82); skull 49.4–55.7 mm. basilar length; interparietal bone with distinct sutures (fig. 51). Thickets in the Valley Grassland, Foothill Woodland, Southern Oak Woodland, up canyon bottoms, and to the Transition Life Zone and other communities in the southern two-thirds of California. Lower and Upper Sonoran life zones. P. 149, fig. 87, Map 35.

Domestic rabbit (*Oryctolagus cuniculus.*) Length 450–600 mm., average about 22 inches; tail 66–88 mm.; hind foot 92–112 mm.; ear (notch) 60–100 mm.; mostly rusty brownish to grayish dorsally but may be many other colors, even spotted. Introduced on some of the San Juan Islands, Washington, possibly when the Hudson's Bay Company controlled them, and on the Farallon Islands, California, well over 100 years ago. (No range map or photograph.)

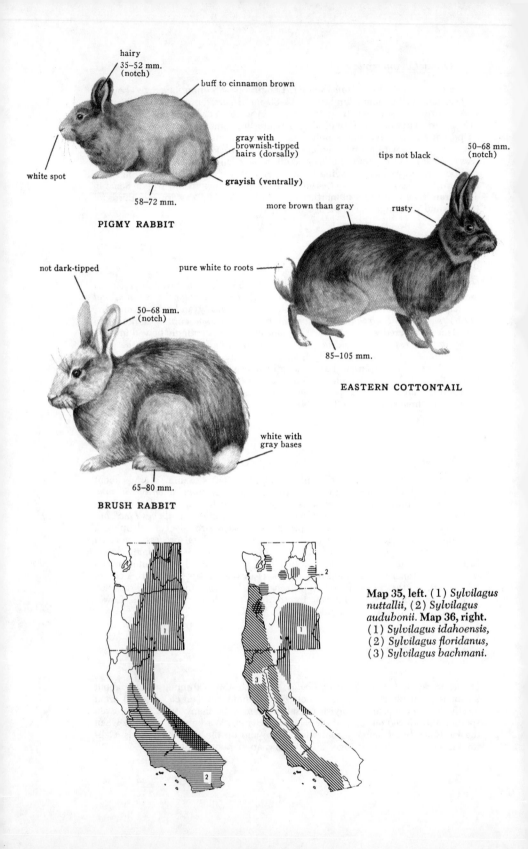

PIGMY RABBIT

hairy
35–52 mm.
(notch)

buff to cinnamon brown

gray with
brownish-tipped
hairs (dorsally)

grayish (ventrally)

white spot

58–72 mm.

EASTERN COTTONTAIL

tips not black

50–68 mm.
(notch)

rusty

more brown than gray

pure white to roots

85–105 mm.

BRUSH RABBIT

not dark-tipped

50–68 mm.
(notch)

white with
gray bases

65–80 mm.

Map 35, left. (1) *Sylvilagus nuttallii*, (2) *Sylvilagus audubonii*. **Map 36, right.** (1) *Sylvilagus idahoensis*, (2) *Sylvilagus floridanus*, (3) *Sylvilagus bachmani*.

Pigmy rabbit (*Sylvilagus idahoensis*). Length 235–95 mm., average about 11 inches; tail 15–30 mm.; hind foot 58–72 mm.; ear from notch 35–52 mm., covered inside and out with fine silky hairs; fulvous across the chest and legs; "peppery," or gray mixed with black fur, dorsally; tail gray with brownish-tipped hairs dorsally, gray below; vibrissae black and white with a white spot on either side of the nostril; antorbital process nearly, or quite, as long as the postorbital process (fig. 82) and both free from the cranium; skull 37–41 mm. basilar length; interparietal bone with distinct sutures (fig. 51). Dense rabbit brush and sagebrush of the Sagebrush Scrub Community; Upper Sonoran Zone. (Some zoologists include this species in the genus *Brachylagus*.) P. 151, fig. 91, Map 36.

Eastern cottontail (*Sylvilagus floridanus*). Length 375–465 mm.; tail 40–65 mm.; hind foot 85–105 mm.; ear (notch) 50–68 mm.; skull about 75 mm. long; brownish dorsally with a tan or brownish rump; ears not black-tipped, back of ears may be darker than back, nape dusky; underparts white; posterior extension of the supraorbital process usually notched and fused to the skull but not extending to the parietal bones (fig. 82). Introduced into Whitman, Clark, Cowlitz, King, and Skogit counties and Whidby Island, Washington, from which it has spread widely. It is common in Kittitas County and Tacoma, Washington, and in Oregon it has been successfully introduced into Benton and Linn counties (Graf, 1955). P. 147, fig. 89, Map 36.

Brush rabbit (*Sylvilagus bachmani*). Length 300–375 mm., average about 13 inches; tail 20–40 mm.; hind foot 65–80 mm.; ear from notch 50–68 mm., sparsely haired all over *without black tips; white hairs of the tail and belly have gray bases; vibrissae all black*; supraorbital process bow-shaped, antorbital process often with blunt tips, basal part of postorbital process usually free from cranium (fig. 82); *skull 47–53.7 mm.* basilar length; interparietal bone with distinct sutures (fig. 51). Chaparral, chiefly Upper Sonoran Life Zone west of the Sierra Nevada and Cascade crests in all three states. P. 149, fig. 88, Map 36.

Fig. 84. Young black-tailed hare (*Lepus californicus*).

Family **Ochotonidae** (Pikas)

Dental Formula 2-0-3-2/1-0-2-3 or 2-0-2-3/1-0-2-3

Pikas (*Ochotona princeps*) are the size of guinea pigs, with nearly round ears and no visible external tail (fig. 85). They live mostly in the taluses below cliffs in the mountains, as well as on lava flows where the rocks are sufficiently broken up to provide protection from enemies and near herbaceous plants and grasses. A pika is not likely to be confused with any other native mammal, since it is the only lagomorph in the region that uses its voice, which is a nasal *eenk*, when alarmed. The call is also a warning to other pikas against invasion of its territory. The pika collects plants and dries them in a "haystack" before storing them deep in the loose rocks for food during the long cold winters (fig. 86). It has been observed to store the dried fecal droppings of marmots in the haystack and later to eat them (Broadbooks, 1963).

The gestation period is about a month. A litter consists of from one to five young, born in May or June. The naked young are altricial and are born with their eyes closed. Martens, weasels, and hawks are probably their worst enemies.

Family **Leporidae** (Hares and Rabbits)

Dental Formula 2-0-3-3/1-0-2-3

All these animals have ears at least twice as long as they are wide and short fluffy tails.

The white-tailed hare (*Lepus townsendii*) is sometimes called the "snowshoe rabbit." It differs from the snowshoe hare in being much larger, in having ears longer than its head, and in having a white instead of a brown undertail (fig. 93). Like the snowshoe hare, however, it has at least two annual molts (fig. 94). Individuals in the colder part of its range become white in winter. These large hares are close relatives of the still larger

Fig. 85. Pika (*Ochotona princeps*). Photograph by Arvil Parker.

Arctic hares (*Lepus arcticus*) of the far north. Where the range of the white-tailed hare overlaps that of the black-tailed hare, the two may be easily distinguished by the color of the undertail. The underside of the white-tailed hare is white; that of the black-tailed hare is brownish. The white-tailed hare tends to live on hills and in mountains, the black-tailed hare in valleys. White-tailed hares feed on creambush, sagebrush, and grasses. They may damage young orchards and timber stands by eating the bark off young trees. The young are precocial; as many as eight are known to occur in a litter, with probably one litter a year. Coyotes, foxes, bobcats, owls, and eagles doubtless are their worst enemies.

The snowshoe hare (*Lepus americanus*) is not likely to be mistaken for any other lagomorph that shares its range (fig. 95). Its ears are scarcely longer than its head, as compared with the ears of the other two native

Fig. 86. Haystack of a pika.

Fig. 87. Audubon cottontail (*Sylvilagus audubonii*).

Fig. 88. Brush rabbit (*Sylvilagus bachmani*).

Fig. 89. Eastern cottontail (*Sylvilagus floridanus*).

Fig. 90. Nuttall cottontail (*Sylvilagus nuttallii*).

hares. Its large hind feet are much longer than those of the cottontails, and the underside of its tail is brown, not white as in the cottontails.

The snowshoe hare has at least two annual molts. In winter most individuals become white, which probably aids escape from enemies. Its food consists of bark and twigs of aspen, willow, alder, and probably coniferous trees. In summer it doubtless feeds on grasses and forbs. Like all true hares, the young of the snowshoe hare are fully furred, with eyes open at birth. The gestation period is 36 to 40 days. Coyotes, foxes, bobcats, Canadian lynx, and horned owls are doubtless this hare's chief enemies. Snowshoe hares are of little economic importance other than as food for valuable fur bearers.

The black-tailed hare (*Lepus californicus*) is likely to be confused only with the white-tailed hare (figs. 92–94). The black-tailed hare ranges from sea level to an altitude of well over 12,000 feet. It is very adaptable and has little difficulty living in the outskirts of large cities, even to the extent of becoming a hazard for planes at airports. Formerly rabbit drives were conducted, when thousands of these animals were killed in an effort to control the population. Its tracks, like those of other hares and rabbits, always show the hind feet ahead of the forefeet in running (fig. 83).

Black-tailed hares eat a great variety of herbs and shrubs, including many cultivated plants. Curiously, this species is *coprophagous,* like European lagomorphs and certain other mammals. Two kinds of pellets are formed in the digestive tract: the hard, normal waste products of digestion are formed in the intestine; the soft pellets are formed in the caecum and are taken directly from the anus and eaten again during the daytime while the animal is resting. The significance of this *refection* or *reingestion* is supposed to be associated with vitamin nutrition.

Breeding of the black-tailed hares may continue the year round, with as many as seven precocial young in a litter. The year-old female produces 14 or more young each year. Besides man with his guns and dogs, these hares have many enemies: eagles, marsh hawks, barn owls, red-tailed hawks, gopher snakes, and rattlesnakes. Dogs may get tapeworm by eating them, and man may get tularemia and plague while handling or skinning diseased individuals. Black-tailed hares may become serious pests in vineyards and on truck farms.

The eastern cottontail (*Sylvilagus floridanus*) (fig. 89) has been introduced at various places in Washington and Oregon (Graf, 1955). It is easily confused with the native cottontails. The eastern species has fur on its rump that is more brown than gray, whereas the native species have dominantly gray rumps. The shape of the posterior part of the supraorbital process is also useful in differentiating the various species (fig. 82). The eastern cottontail lives along fence rows, in fields, and even in the woods at lower elevations. It feeds on grasses, clover, alfalfa, plantain, and many other forbs. It may eat the bark of young dogwood, rose, or apple trees, and become a serious pest to the orchardist. Three litters of five or six naked young are produced each year. Like the native cottontails, the eastern cot-

Fig. 91. Pigmy rabbit (*Sylvilagus idahoensis*).

tontail makes its nest, which is fur-lined, in a depression in the ground. About a week after birth the eyes of the young open and soon they begin to nibble on grasses. Enemies include coyotes, foxes, bobcats, large owls, hawks, and eagles. Escape is by running and "freezing."

The Nuttall cottontail (*Sylvilagus nuttallii*) is mostly an animal of brushy, rocky places in the sagebrush area of the Pacific States (fig. 90). Its white tail and small feet readily distinguish it from the similar-sized snowshoe hare, and the relatively long hairs (5 mm. or more) inside the ears distinguish it from the sparsely-haired ears of the Audubon cottontail

Fig. 92. Black-tailed hare (*Lepus californicus*).

Fig. 93. White-tailed hare (*Lepus townsendii*) in summer pelage. Photograph courtesy of the National Park Service, Yellowstone National Park.

(fig. 87). The latter species usually occupies the plains and lowlands, whereas the Nuttall cottontail lives in thicker cover along streams and on hills. It feeds on sagebrush, junipers, and grasses. The litter consists of as many as eight, born in a furlike nest in early summer. Coyotes, bobcats, horned owls, and large hawks are known to prey on these cottontails. Except that they carry tularemia, they are of little economic importance to man.

The Audubon cottontail (*Sylvilagus audubonii*) is the common rabbit of the lowlands of California and southern Oregon, although locally it may range up into the Transition Life Zone (fig. 87). It might be mistaken for a brush rabbit, except that it is larger, has the hairs on the under parts tipped with white, and the ears tipped with darker fur, whereas the ears of the brush rabbit are uniformly colored. The Audubon cottontail hides in thick brush or under man-made structures, and sometimes in cultivated fields if there is sufficient cover. It is known to eat grass, leaves of various plants, and fallen fruit such as peaches, apples, and acorns. It rarely eats tree bark. The fur-lined nest is made on the ground, usually in the open. The litter may have from one to five young. Like all true rabbits, cottontails are born naked and with eyes closed. The gestation period is 26 to 30 days. The young may be nursed only once in 31 hours (Ingles, 1941). Coyotes, foxes, bobcats, dogs, and large owls are known enemies. Audubon cottontails are of little economic importance, except that they damage gardens and carry tularemia and relapsing fever.

The brush rabbit (*Sylvilagus bachmani*) has unicolored ears and a very small white tail (fig. 88). It seldom feeds more than a few feet from its hiding place in a dense thicket. Its food includes forbs and grasses. The young have very short, fine fur when born, and their eyes are closed, as in the cottontails. Breeding is limited to the first six months of the year. The

Fig. 94. White-tailed hare (*Lepus townsendii*) in winter pelage. Photograph courtesy of the National Park Service, Yellowstone National Park.

Fig. 95. Snowshoe hare (*Lepus americanus*).

gestation period is about 27 days (Mossman, 1955). There are from three to six in a litter, and three or four litters a season.

The pigmy rabbit (*Sylvilagus idahoensis*) has short hind legs (fig. 91). Work (Johnson, 1963) on serum proteins and hemoglobins indicates that it should be separated from the cottontails and is placed by some zoologists in the genus *Brachylagus*. Its short tail is dusky on the upper side and gray on the lower side. It is smaller than other lagomorphs in the Pacific States. It is often erroneously called a "brush rabbit" by local inhabitants. Brush rabbits, however, are found only on the west side of the Sierra Nevada and Cascades. The pigmy rabbit is an inhabitant of the great sagebrush areas that lie east of the Cascades and the Sierra Nevada. It is distributed within its range, however, only where clumps of sagebrush (*Artemisia*) or rabbit brush (*Chrysothamnus*) are dense enough to afford the necessary cover. Tall sagebrush, contrary to previous reports, is not a requirement. Another necessity appears to be soft earth for digging burrows. These are about three inches in diameter, with three or more entrances. Frequently a trough is dug in front of the entrance, where the animal rests. Many tiny fresh fecal pellets, scarcely over 3 mm. in diameter, are a sure sign of the presence of the pigmy rabbit. These lagomorphs range up to 8,500 feet in the vicinity of Bodie State Park, California (Severaid, 1950). They appear to feed largely on sagebrush at night and during the early evening hours. They are rarely seen more than a few feet from their burrows or dense cover. The coyote and long-eared owl are the chief enemies. The pigmy rabbit is of little or no economic importance and occurs in the sagebrush region of all three states. The breeding period is in spring and early summer. Six young have been known to occur in one litter.

9. Order Rodentia

The order Rodentia comprises almost half of all the mammalian species found in the Pacific States. There are probably more individual animals belonging to this order in this area than belong to all the other orders combined. Represented are the familiar gnawing types: mountain beavers, tree squirrels, marmots, ground squirrels, chipmunks, pocket gophers, pocket mice, kangaroo rats, kangaroo mice, beavers, cricetine and microtine mice and rats, and porcupines.

Many species have striking anatomical, physiological, or behavioral adaptations, which enable them to live in just about any terrestrial environment found in the area.

Some rodents meet the vicissitudes of their environment by having periods of *torpor* or *dormancy* when food is in short supply. These dormant periods may be during winter (hibernation) or summer and fall (estivation), or they may occur irregularly during inclement weather. Some species are dormant for periods in both winter and summer, and there seems to be little if any difference in their physiology during these periods of torpor, except that body temperature may be lower in winter.

Warm-blooded animals during dormancy have the body temperature reduced to within a degree or two of the *ambient* temperature of their burrow or den. Their metabolism is greatly reduced and the oxygen consumption may drop to one-thirtieth to one-hundredth of what it was in the active animal. The heartbeat and breathing are slowed down far below that of active life. Small active mammals have a higher metabolic rate but they also lose heat more rapidly than larger mammals. When food is scarce, small species can manage over long periods by becoming dormant. During this state the rodent may rouse long enough to eat food stored in caches in its burrow (chipmunks), or it may simply utilize the energy stored in its body in the form of fat (marmots). A mammal in hibernation or estivation utilizes only a fraction of the energy needed to keep going in an active state. Hence small mammals are thus adapted to live in environments where otherwise they could not exist. A bear, or other large mammal, may live in the same environment and merely become inactive, but not torpid. Its slower metabolic rate and larger size (with less rapid loss of heat) allow it to pass long periods by merely sleeping over them. Animals undergoing such a *winter sleep* are easily aroused to activity, whereas a true hibernator may take many minutes or even hours to warm up enough to become active.

Rodents are of great importance to man because of their numbers. They comprise the basic food species of many predaceous mammals and birds. They may thus act as buffer species. When rodent numbers are reduced greatly, these predators may turn their attention to domestic mammals and birds. Another way in which rodents benefit man's interests is by their continuous burrowing activities. In this way they effect the "plowing" of uncultivated land and the sinking of surface water, especially in the mountains.

Many rodents are destroyers of noxious weeds and other detrimental plants. Chipmunks (*Eutamias*) feed widely on the fruits of the wild gooseberries in the Sierra Nevada of California, for instance, and thus may tend to prevent wider distribution of this detrimental rust-bearing plant that causes so much damage to certain valuable coniferous trees. Some rodents may become carriers of certain diseases that affect man. Sylvatic plague, tularemia, relapsing fever, and Rocky Mountain fever are examples.

Some of the most destructive pests, the vectors of certain diseases, the most important fur bearers, and some of the most interesting of all mammals belong to the order Rodentia.

KEY TO THE RODENTS (Rodentia)

Animals with two upper and two lower incisors and no canines
belong to this order (fig. 12)

1A. Without spines on the back and tail; infraorbital openings smaller than the foramen magnum 2
1B. With heavy sharp spines on the back and tail; infraorbital opening larger than foramen magnum (fig. 31). Usually wherever pines, firs, or junipers are found in all three states. Erethizontidae.
> *Erethizon dorsatum*, porcupine, p. 305, fig. 199.
2A. Like rat or mouse, without external cheek pouches; with three upper cheek teeth on each side (four upper cheek teeth *only* if infraorbital opening is oval-shaped and occupies most of the zygomatic plate); infraorbital opening extending into the dorsal half of the rostrum 8
2B. Like squirrel or beaver, or rat or mouse with external cheek pouches (fig. 129); infraorbital opening limited to the ventral half of the rostrum . 3
3A. Like squirrel or beaver; infraorbital openings slit-shaped or oval (fig. 12) 4
3B. Like pocket gopher, rat, or mouse, with fur-lined cheek pouches; infraorbital openings oval (fig. 136) 6
4A. Like beaver (living near water); apparently tail-less or with round or dorsoventrally flattened tail 5
4B. Like squirrel, marmot, or chipmunk; tail long and hairy; prominent supraorbital processes present (fig. 33). Sciuridae. See key, p. 157.
5A. With a dorso-ventrally flattened or round scaly tail; webbed hind feet. Along lowland streams and lakes in all three states. Castoridae and Capromyidae.
> *Castor canadensis*, beaver, pp. 241, 242, fig. 156.
> *Myocastor coypu*, nutria, p. 308.

5B. With a short tail (apparently tail-less); hind feet not webbed. Streams and seepages in the Transition and Canadian zones of all three states. Aplodontiidae.

> *Aplodontia rufa*, mountain beaver, p. 155, fig. 96.

6A. Tail less than half as long as the head and body length; fossorial. Geomyidae. See key, p. 201.

6B. Tail more than half as long as the head and body length. Heteromyidae
. . . . 7

7A. Soles of hind feet hairy; tail frequently with white lateral stripes with darker ventral and dorsal stripes. *Dipodomys* and *Microdipodops*. See key, p. 224.

7B. Soles of hind feet partly naked; tail without white lateral stripes. *Perognathus*. See key, p. 215.

8A. Tail usually less than one and a half times head and body length; with three cheek teeth; infraorbital opening much wider at the top than at the bottom (fig. 32) 9

8B. Tail about one and a half times longer than the head and body; with four upper cheek teeth; infraorbital opening oval. Zapodidae. See key, p. 301, and figs. 197, 198.

9A. Molars with two rows of cusps (fig. 35), or with prismatic or triangular patterns of dentine bordered by enamel (figs. 42–47, 50). Cricetidae 10

9B. Molars with three rows of cusps (figs. 36, 37). Muridae. See key, p. 295.

10A. Ears large and frequently nearly naked; tail usually more than 80 per cent head and body length; molar teeth with cusps (fig. 35), or with S-shaped figures or with irregular areas of dentine surrounded by enamel (figs. 41–50). Cricetinae. See key, p. 245.

10B. Ears not naked, frequently nearly obscured by the hairs originating in front of them; molar teeth prismatic or with triangular patterns (figs. 42–47); tail usually less than 80 per cent head and body length, but may be equal to or longer than head and body length if animal has a hind foot greater than 50 mm. long. Microtinae. See key, p. 271.

Suborder SCIUROMORPHA

Family **Aplodontiidae** (Mountain Beavers)

Dental Formula 1-0-2-3/1-0-1-3

This primitive family is found only on the Pacific Coast and contains but one species, the lineage of which extends back to Upper Eocene time. Its primitiveness is indicated by the separation of the tibia and fibula and by the development and attachments of the masseter muscles, which originate *entirely* from the lower edge of the zygomatic arch beneath the infraorbital foramen, as distinct from other rodents. The first upper premolar is very small and is nearly cylindrical. The other grinding teeth do not have roots. Their surfaces are peculiar in that they form little cups. The skull is triangular in shape.

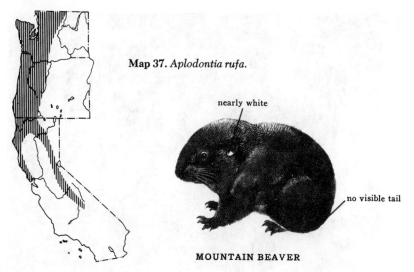

Map 37. *Aplodontia rufa.*

nearly white

no visible tail

MOUNTAIN BEAVER

Mountain beaver (*Aplodontia rufa*). Length 300–470 mm., about 14 inches; *tail 20–40 mm.*; hind foot 55–63 mm.; ear (crown) 13–21 mm.; skull 56–62.3 mm. basilar length, no postorbital process; *blackish-brown* all over, *except for a whitish spot below the ear.* North from Marin and Tulare counties in the Coast Ranges and the Sierra Nevada of California through the western half of Oregon and Washington; seepage slopes and streamside thickets of willow, alder, and creek dogwood, in the Redwood, Yellow Pine, Red Fir, spruce, hemlock, and Lodgepole forests; Transition into Hudsonian life zones. Fig. 96, Map 37.

Mountain Beaver (*Aplodontia rufa*), fig. 96

The open spaces in the forests of western Washington, Oregon, and northwestern California are covered with thimbleberries, salmonberries, and wild blackberries. Where these plants form an almost impenetrable barrier over the fallen logs and rocks, there are almost certain to be burrows of the *Aplodontia,* or mountain beaver. These burrows are about six inches in diameter and frequently are dug so that they run parallel with the surface of the ground for many feet, occasionally opening to the surface through elliptical holes under dense ferns or other thick cover. Sometimes the animal will dig its den where water trickles down through its intricate system of tunnels. More often, however, the burrows are dug in relatively dry ground where logs or roots give adequate protection. The entrances to the subterranean passages are nearly always obscured with thimbleberries, blackberries, and brackens. The holes are about all that most people ever see of this interesting nocturnal mammal, found nowhere but on the West Coast.

The mountain beaver—or boomer, as it is called locally—is quite unlike a beaver in both appearance and habits, and there is nothing about the

Fig. 96. Mountain beaver (*Aplodontia rufa*).

whimpering cry of the creature to suggest the name boomer. The animal is about a foot long, with a very short, stubby tail. It resembles a large, overgrown pocket gopher, but it lacks the external cheek pouches and the nearly naked tail. Some of its habits, too, suggest those of a pocket gopher far more than they do the habits of a beaver; however, it must be remembered that the mountain beaver belongs to a family of its own. Its dense fur is dark brown and is protected with shiny guard hairs. At the base of each ear is a conspicuous white spot. The very long vibrissae are doubtless useful to the animal in running through the dark burrows. The small eyes and ears and long, sharp claws also admirably adapt the mountain beaver to its life, which is mostly spent underground.

Living as it often does near the water, the animal is a fine swimmer. It has been mistaken for a muskrat when seen swimming in small pools or mountain streams.

The mountain beaver is a strict vegetarian. In its native haunts it feeds on thimbleberry, salmonberry, blackberry, creek dogwood, fireweed, bracken fern, skunk cabbage, nettle, lupine, salal, and willow. Entire plants are sometimes jerked into an underlying burrow, in the manner suggesting a pocket gopher. It frequently climbs coniferous trees up to 15 feet to trim off bunches of needles (Ingles, 1960b). The mountain beaver is known to reingest the fecal pellets formed in the caecum. The function of its coprophagy is not known (Ingles, 1961b). The animals are active in winter and frequently burrow through the deep snow 50 yards or more from their den to reach the bark of a young white fir, which they strip from top to bottom. Sometimes a "haystack" is found near the entrance of a burrow.

As compared with the pika, however, the "haymaking" is not as thorough or as complete but probably represents some sort of preparation for the period of adverse weather conditions. After a 28–30 day gestation period, a litter of three or four young is produced in March or April. The young are scantily haired, are helpless, and are blind at birth. They grow very slowly and do not mature until the second year.

Since the mountain beaver in California lives in the forest and high mountain meadows, it rarely does harm to man's interests. Farther north in Oregon and Washington, however, it may become a nuisance, since it does considerable damage to flower gardens, vegetable gardens, and berry patches. The fur of the animal has little value and even when fully prime seldom brings more than 20 cents. Indians are said to use the mountain beaver for food; the meat is reported to be tough and dark-colored.

There is but one species of mountain beaver. It lives in the Transition, Canadian, and Hudsonian life zones along the humid coast, and in the Sierra Nevada as far south as Sequoia National Park, in California.

KEY TO THE TREE SQUIRRELS, GROUND SQUIRRELS, CHIPMUNKS, FLYING SQUIRRELS, AND MARMOTS
(Sciuridae)

The tail is always completely haired. The skull has well-developed postorbital processes (figs. 12, 33). The dental formula is 1-0-2-3/1-0-1-3 or 1-0-1-3/1-0-1-3. The bacula of members of the squirrel family are very useful in identification of the various species (fig. 112). Burt (1960) gives illustrations of many squirrel bacula.

1A. Membrane between fore and hind limbs not present; diurnal . . . 2
1B. Membrane between fore and hind limbs present (for gliding); nocturnal. Transition and Canadian life zones in the northern half of California, but including also the San Bernardino Mountains, and most of Washington and Oregon.
   Glaucomys sabrinus, northern flying squirrel, pp. 195, 200, fig. 128.
2A. With dark and light stripes on the side of the head (usually extending from nose to ear); with infraorbital foramen piercing the zygomatic plate of the maxillary bone (chipmunks) 3
2B. Without stripes on the side of the head; infraorbital foramen passing between the zygomatic plate and the rostrum . . . . 13.
3A. Living in or above the Yellow Pine Forest (about 4,500 feet), from the San Bernardino Mountains in southern California north through Oregon and Washington 4
3B. Living in area from sea level up into the lower part of the Yellow Pine Forest (about 4,500 feet), south of the latitude of San Francisco Bay and west of the Sierra Nevada crest; tail usually over 80 per cent of head and body length; stripes lacking sharp contrast; dark head stripes are brownish; postauricular white spot is indistinct or absent and usually less than the area of the ear; baculum shaft about 4.9 mm. in length, distal part slightly compressed.
   Eutamias merriami, Merriam chipmunk, p. 183, fig. 120.
4A. Hind foot normally more than 35 mm.; skull normally more than 37 mm. 5
4B. Hind foot normally less than 35 mm.; skull normally less than 37 mm. 7

5A. Back of ears clearly bicolored black and gray; tips of nasals not separated
   by a median notch 6
5B. Back of ears unicolored or indistinctly bicolored black and brown, yellowish-brown (summer); light stripes yellowish; dorsal parts reddish; tail
   usually more than 80 per cent of head and body length; a median notch
   separating tips of nasals; baculum shaft 3.0–3.3 mm. in length, with ridges
   on either side of the tip strongly developed. Upper Sonoran Life Zone in
   open or brushy areas in the mountains in California north of San Francisco Bay (usually below 4,500 feet elevation).
   Eutamias sonomae, Sonoma chipmunk, p. 181.
6A. Ears (notch) 15–20 mm. in length, back of ears bicolored; dark stripe below ear, brown; inner light stripes dull yellowish or rusty gray; tail hairs
   edged with gray tips; baculum shaft about 2.2 mm. in length; distal fifth
   is slightly compressed laterally. Transition Life Zone to timberline usually,
   in heavy forests in the coastal and mountainous regions of the northern
   half of California and the western halves of Oregon and Washington.
   Eutamias townsendii, Townsend chipmunk, p. 186, fig. 119.
6B. Ears (notch) 18–26 mm. in length; dark stripe below ear becomes black
   posteriorly; large conspicuous white patch behind ear, which is longer than
   depressed ear; tail hairs tipped with gray; baculum shaft 4.3–5.3 mm. in
   length, distal third slightly compressed laterally. Open brushy places in
   Yellow Pine Forest. Transition Life Zone of the northern and central Sierra
   Nevada of California.
   Eutamias quadrimaculatus, long-eared chipmunk, p. 183.
7A. Hind foot usually more than 31 mm.; skull length more than 31.5 mm.
   Normally living in the timbered areas below 9,000 feet 9
7B. Hind foot usually less than 31 mm.; skull length less than 31.5 mm. Living
   in sagebrush regions of eastern California, Oregon, and Washington, or
   above 9,000 feet in the central Sierra Nevada of California . . . 8
8A. Stripes frequently not sharply defined; dark stripes reddish or brownish,
   never blackish; outer light stripes noticeably wider and brighter than the
   inner light stripes; fur silky; tail conspicuously tipped with blackish (20
   mm. or more), under side light orange, about 75 per cent of head and
   body length; baculum shaft about 2.2 mm. in length, distal third slightly
   compressed. Talus slopes and forest floor in Sierra Nevada of California,
   usually above 9,000 feet.
   Eutamias alpinus, alpine chipmunk, p. 181, fig. 118.
8B. Stripes all well defined, the inner ones continuing to the base of the tail;
   tail 80 per cent or more of head and body length; tail hairs edged with
   lemon buffy; under tail grayish yellow to pale orange; front of ear fulvous,
   posterior half gray; baculum shaft 2.4–4.3 mm. in length, distal half
   slightly laterally compressed (fig. 112). In sagebrush areas in central
   Washington, and in eastern and central Oregon and eastern California.
   Eutamias minimus, least chipmunk, p. 181, fig. 117.
9A. Belly not entirely white 10
9B. Belly and chin mostly whitish with five distinct dark stripes; dark stripes
   on the head mostly black; rump brownish; underside of tail reddish; baculum shaft 4.0–4.6 mm. in length, distal two-fifths of shaft slightly compressed (fig. 112). Northeastern Washington in rocky talus slopes and
   deep forests.
   Eutamias ruficaudus, red-tailed chipmunk, p. 183.
10A. East of the crest of the Sierra Nevada and in extreme northern California,
   and over most of Oregon and Washington; outer dark stripes nearly as
   long as the other stripes, not tending to blend with the sides; grayish
   rump 11

10B. South from Lassen County, California, along both sides of the Sierra Nevada to include Mount Pinos, San Jacinto, San Gabriel, and the San Bernardino Mountains; outer dark stripe less than half as long as the others or nearly obsolete, tending to blend with sides; inner light stripe narrower than the outer light stripe; some black in the dark stripe below the eye; crown gray; tail 70–80 per cent of head and body length; baculum shaft 2.1–3.2 mm. in length, distal two-thirds of shaft strongly compressed laterally (fig. 112). Open and brushy places in Red Fir, Lodgepole, and Subalpine forests in the Canadian and Hudsonian life zones.

Eutamias speciosus, lodgepole chipmunk, p. 185, fig. 115.

11A. Lower dark stripe on the head complete from ear to vibrissae . . . 12

11B. Lower dark stripe on the head nearly obsolete; bright reddish color dorsally, with back of head and rump conspicuously grayish; dorsally flattened skull; baculum shaft about 2.2 mm. in length, distal two-thirds of shaft compressed laterally. Pinyon-Juniper Woodland in Upper Sonoran Life Zone in eastern California.

Eutamias panamintinus, Panamint chipmunk, p. 183.

12A. Inner light stripes often broader, and may be more conspicuous than the outer light stripes; outer dark stripes are often black; crown brownish; under tail deep fulvous; tail hairs tipped with yellowish or reddish; tail 73–85 per cent of head and body length; baculum shaft 2.3–2.9 mm. in length, distal fifth of shaft slightly compressed (fig. 112). Forest floor of the Yellow Pine belt chiefly, but also extends up into the Hudsonian Life Zone of Washington, Oregon, and northern California, and south along the eastern side of the Sierra Nevada to Mono County, California.

Eutamias amoenus, yellow pine chipmunk, p. 185, fig. 116.

12B. Inner light stripes usually not broader or more conspicuous than outer light stripes; lateral dark stripes are dark brown; grayish crown; tail 70–80 per cent of head and body length; baculum shaft 2.5–3.0 mm. in length, distal half of shaft strongly compressed laterally, and curved downward to base of tip (fig. 112). Chiefly in the open Subalpine Forest on the east side of the Sierra Nevada and in the White Mountains of Inyo County, California.

Eutamias umbrinus, Uinta chipmunk, p. 185.

13A. Hind foot over 68 mm.; tail less than half of head and body length; postorbital process broad and projecting at nearly right angles to the longitudinal axis of the skull 14

13B. Hind foot is less than 68 mm.; tail may be more or less than half of head and body length; postorbital processes of skull projecting backward and downward 17

14A. Tail mostly reddish, yellowish, or grayish 15

14B. Tail mostly blackish with some gray- or buffy-tipped hairs; upper tooth rows parallel. Extreme northeastern Washington.

Marmota monax, woodchuck, p. 165.

15A. Upper parts brownish, yellowish, drab, buffy, or grizzly 16

15B. Upper parts, especially over the shoulders, conspicuously covered with light gray or white fur; brown- or black-tipped fur on the rump and head (except the gray nose). Central Washington, mostly in the Cascades in the Hudsonian Life Zone.

Marmota caligata, hoary marmot, p. 165, fig. 101.

16A. With a white bar across the nose more or less distinct; under parts reddish yellow; sides of neck with conspicuous buffy patches; upper parts grizzled with white-tipped hairs; not lighter on the shoulders than on the rump. Sierra Nevada of California, eastern Oregon, and Washington, generally in the arid Transition Life Zone.

Marmota flaviventris, yellow-bellied marmot, p. 165, fig. 99.

Fig. 97. Tracks of yellow-bellied marmot, nearly actual size.

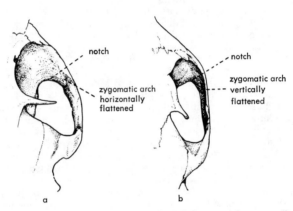

Fig. 98. The zygomatic arch near the notch (a) becomes horizontally flattened in the Beechey ground squirrel, and (b) remains nearly vertically flattened in the western gray squirrel.

16B. With whitish fur around the nose and sometimes with a broad white patch in front of the eyes; upper parts (in adults) usually solid dark brown or yellowish buff or a mixture of both (not grizzled with white-tipped hairs); usually with some black or dark brown on the head and feet; fall molt is usually black on the anterior two-thirds of the body. Hudsonian Life Zone in the Olympic Mountains of Washington.

Marmota olympus, Olympic marmot, p. 165, fig. 100.

17A. Living in trees; tail over half of head and body length, bushy; sides of zygomata flattened from side to side all the way to the notch in the zygomatic plate (fig. 98) (tree squirrels) 18

17B. Living in burrows in the ground; tail length variable; tail hairy or bushy; sides of zygomata flattened from side to side posteriorly but twisted anteriorly until they are flattened from top to bottom before reaching the notch in the zygomatic plate (fig. 98) (ground squirrels) . . . 22

18A. Hind foot over 55 mm.; no black line between the side and the belly; ears not tipped with longer hairs 19
18B. Hind foot less than 55 mm.; summer pelage has a black line separating the sides from the belly; ears tipped with noticeably longer hairs . . 20
19A. Silver gray or rusty gray dorsally; five molariform teeth (rarely four) on each side of the upper jaw 21
19B. Rusty brownish or rarely grayish dorsally; four molariform teeth on each side of upper jaw. Introduced in several cities and campuses from eastern half of the United States.
    Sciurus niger, fox squirrel, p. 193, fig. 124.
20A. Upper parts dark gray or dusky olive; tail hairs tipped with white; under parts yellowish or reddish. Transition into Hudsonian Life Zone in coniferous forests of the northern half of California and the western halves of Oregon and Washington.
    Tamiasciurus douglasii, Douglas squirrel, p. 195, fig. 125.
20B. Upper parts reddish; tail hairs tipped with rusty red; under parts whitish. Coniferous forests in northeastern Oregon and eastern Washington.
    Tamiasciurus hudsonicus, red squirrel, p. 195, fig. 127.
21A. Silver gray dorsally, white ventrally; hind foot usually more than 75 mm. California (Chico) in the Upper Sonoran Life Zone; the humid Transition Life Zone in the Puget Sound area of Washington.
    Sciurus griseus, western gray squirrel, p. 193, fig. 122.
21B. Gray dorsally, often with a wash of rust, especially on the head and tail (sometimes melanistic); hind foot usually less than 75 mm. Introduced into various cities and campuses from the eastern half of the United States.
    Sciurus carolinensis, eastern gray squirrel, p. 193, fig. 123.
22A. Without a light stripe on each side of the body that extends to the hips 26
22B. With a light stripe on each side of the body (sometimes between two black stripes) that extends to the hips 23
23A. Each light stripe not between two black stripes; undertail whitish; crown of skull sloping down to the nuchal line 24
23B. Each light stripe bordered below (outside) by a black stripe; crown of skull sloping up to the nuchal line 25
24A. Upper parts buffy or yellowish; undertail creamy white. Sonoran life zones in western San Joaquin Valley, California, on loam soils.
    Ammospermophilus nelsoni, San Joaquin antelope ground squirrel,
    p. 169, fig. 106.
24B. Upper parts gray; undertail pure white. Dry regions of the Sonoran life zones in southeastern Oregon, and eastern and southeastern California.
    Ammospermophilus leucurus, antelope ground squirrel, p. 169,
    fig. 107.
25A. Light stripe between two long black stripes (fig. 111); head, shoulders, and underparts light yellowish or buffy; hind foot 40–44 mm. Transition into the Hudsonian Life Zone from northeastern Washington south over most of Oregon (except the western foothills of the Cascades and the region west of them), and in the Sierra Nevada and the Salmon, Siskiyou, and San Bernardino mountains of California.
    Callospermophilus lateralis, Sierra Nevada golden-mantled ground
    squirrel, p. 173, fig. 111.
25B. Pale light stripe bordered by two dark stripes, one of which may be indistinct, short, or lacking (fig. 110); head and shoulders and under parts dark tawny; hind foot 43–49 mm. Mostly Canadian and Hudsonian life zones in the Cascade Mountains of Washington.
    Callospermophilus saturatus, Cascades golden-mantled ground
    squirrel, p. 173, fig. 110.

26ᴀ. Plain-colored upper parts, not variegated, mottled, flecked, or spotted   32
26ʙ. Upper parts variegated, mottled, flecked, or spotted   27
27ᴀ. Hind foot usually more than 49 mm.   28
27ʙ. Hind foot usually less than 49 mm.   30
28ᴀ. Tail more than half of head and body length   29
28ʙ. Tail less than half of head and body length; face, thighs, and under parts reddish, or grayish buff; mottled dorsally. Meadows and grasslands in mountains from the Transition Life Zone nearly to timberline in eastern Washington and northeastern Oregon.
   Citellus columbianus, Columbian ground squirrel, p. 171, fig. 104.
29ᴀ. Nape and between the shoulders usually with dark median area; with mostly unflecked lighter fur on the sides of the neck and shoulders but with rump strongly flecked. Central Washington, western Oregon, and most of California except the deserts in all life zones below the Hudsonian.
   Otospermophilus beecheyi, Beechey ground squirrel, p. 173, fig. 105.
29ʙ. Nape and shoulders without dark median area; conspicuously flecked dorsally, even in the light gray area. Pinyon-Juniper belt in the Providence Mountains in southeastern California.
   Otospermophilus variegatus, rock squirrel, p. 173.
30ᴀ. Hind foot usually less than 40 mm.   31
30ʙ. Hind foot usually more than 40 mm.; under parts of tail clay-colored or rusty; dorsally gray dappled with small flecks of cinnamon buff. Transition Life Zone in southeastern Oregon.
   Citellus richardsonii, Richardson ground squirrel, p. 171.
31ᴀ. Upper parts yellowish-gray, lightly flecked with rather tiny indistinct pale dots; upper parts change abruptly to the plain buffy sides and under parts. Transition Life Zone in central Washington, west of the Columbia River, eastern Oregon, and in extreme eastern California.
   Citellus townsendii, Townsend ground squirrel, p. 169, fig. 102.
31ʙ. Upper parts brownish gray marked with distinct lighter spots; under parts buffy; face, thighs, and tail may be dull reddish. North-central Oregon and southeastern Washington east of the Columbia River on sagebrush and grasslands in the Transition Life Zone.
   Citellus washingtoni, Washington ground squirrel, p. 169.
32ᴀ. Hind foot usually less than 39 mm.; dorsal hairs very short, cinnamon, or tipped with white. Deserts of southeastern California   33
32ʙ. Hind foot usually more than 39 mm.; gray sides with a brownish dorsal longitudinal band. Sierra Nevada region of California and eastern Oregon, meadows of the Transition and Canadian life zones.
   Citellus beldingi, Belding ground squirrel, p. 171, fig. 103.
33ᴀ. Undertail buffy, cinnamon, or grayish. Not in the Mojave Desert, California   34
33ʙ. Undertail whitish. Mojave Desert. Dorsally grayish brown with whitish underparts. California in the Lower Sonoran Life Zone.
   Citellus mohavensis, Mohave ground squirrel, p. 171, fig. 108.
34ᴀ. Undertail buffy or cinnamon; dorsally cinnamon; whitish under parts. Colorado Desert of southeastern California in the Lower Sonoran Life Zone.
   Citellus tereticaudus, round-tailed ground squirrel, p. 171, fig. 109.
34ʙ. Undertail grayish; dorsally grayish brown; grayish or buffy under parts. Northeastern California, eastern Oregon, and southeastern Washington in the Upper Sonoran Life Zone.
   Citellus townsendii, Townsend ground squirrel, p. 169, fig. 102.

Family **Sciuridae** (Squirrel Family)

Dental Formula 1-0-2-3/1-0-1-3 or 1-0-1-3/1-0-1-3

This family is composed of two subfamilies: Sciurinae includes marmots (*Marmota*), ground squirrels (*Citellus, Callospermophilus, Otospermophilus,* and *Ammospermophilus*), chipmunks (*Eutamias*), and tree squirrels (*Sciurus* and *Tamiasciurus*); Pteromyinae has one genus, the flying squirrels (*Glaucomys*). The body is variously marked and colored, and the tail is usually more or less bushy. There are four toes on the front feet and five on the hind feet (fig. 97). Internal cheek pouches are present in some of the genera. There is a pointed postorbital process on the frontal bone (figs. 12, 33).

Fig. 99. Yellow-bellied marmot
(*Marmota flaviventris*).

Fig. 100. Olympic marmot
(*Marmota olympus*).

dark bar

grizzled gray or brown
with white-tipped hairs

yellowish

70–90 mm.

YELLOW-BELLIED MARMOT

bar

black

grayish

dark reddish brown

90–115 mm.

HOARY MARMOT

whitish

yellowish or dark brown hairs

68–110 mm.

OLYMPIC MARMOT

no bar

cinnamon brown with
white-tipped hairs

black

68–90 mm.

WOODCHUCK

Marmota Dental Formula 1-0-2-3/1-0-1-3; *summer pelage unless otherwise specified*

Yellow-bellied marmot (*Marmota flaviventris*). Length 500–700 mm.; about 24 inches; tail 130–200 mm.; hind foot 70–90 mm.; ear 15–24 mm.; skull 80–91 mm.; *yellowish grizzly brown with white-tipped hairs, dull yellow below*, with whitish patch in front of eyes behind a *broad dark band*; feet brownish. White Mountains and Sierra Nevada of California across Oregon to Washington. Lives mostly in talus slopes bordering alpine meadows in the Canadian and Hudsonian life zones. P. 167, fig. 99, Map 38.

Hoary marmot (*Marmota caligata*). Length 450–820 mm.; tail 40 to 50 per cent of head and body length, 170–250 mm.; hind foot 90–115 mm.; ear 27 mm.; skull about 88 mm.; *gray and black dorsally*, belly whitish; whitish nose followed by transverse narrow dark band and a large white patch in front of the eye; *tail dark reddish brown*. Sometimes burrow is dug on open slope, but usually it lives in talus slopes near grassy alpine meadows in the Hudsonian Life Zone of the Cascade Mountains of Washington. P. 166, fig. 101, Map 38.

Olympic marmot (*Marmota olympus*). Length 450–785 mm.; tail about 35 to 50 per cent of head and body length, 195–252 mm.; hind foot 68–110 mm; skull about 112 mm.; uniform dark brown, bleaching to yellowish dorsally; whitish nose followed by a transverse narrow dark band and a large white patch in front of the eyes; in the alpine meadows of the Olympic Mountains of Washington; burrows under rocks and on open slopes in the Hudsonian Life Zone. P. 166, fig. 100, Map 38.

Woodchuck (*Marmota monax*). Length 400–660 mm.; tail about 30 to 40 per cent of the head and body length, 100–155 mm.; hind foot 68–90 mm.; skull about 90 mm.; uniformly cinnamon brownish dorsally, crested with white-tipped guard hairs. In the mountains of extreme northeastern Washington (based on a sight record only; it is recorded, however, from nearby British Columbia and Alberta, Canada). P. 167, Map 38.

Marmots (*Marmota*)

There are five species of marmots in North America and all but one are reported from the Pacific States. This one, the Vancouver Island marmot (*Marmota vancouverensis*), lives in the mountains on Vancouver Island only a few miles across the San Juan Strait from Washington. Marmots are the largest members of the squirrel family. They do not possess internal cheek pouches as do the ground squirrels. All of them accumulate layers of fat, almost equal to half the body weight, instead of making food caches before they become dormant for a considerable part of the year. The time spent in dormancy depends on the location and elevation. Some of the yellow-bellied marmots (fig. 99) actually enter estivation late in June. However, others of this species in the Sierra Nevada of California remain active until the first part of October. Dormancy in marmots is apparently similar to that described for certain ground squirrels (see p. 177). The animals may emerge from hibernation the latter part of February in Chelan County, Washington, but not until a month or two later in the high Sierra Nevada, where they live up to 12,000 feet elevation.

The hoary marmot (fig. 101), the Olympic marmot (fig. 100), and the woodchuck frequently dig their dens under single boulders or trees, or even out in the open. Most of the yellow-bellied marmots, however, live in rock slides bordering green meadows, where they are protected from the badgers and wolverines, which might dig them out.

The Olympic marmot undergoes a change of color, from a uniform dark brown in the spring when it emerges from hibernation, to a buffy yellow by late August. Some mammalogists believe that this color change is caused by the bleaching action of the ammonia from the urine excreted in the burrow.

Map 38. (1) *Marmota flaviventris*, (2) *Marmota caligata*, (3) *Marmota olympus*, (4) *Marmota monax*.

Fig. 101. Hoary marmot
(*Marmota caligata*).

Breeding of the yellow-bellied marmot generally occurs in March soon after the animal emerges from hibernation. Half-grown young in June indicate May as the time of birth, since the gestation period is about a month. The single litter per year may have from three to eight young, with four to six being the usual number.

Marmots are generally plant feeders. Their native food is green vegetation and includes tender, nutritious grasses, clovers, vetch, and stonecrops. They may become serious pests when they live near fields of alfalfa or soybeans. Marmots, like ground squirrels and chipmunks, are known to eat animal food. Along the Jordan River in Oregon the skins of 55 large caterpillars of sphinx moths were found in the stomach of a yellow-bellied marmot. The marmots have many enemies besides man and his high-powered rifle with telescopic sights. Along the Columbia River, hunting pressure is becoming so great around towns and cities that the yellow-bellied marmots are becoming partially nocturnal in their activity. Badgers, coyotes, eagles, horned owls, Swainson's hawks, and red-tailed hawks are known to feed on them.

The woodchuck is included with the other marmots of the Pacific States only on the basis of a sight record in northeastern Washington. The other species illustrate *allopatry* in that there is little if any overlap of their geographic ranges.

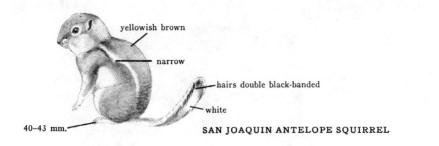

yellowish brown

narrow

hairs double black-banded

white

40–43 mm.

SAN JOAQUIN ANTELOPE SQUIRREL

single black
band on hairs

broad

grayish brown

white

35–40 mm.

ANTELOPE GROUND SQUIRREL

soft, buffy gray

less than 40 mm.

cinnamon, 44–61 mm.

TOWNSEND GROUND SQUIRREL

light spots

reddish

32–65 mm.

WASHINGTON GROUND SQUIRREL

30–38 mm.

Ammospermophilus Dental Formula 1-0-2-3/1-0-1-3

San Joaquin antelope ground squirrel (*Ammospermophilus nelsoni*). Length 218–40 mm., about nine inches; tail 63–79 mm.; *hind foot 40–43 mm.*; ear (notch) 8–9 mm.; skull 39–41.6 mm.; *yellowish brown with one white stripe on each side*; undertail white; tail usually held up over back. Lower Sonoran Life Zone on the western side of the San Joaquin Valley in California on loam soils. P. 176, fig. 106, Map 39.

Antelope ground squirrel (*Ammospermophilus leucurus*). Length 211–33 mm., about nine inches; tail 63–71 mm.; *hind foot 35–40 mm.*; ear (notch) 8–10 mm.; skull 37–41.8 mm.; *grayish brown with one white stripe on each side and no dark stripes*; undertail white; tail usually held closely over the back while running, exposing white under side. Alkali Sink and Creosote Bush Scrub, mostly on rocky or gravelly soil in the Sonoran life zones of California deserts, east of the Sierra Nevada and south of the Tehachapi range, and in southeastern Oregon. P. 176, fig. 107, Map 39.

Citellus Dental Formula 1-0-2-3/1-0-1-3; *summer pelage unless otherwise specified*

Townsend ground squirrel (*Citellus townsendii*). Length 201–33 mm., about nine inches; tail 44–61 mm.; hind foot 29–38 mm.; skull 36–39.3 mm.; *buffy gray with pale dots*; face and hind legs reddish buff; under parts buffy; under surface of slightly flattened tail is cinnamon-colored with white edge. Emerges from dormancy early in the spring and enters dormancy again about July. Upper Sonoran Life Zone in open sagebrush of eastern Oregon and south-central Washington. Fig. 102, Map 39.

Washington ground squirrel (*Citellus washingtoni*). Length 185–245 mm., about nine inches; tail 32–65 mm.; hind foot 30–38 mm.; skull about 39–41 mm.; upper parts brownish gray with distinct large whitish spots 5 mm. or more in diameter; under parts are dark buffy; face, hind legs, and tail are dull reddish. Found on grasslands, low sagebrush, wheat fields, rocky hillsides of southeastern Washington and northern Oregon. Map 39.

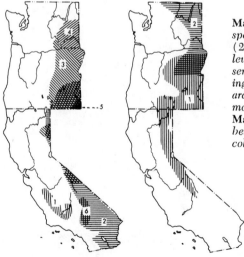

Map 39, left. (1) *Ammospermophilus nelsoni,* (2) *Ammospermophilus leucurus,* (3) *Citellus townsendii,* (4) *Citellus washingtoni,* (5) *Citellus richardsonii,* (6) *Citellus mohavensis.*
Map 40, right. (1) *Citellus beldingi,* (2) *Citellus columbianus*

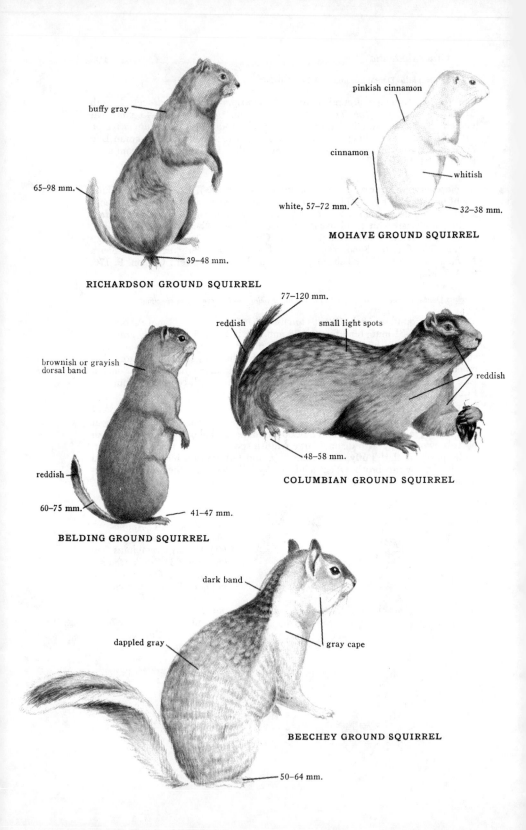

buffy gray

65–98 mm.

39–48 mm.

RICHARDSON GROUND SQUIRREL

pinkish cinnamon

cinnamon

whitish

white, 57–72 mm.

32–38 mm.

MOHAVE GROUND SQUIRREL

brownish or grayish
dorsal band

reddish

77–120 mm.

small light spots

reddish

48–58 mm.

COLUMBIAN GROUND SQUIRREL

reddish

60–75 mm.

41–47 mm.

BELDING GROUND SQUIRREL

dark band

dappled gray

gray cape

BEECHEY GROUND SQUIRREL

50–64 mm.

Richardson ground squirrel (*Citellus richardsonii*). Length 260–340 mm., about 12 inches; tail 65–98 mm.; hind foot 39–48 mm.; ear 13 mm.; skull about 45–48 mm.; *upper parts buffy gray*, shaded with cinnamon buffy and dusky; under parts, sides, and back of ears clear rich buffy (summer) and yellowish (winter); tail hairs tipped with yellowish, under side clay-colored or rusty. Found in grassy places in the Transition Life Zone in southeastern Oregon. Map 39.

Mohave ground squirrel (*Citellus mohavensis*). Length 210–30 mm., about nine inches; *tail 57–72 mm.*; hind foot 32–38 mm.; skull 38–40 mm.; *pinkish cinnamon without stripes or fleckings; under parts white; under surface of tail white;* cheeks brownish. Sandy desert floor in the Alkali Sink and Creosote Bush Scrub of the Lower Sonoran Life Zone in the Mojave Desert, California. P. 176, fig. 108, Map 39.

Belding (or Oregon) ground squirrel (*Citellus beldingi*). Length 254–300 mm., about ten inches; tail 60–75 mm.; hind foot 41–47 mm.; skull 41.3–46.3 mm.; a broad longitudinal band of brownish gray dorsally; buffy or buffy white ventrally and laterally; *no stripes or flecks*; short tail, chestnut below, one and a half times hind foot length; often sits up very straight, hence called "picket pin." Frequently in colonies in meadows in Yellow Pine, Red Fir, Lodgepole, and Northern Juniper Woodland forests in eastern Oregon and northeastern California from the Upper Sonoran Life Zone to the Canadian Life Zone. P. 174, fig. 103, Map 40.

Columbian ground squirrel (*Citellus columbianus*). Length 340–410 mm., about 15 inches; tail 77–120 mm.; hind foot 48–58 mm.; skull 49–57 mm.; upper parts grayish buff mottled with small white dots; back of head and neck are gray; *face, legs, and tail are reddish*; under parts are pale ochraceous or dark fulvous. Grasslands and open timber from the Transition into the Hudsonian Life Zone of eastern Washington and northeastern Oregon. P. 174 and fig. 104, Map 40.

Round-tailed ground squirrel (*Citellus tereticaudus*). Length 232–66 mm., about ten inches; *tail 81–102 mm.*; hind foot 33–40 mm.; skull 35–39.3 mm.; there are two color phases, *plain drab gray or pinkish cinnamon without stripes or fleckings*; under parts whitish; cheeks whitish; *long, nearly unicolored tail, which is round and not bushy*. Wind-blown sand in the Alkali Sink and Creosote Bush Scrub in the lowest, hottest, and driest parts of the Colorado and Mojave deserts of California in the Lower Sonoran Life Zone. Fig. 109, Map 41.

round,
81–102 mm.

grayish cinnamon

33–40 mm.

whitish

ROUND-TAILED GROUND SQUIRREL

no dark band

dappled gray

no higher cape

ROCK SQUIRREL

53–65 mm.

black and white
stripes, long

golden yellow

37–44 mm.

**SIERRA NEVADA GOLDEN-MANTLED
GROUND SQUIRREL**

tawny

variable length

43–49 mm.

**CASCADES GOLDEN-MANTLED
GROUND SQUIRREL**

Otospermophilus Dental Formula 1-0-2-3/1-0-1-3

Beechey (or California) ground squirrel (*Otospermophilus beecheyi*). Length 383–500 mm., about 18 inches; tail longer than half the head and body length, 137–98 mm.; hind foot 50–64 mm.; ear 17–26 mm.; skull 51–62.5 mm.; gray with lighter flecks posteriorly, *a darker band of fur extending from the head down, to spread over the middle of the back; shoulders and sides of head light gray*; under parts light buff. Many plant communities and in all the life zones up to the Hudsonian, from southern California to central Washington. P. 174, fig. 105, Map 41.

Rock squirrel (*Otospermophilus variegatus*). Length 434–510 mm., about 18 inches; tail 198–235 mm.; hind foot 53–65 mm.; skull 58–63.5 mm.; grayish buffy shaded with blackish; mottled, without darker dorsal area, but sometimes with darker head or all completely black. Only in the Providence Mountains in the Mojave Desert, California, in the Pinyon Juniper belt among large rocks. Map 41.

Callospermophilus Dental Formula 1-0-2-3/1-0-1-3

Sierra Nevada golden-mantled ground squirrel (*Callospermophilus lateralis*). Length 235–95 mm., about 11 inches; tail 83–102 mm.; hind foot 37–44 mm.; skull 41–44 mm.; *head and shoulders golden yellow; one white stripe bordered by two long black stripes on each side of the back.* Pine and fir forests of the Transition and Canadian life zones in California, Oregon, and eastern Washington. Fig. 111, Map 42.

Cascades golden-mantled ground squirrel (*Callospermophilus saturatus*). Length 285–315 mm., about a foot long; tail 95–118 mm.; hind foot 43–49 mm.; ear 17 mm.; skull about 44–48 mm.; *one white stripe on each side of the back, bordered by two black stripes, one of which is usually much shorter than the white stripe, or it may be obsolete; head and shoulders tawny.* This species is considered by some zoologists as a subspecies of *Callospermophilus lateralis*. In the higher and eastern Cascade Mountains of Washington in pine, fir, and spruce forests, mostly in the Transition Life Zone. P. 179, fig. 110, Map 42.

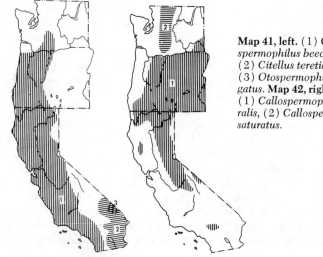

Map 41, left. (1) *Otospermophilus beecheyi,* (2) *Citellus tereticaudus,* (3) *Otospermophilus variegatus.* **Map 42, right.** (1) *Callospermophilus lateralis,* (2) *Callospermophilus saturatus.*

Ground Squirrels (*Citellus, Otospermophilus, Callospermophilus,* and *Ammospermophilus*)

There are 13 species of ground squirrels native to the Pacific States. Some authorities use *Spermophilus* as a generic name for this group (Hall and Kelson, 1959), others simply use *Citellus*. Ground squirrels range in size from the chipmunk (*Eutamias*) to the tree squirrel (*Sciurus*). All of them make their nests in the ground. All have inside cheek pouches which are used to transport seeds and fruits to their burrows. Some become torpid when food is scarce. Most use stored fat to produce energy during estivation and hibernation. Unlike the marmots (*Marmota*), which feed chiefly on leaves and stems of plants, the ground squirrels' diet consists largely of seeds, nuts, and fruits, which some species store in surface caches for use when food is hard to obtain.

Most of the species have skulls that can be distinguished from those of chipmunks by having the infraorbital canal passing *between* the zygomatic plate and the rostrum instead of piercing the zygomatic plate. In ground squirrel skulls the zygomata converge anteriorly and their anterior portions are twisted toward a horizontal plane (whereas in tree squirrels the zygomata are nearly parallel and not twisted) (fig. 98).

The work of Sutton (1962) shows a different number of chromosomes for certain species of ground squirrels. The Belding ground squirrel has 30 chromosomes, the antelope squirrel 32, the Richardson squirrel 34, the round-tailed squirrel 36, the Beechey squirrel 38, and the Sierra golden-mantled squirrel 42. Further work on the groups of chromosomes promises to shed much light on the relationship of the various species. Where two or more species are sympatric, their niches and habitats are always sufficiently different to permit joint occupancy with a minimum of competition.

Most ground squirrels in the Pacific States are easily distinguished from each other. Some have stripes on the back, others have flecking or spots, and still others have a solid color. The Beechey ground squirrel may sometimes be confused with the western gray squirrel. However, the Beechey ground squirrel has a gray-flecked back with a lighter mantle over the shoulders.

All species of ground squirrels are diurnal. They frequently are in conflict with man, especially in regions where predators have been reduced. Perhaps the Beechey ground squirrel (fig. 105) does the greatest damage agriculturally of any mammal in the Pacific States in grain fields and among the almond trees of the Sacramento Valley in California, where it harvests the green nuts. It has crossed the Columbia River and has now spread as far north as Naches, Washington (Armstrong, 1962).

The most destructive ground squirrels in Oregon and Washington are the Belding ground squirrel and the Columbian ground squirrel, respectively (figs. 103, 104). These rodents sometimes live in large colonies and do great damage to grain fields and permanent pastures. The Columbian ground squirrels are called "go-downs" in the eastern part of Washington, probably because they retire deep into their dens and become torpid during

Fig. 102. Townsend ground squirrel (*Citellus townsendii*). OPL photograph by Robert H. Wright.

Fig. 103. Belding ground squirrel (*Citellus beldingi*).

Fig. 104. Columbian ground squirrel (*Citellus columbianus*). Photograph by Arvil Parker.

Fig. 105. Beechey ground squirrel (*Otospermophilus beecheyi*).

the fall and winter months. Large hawks, eagles, coyotes, foxes, wildcats, and badgers are natural enemies and greatly reduce the ground squirrel population. Practically all the species carry fleas that may harbor the germs of sylvatic plague, which can be contracted by man.

The ground squirrel usually breeds shortly after emerging from hibernation, or early in the spring in the case of nonhibernators like the antelope ground squirrel or its close relative, the San Joaquin antelope squirrel (fig. 106). Hawbecker (1958) found no evidence of hypothermy in the San Joaquin antelope ground squirrel. It lives as long as six years and its home range is about 11 acres.

The Columbian ground squirrel has a 24-day gestation period and an average litter of five. The Beechey ground squirrel has a gestation period of a month, and in the lowlands there is normally one litter a year, which averages about seven young. The Washington ground squirrel has from five to 11 young, with an average of eight.

One of the most fundamental concepts in modern biology is the principle of *competitive exclusion*—that two noninterbreeding populations cannot be in the same relationship to their environment indefinitely. Darwin's *On the Origin of Species* (1859) suggested that species of the same genus, because they have much the same structure and habits, are more likely to be competitive than species of different genera. Thus it would appear that two species with exactly the same requirements could not indefinitely occupy the same area—that is, they could not be *sympatric*. There must be different modifications in structure and—what is more likely—in physiology and behavior, which are genetically determined if two closely related species are to live together. These differences are well illustrated by some of the ground squirrels of the Pacific States.

The work by Bartholomew and Hudson (1961) on the antelope ground squirrel and the Mohave ground squirrel demonstrates beautifully how two closely related species can be sympatric (figs. 107, 108). Both these little rodents live in the arid, hot Mojave Desert of California, where summer temperatures are regularly over 100° F., with 115° and higher not uncommon. Only in the spring and early summer are there plenty of food plants. The problem of sufficient food, conservation of water, and intense heat and low humidity is handled by each in its own unique manner.

The antelope ground squirrel carries its short tail close to its back so that the white underside reflects light. It is hyperactive in its movements. When the environmental temperature falls too low, a mammal must maintain body temperature by increasing its metabolic heat. When the outside temperature becomes too high, the animal must cool itself by sweating, panting, or other means. In the case of the antelope ground squirrel, the metabolic rate remains nearly constant when outside temperatures are between 90° and 107°. Between these temperatures the ground squirrel's temperature will be slightly above that of the environment, and it shows no discomfort even when its temperature reaches 110°. When it becomes too hot, it cools itself rapidly by going into an underground burrow, which apparently serves the purpose of unloading heat by conduction, convection, and radiation. When the day is very hot, as a last resort it washes its whole head with drool from its mouth, and thus cools by evaporation. This water loss by evaporation is great, but the superb kidneys are so constructed that the antelope ground squirrel can drink the highly mineralized desert waters and lose a minimal amount of water in the urine in eliminating nitrogenous wastes. Thus the antelope ground squirrel solves the high-temperature problem by having its *thermal neutral zone* (90–107°) higher than any other nonsweating mammal. This feature, with its manner of cooling by salivation, adapts the little rodent to live in one of the hottest and driest regions on earth and, unlike the other small mammals that live there, to be active during the daytime.

The Mohave ground squirrel, living within the range of the antelope ground squirrel, solves the problems of aridity and temperature quite differently. Like the antelope ground squirrel, it has a white underside to its tail to reflect the sun. However, it is larger, much less active, and more placid in temperament. Its life history is not as well known, because for seven months, between August and March, it is underground. Laboratory studies show a similar behavior pattern in captivity, with periods of torpor during this time of year which may last for days at a time, even with normal temperatures. Following a period of torpor, the animal may awaken and become active for a few hours or days, but even in the presence of food it will again soon become inactive. It is not known whether the Mohave ground squirrel stores food in its burrow, but it loses weight if food is not available. The long period underground corresponds to both summer and winter dormancy, or estivation and hibernation, but here there is no apparent difference between these processes. As the animal becomes torpid, its temperature drops nearly to that of the environmental temperature, breathing is suspended for long periods, and the heartbeat is greatly reduced. Its stored fat is doubtless the major source of its energy. It may be aroused by a sound, a touch, or no obvious stimulus. Although the Mohave ground squirrel may take as long as six hours to enter torpor, it may revive

Fig. 106. San Joaquin antelope ground squirrel (*Ammospermophilus nelsoni*). Photograph by Albert C. Hawbecker.

Fig. 107. Antelope ground squirrel (*Ammospermophilus leucurus*). Photograph by George Bartholomew, courtesy of *Scientific American*.

Fig. 108. Mohave ground squirrel (*Citellus mohavensis*). Photograph by George Bartholomew, courtesy of *Scientific American*.

Fig. 109. Round-tailed ground squirrel (*Citellus tereticaudus*).

Fig. 110. Cascades golden-mantled ground squirrel (*Callospermophilus saturatus*).

Fig. 111. Sierra Nevada golden-mantled ground squirrel (*Callospermophilus lateralis*).

in about 20 minutes and become active. It has been observed to be active with body temperatures between 88° and 107°, but its thermal neutral zone is not quite so high as that of the antelope ground squirrel. As in the latter, this tolerance for high body temperatures is a major adaptive factor in its environment in June and July in the desert.

It is obvious that the Mohave ground squirrel meets the exigencies of its environment by conserving energy and becoming dormant during periods when food is scarce, that is, when there may be only enough food for the more active antelope ground squirrel, which does not become dormant. Thus the larger, more sluggish Mohave ground squirrel keeps out of the way of the smaller, more active antelope ground squirrel except in the spring and early summer, when there is enough food for both. Here are two species of ground squirrels that live sympatrically because their ecological niches are different. The antelope ground squirrel is adapted to live in the rigorous environment because of its tolerance for high body temperatures and its extraordinarily efficient kidneys. The Mohave ground squirrel is adapted by its different physiology and behavior, which allow it to live underground and avoid the competition during the months when there is little food for energy.

Bartholomew and Hudson (1960) conclude that this single physiological capacity for dormancy, which may occur from near 32° to 86° of body temperature and is not closely dependent on environmental temperature, allows certain species to avoid periods of drought, high or low temperature, and inadequate food supply. It is this capacity that spells success for the ground squirrels within a range of subtropical deserts to the Arctic.

Sometimes species belonging to different genera appear to occupy the same ecological niche. Actually, however, this is not true if an ecological niche is defined as a functional phenomenon concerned in part with energy relations, food sources, and food chains, and not as a place or environmental situation. Gause's law applies this functional concept of a niche to the principle of competitive exclusion and states that no two species with identical niches can occur together indefinitely without one eliminating the other.

The fact that two species in different genera with slightly different niches can live together is well illustrated by the Cascades golden-mantled ground squirrel (fig. 110) and the yellow pine chipmunk of Washington. Both animals are abundant and are closely associated in the litter-strewn open places in the pine and fir forests on the eastern side of the Cascades. Both eat the same kind of food and appear to use the same places for their burrows. There seems to be little competition between them, probably because of the difference in niches.

The Cascades golden-mantled ground squirrel gets nuts and seeds after they fall. The yellow pine chipmunk climbs bushes and high trees for the same food. The ground squirrel puts on thick layers of fat to provide it with energy during hibernation. The chipmunk draws from food stores in its winter burrow during torpid periods. Thus these two species live successfully sympatrically without serious competition.

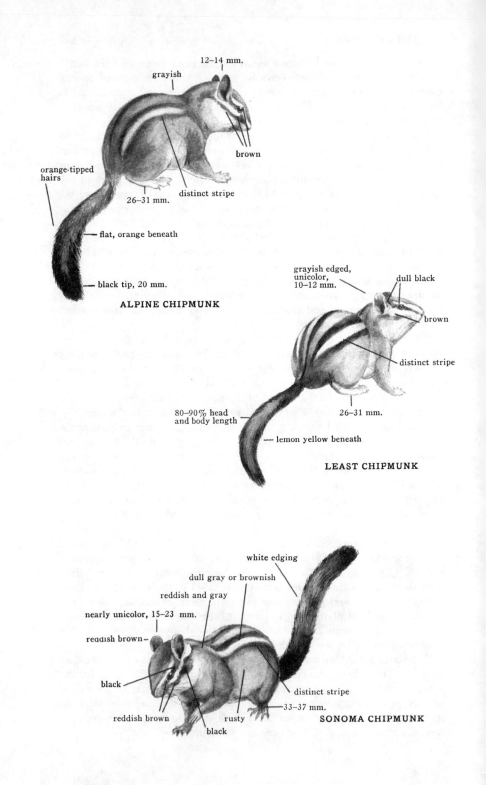

ALPINE CHIPMUNK

12–14 mm.

grayish

brown

orange-tipped hairs

distinct stripe

26–31 mm.

flat, orange beneath

black tip, 20 mm.

LEAST CHIPMUNK

grayish edged, unicolor, 10–12 mm.

dull black

brown

distinct stripe

80–90% head and body length

26–31 mm.

lemon yellow beneath

SONOMA CHIPMUNK

white edging

dull gray or brownish

reddish and gray

nearly unicolor, 15–23 mm.

reddish brown

distinct stripe

33–37 mm.

black

reddish brown

rusty

black

Eutamias Dental Formula 1-0-2-3/1-0-1-3

Alpine chipmunk (*Eutamias alpinus*). Length 166–84 mm.; tail 63–85 mm.; hind foot 26–31 mm.; ear 12–14 mm., skull 29–32 mm.; baculum length about 2.2 mm., distal half slightly compressed laterally; fur long and silky; crown gray with conspicuous postauricular patches; dark lateral stripes are reddish or brownish but never blackish; medium dark stripe may be blackish; dark stripes on head are brown except for dusky spot before and after each eye: outer light stripes noticeably wider and brighter than the inner light stripes; tail is much broader than deep *and is light orange yellow on the under side*; tail tipped with black for about 20 mm. or more. Talus slopes and forest floor in Subalpine Forest and Alpine Fell-fields (generally above 9,000 feet) in the Hudsonian and Alpine-Arctic life zones of the high central Sierra Nevada of California. P. 191, fig. 118, Map 43.

Least chipmunk (*Eutamias minimus*). Length 173–203 mm.; tail 72–88 mm.; hind foot 26–31 mm.; ear 9–12 mm.; skull 29–30.5 mm.; baculum length 2.4–4.3 mm., distal half slightly compressed laterally (fig. 112); short harsh, grayish fur with contrasting stripes; the dorsal stripe is black; the outer light stripe is white; all stripes extend to the base of the tail; *ear nearly unicolored on back side*; tail is long, narrow, round, and is *lemon yellow or grayish yellow on the under side*; dark facial stripes are almost black at their centers. Northern Juniper Woodland and Sagebrush Scrub, mostly in the Upper Sonoran Life Zone but also up to 10,500 feet in the mountains of eastern California, eastern Oregon, and central Washington. P. 191, fig. 117, Map 43.

Sonoma chipmunk (*Eutamias sonomae*). Length 220–77 mm.; tail 93–123 mm.; hind foot 33–37 mm.; ear 15–23 mm.; skull 36.6–39.7 mm.; baculum length about 2.2 mm., distal one-fifth is slightly compressed laterally; *upper incisors strongly incurved, with a notched occlusive surface* (fig. 114); dorsal and lateral coloration *noticeably reddish*; dull yellowish gray or brownish outer light stripes; all dorsal stripes about the same width and *may not be sharply demarcated from one another; back side of ear is unicolored or indistinctly bicolored; lower dark stripes on the head are reddish, with black behind the eyes and below the ears*; postauricular patch distinct; tail edging buffy. Chaparral and open places in the Redwood Forest and in the lower and drier Yellow Pine Forest; Transition and Upper Sonoran life zones in northwestern California. P. 191, Map 43.

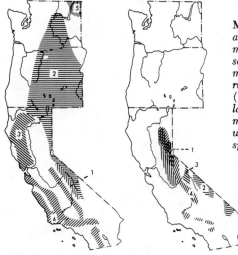

Map 43, left. (1) *Eutamias alpinus*, (2) *Eutamias minimus*, (3) *Eutamias sonomae*, (4) *Eutamias merriami*, (5) *Eutamias ruficaudus*. Map 44, right. (1) *Eutamias quadrimaculatus*, (2) *Eutamias panamintinus*, (3) *Eutamias umbrinus*, (4) *Eutamias speciosus*.

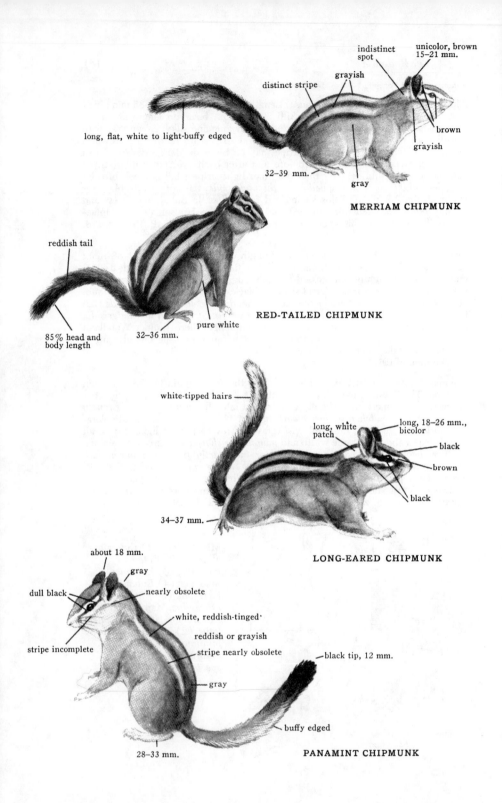

indistinct spot

unicolor, brown 15–21 mm.

grayish

distinct stripe

long, flat, white to light-buffy edged

brown

grayish

32–39 mm.

gray

MERRIAM CHIPMUNK

reddish tail

RED-TAILED CHIPMUNK

pure white

85% head and body length

32–36 mm.

white-tipped hairs

long, 18–26 mm., bicolor

long, white patch

black

brown

black

34–37 mm.

LONG-EARED CHIPMUNK

about 18 mm.

gray

dull black

nearly obsolete

white, reddish-tinged·

reddish or grayish

stripe incomplete

stripe nearly obsolete

black tip, 12 mm.

gray

buffy edged

28–33 mm.

PANAMINT CHIPMUNK

Merriam chipmunk (*Eutamias merriami*). Length 210–80 mm.; tail 89–140 mm.; *tail long, usually over 80 per cent of head and body length*; hind foot 32.5–39 mm.; ear 15–21 mm.; skull 36.2–40 mm.; baculum length about 4.9 mm., distal one-tenth slightly compressed laterally; general coloration grayish; *all light stripes gray and dark stripes brown, stripes lack clear demarcation; back side of ear is unicolored, grayish, or buffy; all brownish stripes on the head, with dull black spots only before and behind the eyes*; postauricular spot is indistinct or absent; tail edgings white or light buff. Upper Sonoran Life Zone in the solid stands of Chaparral or in the Foothill Woodland in the southern half of California. In southern California woodlands this species may extend up to 7,000 feet into open coniferous forests or Pinyon-Juniper Woodland. P. 191, fig. 120, Map 43.

Red-tailed chipmunk (*Eutamias ruficaudus*). Length 220–50 mm.; tail 100–120 mm.; hind foot 31–36 mm.; ear 18 mm.; skull 34–36 mm.; *baculum length 4.0–4.6 mm.*, distal two-fifths slightly compressed (fig. 112); rump brownish; under parts mostly whitish, with five distinct dark stripes; dark stripes on the head mostly black; tail reddish. In and above the yellow pine belt of northeastern Washington. (Some mammalogists suggest this species may be synonymous with *Eutamias amoenus*.) Map 43.

Long-eared chipmunk (*Eutamias quadrimaculatus*). Length 200–255 mm.; tail 85–118 mm.; hind foot 34–37 mm.; ear 18–26 mm.; skull 36.2–38.5 mm.; baculum length 4.3–5.3 mm., distal one-third slightly compressed laterally; *ears long, slender, and pointed*; bright reddish with contrasting stripes (especially on the face); *large conspicuous white patch behind the ear*, which is longer than the depressed ear; *dark stripe immediately below the ear contains much black*, stripe in front of eye is brown; undertail is reddish brown; tail hairs are white-tipped. Open, brushy and rocky places in the Yellow Pine and Douglas Fir forests in the Transition Life Zone of the northern Sierra Nevada of California. Map 44.

Panamint chipmunk (*Eutamias panamintinus*). Length 190–214 mm.; hind foot 28–33 mm.; ear 18 mm.; skull 33–34 mm.; baculum length about 2.2 mm., distal two-thirds compressed laterally; reddish gray; *crown of head noticeably gray; shoulders and back reddish; lower dark stripe on the head is brown and does not extend to the vibrissae and rarely under the ear;* median dark stripe is darkest, and *outer dark stripes, below the outer white stripes, are nearly or quite obsolete;* other dorsal dark stripes are reddish or grayish; *dark stripe through the eye is partly black;* ears rounded; postauricular patch distinct. Pinyon-Juniper Woodland among the boulders and on the cliffs in the Upper Sonoran Life Zone of eastern California. Map 44.

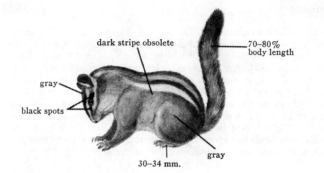

dark stripe obsolete

70–80% body length

gray

black spots

gray

30–34 mm.

UINTA CHIPMUNK

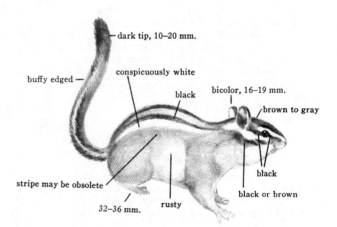

dark tip, 10–20 mm.

buffy edged

conspicuously white

black

bicolor, 16–19 mm.

brown to gray

black

stripe may be obsolete

black or brown

32–36 mm.

rusty

LODGEPOLE CHIPMUNK

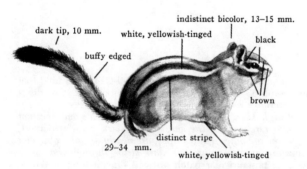

indistinct bicolor, 13–15 mm.

dark tip, 10 mm.

white, yellowish-tinged

black

buffy edged

brown

distinct stripe

29–34 mm.

white, yellowish-tinged

YELLOW PINE CHIPMUNK

Uinta chipmunk (*Eutamias umbrinus*). Length 210–25 mm.; tail 86–103 mm.; hind foot 30–34.5 mm.; ear 16–19 mm.; skull 34–36 mm.; baculum length 2.5–3.0 mm., width of base more than one-third the length of the shaft, distal two-thirds strongly compressed laterally and curved downward at the tip (fig. 112); back of neck and crown grayish; outer light stripes *pure white* and usually not broader than the inner light stripes; except for dull black spots before and behind each eye, the dark facial stripes are brown but are *nearly obsolete anteriorly*; dorsal stripes well demarcated, outer dark stripes nearly or quite obsolete; dark stripes are more black than reddish but *never grayish*; tail edging buffy; dark end of tail less than 15 mm. long; resembles *E. speciosus*. Subalpine Forest of the Canadian and Hudsonian life zones near timberline in southern Mono and northern Inyo counties, California. Map 44.

Lodgepole chipmunk (*Eutamias speciosus*). Length 197–230 mm.; tail 70–103 mm.; hind foot 32–36 mm.; ear 16–19 mm.; skull 34–36 mm.; incisors straight (fig. 114); baculum length 2.1–3.2 mm., distal two-thirds strongly compressed laterally (fig. 112); brown to grayish head and shoulders, crown grayish to grizzly brown; *outer light stripes pure white and broader than the inner light stripes; they contrast strongly with the dark stripes*; except for dull black spots before and behind each eye, the *dark facial stripes are black and brown and sometimes are nearly obsolete anteriorly; dark stripes are more black than reddish, never grayish; outer dark stripes nearly or quite obsolete; tail edgings buffy; dark end of tail less than 15 mm. long*. Subalpine, Red Fir, and Lodgepole forests, chiefly in the Canadian and Hudsonian life zones of California in the central and northern Sierra Nevada, in the San Bernardino and San Gabriel ranges, and on Mount Pinos in Ventura County (fig. 113). P. 191, fig. 115, Map 44.

Yellow pine chipmunk (*Eutamias amoenus*). Length 180–240 mm.; tail 73–108 mm.; hind foot 29–35 mm.; ear 13–15 mm.; skull length 31–35.5 mm.; baculum length 2.3–2.9 mm.; distal fifth of shaft slightly compressed (fig. 112); ears indistinctly bicolored; color bright, with *inner light stripes often broader and more conspicuous than outer light stripes*; outer dark stripes black; undertail deep fulvous; tail 73–85 per cent of head and body length; some black in stripe that is in front and back of eye. Open forests of yellow pine chiefly, but also up into the Canadian and Hudsonian life zones of Washington, Oregon, and northern California, and along the east slope of the Sierra Nevada south to Mono County, California. P. 191, and fig. 116, Map 45.

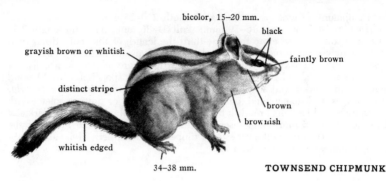

bicolor, 15–20 mm.

black

grayish brown or whitish

faintly brown

distinct stripe

brown

brownish

whitish edged

34–38 mm.   **TOWNSEND CHIPMUNK**

Townsend chipmunk (*Eutamias townsendii*). Length 227–77 mm.; tail 91–126 mm.; hind foot 34–38 mm.; ear 15–20 mm.; baculum length about 2.2 mm., distal one-fifth is slightly compressed; upper incisors moderately incurved with a smoothly curved occlusive surface (fig. 114); grayish or "dirty white" light stripes; tail edgings white or faint buffy; *undertail reddish brown* or tawny; specimens from the western parts of California, Oregon and Washington have a reddish wash over the back, with the inner light stripes being mostly brownish; those from the Sierra have whitish outer light stripes; stripes are sometimes not clearly demarcated; *back side of the ear is bicolored, blackish in front and grayish behind; dark stripe below the ear is brown and has no black.* Floor of Yellow Pine, Redwood, hemlock, and fir forests, mostly in the Transition Life Zone of California, north of San Francisco and the central Sierra Nevada to include the western half of Oregon and Washington. (Sutton, 1963, proposed a revision, based largely on the bacula, which would make four species of the present species: *Eutamias townsendii* [to include the subspecies *townsendii* and *cooperi*], *E. siskiyou, E. ochrogenys,* and *E. senex.*) P. 191, fig. 119, Map 46.

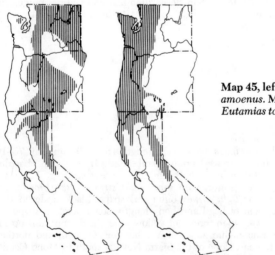

Map 45, left. *Eutamias amoenus.* **Map 46, right.** *Eutamias townsendii.*

Chipmunks (*Eutamias*)

There are 11 species of chipmunks in the Pacific States, some of which are so similar that it is frequently necessary to refer to the peculiarities of the bacula (fig. 112) or a series of characters including the geographical and ecological distribution to identify them. The work of Sutton (1962) on chromosomes shows promise of uncovering obscure relationships as well as valuable aids in identification. Chipmunks have 38 chromosomes insofar as they have been examined, but some of the species show different numbers of large chromosomes and small chromosomes and different positions of the centromeres on them. The members of this genus are not likely to be confused with other genera except with certain ground squirrels (*Callospermophilus*), which, unlike chipmunks, lack the stripes on the sides of the head, although these ground squirrels have dorsal stripes.

Like the ground squirrels, these rat-sized rodents are hibernators and have internal cheek pouches in which they carry food. Like them also, all chipmunks are diurnal. Unlike most ground squirrels, which store fat for energy during dormancy, the chipmunks have large underground caches of food for the occasional periods of waking and for use in early spring when snow still covers the ground. Seeds and fruits constitute most of the chipmunk's diet. The least chipmunk eats insects, especially Lepidoptera larvae, in the spring of the year, but it gradually becomes more of a seed-

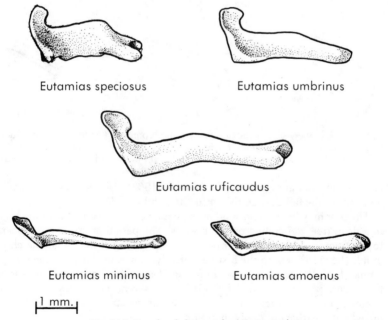

Eutamias speciosus   Eutamias umbrinus

Eutamias ruficaudus

Eutamias minimus   Eutamias amoenus

1 mm.

Fig. 112. Bacula of chipmunks (*Eutamias*).

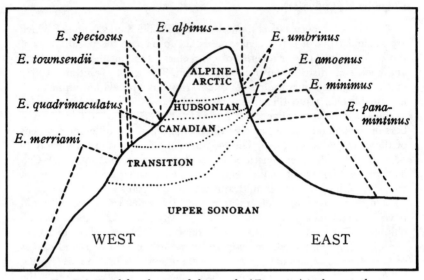

Fig. 113. Zonal distribution of chipmunks (*Eutamias*) in the central Sierra Nevada.

Fig. 114. Side view of the rostrum of certain chipmunks (*Eutamias*). (a) Short incurved incisors of *Eutamias townsendii*, (b) notched, strongly incurved incisors of *Eutamias sonomae*, and (c) short straight incisors of *Eutamias speciosus*.

eater as autumn approaches (D. Johnson, 1963). Chipmunks are usually no fatter in the fall than in the spring after hibernation.

The nest may be underground or in an abandoned woodpecker hole high in a dead tree, depending on the species. The period of gestation appears to be a month. The single litter of three to six young of the lodgepole chipmunk (fig. 115) is born the first part of July. A nest of the Townsend chipmunk (fig. 119) has been found of sedge leaves and lichen, and a nest of the yellow pine chipmunk (fig. 116) with seven young was found in a chamber in an underground burrow. It was constructed of sedge leaves mixed with feathers of the blue grouse.

Fig. 115. Lodgepole chipmunk (*Eutamias speciosus*).

Fig. 116. Yellow pine chipmunk (*Eutamias amoenus*).

Fig. 117. Least chipmunk (*Eutamias minimus*).

Fig. 118. Molting alpine chipmunk (*Eutamias alpinus*).

Fig. 119. Townsend chipmunk (*Eutamias townsendii*).

Fig. 120. Merriam chipmunk (*Eutamias merriami*).

The yellow pine chipmunk in the Cascade Mountains probably mates in April (Broadbooks, 1958), and the young are born in May or early June. The young do not breed until the following spring, with one litter of four to six each year. The life span is over five years. Their nest is in the ground, and by the middle of November most of the animals are underground. They seem to be partial hibernators and revive occasionally to feed. One underground cache was found to include some 35,000 seeds from 20 different kinds of plants and to weigh 140 grams.

The yellow pine chipmunk is associated closely with the Cascades golden-mantled ground squirrel in many places. Both occupy the same habitat without apparent competition. The niches are different, with the chipmunk climbing high in the conifers to obtain seeds, while the ground squirrel gets the same kinds of seeds after they fall to the ground. Chipmunks in general select seeds for food, while ground squirrels eat more stems and leaves. Ground squirrels depend upon body fat for energy during hibernation; chipmunks depend upon food caches deep in their winter dens. The yellow pine chipmunk is closely related to the red-tailed chipmunk and in many cases can be distinguished from it only by its shorter baculum.

The least chipmunk (fig. 117) which inhabits mountains up to 10,500 feet, may also be found living far out in the vast expanse of sagebrush. All the other species live in the humid coastal forests or arrange themselves zonally on the wetter western and drier eastern sides of the great mountain ranges (fig. 113). Thus the community, life zone, and habitat are useful in making tentative field identifications of chipmunks.

The chipmunks of the Western states illustrate very well the biological principle of Gloger, that a species of mammal is more heavily pigmented in the more humid areas. The chipmunks in the humid coastal forest, such as the Townsend chipmunk (fig. 119), are much darker than the same species farther east or the lodgepole chipmunk of the less humid western Sierra Nevada. This latter species, in turn, is darker than the least chipmunk, which lives in the still drier sagebrush areas farther east (fig. 117).

The brightness of the stripes, too, is related to the habitat. The Sonoma chipmunk and the Merriam chipmunk (fig. 120) have stripes that are not clearly demarcated. Both these species live in dense chaparral, where the shadows of small twigs are weak and not sharp. The alpine chipmunk, which lives in talus slopes and on the open rocky floor of the Alpine forests, also has poorly defined stripes (fig. 118). Other species, such as the least, the lodgepole, and the yellow pine chipmunks, that inhabit sunlit open forests where light-bathed twigs cast dark shadows, have well-demarcated light and dark stripes.

75–90% head and body length

dark gray with rusty wash

55–75 mm.

white

EASTERN GRAY SQUIRREL

silvery gray, not rusty

white-edged hairs

white

72–82 mm.

WESTERN GRAY SQUIRREL

grizzled reddish gray

short ears

reddish

reddish or orange

FOX SQUIRREL

Sciurus Dental Formula 1-0-1-3/1-0-1-3 or 1-0-2-3/1-0-1-3

Eastern gray squirrel (*Sciurus carolinensis*). Length 385–500 mm., about 18 inches long; tail 165–240 mm.; hind foot 55–75 mm.; skull about 62 mm.; *five cheek teeth on each side of the upper jaw;* upper parts gray with a reddish wash (summer); underparts whitish; tail with long white-tipped hairs; melanism may occur. Introduced from the eastern half of the United States into Seattle, Washington, in 1925, into Golden Gate Park, San Francisco, and into other cities, campuses, and large private estates. P. 196, fig. 123 (no range map).

Western gray squirrel (*Sciurus griseus*). Length 500–575 mm., about 22 inches; tail very bushy, edged with white, 240–80 mm.; hind foot 72–82 mm.; ear (crown) 28–36 mm.; skull 65–70 mm.; *five cheek teeth on each side of upper jaw; "salt and pepper" to silvery gray above, white below.* From Tehachapi Mountains north along the Sierra Nevada and in the Coast Ranges in California, north from the Mexican border. Through western Oregon into central and western Washington, chiefly in the oaks of the Upper Sonoran and Transition Life Zones. P. 196, fig. 122, Map 47.

Fox squirrel (*Sciurus niger*). Length 474–565 mm., about 20 inches; tail 225–65 mm.; hind foot 62–80 mm.; skull 62–70 mm.; *four cheek teeth on each side of the upper jaws;* three color phases; upper parts usually rusty or reddish gray, lower parts rusty yellow or orange; there may be pure steel gray individuals with no rust, which are difficult to distinguish from the eastern gray squirrel, or some that are gray with a little rusty coloration on the legs, but with blackish heads, white noses, and white ears. Some tend to be melanistic. Introduced into several cities, campuses, and large private estates from the eastern half of the United States. They are known to occur in the Seattle area, in Asotin County, and along Okanogan creek in Okanogan County, Washington. They are rather common in the country around Ventura, California, and on the Stanford University campus in Palo Alto, California, where the gray phase is frequently seen; it is also common in Fresno, California, but it is at present only in the city limits. P. 196, fig. 124 (no range map).

longer hairs

whitish edge

rusty or
yellowish

dark line

DOUGLAS SQUIRREL

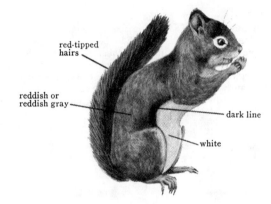

red-tipped
hairs

reddish or
reddish gray

dark line

white

RED SQUIRREL

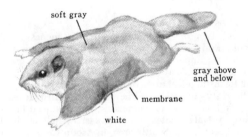

soft gray

gray above
and below

membrane

white

NORTHERN FLYING SQUIRREL

Tamiasciurus Dental Formula 1-0-1-3/1-0-1-3 or 1-0-2-3/1-0-1-3

Douglas squirrel (*Tamiasciurus douglasii*). Length 270–357 mm., about 14 inches; hind foot 50–55 mm.; ear 23–24 mm.; skull 49–50 mm.; *upper parts dusky olive; whitish-tipped tail hairs; underparts yellowish white to deep orange,* separated from the sides by a dark stripe (summer); ears tipped with long hairs (winter). Coniferous forests of the upper pine belt and in the forests of fir, spruce, and hemlock from the Transition to the Hudsonian Life Zone, from San Francisco, California, north through the Coast Ranges, in the Sierra Nevada and Cascades of Oregon and Washington. P. 199, fig. 125, Map 48.

Red squirrel (*Tamiasciurus hudsonicus*). Length 330–80 mm., about 15 inches; tail 92–158 mm.; hind foot 35–55 mm.; ear 23–24 mm.; skull about 48 to 50 mm.; *upper parts reddish or reddish gray; reddish-tipped tail hairs; underparts white,* separated from the sides by a black stripe (summer), ears tipped with long hairs (winter). Coniferous forests of pine, spruce, and hemlock in eastern Washington and northeastern Oregon, from Transition Life Zone up into the Hudsonian Life Zone. P. 199, fig. 127, Map 48.

Glaucomys Dental Formula 1-0-2-3/1-0-1-3

Northern flying squirrel (*Glaucomys sabrinus*). Dental Formula 1-0-2-3/ 1-0-1-3. Length 258–310 mm., about 11 inches; tail 116–45 mm.; hind foot 36–39 mm.; ear (crown) 17–26 mm.; skull 40–42 mm.; *with a fur-covered skin membrane between the fore and hind limbs;* lead gray above, dull creamy white below; both sides of the flat tail are gray, fur not separated into guard hairs and underfur; large eyes. Forested areas of yellow pine, red fir, spruce, hemlock, and redwood forests in Transition and Canadian life zones of all three states. P. 200, fig. 128, Map 49.

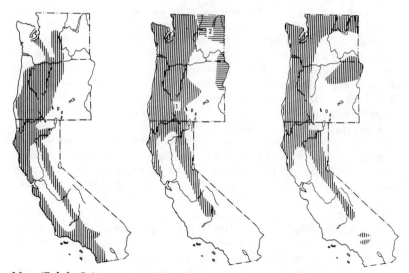

Map 47, left. *Sciurus griseus.* **Map 48, center.** (1) *Tamiasciurus douglasii,* (2) *Tamiasciurus hudsonicus.* **Map 49, right.** *Glaucomys sabrinus.*

Tree Squirrels (*Tamiasciurus, Sciurus, and Glaucomys*)

The animals belonging to these genera are chiefly arboreal and will be considered together, even though they represent two separate subfamilies (Sciurinae and Pteromyinae).

The long bushy tails, the lack of dorsal stripes, spotting, or flecking, and the absence of internal cheek pouches are features that distinguish the tree squirrels from the ground squirrels and chipmunks. Tree squirrels do not hibernate, and all except the northern flying squirrel are diurnal. Tree squirrels, like all other members of the Sciuridae, have four toes on the forefeet and five on the hind feet (fig. 121).

Fig. 121. Tracks of western gray squirrel, nearly actual size.

Two species have been brought into the Pacific States, the eastern gray squirrel (fig. 123) and the fox squirrel (fig. 124). They have been introduced into city parks, college campuses, and large estates, but rarely have they been able to extend their range into the forests of the surrounding rural areas, although the fox squirrel is extending into the countryside around Ventura, California. The eastern gray squirrel has a different pelage in winter and summer, and the fox squirrel is represented in the Pacific States by at least two of its three color phases; hence these two introduced species are easily confused (see drawings, photographs, and brief descriptions), and it is often necessary to observe the dentition to make accurate identification. The fox squirrel is known to live over seven years, and the eastern gray squirrel over 14 years. The gestation period for both is about 45 days. There are three or four in a litter with two litters a year.

The western gray squirrel is primarily an acorn eater and most of its range includes oak trees of various species. When the acorns fall in autumn, it spends considerable time on the ground gathering and burying each acorn in a hole three to four inches deep. Observation and experiment have shown that the acorns are retrieved by the sense of smell.

The western gray squirrel usually enlarges an old woodpecker or flicker hole for its brood den. Then, in late winter or spring, after a 44-day gestation period, its single litter of three or five young is born. The den may be in a leafy nest far out on the branches of a large tree. The gray squirrel is not as quick or as nimble in trees as the other species of tree squirrels. Its main enemies, such as the coyote, fox, bobcat, large hawk, and owl,

Fig. 122. Western gray squirrel (*Sciurus griseus*).

Fig. 123. Eastern gray squirrel (*Sciurus carolinensis*).

Fig. 124. Fox squirrel (*Sciurus niger*).

Fig. 125. Douglas squirrel (*Tamiasciurus douglasii*).

Fig. 126. Jeffrey pine cones cached by Douglas squirrel.

Fig. 127. Red squirrel (*Tamiasciurus hudsonicus*).

Fig. 128. Northern flying squirrel (*Glaucomys sabrinus*).

catch it on the ground; in the trees it is reasonably safe. This is part of the normal niche of the western gray squirrel. Sometimes, however, it extends its range up the mountains into the Canadian Life Zone, where there are no oaks and where the deadly enemy of all tree squirrels, the marten (*Martes americana*), lives. Here the winters are long, the snow may reach 15 feet on the level and stay on the ground for months. In such an environment the western gray squirrel may last for a year or two, and even raise a litter of young. When the snow becomes deeper, the marten comes lower down the mountains to find food. It can easily catch this slow-moving squirrel in the trees or in the enlarged hole it uses for a winter nest. The deep snow is probably its worst enemy because of its practice of burying a single fungus or pine nut in one small hole.

The Douglas squirrel and the red squirrel live mostly in the Transition, Canadian, and Hudsonian life zones. Their niches are quite different from that of the western gray squirrel. Both live largely on conifer cones, which they cut off the trees early in autumn. The cones are then stored in large caches in moist places, under logs, in old stumps, or even in small slow-moving streams (fig. 126). Here they may remain for as long as three years. When the deep snow comes, a single burrow down through it makes the entire cache (sometimes hundreds of cones) available.

The chattering Douglas squirrel and the red squirrel are extremely agile. The old woodpecker holes or the openings between rocks of a talus slope where the Douglas squirrel makes its nest are often too small for the marten. Coyotes, foxes, bobcats, goshawks, and horned owls doubtless catch a few on the ground. After the Douglas squirrel has dropped a large Jeffrey pine cone from as high as 150 feet, it races down the tree trunk to drag its heavy meal to the base of the tree, which prevents surprise attack from the rear as it deftly cuts away the scales to expose the nutritious nuts. Both the Douglas squirrel and the red squirrel are well suited to the arboreal life in coniferous forests, where even if the cone crop fails, they eat various fungi. It is doubtful if either could exist long in the plant communities that constitute the Upper Sonoran Zone, where the western gray squirrel is eminently successful. The gestation period is believed to be between 36 and 40 days. Five young is the average litter for the Douglas squirrel. There may be two litters a year, since nursing females have been taken early in June and late in October in Washington.

The only nocturnal squirrel in the Pacific States is the beautiful soft-furred northern flying squirrel, which actually does not fly at all. It has very large eyes, long vibrissae, and a flat furry membrane that extends along each side of the body between the ankle and wrist. These structures enable it to jump from high in a tree and glide to the base of another tree, sometimes over 150 feet, thus avoiding coyotes, foxes, and bobcats, as well as martens, but it is frequently caught by large owls, which are its worst enemy.

Like other arboreal squirrels, the northern flying squirrel does not hibernate, although it frequents coniferous forests of high mountains where there are long-persisting deep snows. Unlike the Douglas squirrel and the red squirrel, it does not collect food for winter. Instead, it lives largely on fungi in summer, and in winter gets energy from the hair moss (*Alectoria fremonti*), a lichen that hangs from the foliage. Although it is not primarily a seed eater, it is known to eat nuts, fruit, meat bait, oatmeal, raisins, eggs, and insects.

The nest of the northern flying squirrel is made in an old woodpecker hole or other tree cavity. This species in British Columbia is reported to live in tree cavities in winter but to make outside nests of shredded bark and lichens for the summer. After a gestation period of 40 days, the three or four young are born in May or June in the outside nest.

Thus the nonhibernating tree squirrels of the Pacific States are adapted to food-getting and food storage in different ways in the same environment.

KEY TO POCKET GOPHERS (Geomyidae)

There are fur-lined pouches on either side of the mouth, and the tail is always shorter than the combined head and body length. All pocket gophers in the Pacific States belong to the genus *Thomomys*. The dental formula is 1-0-1-3/ 1-0-1-3. Pocket gophers are difficult to identify on external features alone. Differences in the skull (fig. 136) and baculum (fig. 137) are much more dependable. Sometimes there are considerable differences in size of the sexes.

1A. Hind foot, male, over 34 mm., female, over 30 mm.; basal end of baculum (viewed dorsally) divided by longitudinal groove (fig. 137) . . . 2

1B. Hind foot, male, usually less than 34 mm., female, usually less than 30 mm.; basal end of baculum (viewed dorsally) undivided (fig. 137) . . 3

2A. Hind foot, male, usually over 40 mm., female, usually over 38 mm.; baculum 8.8–9.5 mm. (fig. 137). Only in the Willamette Valley, Oregon.
   Thomomys bulbivorus, Camas pocket gopher, p. 203, fig. 135.

2B. Hind foot, male, usually less than 40 mm.; female, usually less than 38 mm.; baculum 9.2–11.0 mm. (fig. 137); ears oval, 6–7 mm. In southeastern Oregon and northeastern California.
   Thomomys townsendii, Townsend pocket gopher, p. 203, fig. 134.

3A. Washington, Oregon (except extreme southwestern part), and California north of the Feather River, in the high Sierra Nevada, and in the sagebrush area east of the Sierra. Postauricular dark patch two or more times the area of the oval or pointed ear; snout and rostrum narrow and slender, with abrupt arch in front of the premolars (fig. 136); incisive foramen is anterior to the infraorbital canal; sphenoidal fissure absent or very narrow (fig. 136) 4

3B. Extreme southwestern Oregon and all of California except the driest areas and those areas that lie north of the Feather River and east of or high in the Sierra Nevada; postauricular dark patch usually about the same size as the round ear (some races much larger); snout and rostrum broad and deep, sloping up gradually in front of the premolars (fig. 136); incisive foramen is posterior to the anterior opening of the infraorbital canal; distinct sphenoidal fissure present (fig. 136); baculum 9.1–13.0 mm. (fig. 137).
   Thomomys bottae, Botta pocket gopher, p. 205, figs. 129, 130.

4A. North of the Feather River in California and over Oregon and Washington 5

4B. North in the high Sierra Nevada (mostly above 6,000 feet) to the Feather River in California; ears pointed and oval, 7–9 mm. long; mammae eight (two pairs pectorally); baculum 12–15 mm. (fig. 137); upper incisors all yellow, with a distinct groove near the inner edge of each tooth.
   Thomomys monticola, mountain pocket gopher, p. 203, fig. 132.

5A. Northeastern and eastern California, Oregon and Washington east of the southern Cascades and Vancouver area. Ears more rounded than pointed, 5–6 mm. long; mammae eight–ten (three pairs pectorally); upper incisors more or less white-tipped; baculum 12–17 mm.
   Thomomys talpoides, northern pocket gopher, p. 205, fig. 133.

5B. Northwestern California; Oregon west of the Cascade range and in the Bend area; Washington on scattered lowland areas south of Puget Sound to the Columbia River and in the Olympic Mountains. Ears pointed, 7–8 mm. long; upper incisors all yellow; baculum 21–31 mm. (fig. 137).
   Thomomys mazama, Mazama pocket gopher, p. 205.

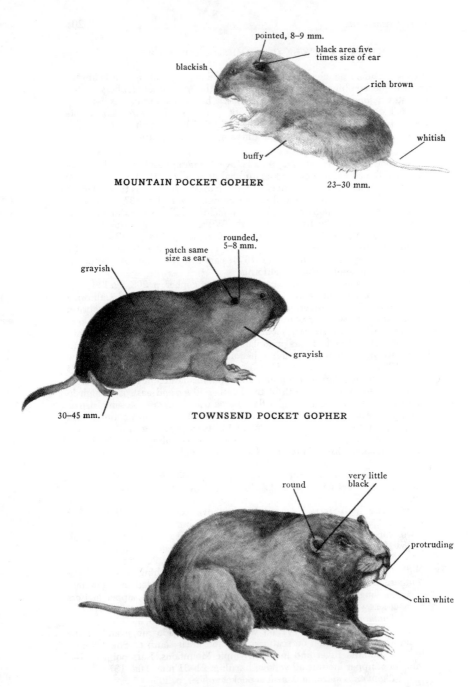

MOUNTAIN POCKET GOPHER

pointed, 8–9 mm.

black area five times size of ear

blackish

rich brown

whitish

buffy

23–30 mm.

TOWNSEND POCKET GOPHER

rounded, 5–8 mm.

patch same size as ear

grayish

grayish

30–45 mm.

CAMAS POCKET GOPHER

round

very little black

protruding

chin white

Thomomys Dental Formula 1-0-1-3/1-0-1-3

Mountain pocket gopher (*Thomomys monticola*). Length, male, 190–273 mm., about nine inches; tail 55–97 mm.; hind foot 23–30 mm. Length, female, 167–235 mm.; tail 42–84 mm.; hind foot 22–24 mm.; *ears 7–9 mm., pointed*; postauricular dark patch about three times the area of the ear; normally eight mammae with two pairs pectorally located. Skull 32–37 mm.; *no sphenoidal fissure* (fig. 136); incisive foramen in front of the front edge of the infraorbital canal; *under side of the rostrum slopes sharply upward in front of the premolar* (fig. 136); temporal ridges diverge posteriorly; *upper incisors yellow; baculum length 12.0–15.0 mm.* (fig. 137); in summer, upper parts russet brown or tawny, in winter, pale grayish brown; under parts grayish washed with buffy; *snout somewhat darker than the rest of the face*. Meadows and rocky slopes in the pine, fir, spruce, and hemlock forests in the Transition and Canadian life zones in the high Sierra Nevada and on south Yolla Bolly Mountain in California. Pp. 206, 207, fig. 132, Map 50.

Townsend pocket gopher (*Thomomys townsendii*). Length, male, 230–335 mm., about 11 inches; tail 53–100 mm.; *hind foot 34–45 mm.* Length, female, 225–64 mm.; tail 69–86 mm.; hind foot 30–36 mm.; *ears 5–8 mm., ovate*; postauricular dark patch usually smaller than the area of the ear; normally eight mammae. Skull, male, 43–49 mm., pterygoids flat and straight; *sphenoidal fissure present*; the front of the opening of the infraorbital canal is at the same level or in front of the anterior palatine foramen; *baculum length 9.2–11.0 mm.* (fig. 137); two color phases: slaty black or sooty gray above; two or more litters of three to ten a year. Deep soils of river bottoms or old lake beds in the Upper Sonoran Life Zone of northeastern California and southeastern Oregon. Fig. 134, Map 50.

Camas pocket gopher (*Thomomys bulbivorus*). Length, male, 285–300 mm.; tail 70–90 mm.; hind foot 40–45 mm.; ear 5 mm. Length, female, 254–85 mm.; tail 81 mm.; hind foot 39 mm.; ear 5 mm. Skull, male, about 58 mm.; skull, female, 50–55 mm.; zygomatic arch widest posteriorly; sphenoidal fissure present (fig. 136); pterygoids concaved on the inner surface; *baculum 8.8–9.5 mm.* (fig. 137); tail nearly naked; normally eight mammae; greatly protruding incisors; dark sooty brown above and nearly the same below; chin and anal spot white. Transition Life Zone only in the deep soil of the Willamette Valley of Oregon. Fig. 135, Map 50.

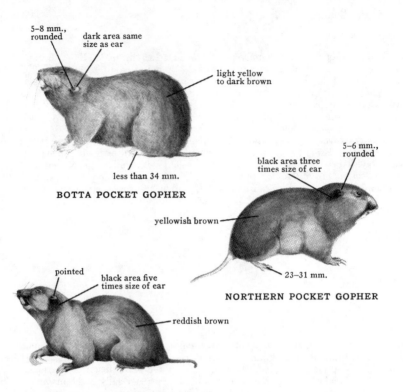

5–8 mm., rounded

dark area same size as ear

light yellow to dark brown

less than 34 mm.

BOTTA POCKET GOPHER

5–6 mm., rounded

black area three times size of ear

yellowish brown

23–31 mm.

NORTHERN POCKET GOPHER

pointed

black area five times size of ear

reddish brown

MAZAMA POCKET GOPHER

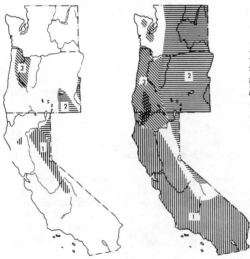

Map 50, left. (1) *Thomomys monticola*, (2) *Thomomys townsendii*, (3) *Thomomys bulbivorus*. **Map 51, right.** (1) *Thomomys bottae*, (2) *Thomomys talpoides*, (3) *Thomomys mazama*.

Botta pocket gopher (*Thomomys bottae*). Length, male, 190–273 mm., about nine inches; tail 55–97 mm.; hind foot 26–34 mm. Length female, 167–235 mm.; tail 42–84 mm.; hind foot 22–26 mm.; normally eight mammae. Skull, male, 35–43 mm.; *sphenoidal fissure present* (fig. 136); *under side of rostrum slopes gradually from the premolars to the top of the arch; baculum length 9.1–13.0 mm.* (fig. 137); buffy brownish to light gray above, under parts gray to white; *ears 5–8 mm., rounded;* postauricular dark patch about the same area as the ear, but in some races it may be longer; the incisive foramen is behind the front of the opening of the infraorbital canal. Lower Sonoran Life Zone, and up into the Canadian Life Zone; locally in southwestern Oregon; in all of California except the high mountains, sagebrush area, and parts of the dry deserts. Pp. 207, 210, fig. 130, Map 51.

Northern pocket gopher (*Thomomys talpoides*). Length, male, 175–227 mm., about eight inches; tail 50–70 mm.; hind foot 24–31 mm. Length, female, 171–211 mm.; tail 45–67 mm.; hind foot 23–31 mm.; *ears 5–6 mm., rounded;* postauricular dark patch about three times the area of the ear; normally ten mammae with three pairs pectorally located. Skull, male, 35–37 mm.; *no sphenoidal fissure* (fig. 136); the front of the opening of the infraorbital canal is behind the anterior palatine foramen; interparieto-parietal and fronto-parietal suture jagged and serrate; temporal ridges nearly parallel; *distal part of upper incisors white; baculum length 12–17 mm.* (fig. 137); in summer yellowish brown or gray brown above, gray below, sometimes with considerable white under the chin and on the throat; nose sometimes blackish or lead-colored. Chiefly in deep soil along streams and in meadows, but may occur in coarse rocky soil on the dry slopes; Upper Sonoran and Transition life zones, northeastern California and east of the Cascades, and eastern Oregon and Washington in sagebrush areas mostly. P. 211, fig. 133, Map 51.

Mazama pocket gopher (*Thomomys mazama*). Length, male, 196–233 mm.; tail 55–78 mm.; hind foot 25–31 mm.; skull about 46 mm. Length, female, 191–220 mm.; tail 53–71 mm.; hind foot 27–31 mm.; no sphenoidal fissure (fig. 136). *Baculum length 22–31 mm.* (fig. 137); reddish brown dorsally (some are melanistic); subauricular dark patch of fur, sometimes five to six times the area of the ear; slight groove near the inside on upper incisor; interparietal and fronto-parietal suture smooth; temporal ridges tend to diverge posteriorly. Along the lower Umpqua River in western Oregon is an entirely black subspecies, *T. m. niger.* From prairies to alpine meadows west of the Cascade Mountains in Washington, Oregon, and northwestern California. (Except for the baculum, this species is perhaps indistinguishable from *T. talpoides.*) P. 210, Map 51.

Family **Geomyidae** (Pocket Gophers)

There is one genus (*Thomomys*) of six species in this family living in the Pacific States. The dental formula is 1-0-1-3/1-0-1-3. These fossorial rodents have fur-lined cheek pouches for carrying food (fig. 129) and a tail much shorter than the combined head and body length. The mastoid bones are restricted to the occiput, and the infraorbital canal (fig. 137) opens low on the side of the rostrum through a small foramen, as in the squirrels. The premolars are larger than the molars and all the cheek teeth are rooted.

The pocket gopher is a solitary animal, and usually expels intruders from its burrow system. However, this behavior pattern is relaxed considerably during the breeding season, when the female even permits other females to enter its private domain. The territories are re-established in the autumn. The burrow system must be large enough to provide food in the form of roots, stems, and leaves for the occupant and, if a female, for its young. The burrow system of the mountain pocket gopher covers from 200 square feet for young animals to 2,000 square feet for old established females. The earth mounds of a pocket gopher (fig. 131) can be distinguished from those of a mole (fig. 68) by a distinct earthen "plug" at the center or, more frequently, at the side of the mound. Mole workings often have clods and lack these plugs.

The underground life of a pocket gopher has affected the evolution of its body parts as well as its behavior patterns. Certain adaptations are easily observed in external features. The small ears and eyes do not become filled or clogged with dirt. The sensitive vibrissae and short, nearly naked tail enable the animal to run rapidly forward or backward through the dark tunnel. The long sharp claws on the forefeet and the heavy musculature in the shoulders equip it superbly for digging. When burrowing becomes

Fig. 129. Botta pocket gopher, showing fur-lined cheek pouches.

Fig. 130. Botta pocket gopher (*Thomomys bottae*).

hard, the long incisors bite off chunks of the hard earth or roots. The dirt is kept out of the mouth by a perforated furry membrane that crosses the buccal cavity *behind* the incisors. The ever-growing incisors wear down rapidly in digging. Studies have shown that the combined growth of the four incisors of a Botta pocket gopher may be as much as 46 inches a year, measured from the gums, or an average of 11.5 inches each, a rate more than twice that of the Norway rat.

One of the most remarkable adaptations of the pocket gopher is of the pelvis. The hips must remain small so that it can turn readily and rapidly to escape an enemy. The opening through the pelvic basin, however, must remain large enough to permit passage of the young at birth. Solution of this problem illustrates how physiology can aid in adaptation by changing the anatomy. The pubic bones are united across the symphysis and the hips remain small in virgin females. When the animal becomes pregnant, the connection across the pubic bones disappears, apparently as a result of hormonal action, and the opening through which the young are born becomes changed from O-shaped to U-shaped, thus permitting the birth of the relatively large young.

Another equally important adaptation is in the peculiar patterns of inherited behavior. Many other animals inhabit the burrows and nests of the mountain pocket gopher, which provide a microclimate essential for their existence when the weather is extreme. Certain species of arthropods are known only from mountain gopher nests (Ingles, 1952); in addition, salamanders, toads, snakes, mice, and weasels may also enter the burrows. Therefore the practice of plugging all entrances to the burrow not only helps keep out enemies, but also provides temperature and humidity conditions agreeable to the pocket gopher and its guests.

Pocket gophers are eaten by owls, hawks, coyotes, foxes, badgers, weasels, and snakes. The animal is most vulnerable when it must open its burrow and push out the fresh earth it accumulates as it digs for food. The young is forced from the burrow after weaning and unless it can find an empty burrow or quickly establish one of its own, it has little chance of survival. The pocket gopher does not hibernate or become inactive at any

Fig. 131. Mound of mountain pocket gopher, showing earthen plug at the center.

Fig. 132. Mountain pocket gopher (*Thomomys monticola*).

Fig. 133. Northern pocket gopher (*Thomomys talpoides*).

Fig. 134. Townsend pocket gopher (*Thomomys townsendii*).

Fig. 135. Camas pocket gopher (*Thomomys bulbivorus*).

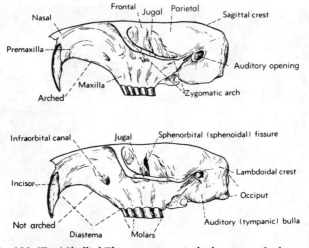

Fig. 136. *(Top)* Skull of *Thomomys monticola* showing arched rostrum. *(Bottom)* Skull of *Thomomys bottae* showing sphenoidal fissure.

time of the year. Instead, it may burrow through the snow and feed on the stems of grass and other plants at the surface of the ground. Large food caches are frequently made underground during winter, but the grassy nest, which is about a foot in diameter, occasionally is made in the snow. As the snow melts, the animal goes underground and pushes earth up into the snow burrow. These long earthen cores, some 40 feet long, lie over one another on the surface of the ground.

Pocket gophers rarely live beyond three years, but they produce many young each year. The gestation period appears to be 18 or 19 days. Although the average size of a litter is five or six, as many as 12 have been found, and the Botta pocket gopher, for one, may have at least three litters a year. Predator control has greatly increased the number of pocket gophers in agricultural and grazing areas. As many as 30 to an acre of grazing land have been found in the San Joaquin Valley in California. The encouragement of broad-winged hawks, owls, gopher snakes, weasels, badgers, foxes, and coyotes would help materially in keeping the pocket gopher population greatly reduced.

Pocket gophers genetically appear to be a very plastic group, and there is much evidence that natural selection has adapted the fur of certain populations to match closely the soil color in which they live. Other populations appear to have developed as a result of genetic drift, with little or no selective pressure. It has been pointed out that the black pocket gopher (*Thomomys mazama niger*) of western Oregon closely matches the dark moist soil of its environment (Walker, 1955).

Economically, the pocket gopher may be considered either beneficial or harmful, depending on where it establishes its burrow system. High in the mountain meadows where predators still exert considerable influence in the population, the gopher is doubtless beneficial, since it is the only

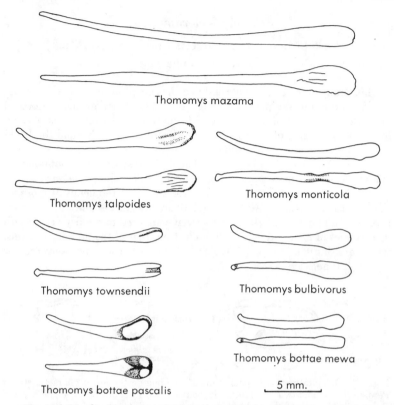

Thomomys mazama

Thomomys talpoides

Thomomys monticola

Thomomys townsendii

Thomomys bulbivorus

Thomomys bottae mewa

Thomomys bottae pascalis

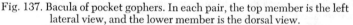

5 mm.

Fig. 137. Bacula of pocket gophers. In each pair, the top member is the left lateral view, and the lower member is the dorsal view.

means of "plowing" the land, and tons of soil are brought to the surface on an acre each year (Ingles, 1952). Through the burrow systems, water from the melting snow sinks to provide permanent springs and to prevent run-off floods further down the mountains (Ingles, 1949b). The continued work of this rodent has done much to gradually wear away the mountains to form fertile meadows and alluvial fans in the valleys. Even in established alfalfa fields in Washington, northern pocket gophers (fig. 133) are considered beneficial by some people, who claim that the plants are stimulated to grow larger and healthier as a result of pocket gopher feeding and cultivation (Dalquest, 1948), and direct observation bears out this contention.

However beneficial the pocket gopher is under certain conditions, it is still a great pest where the land has been overgrazed, where it must be irrigated, or in the vineyards, orchards, and grain fields where its natural foods are eliminated. There is some evidence that the "hog-wallow" land of the San Joaquin Valley in California and the "mima prairie" of Washington are the result of the work of pocket gophers over long periods.

Family **Heteromyidae**

(Pocket Mice, Kangaroo Rats, and Kangaroo Mice)

Dental Formula 1-0-1-3/1-0-1-3

This family of long-tailed rats and mice has deep fur-lined cheek pouches similar to those of the pocket gopher (fig. 129). There are no postorbital processes on the frontal bones. The infraorbital canal opens as a small foramen on the side of the rostrum, which projects well beyond the back-ward-slanting incisors. The auditory bullae are large.

There are two subfamilies in the Pacific States: the *Perognathinae* includes one genus, the *Perognathus*, or pocket mice; the *Dipodomyinae* includes the genus *Dipodomys*, or kangaroo rats, and the genus *Microdipodops*, or kangaroo mice. All live in relatively arid places and all are gramnivorous and nocturnal. The way they have adapted to the dry desert with its extremes of heat and cold is different from that of the ground squirrels, which are diurnal (see p. 177). Parts of the desert are snow-covered for days at a time.

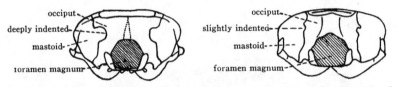

Fig. 138. Occipital region in pocket mice. The one on the left is characteristic of *Perognathus spinatus, P. formosus, P. penicillatus, P. californicus, P. fallax,* and *P. baileyi.* The one on the right is characteristic of *P. longimembris, P. inornatus, P. parvus,* and *P. alticolus.*

Bartholomew and Cade (1957) have studied the little pocket mouse in the field and the laboratory. It is one of the smallest of North American rodents and, like all small, warm-blooded (*homoiothermal*) animals, has a high metabolic rate and loses body heat rapidly (see discussion on surface-volume relationship, p. 93). It must have a continually available food supply in order to maintain its high metabolic rate during periods of extreme weather and food shortage. The little pocket mouse is known to store some food, but the ability to become dormant for only a few bad nights is an important factor in its survival. Captive pocket mice remain active in the laboratory as long as their deep body temperature ranges between 90 and 102° F., but when the ambient temperature exceeds the body temperature of an active animal, *hyperthermia* results and the animal must cool itself or die. When the pocket mouse is kept at 68°, it occasionally becomes torpid, and will always do so if food is withheld for 24 to 36 hours.

While the animal is becoming torpid, the temperature of its body declines rapidly to within a degree or less of the ambient temperature and the breathing and heartbeat are greatly reduced. The metabolic rate becomes much lower, and hence energy is conserved. Since it may become torpid when environmental temperatures are between 36° and 77°, the little pocket mouse is a good species to use in studying hibernation (winter torpor) and estivation (summer torpor), the only difference being the lower temperature of hibernation. The periods of dormancy of the little pocket mouse are not predictable, as they are in the daily torpor of bats (p. 107) or the seasonal torpor of marmots and ground squirrels (p. 177). Dormancy in the little pocket mouse is dictated by extreme weather conditions and food shortage.

Pocket mice in captivity live longer than would be expected of such small mammals. The San Diego pocket mouse has been known to live over eight years, four months, and the Great Basin mouse (fig. 139) over four years, six months. The burrow of the Great Basin pocket mouse (fig. 139), found in all three states, is generally placed under sagebrush in friable soil and is usually plugged during the daytime. The burrow is two or three feet deep and has a nest cavity and one or more storage chambers containing seeds of wild mustard, dock, nettles, sunflowers, and pigweed. Water is probably obtained in the food. It has a litter of three to five, probably born in the summer months. Rattlesnakes, owls, and badgers are known enemies. The Great Basin pocket mice, where numerous, may check the reseeding of certain grasses.

Fig. 139. Great Basin pocket mouse (*Perognathus parvus*).

Fig. 140. Desert pocket mouse (*Perognathus penicillatus*).

Fig. 141. California pocket mouse (*Perognathus californicus*).

KEY TO THE POCKET MICE (Heteromyidae in part; *Perognathus*)

Animals belonging to this family have external fur-lined cheek pouches, a tail that is always longer than the head and body length, and no white stripes across the hips. The dental formula is 1-0-1-3/1-0-1-3.

1A. Sole of hind foot usually with some hairs near the ankle (may be naked in *P. formosus*); pelage soft without stiff coarse hairs on flanks; interparietal bone usually not as wide as the interorbital width; auditory bullae nearly meeting anteriorly 2
1B. Sole of hind foot usually naked to the heel; pelage usually harsh, frequently with stiff coarse hairs or spines on the rump and hips; interparietal bone as wide as or wider than the interorbital width; auditory bullae separated anteriorly by nearly the full width of the basisphenoid 7
2A. Hind foot normally more than 20 mm.; mastoids projecting posteriorly to the level of the occiput 3
2B. Hind foot normally 20 mm. or less; mastoids projecting posteriorly distinctly beyond the level of the occiput 6
3A. Tail normally 95 mm. or less, with hairs on its crest or tuft normally 15 mm. or less; mastoids not deeply indenting the supraoccipital (fig. 138) . 4
3B. Tail normally 95 mm. or more in length; hair on its dark crest and tuft more than 15 mm. long; ear more than 10 mm. from notch; mastoids deeply indent supraoccipital (fig. 138). Dry stony ground in eastern and southeastern California in the Sonoran life zones.
    Perognathus formosus, long-tailed pocket mouse, p. 221.
4A. Inside ears with white or yellowish hairs; tail pale yellowish. Tree yucca and pine belts of Tehachapi and San Bernardino mountains of California 5
4B. Inside ears lacking white or yellowish hairs; dark dorsally, white below, sometimes with reddish tinge; tail not crested but with terminal hairs up to 15 mm. long. Eastern parts of Washington, Oregon, and California in Upper Sonoran and Transition life zones.
    Perognathus parvus, Great Basin pocket mouse, p. 221, fig. 139.
5A. Dorsal parts buffy; hairs inside ears yellow; tail distinctly penicillate. West side of Walker Pass, Kern County, California, in Upper Sonoran Life Zone.
    Perognathus xanthonotus, yellow-eared pocket mouse, p. 223, fig. 144.

Fig. 142. San Joaquin pocket mouse (*Perognathus inornatus*).

Fig. 143. Little pocket mouse (*Perognathus longimembris*).

Fig. 144. Yellow-eared pocket mouse (*Perognathus xanthonotus*).

5B. Dorsal parts predominantly blackish; hairs inside ears white; tail with terminal hairs about 5 mm. long. Little Bear Valley in the San Bernardino Mountains and in a restricted area west of Lebec in the Tehachapi Mountains of California in the Upper Sonoran Life Zone.

Perognathus alticolus, white-eared pocket mouse. p. 221.

6A. Sonoran life zones in mountains and deserts (other than the Salinas and San Joaquin valleys) of California and southeastern Oregon. Under parts tawny, buffy, or white; tail nearly unicolored, with terminal hairs 3–7 mm. long; baculum less than 5.5 mm. in length; interparietal width 3.5–3.8 mm.

Perognathus longimembris, little pocket mouse, p. 219, fig. 143.

6B. Sonoran life zones in the Salinas and San Joaquin valleys of California. Under parts white; tail with terminal hairs 3–6 mm. long; tail faintly bicolored, nearly unicolored; interparietal width about 3.5 mm.

Perognathus inornatus, San Joaquin pocket mouse, p. 221, fig. 142.

7A. Rump, and sometimes flanks, with distinct bristly white or black hairs or with spines mixed with the shorter fur 8

7B. Rump without conspicuous spines or bristles 10

8A. Buffy or fulvous lateral line (sometimes faintly represented) along the body between the belly and the sides 9

8B. No buffy or fulvous lateral line along the sides of the body; ear 6–9 mm. from notch; tail crested with tuft 15–25 mm. long; white bristles on rump and frequently along sides to the shoulders. Mostly Lower Sonoran Life Zone in southern California.

Perognathus spinatus, spiny pocket mouse, p. 221.

9A. Ear 9–14 mm. from notch; tail tuft 9–14 mm. long; white bristles only on hips and rump; skull usually more than 27.5 mm. Sonoran and Transition life zones west of the deserts, and the Sierra Nevada of California.

Perognathus californicus, California pocket mouse, p. 223, fig. 141.

9B. Ear 7–11 mm. from notch; tail tuft 12–16 mm. long; black grooved hairs on the rump (may be inconspicuous until fur is raised by rubbing it backward) and long white spines on the hips; skull usually less than 27.5 mm. Sonoran life zones of extreme southwestern California.

Perognathus fallax, San Diego pocket mouse, p. 219.

10A. Usually less than 210 mm. total length; yellowish brown dorsally; tail sometimes annulated and crested with a buffy tuft, 15–25 mm. long; hind foot usually less than 26 mm. Sandy deserts in the Lower Sonoran Life Zone of southern California.

Perognathus penicillatus, desert pocket mouse, p. 223, fig. 140.

10B. Usually more than 210 mm. total length; grayish dorsally; tail tuft about 10 mm. long; hind foot usually 26 mm. or more. Chiefly Upper Sonoran Life Zone in extreme southern California.

Perognathus baileyi, Bailey pocket mouse, p. 219.

Pocket Mice (*Perognathus*)

The external fur-lined cheek pouches and naked soles of the hind feet identify a pocket mouse from any other similar-sized mammal in the Pacific States. The 11 species have moderately long hind feet, the tails are as long as or longer than the head and body, and the ears are small. Some species have very soft, fine fur; others have thick spines or bristles. Some of the pocket mice are very difficult to identify; one must resort to features of the skull or to the geographic location of the place of capture.

Like other seed-storing mammals, pocket mice are ordinarily solitary.

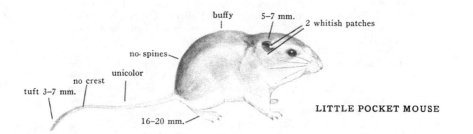

buffy 5–7 mm. 2 whitish patches

no· spines

unicolor

no crest

tuft 3–7 mm.

16–20 mm.

LITTLE POCKET MOUSE

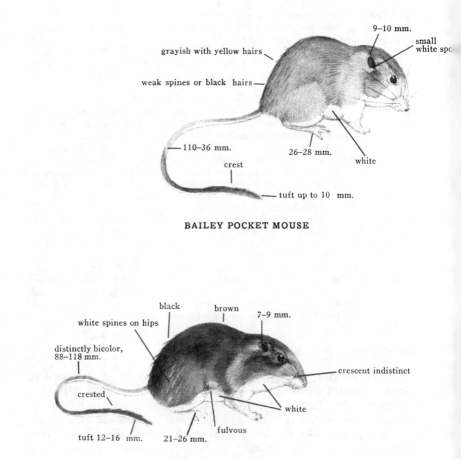

9–10 mm.

small
white spo

grayish with yellow hairs

weak spines or black hairs

110–36 mm.

26–28 mm.

white

crest

tuft up to 10 mm.

BAILEY POCKET MOUSE

black brown 7–9 mm.

white spines on hips

distinctly bicolor,
88–118 mm.

crescent indistinct

crested

white

tuft 12–16 mm. 21–26 mm.

fulvous

SAN DIEGO POCKET MOUSE

Perognathus Dental Formula 1-0-1-3/1-0-1-3

Little pocket mouse (*Perognathus longimembris*). Length 112–55 mm., about five inches; *tail unicolored, 61–77 mm., with tuft 3–7 mm.; hind foot 16–20 mm.*; skull about 23 mm.; mastoids projecting well beyond the occiput; occiput without lateral indentation by the mastoids (fig. 138); interparietal width 3.5–3.8 mm.; baculum length less than 4.7 mm.; *pelage grayish yellow, soft, no bristles or spines; two small but conspicuous patches of lighter hairs at the base of the ear.* Fine, firm, gravelly soil below sandy soils in the Lower and Upper Sonoran life zones of southern and eastern California and southeastern Oregon. Fig. 143, Map 52.

Bailey pocket mouse (*Perognathus baileyi*). Length 200–231 mm., about eight inches; pelage soft, with grayish yellow hairs; *tail 110–36 mm.*, with tuft about 10 mm., yellowish dorsal stripe of tail only a little narrower than light ventral stripe; *hind foot 26–28 mm.*; ear (crown) 9–11 mm.; skull 29.5–33 mm.; mastoids deeply indenting the occiput and projecting somewhat beyond the plane of the occiput (fig. 138); baculum length 10–11 mm.; interparietal width about 6.8 mm.; lower premolar equal to or slightly smaller than the last molar. Rocky sloping terrain on the low desert slopes of the Coast Ranges of extreme southern California, chiefly Upper Sonoran Life Zone. Map 52.

San Diego pocket mouse (*Perognathus fallax*). Length 176–200 mm., about 7.5 inches; *tail 88–118 mm.*, with tuft 12–16 mm.; *hind foot 21–26 mm.*; ears short, 7–9 mm. from notch; skull 26–27 mm.; mastoids large, deeply indenting the sides of the occiput, but barely projecting beyond the level of the occiput (fig. 138); interparietal width about 7.8 mm.; *tail distinctly bicolored and strongly crested, with dark dorsal stripe narrower than light ventral stripe*; pelage harsh, often with black, grooved hairs or spines on the rump and white spines on the hips; buffy band between the belly and the sides. Open, sandy, weed-grown areas in the low desert and foothills in the Lower and Upper Sonoran life zones of southwestern California. Map 52.

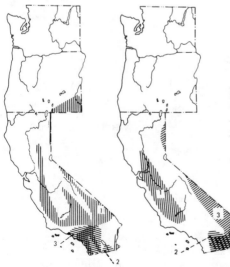

Map 52, left. (1) *Perognathus longimembris*, (2) *Perognathus baileyi*, (3) *Perognathus fallax*. **Map 53, right.** (1) *Perognathus inornatus*, (2) *Perognathus spinatus*, (3) *Perognathus formosus*.

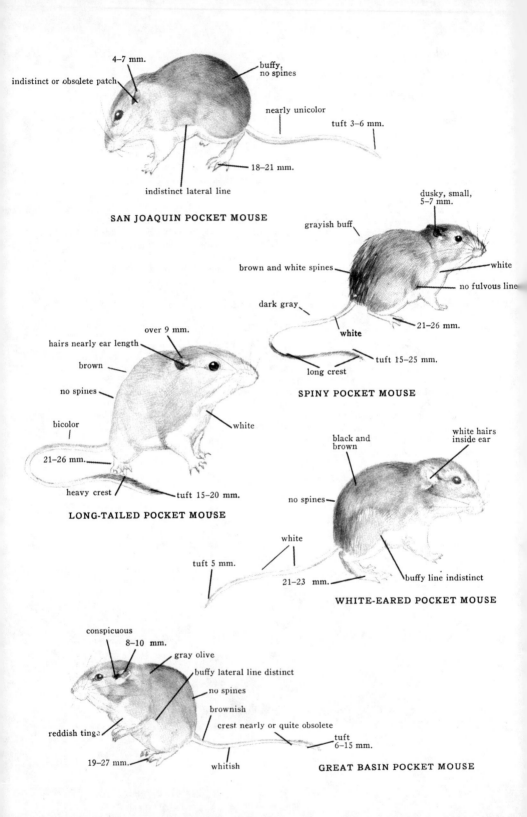

SAN JOAQUIN POCKET MOUSE

4–7 mm.

indistinct or obsolete patch

buffy, no spines

nearly unicolor

tuft 3–6 mm.

18–21 mm.

indistinct lateral line

SPINY POCKET MOUSE

dusky, small, 5–7 mm.

grayish buff

brown and white spines

white

no fulvous line

dark gray

21–26 mm.

white

tuft 15–25 mm.

long crest

LONG-TAILED POCKET MOUSE

over 9 mm.

hairs nearly ear length

brown

no spines

bicolor

21–26 mm.

white

heavy crest

tuft 15–20 mm.

WHITE-EARED POCKET MOUSE

black and brown

white hairs inside ear

no spines

white

tuft 5 mm.

21–23 mm.

buffy line indistinct

GREAT BASIN POCKET MOUSE

conspicuous

8–10 mm.

gray olive

buffy lateral line distinct

no spines

brownish

crest nearly or quite obsolete

reddish tinge

tuft 6–15 mm.

19–27 mm.

whitish

San Joaquin pocket mouse (*Perognathus inornatus*). Length 128–60 mm., about six inches; *tail nearly unicolored, 65–78 mm., with tuft 3–6 mm.; hind foot 18–21 mm.;* ear 4–7 mm.; skull 24–28 mm.; mastoids projecting posteriorly beyond the level of the occiput; occiput not deeply indented laterally by the mastoids (fig. 138); baculum length 6.1 mm.; *pelage orange buffy, soft, no bristles or spines; sometimes patches of lighter hairs at the base of the ear.* Grassy or weedy fine-textured soil in the Lower and Upper Sonoran life zones of the San Joaquin Valley in California. Fig. 142, Map 53.

Spiny pocket mouse (*Perognathus spinatus*). Length 154–204 mm., about seven inches; tail 75–122 mm., crested with tuft 15–25 mm.; hind foot 21–26 mm.; ear dusky and small, 5–7 mm.; skull 24–27 mm.; mastoids small, not reaching to the posterior level of the occiput; mastoids deeply indenting the sides of the occiput (fig. 138); baculum length 9.5–11.3 mm.; interparietal width 7.6–7.7 mm.; pelage harsh, with grooved, conspicuous white spines on the rump, some-times extending to shoulders; no fulvous stripes on the sides; pale yellowish buff or grayish buff. Rough, hot desert terrain among xerophilous plants in the Lower Sonoran Life Zone of southeastern California. Map 53.

Long-tailed pocket mouse (*Perognathus formosus*). Length 164–210 mm., about seven inches; pelage soft, no bristles or spines; long hairs from the front edge of the ear nearly reach across the ear; antitragus of ear narrow at base; light spot at base of ear nearly or quite obsolete; upper parts slate gray or brown; tail bi-colored, 97–118 mm., *heavily crested with tuft 15–20 mm., the tail crest darker than the rest of the body;* hind foot 21–26 mm.; ear over 9 mm., from notch; skull 26-28 mm.; posterior part of the occiput and the mastoids on about the same level; occiput deeply indented by the sides of the mastoids (fig. 138); baculum length 8.8 mm.; interparietal width about 5.8 mm. Gravelly or rocky ground, frequently in or near hot desert canyons; chiefly Lower Sonoran Life Zone in southeastern California. Map 53.

White-eared pocket mouse (*Perognathus alticolus*). Length 147–81 mm., about six inches; tail white, 72–91 mm., with tuft about 5 mm.; hind foot 21–23 mm.; dark (black predominating) dorsally, with *white hairs inside ears;* skull 25.4 mm.; mastoids not deeply indenting the occiput laterally (fig. 138); pelage soft, no bristles or spines. Open grassy places or dry bracken beds of the Yellow Pine Forest and Joshua Tree Woodland in the Transition Life Zone of the Tehachapi and San Bernardino mountains of California. Map 54.

Great Basin pocket mouse (*Perognathus parvus*). Length 148–97 mm., about seven inches; tail 72–101 mm., not crested but with tuft 6–15 mm.; ochraceous buffy overlaid with dark hairs dorsally, with some dark hairs inside the ears; antitragus of ear broad at the base; *hind foot 19–27 mm.;* skull about 27 mm.; posterior level of the occiput and mastoids about equal; occiput not deeply in-dented by the sides of the mastoids (fig. 138); interparietal width about 5.4 mm.; baculum length about 7.5 mm.; gray olive above, white below with a reddish tinge; buffy lateral line; pelage soft, no bristles or spines. Slopes and flats of the Sagebrush, Scrub, and Pinyon-Juniper Woodland, saltbrush and greasewood; chiefly Upper Sonoran Life Zone of the eastern parts of all three states. P. 213, fig. 139, Map 54.

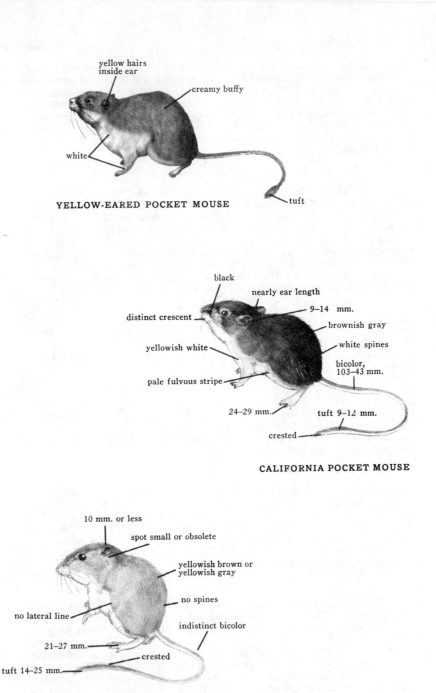

YELLOW-EARED POCKET MOUSE

yellow hairs
inside ear

creamy buffy

white

tuft

black

nearly ear length

distinct crescent

9–14 mm.

brownish gray

yellowish white

white spines

pale fulvous stripe

bicolor,
103–43 mm.

24–29 mm.

tuft 9–12 mm.

crested

CALIFORNIA POCKET MOUSE

10 mm. or less

spot small or obsolete

yellowish brown or
yellowish gray

no spines

no lateral line

indistinct bicolor

21–27 mm.

crested

tuft 14–25 mm.

DESERT POCKET MOUSE

Yellow-eared pocket mouse (*Perognathus xanthonotus*). Length about 170 mm.; tail about 85 mm. and tufted; hind foot about 23 mm.; dorsally ochraceous buffy to cream buffy; with *all yellow hairs inside the ears*; feet and ventral surface white; penicillate tail, white beneath, cream buffy dorsally; mastoids at about the same level as the occiput; occiput not deeply indented by the mastoids (fig. 138); no spines or bristles. Upper Sonoran Life Zone in Kelso Valley, Walker Pass, Tehachapi Mountains, California. Fig. 144, Map 54.

California pocket mouse (*Perognathus californicus*). Length 190–224 mm., about eight inches; *tail bicolored,* 103–43 mm., *with a tuft 9–14 mm.; hind foot 24–29 mm.;* ear elongated, 9–14 mm.; skull 28–30 mm.; mastoids exceedingly small and not reaching the posterior level of the occiput; occiput deeply indented by the sides of the mastoids (fig. 138); baculum length 9.7–10.8 mm.; interparietal width 8.1–8.3 mm.; pelage harsh with conspicuous white, grooved hairs or spines on the rump; *long black or buffy hairs at the forward base of ear nearly as long as the ear; under parts and feet yellowish white*; definite fulvous stripe along the sides. As a rule, on slopes with chaparral growth from the Lower Sonoran into the Transition Life Zone of California, south of San Francisco Bay and west of the Sierra Nevada. Fig. 141, Map 55.

Desert pocket mouse (*Perognathus penicillatus*). Length 153–216 mm., about seven inches; *tail 91–121 mm., indistinctly bicolored, sometimes annulated, and crested with buffy tuft, 14–25 mm.;* hind foot 21–27 mm.; *ear less than 10 mm. from notch with antitragus narrow at base*; skull 25–29 mm.; mastoids hardly projecting to the posterior level of the occiput; occiput very deeply indented by the mastoids laterally (fig. 138); baculum length 9.7–12.5 mm.; interparietal width about 6.9–7.6 mm.; pelage harsh, often with *inconspicuous bristles but no spines on the rump*; very small light spot at the base of the ear (may be obsolete) and no lateral line. Sandy desert floor in the Lower Sonoran Life Zone of southeastern California. Fig. 140, Map 55.

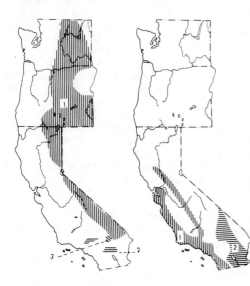

Map 54, left. (1) *Perognathus parvus,* (2) *Perognathus alticolus,* (3) *Perognathus xanthonotus.* **Map 55, right.** (1) *Perognathus californicus,* (2) *Perognathus penicillatus.*

KEY TO KANGAROO MICE AND KANGAROO RATS
(Heteromyidae in part; *Dipodomys* and *Microdipodops*)

Animals in this family have external fur-lined cheek pouches and a tail that is always longer than the head and body length. The bacula (fig. 146) are useful in determining the species. The dental formula is 1-0-1-3/1-0-1-3.

1A. Tip of tail without tuft of hairs 10 mm. or more in length; hind foot less than 32 mm. 2
1B. Tip of tail with tuft of long hairs over 10 mm. in length; hind foot more than 32 mm. 3
2A. Blackish or brownish dorsally; postauricular patches buffy; fur on under parts white-tipped, more or less lead-colored at the base; hind foot 23–25 mm.; premaxillae extending a short distance (less than 1 mm.) behind the nasals. Upper Sonoran Life Zone in eastern California, central and perhaps southeastern Oregon.

> *Microdipodops megacephalus,* dark kangaroo mouse, p. 233, fig. 148.

2B. Pale or buffy yellowish dorsally; postauricular patches white; fur on under parts white to the base; hind foot 25–27 mm.; premaxillae extending 1–2 mm. behind the nasals. Upper Sonoran Life Zone in extreme eastern California.

> *Microdipodops pallidus,* pallid kangaroo mouse, p. 233.

3A. With only four toes on the hind foot (no small functionless claw on the side of the foot) 4
3B. With four functional toes and a small claw or toe about a third of the way from the tip of the inside toe (outside on skins) to the ankle . . . 7
4A. Hind foot less than 50 mm. 5
4B. Hind foot more than 50 mm.; pale ochraceous buff dorsally; no ventral tail stripe. Wind-drifted sand in Lower Sonoran Life Zone of southeastern California.

> *Dipodomys deserti,* desert kangaroo rat, p. 233, fig. 149.

5A. Less than 267 mm. total length; total length of skull less than 38 mm. 6
5B. More than 267 mm. total length; total length of skull more than 38 mm. North of a line between San Francisco Bay and Mariposa County, and northwest of Honey Lake, Lassen County, west of Clear Lake, Modoc County, California, and north into central southern Oregon.

> *Dipodomys heermanni,* Heermann kangaroo rat, p. 227, fig. 155.

6A. White lateral tail stripes at least as wide or wider than the dark dorsal tail stripe. In Sonoran life zones in the deserts of the southern third of California (not in the San Joaquin Valley).

> *Dipodomys merriami,* Merriam kangaroo rat, p. 231, fig. 154.

6B. White lateral tail stripe noticeable, not as wide as the dark dorsal tail stripe. Lower Sonoran Life Zone in the San Joaquin Valley of California.

> *Dipodomys nitratoides,* San Joaquin kangaroo rat, p. 231, fig. 151.

7A. Hind foot usually less than 48 mm.; skull usually less than 45 mm. . 8
7B. Hind foot usually 48 mm. or more; skull over 45 mm.; among ephedra of the Lower Sonoran Life Zone along the western side of the San Joaquin Valley, California.

> *Dipodomys ingens,* giant kangaroo rat, p. 233, fig. 150.

8A. West of the Sierra Nevada, but also north from within southern Santa Barbara and Kern counties, California 9
8B. East of the Sierra Nevada and Cascade Mountains, but also south of Santa Barbara and Kern counties, California 11

9A. Ear from crown usually more than 15 mm.; maxillary arch with angle weak and rounded (fig. 145); from San Francisco Bay south into Santa Barbara County 10

9B. Ear from crown usually less than 15 mm.; maxillary arch with a strong or weak angle (fig. 145); north from within Santa Barbara and Kern counties.

Dipodomys heermanni, Heermann kangaroo rat, p. 227, fig. 155.

10A. Ear mostly brownish, 16.5 mm. or more from crown; at mid-length, the dark ventral tail stripe is narrower than the lateral white stripe. Chiefly Upper Sonoran Life Zone in or near San Benito County, California.

Dipodomys elephantinus, big-eared kangaroo rat, p. 229.

10B. Ear mostly blackish, usually 16.5 mm. or less from crown; at mid-length the dark ventral stripe is wider than the lateral white stripe. In the Upper Sonoran Life Zone from San Francisco Bay south to San Luis Obispo County, California.

Dipodomys venustus, Santa Cruz kangaroo rat, p. 229.

11A. Lower incisors awl-shaped, each tooth usually less than 1 mm. wide (fig. 145) 12

11B. Lower incisors chisel-shaped, each tooth usually at least 1 mm. wide (fig. 145); dark ventral tail stripe wider than the white lateral stripe and extends to the tip of the caudal vertebrae; width of maxillary arch less than 3.9 mm., strongly angled (fig. 145); tail ratio to head and body 130 to 150 per cent. Upper Sonoran Life Zone in dry regions of southeastern Oregon and eastern California.

Dipodomys microps, Great Basin kangaroo rat, p. 231, fig. 153.

12A. Mojave Desert, San Jacinto Valley (Riverside County), and other dry regions of southern and eastern California, eastern Oregon, and south-central Washington 13

12B. Coast ranges south from Santa Barbara County and east into the Tehachapi, San Bernardino, and San Gabriel mountains, California. Maxillary arch weakly angled, width usually over 4 mm. (fig. 145); tail ratio to head and body about 155 per cent.

Dipodomys agilis, Pacific kangaroo rat, p. 233.

13A. Total length usually more than 280 mm.; width of maxillary arch usually more than 5 mm. (fig. 145). Eastern and southern California . . . 14

13B. Total length usually less than 280 mm.; width of maxillary arch usually less than 5 mm.; dark tail stripe about as wide as the lateral white stripe and does not extend to the end of the caudal vertebrae; tail ratio to head and body about 120 to 130 per cent. Extreme eastern California, eastern half of Oregon, and extreme south-central Washington in Upper Sonoran Life Zone.

Dipodomys ordii, Ord kangaroo rat, p. 227 fig. 152.

14A. San Jacinto Valley in Riverside and San Bernardino counties, California, in lower Sonoran Life Zone. Hind foot ordinarily less than 42.5 mm.; tail 145 to 154 per cent of head and body length; white tail stripe about half as wide as the dorsal tail stripe, dark ventral stripe extends to the end of caudal vertebrae; angle on the maxillary arch with a distinct heel (fig. 145) and usually more than 5 mm. wide.

Dipodomys stephensi, Stephens kangaroo rat, p. 229.

14B. San Bernardino County and north through eastern California to Sierra County. Hind foot ordinarily more than 42.5 mm.; tail about 140 per cent of head and body with dark ventral stripe not extending to the end of the caudal vertebrae; maxillary arch with a prominent angle (fig. 145) and usually more than 5 mm. wide

Dipodomys panamintinus, Panamint kangaroo rat, p. 229.

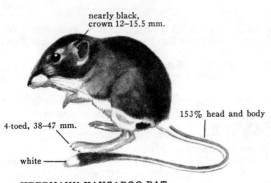

nearly black,
crown 12–15.5 mm.

153% head and body

4-toed, 38–47 mm.

white

HEERMANN KANGAROO RAT

(North from San Francisco Bay and Mariposa County)

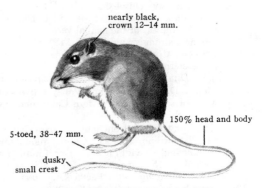

nearly black,
crown 12–14 mm.

150% head and body

5-toed, 38–47 mm.

dusky,
small crest

HEERMANN KANGAROO RAT

(South from San Francisco Bay and San Joaquin County)

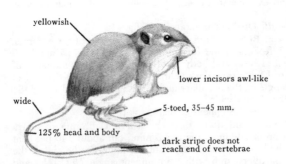

yellowish

lower incisors awl-like

wide

5-toed, 35–45 mm.

125% head and body

dark stripe does not
reach end of vertebrae

ORD KANGAROO RAT

Heermann kangaroo rat (*Dipodomys heermanni*). Length 269–340 mm., about 12 inches; tail 160–217 mm.; hind foot 38–47 mm.; ear (crown) 12–15.5 mm., *dusky or nearly black*; skull 38–41.2 mm.; *maxillary arch with a prominent angle,* width 4–6 mm. (fig. 145); baculum length 11.2 mm. (fig. 146); auditory bullae not as high as skull when viewed posteriorly; normally four toes on the hind foot of those found north of San Francisco Bay and Coulterville, Mariposa County, California; but with five toes, including the small claw on the side of the foot, south of San Francisco Bay and San Joaquin County; *tail light gray or abruptly whitish, tipped with little or no crest,* and about 150 per cent of the head and body length; ears frequently appear blackish. Valley Grassland and Foothill Woodland of California north of Ventura County and west of the Sierra Nevada to southwestern Oregon in the Lower and Upper Sonoran life zones. P. 236, fig. 155, Map 56.

Ord kangaroo rat (*Dipodomys ordii*). Length 228–61 mm., about 9.5 inches; tail 127–39 mm.; *hind foot 35–45 mm.*; ear (crown) 9–13 mm.; skull 35.1–37.8 mm.; maxillary arch width about 3.9–4.7 mm. (fig. 145), with prominent angles; nasals 12.7–14.4 mm.; baculum length 11.3 mm. (fig. 146); *five-toed*, including the small claw on the side of the hind foot; tail crested about 40 per cent of the way up from the tip; tail ratio to head and body about 120 to 130 per cent; *white tail stripe is as wide as or wider than the ventral dark tail stripe; ventral tail stripe never reaches the end of the vertebrae;* more yellowish than brown dorsally; *lower incisors awl-shaped, with rounded surfaces in front* (fig. 145); weight about 45 grams; black whisker patch small or lacking; *lining of the cheek pouches white.* Sagebrush Scrub in open sandy areas in the Upper Sonoran Life Zone of extreme eastern California, and in the eastern half of Oregon and extreme southern Washington. P. 236, fig. 152, Map 57.

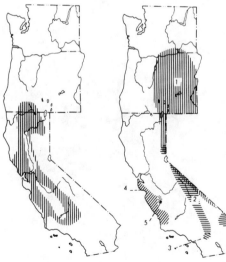

Map 56, left. *Dipodomys heermanni.* **Map 57, right,** (1) *Dipodomys ordii,* (2) *Dipodomys panamintinus,* (3) *Dipodomys stephensi,* (4) *Dipodomys venustus,* (5) *Dipodomys elephantinus.*

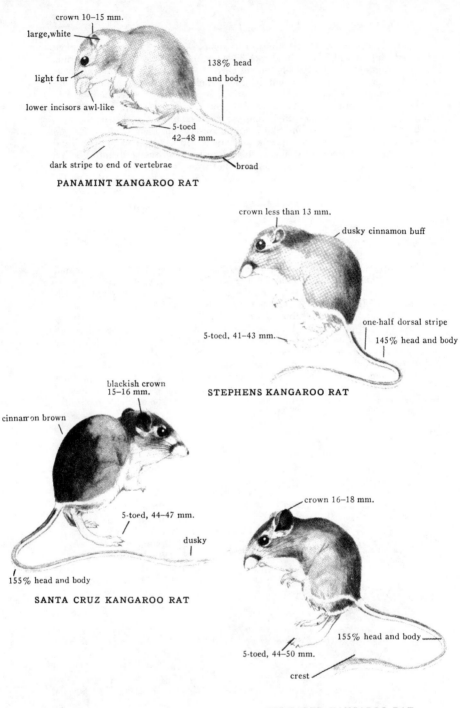

crown 10–15 mm.

large, white

light fur

lower incisors awl-like

138% head
and body

5-toed
42–48 mm.

dark stripe to end of vertebrae

broad

PANAMINT KANGAROO RAT

crown less than 13 mm.

dusky cinnamon buff

one-half dorsal stripe

5-toed, 41–43 mm.

145% head and body

STEPHENS KANGAROO RAT

blackish crown
15–16 mm.

cinnamon brown

5-toed, 44–47 mm.

dusky

155% head and body

SANTA CRUZ KANGAROO RAT

crown 16–18 mm.

155% head and body

5-toed, 44–50 mm.

crest

BIG-EARED KANGAROO RAT

Panamint kangaroo rat (*Dipodomys panamintinus*). Length 285–315 mm.; about 12 inches; tail 156–82 mm.; hind foot 42–48 mm.; ear (crown) 10–15 mm., sometimes almost black; skull 35.8–42 mm.; maxillary arch with a *prominent rounded angle,* its width about 4.9–6.1 mm. (fig. 145); baculum length 10.7 mm. (fig. 146); five-toed, including the small claw on the side of the hind foot; *light cheek patches,* sometimes obscured by dusky, dark whisker patches, may or may not join over the nose; large white spot behind ear; *tail ratio to head and body about 138 per cent; ventral tail stripe extends to end of vertebrae;* weight usually more than 70 grams; *lower incisors rounded on the outer surface* similar to those of *D. ordii* (see fig. 145). Joshua trees on gravelly desert flats in the Creosote Bush Scrub and Pinyon-Juniper Woodland from Mono County south to the Mojave Desert, California, in the Upper Sonoran and the lower part of the Transition life zones. Map 57.

Stephens kangaroo rat (*Dipodomys stephensi*). Length 277–300 mm., about 11.5 inches; tail 164–80 mm.; hind foot 41–43 mm.; *ear (crown) about 12 mm.;* skull 38.3–40.6 mm.; *width of maxillary arch 5.1–6 mm.* (fig. 145); auditory bullae are elongate globose when viewed from above, and are as high as the skull when viewed from behind; *white tail stripe about half as wide as the dorsal tail stripe at mid-tail; five-toed,* including the small claw on the side of the hind foot; tail ratio to the head and body about 145 per cent; *dusky cinnamon buff.* Only in San Jacinto Valley in southern California, chiefly in the Lower Sonoran Life Zone. Map 57.

Santa Cruz kangaroo rat (*Dipodomys venustus*). Length 293–332 mm., about 12 inches; tail 175–203 mm.; *hind foot 44–47 mm.; ear (crown) 15–16 mm.; skull 41–43 mm.;* maxillary arch width 4.8–5.7 mm., with rounded angle (fig. 145); nasals 15.3–15.8 mm.; *five-toed,* including the small claw on the side of the hind foot; black top of the nose connects black whisker patches; *tail dusky-tipped and crested,* dull white at the bases of the hairs; tail ratio to head and body about 155 per cent. Chaparral and Foothill Woodland, chiefly Upper Sonoran Life Zone of west-central California. (Some mammologists believe this species may not be specifically distinct from *D. agilis.*) Map 57.

Big-eared kangaroo rat (*Dipodomys elephantinus*). Length 305–36 mm., about 13 inches; tail 183–210 mm.; *hind foot 44–50 mm.; ear (crown) 16–18 mm.; skull 41.7–43.9 mm.;* maxillary arch width 4.8–5.8 mm., with a moderate angle (fig. 145); nasals 14.9–16.4 mm.; *five-toed,* including the small claw on the side of the hind foot; *tail heavily crested and tufted, tipped with dark hairs with gray bases;* tail ratio to head and body about 155 per cent. Chaparral in the Upper Sonoran Life Zone of west-central California. Map 57.

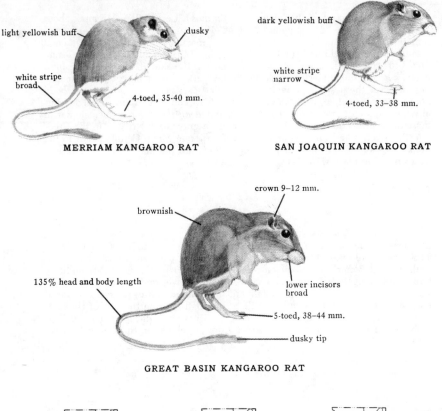

light yellowish buff

dusky

white stripe broad

4-toed, 35-40 mm.

MERRIAM KANGAROO RAT

dark yellowish buff

white stripe narrow

4-toed, 33–38 mm.

SAN JOAQUIN KANGAROO RAT

crown 9–12 mm.

brownish

135% head and body length

lower incisors broad

5-toed, 38–44 mm.

dusky tip

GREAT BASIN KANGAROO RAT

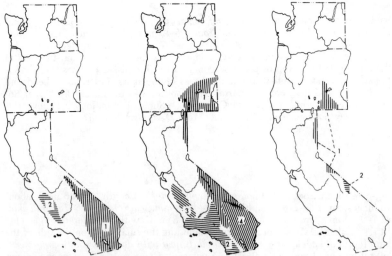

Map 58, left. (1) *Dipodomys merriami*, (2) *Dipodomys nitratoides*. **Map 59, center.** (1) *Dipodomys microps*, (2) *Dipodomys agilis*, (3) *Dipodomys ingens*, (4) *Dipodomys deserti*. **Map 60, right.** (1) *Microdipodops megacephalus*, (2) *Microdipodops pallidus*.

Merriam kangaroo rat (*Dipodomys merriami*). Length 220–60 mm., about 9.5 inches; tail 123–57 mm.; hind foot 35–40 mm.; ear (crown) 10–12 mm.; skull 33.6–37.3 mm.; width of maxillary arch 4.6–5.5 mm. (fig. 145), *with rounded angle;* baculum length 8–11 mm. (fig. 146); *four-toed,* small claw on the side of the hind foot lacking; dark whisker patches not connected across nose; *white tail stripe is always noticeably wider than the dark tail stripes;* tail tuft is brown or blackish, and there is a *dorsal crest* that extends 40 per cent of the way up from the tip; tail slender, ratio to head and body length about 145 per cent; *light yellowish buff above.* Mostly below the pinyon belt on the Alkali Sink, Creosote Bush Scrub, Shadscale Scrub, and Sagebrush Scrub south of the Tehachapi Mountains in southern California deserts in the Lower and Upper Sonoran life zones. P. 235, fig. 154, Map 58.

San Joaquin kangaroo rat (*Dipodomys nitratoides*). Length 211–67 mm., about 9.5 inches; tail 120–62 mm.; hind foot 33–38 mm.; ear (notch) 11–13 mm.; skull 30.7–35.6 mm.; width of maxillary arch 4.1–5 mm., with a sharp angle (fig. 145); baculum length 13.3 mm. (fig. 146); *four-toed,* small claw on the side of the hind foot is lacking; *tail buffy-tipped, with a crest of longer hairs* on the distal third; dark whisker patches connected by dark fur across the nose; *light tail stripes never noticeably wider than the dark tail stripes;* tail ratio to head and body about 142 per cent; *dark yellowish buff.* Often on alkaline soil in the Valley Grassland in western San Joaquin Valley, California, in the lower Sonoran Life Zone. Fig. 151, Map 58.

Great Basin kangaroo rat (*Dipodomys microps*). Length 244–90 mm., about 11 inches; tail 140–73 mm.; hind foot 38–44 mm.; ear (crown) 9–12 mm.; skull 34.4–38.9 mm.; *maxillary arch width 3.0–3.8 mm.* with a weak angle (fig. 145); nasals 11.9–13.5 mm.; baculum length 8.4 mm.; *weight 55–75 grams; five-toed, including the small claw on the side of the hind foot; lower incisors with flat chisel-like outer surfaces* (fig. 145); *tail ratio to head and body about 130 to 140 per cent; white tail stripe narrower than the dark dorsal and ventral tail stripes;* dark ventral stripe goes all the way to the tip of the vertebrae; more brown than yellow dorsally. Sagebrush Scrub, Shadscale Scrub, and Pinyon-Juniper Woodland in the Upper Sonoran Life Zone of northeastern California and southeastern Oregon in low hot valleys. Fig. 153, Map 59.

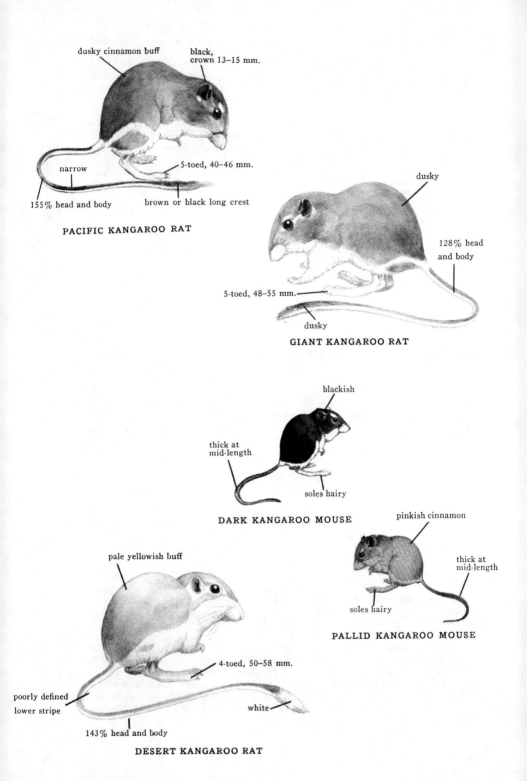

dusky cinnamon buff

black,
crown 13–15 mm.

narrow

5-toed, 40–46 mm.

155% head and body

brown or black long crest

PACIFIC KANGAROO RAT

dusky

128% head
and body

5-toed, 48–55 mm.

dusky

GIANT KANGAROO RAT

blackish

thick at
mid-length

soles hairy

DARK KANGAROO MOUSE

pinkish cinnamon

thick at
mid-length

soles hairy

PALLID KANGAROO MOUSE

pale yellowish buff

4-toed, 50–58 mm.

poorly defined
lower stripe

white

143% head and body

DESERT KANGAROO RAT

Pacific kangaroo rat (*Dipodomys agilis*). Length 265–319 mm., about 12 inches; tail 155–97 mm.; *hind foot 40–46 mm.; ear (crown) 13–15 mm.*; maxillary arch weakly angled, width about 4.1–5.3 mm. (fig. 145); nasals 13.2–15 mm.; baculum length 9.6 mm. (fig. 146); *five-toed*, including the small claw on the side of the hind foot; *white tail stripes almost as wide as the dorsal tail stripe at mid-tail*; tail ratio to head and body about 155 per cent; average weight is less than 70 grams; *dusky cinnamon buff; tail tuft and crest is dull brownish black,* with gray at the bases of the hairs. Coastal Sagebrush Scrub, chiefly Upper Sonoran Life Zone of southwestern California. (Some mammalogists believe this species may not be specifically distinct from *D. heermanni.*) Map 59.

Giant kangaroo rat (*Dipodomys ingens*). Length 311–47 mm, about 13 inches; tail 174–98 mm.; *hind foot 48–55 mm.*; ear (crown) 13 mm.; skull 43.3–46.6 mm.; width of maxillary arch 5.6–6.2 mm., with rounded angle (fig. 145); baculum length 12.7 mm. (fig. 146); *five-toed*, including the small claw on the side of the hind foot; *tail ratio to head and body about 128 per cent*; all tail stripes well developed and *tip is dusky.* Valley Grassland among ephedra, filaree, and peppergrass in western San Joaquin Valley in California in the Lower Sonoran Life Zone. P. 239, fig. 150, Map 59.

Desert kangaroo rat (*Dipodomys deserti*). Length 305–77 mm., about 14 inches; tail 180–215 mm.; *hind foot 50–58 mm.*; ear (crown) 12–15 mm.; skull 42–47.7 mm.; *maxillary arch width about 3.6–4.8 mm.*, with a moderate angle (fig. 145); nasals 15.3–17.9 mm.; baculum length 9.5 mm. (fig. 150); weight 80–130 grams; *four-toed*, small claw on the side of the hind foot is lacking; *dark ventral tail stripe is lacking or poorly defined; white-tipped tail* with moderate crest; tail ratio to head and body 143 to 161 per cent. Wind-drifted sand in the Alkali Sink, Shadscale Scrub, and Creosote Bush Scrub in the Lower and Upper Sonoran life zones of southeastern California. Fig. 149, Map 59.

Dark kangaroo mouse (*Microdipodops megacephalus*). Length 148–77 mm., about 6.5 inches; tail 74–100 mm.; hind foot 23–25 mm.; skull about 30 mm.; with premaxillae extending a little back of the nasals (less than 1 mm.); *upper parts blackish or grayish brown with reddish hue*; fur on under parts white-tipped, with lead-colored base; *tail thicker at mid-length than at either end*; tail without tuft or longitudinal stripes; soles of hind feet entirely covered with hair; *tail dorsally and distally tipped with black.* Northeastern border of California from the east side of Mono Lake north to southeastern Oregon; Shadscale Scrub, Sagebrush Scrub, and Alkali Sink, in the fine loose sands and gravels in the Upper Sonoran Life Zone. P. 240, fig. 148, Map 60.

Pallid kangaroo mouse (*Microdipodops pallidus*). Length 150–69 mm., about 6.5 inches; tail 74–94 mm.; hind foot 25–27 mm.; skull about 30 mm, with premaxillae extending well behind the nasals; fur, *light pinkish cinnamon above and white to the base below*; upper part of the distal end of the tail same color as back; *tail thicker at mid-length than at the ends*; tail without tuft or longitudinal stripes. Valley lying east of the White Mountains in Mono and Inyo counties of California, fine wind-blown sand of the Alkali Sink and Shadscale Scrub in the Upper Sonoran Life Zone. Map 60.

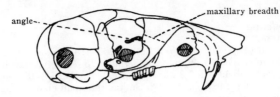

Skull of *Dipodomys* showing position of maxillary arch

Dipodomys ordii, showing awl-shaped lower incisors

Dipodomys microps, showing chisel-shaped lower incisors

*Dipodomys
heermanni californicus*

*Dipodomys
heermanni swarthi*

*Dipodomys
panamintinus mohavensis*

Dipodomys stephensi

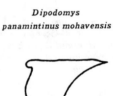

Dipodomys merriami

Dipodomys nitratoides

Dipodomys ingens

Dipodomys ordii

Dipodomys agilis

*Dipodomys
venustus sanctiluciae*

*Dipodomys
venustus venustus*

Dipodomys elephantinus

Dipodomys microps

Dipodomys deserti

Fig. 145. Shape of the maxillary arch and lower incisors in various species of kangaroo rat.

Kangaroo Rats (*Dipodomys*)

The kangaroo rat has deep fur-lined cheek pouches, large hind legs, and tail always longer than the head and body. The hind feet have hairy soles. There are four functional toes with or without a functionless fifth toe high up on the inside of the foot. The tail in most species has dark dorsal and ventral longitudinal bands with white lateral longitudinal stripes, and is tufted with longer hairs. There is usually a white band of fur that crosses the hip from the base of the tail. The ears are small. The tracks left by hopping show only the hind feet and tail marks (fig. 147). The shape of the maxillary bone is different in the various species; therefore it is important in classification (fig. 145), as are the bacula (fig. 146).

Kangaroo rats are usually solitary animals. The Merriam kangaroo rat is perhaps the most common species in California deserts. Its home range covers a little less than half an acre (Reynolds, 1960). The male and female ranges do not overlap (the female's range is slightly smaller than the male's), and hence they may be considered *territories* from which other

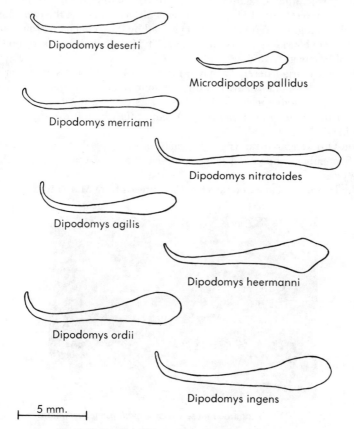

Dipodomys deserti

Microdipodops pallidus

Dipodomys merriami

Dipodomys nitratoides

Dipodomys agilis

Dipodomys heermanni

Dipodomys ordii

Dipodomys ingens

5 mm.

Fig. 146. Bacula of kangaroo rats and kangaroo mice.

Fig. 147. Tracks of kangaroo rat.

individuals are excluded. This animal shows two peaks of activity nightly, one about 9 P.M., the other near 4 A.M. There are two peaks of pregnancy that correspond to the periods of growth of new vegetation in the spring and fall. The gestation period is from 17 to 23 days, with normally two young in each litter. Captives have lived at least five years.

The San Joaquin kangaroo rat (fig. 151) is closely related to the Merriam kangaroo rat (fig. 154), and it is difficult to distinguish the two. However, their ranges in California are separated by the Tehachapi Mountains, and they are considered separate species. The San Joaquin rat feeds on the seeds of brome grass and wild oats.

The much larger desert kangaroo rat (fig. 149) has a gestation period of 29 to 32 days and usually has three to four young in a litter. It appears to be a *stenoecious* species with respect to its habitat, for it can live only in a narrow range of environment—it occurs *only* where it can dig its burrows in wind-blown sand.

The Ord kangaroo rat (fig. 152) may breed twice between February and September. The young may reproduce the same year in which they were born.

The Heermann kangaroo rat (fig. 155) breeds from March to August. It

Fig. 148. Dark kangaroo mouse (*Microdipodops megacephalus*).

Fig. 149. Desert kangaroo rat (*Dipodomys deserti*).

Fig. 150. Giant kangaroo rat (*Dipodomys ingens*).

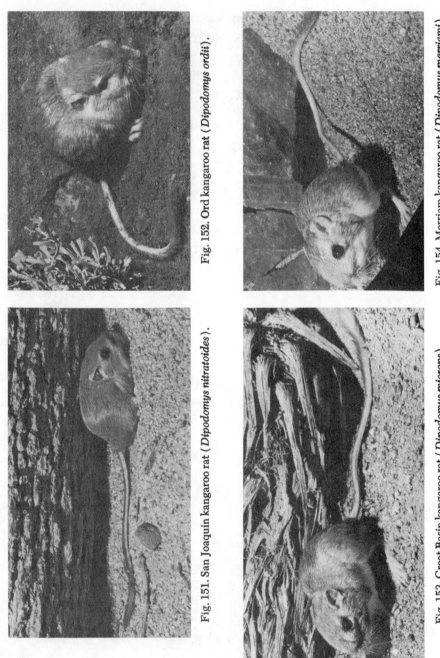

Fig. 152. Ord kangaroo rat (*Dipodomys ordii*).

Fig. 154. Merriam kangaroo rat (*Dipodomys merriami*).

Fig. 151. San Joaquin kangaroo rat (*Dipodomys nitratoides*).

Fig. 153. Great Basin kangaroo rat (*Dipodomys microps*).

may have as many as three litters of two to five young each. Females born in the first litter may have two litters of their own before winter. Thus one female in the spring may be responsible for 30 pregnancies in one season.

As might be expected of animals with such a high reproductive potential, the life span is relatively short. In a study of more than 2,100 animals live-trapped over a four-year period in an 80-acre area, less than 5 per cent lived beyond one year. One desert kangaroo rat, however, is known to have lived more than five years.

The giant kangaroo rat (fig. 150) of the San Joaquin Valley in California dries seeds in thimble-like holes around the entrance to its burrow before it takes them underground. It is known to consume daily 18 grams of food per 100 grams of its weight.

Kangaroo rats, although they live in the hot, waterless desert, have the same body water content as do other mammals—about 65 per cent of the body weight. Two investigators (Schmidt-Nielsen and Schmidt-Nielsen, 1953), working with the banner-tailed kangaroo rat of Arizona (*Dipodomys spectabilis*) and the Merriam kangaroo rat (*Dipodomys merriami*), found that they do not store water in their bodies for later use. They actually increase their water content when fed dry seeds with no drinking water at all. It is now known that much of the water comes from food oxidation. It was found that one gram of carbohydrates will produce .6 gram of water when oxidized; fats make 1.1 grams, and proteins .3 gram. Some free water, of course, is absorbed in the seed, depending on the amount of moisture in the air. All of this, however, is a very small amount of water for an animal the size of a kangaroo rat. Then it was found that water was conserved by means of the kidneys, which are able to dispose of nitrogenous wastes with an extremely small output of water. The concentration of urea in the urine may run as high as 24 per cent, whereas in man it rarely is over 6 per cent. Thus the kangaroo rat needs only one-fourth as much water to eliminate a given amount of urea as man. Like other rodents, it does not cool itself by sweating or panting, and the feces contain little water.

The work of Church (1962) shows that the maritime Santa Cruz kangaroo rat (*Dipodomys venustus*) is not nearly so efficient in water conservation. When deprived of free water, it loses weight rapidly. Apparently the desert-dwelling species have become genetically different in their physiology.

The ability to metabolize dry food and the specialized kidneys are still not enough to maintain the necessary body water content. Actual tests demonstrate that the animal can maintain its water balance while subsisting on a dry diet only if the moisture in the air is equal to that present when the relative humidity is greater than 10 per cent at an air temperature of 75° F. The desert air is often somewhat drier than this during the day. But the kangaroo rat is a nocturnal animal, remaining in its den during the day, where there is more moisture in the air, and coming out at night, when there is less evaporation and the humidity is higher.

Fig. 155. Heermann kangaroo rat (*Dipodomys heermanni*).

Kangaroo Mice (*Microdipodops*)

There are two species in this genus. The kangaroo mice have deep fur-lined cheek pouches like the pocket mice (*Perognathus*) and kangaroo rats (*Dipodomys*). They differ from the pocket mice in having densely haired soles on the hind feet and from the kangaroo rats in not having dark dorsal and ventral longitudinal bands along the tail. They differ from both in having a fat tail with its largest diameter at mid-length. Fat is stored in this thick, nonpenicillated tail. The tail is also used for balancing (Hall, 1946).

Kangaroo mice are nocturnal and are found on sandy, mellow soil among the sagebrush. Their burrows, usually closed during the day, are not easily found. They are frequently trapped by making a trench an inch or two deep. Along the trench a few seeds or rolled oats are sprinkled and a trap is set.

The favorite food of the dark kangaroo mouse (*Microdipodops megacephalus*) (fig. 148), in southeastern Oregon, according to Bailey (1936), appears to be the black seeds of the desert star (*Mentzelia albicaulis*).

The burrows of kangaroo mice are from four to six feet long and about one foot below the surface. They usually have at least two entrances and no nest or food chambers (at least in summer). The young average four to a litter, with a range of from one to six or seven. Owls, foxes, badgers, and weasels are probably the chief enemies. Kangaroo mice are of little or no economic importance.

The pallid kangaroo mouse, like the kangaroo rats and pocket mice, lives in the desert. Like the little pocket mouse, it shows well-developed patterns of irregular hibernation and estivation (Bartholomew and MacMillen, 1961). These mice may become dormant at ambient temperatures ranging from $41°$ to $79°$ F. The metabolism can be lowered in summer and winter, which conserves water as well as energy.

Family **Castoridae** (Beavers)

Dental Formula 1-0-1-3/1-0-1-3

There is one species in this rodent family in North America, the beaver (*Castor canadensis*) (fig. 156). It is the largest rodent in North America, weighing up to 74 pounds. Its large size, flat scaly tail, and webbed hind feet easily distinguish the beaver from any other native mammal, and even from the feral similar-sized South American nutria, which has a round tail. There is no postorbital process on the frontal bone, and the antorbital foramen is smaller than the *foramen magnum*. The intestine and urogenital system open into a common cloaca, which makes the identification of sex difficult.

Certainly no other animal was more responsible for the early development of the nation west of the Appalachian Mountains than the beaver. The quest for its valuable pelt led the trappers to make friends with the Indians and to become acquainted with the country and the routes over which they later were to guide the long wagon trains to Oregon and California. Beavers are still rather numerous locally at various places in the Pacific States. The trapping season is usually closed on beavers, but where they do damage or become too numerous, they are taken under special permit.

A great deal of beaver lore does not stand the test of scientific inquiry. A few misconceptions are discussed in the hope of encouraging more accurate observations and ultimately a truer understanding of these large rodents.

Beavers fell trees toward the water, not because they are good woodsmen but because stream-side trees generally lean that way. A beaver dam is arched across the stream, not because the beaver is a good engineer but because the current carries the material that way while the dam is being built. Moreover, a beaver dam arches downstream or upstream depending upon whether its construction is started from the banks or from some favorable anchor in the stream itself. There is no evidence to support the belief that a beaver "mates for life" or the stories about old male beavers remaining "bachelors" after their mates have been killed. There are stories about the beaver carrying loads on its broad tail as it swims along and pictures showing the paddle-like organ used as a trowel to plaster mud on its dams and houses. However, competent mammalogists have never observed these alleged uses of a beaver's tail.

Yet there is much about the beaver that is interesting if we interpret its behavior as a rodent and not as a being endowed with moral and intellectual understanding.

Most native beavers living in the valleys have nests in burrows in the banks of deep streams and are not so inclined to construct dams and houses (fig. 157) as are the beavers introduced from other places. In shallow mountain streams the beaver, which does not hibernate, would find it difficult to get food in winter were it not for the deep ponds that fill behind its

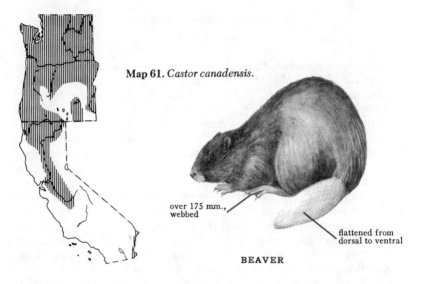

Map 61. *Castor canadensis.*

over 175 mm., webbed

flattened from dorsal to ventral

BEAVER

Beaver (*Castor canadensis*). Length 1,025–1,200 mm., about four feet; tail 350–420 mm.; hind foot 175–205 mm.; ear (crown) 23–28 mm.; skull 113–30 mm. basilar length; largest of all North American rodents, weight sometimes over 60 pounds; *hind feet large and fully webbed, with a divided claw on the second digit; tail scaly and flattened from top to bottom*; golden to dark brown above, somewhat lighter below. Native in the lowlands along Colorado, San Joaquin, Sacramento, Pit, and Klamath rivers of California and Oregon; beavers from other states have now been introduced widely along the Columbia River and up into the Canadian Life Zone in the Cascades of Washington. P. 241, fig. 156, Map 61.

dams. Green twigs and sticks are "mudded down" on the bottoms of these ponds in autumn, and the bark is peeled off and eaten after the pond freezes over. However, even in the lowlands, where food is always plentiful, beavers build dams and houses if deep water is not readily available for safety.

It is interesting to watch a beaver pond late in the afternoon when the animal begins its nocturnal activities. Usually the first sign of its presence is a V-shaped series of ripples on the quiet surface of the water. Closer inspection shows the nostrils, eyes, and ears of a beaver silently swimming at the convergence of the lines of waves. In the water the tail seems to be used as a rudder rather than a propeller. If the observer moves, there is a resounding plop as the beaver slaps its tail on the surface and dives to an underwater entrance of its house or burrow. This sound serves to warn other beavers of danger. If there is no alarm, the animal dives to bring up a load of mud, held between the forepaws and the chin, and places it on the dam. After circling the pond, it silently leaves the water, ambling awk-

Fig. 156. Beaver (*Castor canadensis*).

Fig. 157. Beaver dam and house.

wardly up a trail to the base of a willow, cottonwood, or aspen. Here the big creature sits up on its hind legs, using its tail as a prop, and gnaws chips from the tree. Most of the trees felled are less than a foot in diameter. Once the tree is down, the twigs and smooth green bark are eaten or cut into suitable lengths and stored in the pond for winter use. Besides green bark, beavers eat willow rootlets, grasses, cattails, tules, and pond lilies.

Each sex has two pairs of large glands in its abdomen, which open through the cloaca. One pair secrets a yellow substance called castoreum, and the other pair secretes an oil; both are used extensively during the mating season. The function of the glands is not well known; but the secretions are deposited on piles of leaves, sticks, and mud at the water's edge, supposedly to pass along information.

A litter consists of two to six young, called kits, which are born in April and May in the house or burrow. They are well furred at birth. A typical colony consists of an adult male and female and two litters.

Man is the beaver's worst enemy. The coyote, bobcat, and mountain lion may kill and eat a few of these rodents when they venture far from the deep water. Beavers harbor a number of internal worm parasites, and a species of beetle that lives in the fur is found only on beavers.

Sometimes the animals do considerable damage by damming irrigation canals and thus causing breaks in levees, and by flooding roads and fields when they build dams across small streams. However, the dams may raise the water level in a meadow so that the entire pasture is kept green by sub-irrigation during a dry season. In Plumas County, California, six beavers were introduced one winter by the United States Forest Service into a stream that would have dried up entirely in summer because of a recent forest fire. The beavers established a series of dams, which impounded the winter and spring runoff. As a result, the small stream now runs throughout the year and hundreds of acres of meadowland farther down the stream are subirrigated and kept green, thus supporting cattle for weeks longer than before the beavers were introduced.

Two pairs of beavers were introduced on Sagehen Creek, Nevada County, California, in 1945. They had increased to about 30 animals ten years later and were distributed in five colonies along the stream. Here the interaction between the beaver and its two chief food and building materials (willows and aspens) were studied by Hall (1960). Aspen is preferred to willow as food, although willow is readily eaten as the aspen decreases. After all the trees are cut near the colony, the animals move up or down the stream to a new location, leaving the cut-over area to reforest. Willows are cut on a sustained-use basis as practiced by foresters. Beavers introduced into the Mad River drainage in northwestern California in 1942 and 1946 had become well established by 1960. They were originally not present in this region. Under adequate protection beavers are once again well established in our fauna after reaching a low level in population numbers a few years ago.

Family **Cricetidae**

Dental Formula 1-0-0-3/1-0-0-3

These mice and rats have the infraorbital canal running high up on the rostrum (fig. 32). Its widest part is at the top and transmits part of the masseter muscle; its lower part carries a nerve to the face. There are no postorbital processes.

The cricetid or New World rodents differ from the Muridae or Old World rodents in that the tubercles (cusps) or prisms on the molars are arranged in two longitudinal rows (figs. 3, 35) instead of three (fig. 36). Two kinds of cricetid rodents are readily distinguishable: the cricetine (Cricetinae) species, in which the cheek teeth are crowned with tubercles or cusps (fig. 35), and the microtine (Microtinae) species, in which the cheek teeth are crowned with prisms (figs. 42–47). The presence or absence of accessory cusps (fig. 158) and the bacula are also useful in the classification of certain genera (fig. 159). The hair in front of the ear of cricetines is rarely long enough to obscure any part of the ear. The hair of microtines, however, frequently covers a considerable part of the ear. Apparently some of the cricetid species may become dormant. (See Richard E. MacMillen [1965], *Comp. Biochem. & Physiol.* **16**: 227–48.) Many of the species have high-pitched songs reminiscent of that of songbirds. A key to the species is provided for the Cricetinae and a separate key for the Microtinae.

Subfamily **Cricetinae** (Cricetine Mice)

The mice and rats belonging to this subfamily are characterized by a number of features that apply to most of the species. All except the cotton rat (*Sigmodon hispidus*) have large membranous ears *not* covered by the hairs that grow in front of them. Except for the grasshopper mice (*Onychomys*), all have tails over three-fourths of the head and body length. The cricetine mice have cusps on the unworn molars (fig. 35), and the rats have flattened crowns on their molars (figs. 49, 50).

KEY TO THE CRICETINE MICE AND RATS (Cricetinae)

The mice and rats of this subfamily are without external cheek pouches and have tails which in most species are nearly as long as or longer than the head and body. The ears usually do not have long fur on their anterior sides that tend to cover them. The molar crowns are composed of two rows of cusps in these mice and are filled with little "puddles" of dentine surrounded by enamel in the rats (figs. 41, 49, 50). The features on the crown of the unworn M^1 (fig. 3) are important in making identification of certain species. The bacula are also useful in making specific determinations of many of these species (fig. 159). The dental formula is 1-0-0-3/1-0-0-3.

1A. With longitudinal grooves on front face of upper incisors (fig. 160) . 2

1B. Without longitudinal grooves on upper incisors 3

2A. Tail distinctly bicolored; under parts grayish white, often buffy-tinged. Not occurring in the salt marshes in San Francisco Bay, California, but occurring elsewhere in the state and in Oregon and Washington.
Reithrodontomys megalotis, western harvest mouse, p. 249, fig. 161.

2B. Tail unicolored or indistinctly bicolored; under parts brown or pinkish cinnamon. Occurring in salt marshes around San Francisco Bay, California.
Reithrodontomys raviventris, salt marsh harvest mouse, p. 249.

3A. Mouselike; usually less than 260 mm. total length; hind foot usually less than 30 mm. 4

3B. Ratlike; usually more than 260 mm. total length; hind foot usually 30 mm. or more 13

4A. Tail usually less than 70 per cent of head and body length; coronoid process of the jaw as high as or higher than the condyloid process (fig. 38) 5

4B. Tail usually more than 70 per cent of head and body length; coronoid process of the jaw lower than the condyloid process (fig. 38) . . . 6

5A. Tail normally less than 50 per cent of head and body length; M¹ less than half of the length of the molar tooth row. Northeastern California, eastern Oregon, and Washington.
Onychomys leucogaster, northern grasshopper mouse, p. 262.

5B. Tail normally more than 50 per cent of head and body length; M¹ is equal to or more than half of the length of the molar tooth row. Dry regions in the southern half of California.
Onychomys torridus, southern grasshopper mouse, p. 262, fig. 169.

6A. Tail bicolored or not, but usually more than 90 per cent of head and body length 7

6B. Tail bicolored but usually less than 90 per cent of head and body length; maxillary bones not extending posterior to the nasals; M¹ with anterocone inclined toward the labial side, clearly bicuspidate with outer anteroconule approaching in size each of the four major cones, inner anteroconule suppressed, accessory cusp (anterostyle) in the first primary fold, posterior margin not indented (fig. 3). Living in nearly all plant communities and zones throughout all three states.
Peromyscus maniculatus, deer mouse, p. 255, fig. 165.

7A. Hind foot 24 mm. or less 8

7B. Hind foot 25 mm. or more; tail usually not sharply bicolored; premaxillary bones extending posterior to the nasals; M¹ with no anterostyle outside the first primary fold, outer anteroconule as large as or larger than the paracone. Chaparral, Foothill Woodland in the Upper Sonoran Life Zone west of the Sierra Nevada and south of San Francisco Bay in California.
Peromyscus californicus, California mouse, p. 253, fig. 162.

8A. Ear usually 21 mm. or less (from notch), less than hind foot length . 9

8B. Ear usually 21 mm. or more (from notch), about equal to or more than hind foot length; tail frequently sharply bicolored; premaxillary bones extending to or sometimes posterior to (1 mm. or more) the nasals; M¹ with compressed anterocone inclined toward the labial side, the outer conule smaller than the major cones but noticeably larger than the inner conule. Foothill Woodland and Pinyon-Juniper Woodland in the Upper Sonoran Life Zone from Oregon through California.
Peromyscus truei, pinyon mouse, p. 255, fig. 168.

9A. More grayish, yellowish, or buffy than brownish dorsally; sole of hind foot naked to heel 12

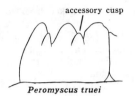

accessory cusp

Peromyscus truei

Fig. 158. M¹ of *Peromyscus truei* showing
accessory cusps between the major cusps.
(For anterostyle and mesostyle, see fig. 3, p. 9.)

9B. More brownish dorsally than grayish, yellowish, or buffy; sole partially
haired near the heel 10

10A. Western half of Washington, western third of Oregon, extreme northwestern California. Dark cinnamon, reddish, or dark brown; tail sharply
bicolored, brown dorsally 11

10B. Most of California except the northwestern humid forests, the low central
valleys and the southeastern deserts. Tail 90–120 mm. long and not usually
sharply bicolored; M¹ with anterocone wide and not noticeably inclined
toward the labial side but deeply indented at the major fold, slightly indented at the minor fold, conules on the anterocone about the same size.
Peromyscus boylii, brush mouse, p. 253, fig. 167.

11A. Western Washington to the foothills on the eastern slopes of the Cascades,
in coniferous Alpine forests (usually above 2,700 ft. elevation). Tail usually
bicolored and over 103 mm. in length, frequently white-tipped (fig. 166);
M¹ with anterocone inclined toward the labial side, both anteroconules
about the same size but the outer conule tending to be more angular than
rounded, posterior end of tooth indented; head and body reddish to dark
brown dorsally.
Peromyscus oreas, forest deer mouse, p. 255, fig. 166.

11B. Western Washington through western Oregon to extreme northwestern
California in lowland coniferous forests (usually below 2,700 ft. elevation);
tail usually less than 103 mm. in length; M¹ with anterocone inclined toward
the labial side, outer anteroconule tending to be more rounded than angular,
posterior end of tooth not indented (fig. 3); dark brown or dark cinnamon
with blackish dorsally.
Peromyscus maniculatus (races *rubidus* or *austerus*), deer mouse,
p. 255, fig. 165.

12A. Tail terminated with hairs 4–10 mm. long; premaxillary bones not noticeably extending posterior to the nasals; M¹ has both anterior and posterior
ends indented, minor fold narrow and deep. Rocky places in central and
eastern Oregon and eastern California, mostly in dry regions in the Sonoran
life zones.
Peromyscus crinitus, canyon mouse, p. 253, fig. 164.

12B. Tail terminated with hairs 2–4 mm. long at the tip; premaxillary bones
extending posterior to the nasals (1 mm. or more); M¹ has rounded anterior
and posterior ends, minor fold about as wide as deep, both conules on the
anterocone indistinguishably fused into one. Southern third of California
in low arid regions in the Lower Sonoran Life Zone.
Peromyscus eremicus, cactus mouse, p. 253, fig. 163.

13A. Guard hairs at the lower anterior edge of the ear less than half as long as
the ear; palate not extending posteriorly beyond the M³ 14

13B. Guard hairs at the lower anterior edge of the ear more than half as long
as the ear; blackish fur tipped with brown; palate extending behind the
M³. Cattail marshes along the Colorado River, California.
Sigmodon hispidus, hispid cotton rat, p. 264, fig. 170.

14A. Tail scaly or with hairs less than 10 mm. long; hind foot naked from heel along the outside to the posterior tubercle 15

14B. Tail covered with hair more than 10 mm. long; hind foot furred from heel to posterior tubercle. Sagebrush and forested regions from the Upper Sonoran or Transition to the Canadian Life Zone throughout eastern and northern California and all of Oregon and Washington.

    Neotoma cinerea, bushy-tailed wood rat, p. 267, fig. 173.

15A. Hind foot normally more than 31 mm.; hairs on throat white to roots . 16

15B. Hind foot normally less than 33 mm.; hairs on throat mostly lead-colored to the roots; posterior re-entrant angle on the cheek side of the M^3 is slightly bent posteriorly or is straight (fig. 49). Southeastern Oregon and the extreme eastern and southern half of California in the Sagebrush Scrub, Chaparral, and Foothill Woodland of the Sonoran life zones.

    Neotoma lepida, desert wood rat, p. 267, fig. 174.

16A. Not in the desert regions of Riverside and Imperial Counties or along the Colorado River, California. Hind foot normally 33–47 mm. in length; posterior external angle of the M^3 bent posteriorly at about a 45° angle. Various communities from Lower Sonoran up into the Transition Life Zone in California and Oregon west of the eastern dry regions.

    Neotoma fuscipes, dusky-footed wood rat, p. 267, fig. 171.

16B. Along the Colorado River and in the desert regions of Riverside and Imperial counties, California. Hind foot normally 31–37 mm. in length; posterior external angle of M^3 straight. Under mesquite trees in the Creosote Bush Scrub of the Lower Sonoran Life Zone.

    Neotoma albigula, white-throated wood rat, p. 267.

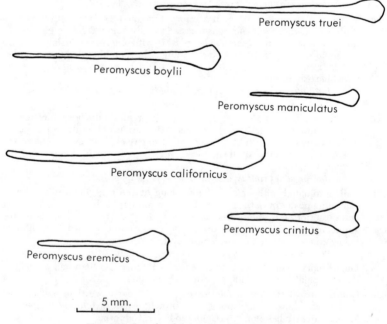

Fig. 159. Bacula of deer mice (*Peromyscus*).

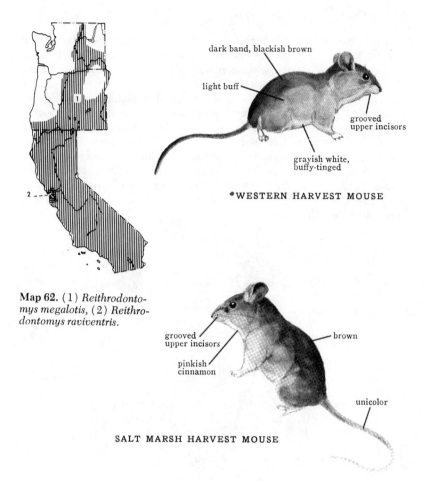

Map 62. (1) *Reithrodonto-mys megalotis*, (2) *Reithro-dontomys raviventris*.

dark band, blackish brown

light buff

grooved upper incisors

grayish white, buffy-tinged

•WESTERN HARVEST MOUSE

grooved upper incisors

brown

pinkish cinnamon

unicolor

SALT MARSH HARVEST MOUSE

◦Western harvest mouse (*Reithrodontomys megalotis*). Length 130–70 mm., about six inches; *tail 55–96 mm.; hind foot 15–19 mm.; ear 12–18 mm.; skull 20.5–22 mm.*; brownish or buffy and black above, sometimes forming an indistinctly bordered, dark dorsal band; *grayish tinged with buff beneath*; sides buffy; tail indistinctly bicolored; upper incisors with deep grooves on outer surface. In many communities and in life zones up to the Hudsonian, all over California, and the eastern halves of Oregon and Washington. P. 250, fig. 161, Map 62.

Salt marsh harvest mouse (*Reithrodontomys raviventris*). *Length 120–62 mm.,* about 5.5 inches; *tail 64–88 mm.; hind foot 15–19 mm.; skull (average) 21.2 mm.*; upper incisors with deep grooves; upper parts rich brown; *under parts pinkish cinnamon to whitish; tail unicolored.* Coastal Salt Marsh, Lower Sonoran Life Zone around San Francisco Bay, California. P. 250, Map 62.

Harvest Mice (*Reithrodontomys*)

There are two species of this genus in the Pacific States: the western harvest mouse (*Reithrodontomys megalotis,* fig. 161) and the salt marsh harvest mouse (*Reithrodontomys raviventris*). All harvest mice are easily distinguished from other cricetine mice by their grooved upper incisors (fig. 160). Harvest mice might be confused with jumping mice (*Zapus*), which also have grooved upper incisors and no external cheek pouches. Jumping mice have long tails that are about 150 per cent of the head and body length, and they have pure white bellies. Harvest mice are nocturnal and they are more active on moonlight nights. They are primarily seed and fruit eaters and seem to prefer wild plants. They build their birdlike nests above the ground in thick grass or weeds. The inside is frequently lined with fine grasses or down. These mice frequently use the runways of meadow mice (*Microtus*).

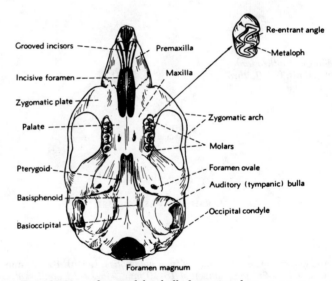

Fig. 160. Ventral view of the skull of a western harvest mouse
showing the grooved upper incisors and bones.

Pearson (1960b) also found that these mice consume a minimum of 2.5 cc. of oxygen per gram of weight per hour when the ambient temperature is 91° F. and the zone of thermal neutrality is not more than 3°. The use of a nest reduces the metabolism as much as 24 per cent, and huddling at 34° reduces the rate of metabolism 28 per cent.

Both these mice can drink 100 per cent seawater. MacMillen (1964a) suggests that, in view of the predominantly inland distribution of the west-

Fig. 161. Two views of the western harvest mouse
(*Reithrodontomys megalotis*).

ern harvest mice, they both are probably generally adapted for aridity, and thus "*preadapted*" for drinking salt water.

There are probably several litters a year, since pregnant females have been taken in nearly every month. The litter ranges from four to six young. They are preyed upon by owls, snakes, and many mammal predators. Harvest mice are rarely of any economic importance.

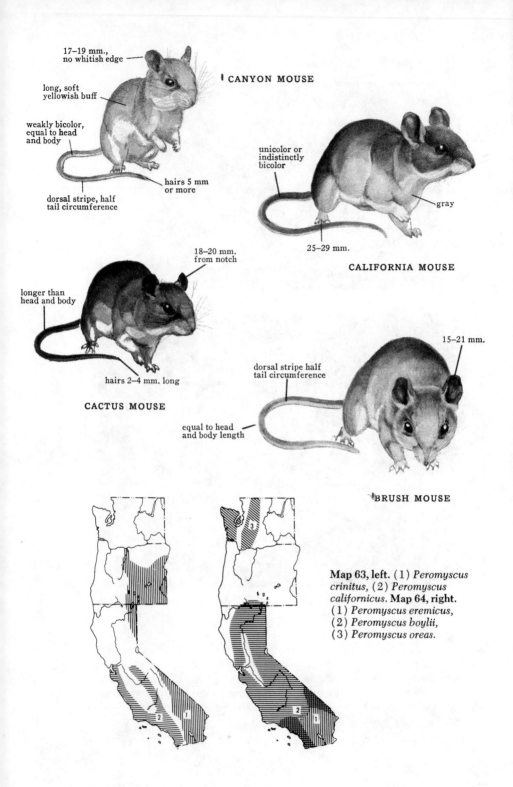

17–19 mm., no whitish edge

CANYON MOUSE

long, soft yellowish buff

weakly bicolor, equal to head and body

unicolor or indistinctly bicolor

hairs 5 mm or more

dorsal stripe, half tail circumference

gray

25–29 mm.

CALIFORNIA MOUSE

18–20 mm. from notch

longer than head and body

15–21 mm.

dorsal stripe half tail circumference

hairs 2–4 mm. long

equal to head and body length

CACTUS MOUSE

BRUSH MOUSE

Map 63, left. (1) *Peromyscus crinitus*, (2) *Peromyscus californicus*. **Map 64, right.** (1) *Peromyscus eremicus*, (2) *Peromyscus boylii*, (3) *Peromyscus oreas*.

* Canyon mouse (*Peromyscus crinitus*). *Length 163–92 mm.*, about seven inches; tail 80–118 mm.; *hind foot 17–23 mm.*; ear, notch, 17–21 mm.; skull 23–26.8 mm.; fur long and soft, pale yellowish buff above and whitish below; feet white; *tail usually longer than the head and body, with broad, light brown dorsal stripe,* creamy white below; *hairs on tip of tail 5–10 mm.;* ear without a white edge; accessory cusps *usually not present on the M^1* (figs. 3, 158); *premaxillary bones not extending noticeably beyond the nasals posteriorly.* Rocky places on desert mountains in all three states in the Upper Sonoran and Transition life zones. P. 256, fig. 164, Map 63.

California mouse (*Peromyscus californicus*). *Length 220–26 mm.*, about ten inches; tail 117–48 mm.; *hind foot 25–29 mm.*; ear 20–28 mm.; skull 29–32.1 mm.; premaxillary bones extending posteriorly to the ends of the nasals; yellowish brown or gray mixed with black above, grayish below; *tail longer than head and body, unicolored, or indistinctly bicolored, with broad brown dorsal stripe above and lighter brown below*; no accessory cusps on the M^1; Chaparral and Foothill Woodland, Upper Sonoran Life Zone in the southern half of California. P. 256, fig. 162, Map 63.

Cactus mouse (*Peromyscus eremicus*). *Length 170–218 mm.*, about eight inches; tail 89–128 mm.; *hind foot 18–22 mm.*; ear 18–20 mm.; skull 24.5–26.5 mm.; buffy gray above, white below; feet white and sole naked to heel; *tail nearly always longer than the head and body, not distinctly bicolored, has a broad, dorsal, brownish stripe*, is sparsely covered with *hairs about 2–4 mm. long at its tip*; ear without a white edge; ordinarily *no accessory cusps on the M^1; premaxillary bones extending noticeably beyond the ends of the nasals posteriorly.* In low arid regions in the Lower Sonoran Life Zone of southern California. P. 256, fig. 163, Map 64.

* Brush mouse (*Peromyscus boylii*). *Length 180–238 mm.*, about eight inches; tail 91–123 mm.; *hind foot 20–26 mm.; ear, notch, 15–20 mm.*; skull 27.5–28.5 mm.; dark brown to brown above, whitish beneath; feet whitish, proximal part of sole hairy; *tail generally longer than head and body, more or less bicolored, width of dorsal stripe about half the circumference of the tail; accessory cusps (anterostyles) between the major cusps on the M^1* (see figs. 3, 158); premaxillary bones extending posteriorly to the end of the nasals. Chaparral and rocky areas in the Upper Sonoran Life Zone of California. P. 256, fig. 167, Map 64.

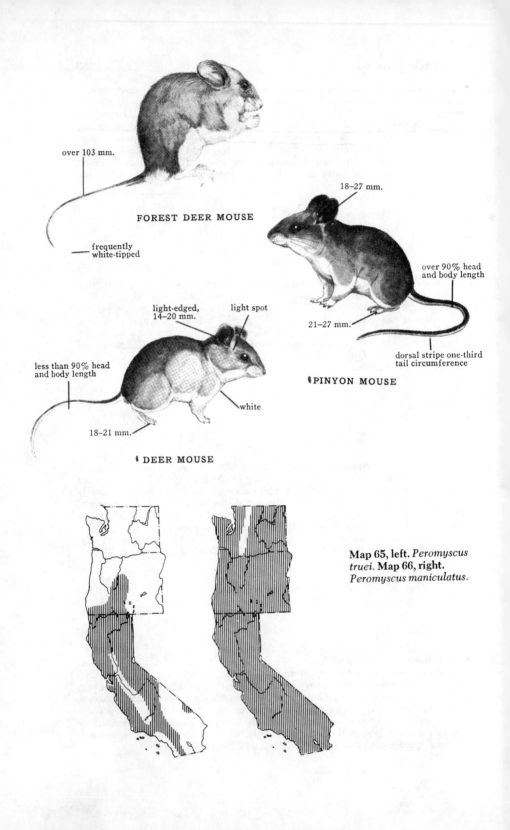

over 103 mm.

FOREST DEER MOUSE

frequently
white-tipped

18–27 mm.

over 90% head
and body length

21–27 mm.

dorsal stripe one-third
tail circumference

PINYON MOUSE

light-edged,
14–20 mm.

light spot

less than 90% head
and body length

white

18–21 mm.

DEER MOUSE

Map 65, left. *Peromyscus truei.* Map 66, right. *Peromyscus maniculatus.*

Forest deer mouse (*Peromyscus oreas*). Length 181–201 mm.; tail usually over 50 per cent of the total length and frequently white-tipped; hind foot 21–23 mm.; ear 16–18 mm.; skull 26–29 mm.; accessory cusps on the M¹ (figs. 3, 158). West from the eastern slopes of the Cascade range to the Pacific Ocean except for Puget Sound and an area running south from it to the Columbia River; mostly in the dense Douglas and white fir forests. (This species is considered by some mammalogists to be a race of *Peromyscus maniculatus* on the basis of a study of its protein chemistry by Johnson (1963).) P. 256, fig. 166, Map 64.

Pinyon mouse (*Peromyscus truei*). Length 170–231 mm., about eight inches; tail 76–123 mm.; *hind foot 20–27 mm.; ear, notch, 18–27 mm.;* skull 27–30.7 mm.; brown to dark brown above, creamy white beneath; tail bicolored, with the width of the dorsal stripe about one-third the circumference of the tail, *whitish below and over 90 per cent of the head and body length*; feet whitish; *accessory cusps (anterostyles) on the M¹* (figs. 3, 158); premaxillary bones about as long as the nasals or extending slightly behind them. Foothill Woodland and Pinyon-Juniper Woodland of California and brushy places in central Oregon in the Upper Sonoran Life Zone. P. 256, fig. 168, Map 65.

Deer mouse (*Peromyscus maniculatus*). Length 148–200 mm., about seven inches; *tail 60–90 mm.; hind foot 18–22 mm.;* ear 14–20 mm.; skull 24–26.5 mm.; yellowish brown to grayish above, pure white below; feet white; *tail usually less than 90 per cent of head and body, bicolored* (may be as long as or longer than the head and body in the subspecies *P.m.austerus* and *P.m.rubidus* along the coast), with the width of the dorsal stripe about half the circumference of the tail; frequently a lighter spot in front of the ear and a delicate lighter edge around the ear; *accessory cusps (anterostyles) on the M¹* (figs. 3, 158); premaxillary bones not extending posterior to the ends of the nasals. Nearly all communities and life zones in all three states. P. 256, fig. 165, Map 66.

Deer Mice (*Peromyscus*)

There are seven species of deer mice in the Pacific States: the canyon mouse (*Peromyscus crinitus*), the California mouse (*Peromyscus californicus*), the cactus mouse (*Peromyscus eremicus*), the deer mouse (*Peromyscus maniculatus*), the forest deer mouse (*Peromyscus oreas*), the brush mouse (*Peromyscus boylii*), and the pinyon mouse (*Peromyscus truei*).

They are distinguished from other mice by large membranous ears, grooveless upper incisors, no external cheek pouches, a tail more than 70 per cent of the head and body length, and the coronoid process of the jaw not as high as the condyloid process (fig. 38). The deer mice might be confused with the much less common grasshopper mice (*Onychomys*), which have the coronoid process higher than the condyloid process and a tail less than 70 per cent of the head and body length. Deer mice may be distinguished from the house mouse (*Mus musculus*) by their white or gray under parts and white feet, which contrast with the color of the back. There are two rows of tubercles (cusps) on the molars (fig. 35) instead of three rows as in the house mouse. In many places the more aggressive house mouse from the Old World seems to be replacing the deer mouse.

These mice all have two rows of cusps running down the molars (fig. 35). In order to avoid confusion, see the drawing of the teeth of a house mouse (fig. 36). The outer surfaces of the upper incisors of deer mice are smooth, not grooved as in the harvest mice (fig. 160). The coronoid process of the lower jaw is lower than the condyloid process in deer mice (fig. 38). (See fig. 3 for orientation of M^1.)

The basic number of diploid chromosomes in *Peromyscus* is 48. The cac-

Fig. 162. California mouse (*Peromyscus californicus*).

tus mouse, however, is reported to have 58, and—what is even more interesting—a subspecies of deer mouse differs from six related species in
having 52 instead of 48, and these chromosomes are smaller in size and lack
an apparent constriction (Tamsitt, 1960).

The seven species of deer mice may be distinguished from each other by
certain external and internal features. The canyon mouse and the cactus
mouse are buffy or gray on the back, compared with the brownish back of
the other species. The premaxillary bones extend posteriorly beyond the
nasal bones in the cactus mouse, but in the canyon mouse all these bones
end at about the same level. The habitat usually serves to separate these
two species of desert mice: the cactus mouse (fig. 163) inhabits the lowlands, the canyon mouse (fig. 164) the rocky outcrops.

The California mouse (fig. 162) can usually be distinguished from the
deer mouse (fig. 165), brush mouse (fig. 167), and pinyon mouse (fig.
168) by its longer hind foot (25–29 mm.). It has no accessory cusps on the
upper first molar (M^1), whereas the other three do (figs. 3, 158).

The large ears (18–27 mm.) usually distinguish the pinyon mouse from
the brush mouse and the deer mouse. The dorsal stripe on its tail covers
one-third the circumference, whereas in the brush mouse and deer mouse
it covers half.

The forest deer mouse was given specific status by Sheppe (1961); however, work by Murray Johnson (1963) indicates that it is not specifically
different from the deer mouse in its protein chemistry. It can readily be
separated from most of the races of deer mice by its much longer tail, which
is always longer than the head and body and rarely less than 103 mm. in
length. The tail is frequently white-tipped.

Finally, most of the subspecies of deer mice (*P. maniculatus*) can usually
be distinguished from the brush mouse by their shorter tails (less than 90
per cent of head and body length); the tail of the brush mouse is about as
long or longer than the head and body length. Two subspecies of deer
mouse, however, do have tails as long as or longer than the head and body.
These are the subspecies *rubidus* and *austerus* of northwestern California,
western Oregon, and Washington. The range of the brush mouse overlaps
that of *rubidus*, but positive identification can usually be made by checking
pelage color and skull features. The dark reddish brown fur of *P.m.rubi-
dus*, which lives mostly in the humid coastal forest, distinguishes it readily
from the lighter grayish brown brush mouse. The premaxillary bones do
not extend behind the nasals in the deer mouse; they do extend slightly
beyond the nasals in the brush mouse.

Deer mice are primarily nocturnal; some species will be found in just
about any terrestrial habitat in North America where other mammals are
found. In many places this rodent is so numerous that it is necessary to trap
it out before the other species can be captured.

It has recently been shown that the white-footed mice perform a great
service in the forests in other parts of the United States by feeding on certain larvae and pupae of insects that are detrimental to the trees. Detailed
studies of their ecological relation to Western forests are yet to be made,

Fig. 163. Cactus mouse (*Peromyscus eremicus*).

Fig. 164. Canyon mouse (*Peromyscus crinitus*).

Fig. 165. Deer mouse (*Peromyscus maniculatus*).

Fig. 166. Forest deer mouse (*Peromyscus oreas*).

although the Oregon State Board of Forestry has done some work in this field. Certainly a mammal that is so numerous must play an important part in the ecology of any biotic community in which it lives. Deer mice eat nearly all kinds of seeds, fruits, cheese, bacon, and butter, but they seldom consume grass, bark, or leaves as do the meadow mice (*Microtus*). They store large caches of food and are active above the snow all winter.

These rodents are known to feed largely on lepidopterous larvae and other insects in the spring, but seeds become much more important in the fall diet (Donald Johnson, 1963).

The nest is usually in a rotting log, among rocks, or even in a burrow. It is made of fine grass, usually with some down or wool inside.

The gestation period is from 22 to 25 days. There are from three to six young in a litter and there may be three or four litters a year.

The pelage of the immature mouse is frequently very different from that of the adult. It is usually bluish gray and lasts for about six weeks.

The deer mice (*Peromyscus maniculatus*) may number five to ten per acre in the wilds of the Sierra Nevada in California. Some may have a home range of five to six acres.

Almost every bird and mammal predator feeds on these little mice and helps keep the population down. Where predators have been reduced, these mice may become serious pests.

Perhaps no group of mammals illustrates speciation, or evolution in action, better than the genus *Peromyscus*. One species, the deer mouse (*P. maniculatus*, fig. 165), ranges from central Alaska to the mountains south of Mexico City. Its range extends from the Pacific Ocean eastward to Labrador on the Atlantic Ocean and covers an area of over five million square miles. This species has a wide range of habitats. Within this enormous range, evolution of the species has resulted in the differentiation of more than 60 forms of varying degrees of distinctness, which are designated as subspecies or geographic races. These subspecies are mostly interfertile when tested in the laboratory, and there seem to be no barriers other than occasional geographic or ecological ones to prevent free dispersal. How do these races maintain their uniqueness if other genes flow into their populations? There is great local variability in *Peromyscus,* and a considerable part of it probably is genetically based. Sumner (1932) experimented by breeding the pale deer mice from the deserts with those in the humid coastal region, where the native deer mice are dark. Generation after generation of breeding the pale deer mice together resulted in their remaining pale, indicating that there was a genetic basis for paleness and that it was not a response to the environment in the Lamarckian sense.

Some of these subspecific characters are known to be correlated with certain environmental features. The humid regions, for instance, with the resulting dark soils of the West Coast coniferous forests and on the tops of isolated desert mountains, have produced dark races of *Peromyscus maniculatus* as well as of other vertebrates. But dark forms have also been produced on black lava flows where the air is also very dry. The deer mice that live in the dry air of the deserts on the much lighter soils tend to match

Fig. 167. Brush mouse (*Peromyscus boylii*).

the color of the surface soil (Dice and Blossom, 1937). The deer mice
(*Peromyscus maniculatus gambeli*) that live between these regions of extremes in humidity are intermediate in character and form a long, narrow
range over 1,200 miles in length from Washington to Baja California. Thus
some mammalogists (Dice, 1940) interpret development of a subspecies
as an inherited ecological response rather than one of descent. Similar ecological conditions act as selectors on the general population and may cause
two or more populations of deer mice to become dark and look exactly alike,
even though they are found only on desert mountaintops hundreds of miles
apart and are surrounded by light-colored deer mice living on light-colored
desert soils. It seems more reasonable to believe that these dark populations of mountaintop mice have developed independently from their light-
colored desert relatives than that they once had a continuous range and
were left stranded on the cool mountaintops after the withdrawal of the
glaciers (Dice, 1940).

Many other races and species of other small mammals that prefer rocky
habitats have developed a dark coloration on relatively recent black lava
flows, even though they were completely surrounded by light desert soils
and in air with low humidity.

It has been shown experimentally that laboratory-raised races of the deer
mouse (*Peromyscus maniculatus*) have an innate tendency to select habitats similar to those of the same race living wild (Harris, 1952).

Another kind of geographic variation, called a *cline*, is a long geographic
gradient of *one* character. Thus, the ear of a certain species may gradually
get longer over the range of one or more of the subspecies, in a given direction. Clines are not to be confused with differences in *subspecies* or geographic races, which represent a population on a part of the range of the
species. The subspecies differs in one or more characters from other populations within the species.

These studies on races and species of *Peromyscus* under the varying environmental conditions of the Southwest indicate that evolution may be much speeded up, especially where environmental or ecological factors select one genetically based character over another.

An interesting experiment to test the effectiveness of natural selection in the evolution of protective coloration in *Peromyscus* was made by Dice (1947).

Fig. 168. Pinyon mouse (*Peromyscus truei*).

Owls were the predators, and differently colored races of deer mice (*Peromyscus maniculatus*) were the prey. Four animals with dorsal coloration that matched the soil and four that contrasted with it were used in each experiment. Several types of soils were used in a simulated "desert" over which the light could be controlled to total darkness. After taking precautions to assure that the owls would have to use their eyes as well as their ears to locate the mice, a large series of experiments were begun to learn if the animals that matched the soils had any selective advantages over those that did not. The results of the experiments were tested with a mathematical formula known as the selective index, which may vary between $+1.0$ and -1.0, with 0.0 indicating no selective effect at all. The significance of the deviation from 0.0 was tested by the usual chi-square formula for a 1 : 1 ratio. In every experiment in which the owl depended mostly on its sense of sight to locate the prey, a *significantly* greater number of the contrastingly colored mice were caught. It was thus concluded that natural selection can theoretically produce very rapid evolution whenever a genetically variable population is exposed to its action.

Thus, of the genetically pliable genus of deer mice (*Peromyscus*) living in the ecologically variable West and Southwest, a large number of subspecies have been developed that are interfertile with the contiguous races, but they are able to maintain themselves by the constantly selective action of the environmental factors.

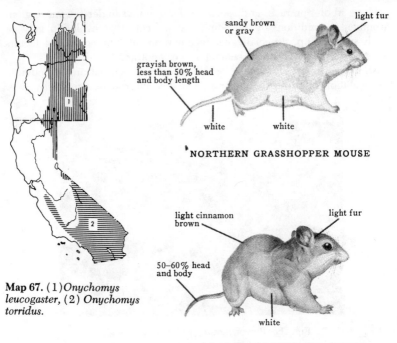

light fur

sandy brown
or gray

grayish brown,
less than 50% head
and body length

white   white

NORTHERN GRASSHOPPER MOUSE

light cinnamon   light fur
brown

50–60% head
and body

white

Map 67. (1)*Onychomys*
leucogaster, (2) *Onychomys*
torridus.

SOUTHERN GRASSHOPPER MOUSE

Northern grasshopper mouse (*Onychomys leucogaster*). Length 131–90 mm., about 5.5 inches; tail 32–60 mm.; hind foot 17–25 mm.; ear, crown, 13–16 mm.; skull 27–28 mm.; upper parts pale sandy brown *or* gray, sharply marked off from the pure white under parts; *ear edged with white*, with a lighter spot at its anterior base; feet white; *tail usually less than half the head and body length*, bicolored; *upper M^1 usually less than half the length of the molar tooth row.* Sagebrush Scrub; chiefly in Upper Sonoran Life Zone, in southeastern Washington, eastern Oregon, and northeastern California. P. 263, Map 67.

Southern grasshopper mouse (*Onychomys torridus*). Length 120–60 mm., about 5.5. inches; *tail 39–52 mm.; hind foot 18–23 mm.; ear, crown, 11–18 mm.;* skull 24.3–25.8 mm.; light cinnamon above, white below; *tail between 50 and 60 per cent of head and body length, its basal two-thirds like upper parts dorsally; upper M^1 usually more than half the length of the tooth row.* Valley Grassland; Lower Sonoran Life Zone over most of the southern half of California. P. 263, fig. 169, Map 67.

Grasshopper Mice (*Onychomys*)

There are two species of grasshopper mice inhabiting the more arid places in the Pacific States: the northern grasshopper mouse (*Onychomys leucogaster*) and the southern grasshopper mouse (*Onychomys torridus*, fig. 169). They have large membranous ears and white under parts and resemble the deer mice (*Peromyscus*). However, they differ in having a tail that is less than 70 per cent of the head and body length and in having the coronoid process of the jaw as high as or higher than the condyloid process (fig. 38).

Fig. 169. Southern grasshopper mouse (*Onychomys torridus*).

These mammals include about 90 per cent animal food in their diet, of which 80 per cent is arthropods. Their stomachs are peculiarly adapted to handle the rough chitinous food in having the glandular fundic portion nearly "pinched off" from the cardiac and pyloric parts. The fundic part is connected to the rest of the stomach by only a small lumen (Taylor, 1963).

Grasshopper mice are nocturnal. They have a high-pitched voice, which can be heard long before they are seen. They prefer grasshoppers but will eat seeds and other insects, including the hard-shelled tenebrionid beetles, and even lizards. The nest is usually made in a burrow dug by another mammal. The gestation period is between 32 and 38 days. Pregnant females have been taken in about every month of the year, especially in the warmer parts of its range. There may be more than one litter of three to six young a year. They are born naked, but within three weeks the young are covered with fur, and the eyes and ears are open. If the nest is disturbed, the young attach themselves to the mother's teats and are dragged to safety —a method of escape employed by many small rodents.

Snakes, weasels, and owls are known enemies. Probably coyotes, foxes, bobcats, and badgers also are. Grasshopper mice are beneficial, since they eat many detrimental insects.

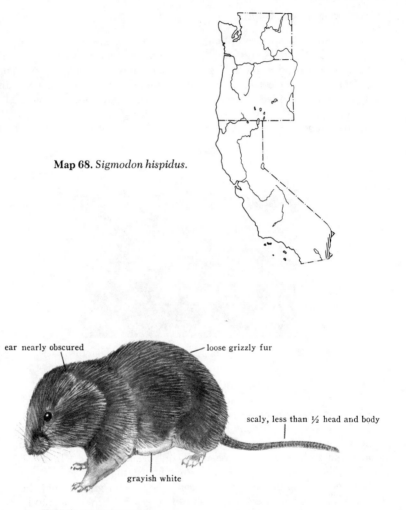

Map 68. *Sigmodon hispidus.*

ear nearly obscured   loose grizzly fur

scaly, less than ½ head and body

grayish white

HISPID COTTON RAT

Hispid cotton rat (*Sigmodon hispidus*). Length 268–338 mm., about 12 inches; tail 112–43 mm., less than half the head and body length, *sparsely haired, with scales clearly showing;* hind foot 32–37 mm.; skull about 50 mm. total length, with a deep notch at the antorbital foramen (fig. 39); *flat grinding surfaces of the molars have roughly S- or Σ-shaped ridges* (fig. 41); *ears nearly covered with hair;* pelage grizzly, blackish-based hairs, with brown tips above and whitish below. Cattail marshes along the Colorado River in California. Lower Sonoran Life Zone. P. 265, fig. 170, Map 68.

Cotton Rats (*Sigmodon*)

These rat-sized rodents are represented by one species (*Sigmodon his-pidus,* fig. 170) in the Pacific States. It is found only along the Colorado River in southeastern California. The scaly tail is shorter than the head and body. The fur is harsh and rough, or hispid. The large roundish ears are nearly covered by long hairs that grow from the base. The shape of the ear and its excessive hairiness serve to distinguish the cotton rat from the Old World Norway rat.

Fig. 170. Hispid cotton rat (*Sigmodon hispidus*).

The most characteristic feature of the cotton rat, however, is the S- or Σ-shaped crowns (fig. 41) on the molar teeth, from which the genus gets its name (*sigma*-shaped; *odontos,* tooth).

Cotton rats are active both day and night. They are like large meadow mice (*Microtus*) in the way they make runways through the grassy or weedy places they live in, and in their food, which is mostly vegetable matter. However, insects are sometimes eaten. They do not store food and never become dormant.

The grassy nest is frequently placed in a shallow runway or tunnel. The gestation period is 27 days. There may be as many as nine litters over a period of ten months, with about six young to a litter, although 11 have been known to occur.

Cotton rats are preyed upon by coyotes, foxes, weasels, skunks, hawks, and owls. Where predators have been reduced and cover allowed to grow thick, they may become agricultural pests as their numbers increase.

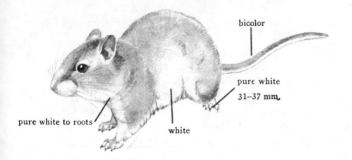

bicolor

pure white
31–37 mm.

pure white to roots

white

WHITE-THROATED WOOD RAT

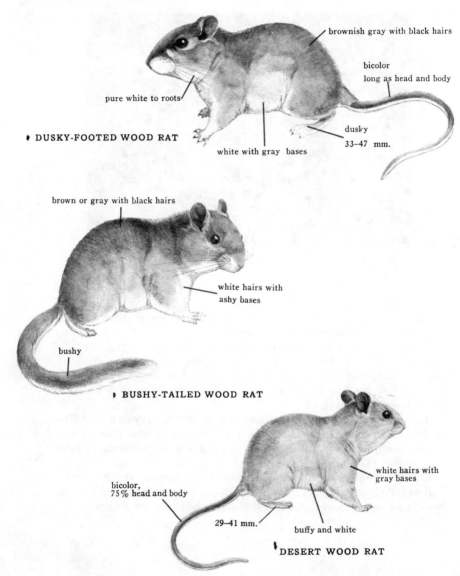

brownish gray with black hairs

bicolor
long as head and body

pure white to roots

♦ **DUSKY-FOOTED WOOD RAT**

dusky
33–47 mm.

white with gray bases

brown or gray with black hairs

white hairs with
ashy bases

bushy

♦ **BUSHY-TAILED WOOD RAT**

white hairs with
gray bases

bicolor,
75% head and body

29–41 mm.

buffy and white

♦**DESERT WOOD RAT**

White-throated wood rat (*Neotoma albigula*). Length 282–400 mm., about 12–15 inches; tail 75–185 mm.; hind foot 31–38 mm.; skull 36.3–40.5 mm., basilar length; molars with little "puddles" of dentine surrounded with enamel on the flat grinding surface; first upper molar with re-entrant angle on the tongue side less than halfway across the tooth, the last upper molar with a deep re-entrant angle on the tongue side and with a straight re-entrant angle on the cheek side; pinkish buff above, *throat and pectoral region pure white to the roots of the hairs; tail bicolored.* Lives in burrows under mesquite trees in the Creosote Bush Scrub; Lower Sonoran Life Zone, in extreme southeastern California. P. 268, Map 69.

♦Dusky-footed wood rat (*Neotoma fuscipes*). Length 335–470 mm., about 16 inches; tail 152–241 mm., short hairs covering the scales of the tail; *hind foot 33–47 mm.;* skull 36.3–44.7 mm., basilar length; molars with little "puddles" of dentine surrounded by enamel on the flat grinding surface; *one deep re-entrant angle on the tongue side of the last molar and the posterior re-entrant angle on the cheek side are bent* (fig. 50); *tail almost as long as the head and body; brownish or blackish above*; under parts, undertail, and upper parts of the feet white. Various communities; Lower Sonoran into the Transition Life Zone in western Oregon and most of California west of the Sierra Nevada. P. 268, fig. 171, Map 69.

● Bushy-tailed wood rat (*Neotoma cinerea*). Length 282–470 mm., about 12 inches; tail 120–223 mm.; hind foot 33–52 mm.; skull 38.1–46.1 mm., basilar length; molars with little "puddles" of dentine surrounded by enamel on the flat grinding surface; *two re-entrant angles on the tongue side of the first molar; tail, with hairs, over 20 mm. long*; cinnamon brown to buffy, sometimes tipped with black above; white or grayish below. Sagebrush Scrub, Yellow Pine Forest, Red Fir Forest, Lodgepole Forest and Northern Juniper Woodland; Upper Sonoran, Transition, and Canadian life zones over all of Washington and Oregon, the mountains of northern California, and the Sierra Nevada. P. 268, fig. 173, Map 70.

◀ Desert wood rat (*Neotoma lepida*). Length 225–380 mm., about 11.5 inches; tail 95–185 mm., short hairs covering the scales of the tail; *hind foot 28–41 mm.;* skull 29.9–36 mm., basilar length; molars with little "puddles" of dentine on the flat grinding surface; *last upper molar with a shallow re-entrant angle on the tongue side, and a straight or slightly bent posterior re-entrant angle on the cheek side* (fig. 49); tail about three-fourths the length of the head and body; *grayish mixed with black hairs above*, under parts white or buffy; Sagebrush Scrub, Chaparral, chiefly Lower and Upper Sonoran life zones over most of the southern half of California and southeastern Oregon. P. 268, fig. 174, Map 71.

Wood Rats (*Neotoma*)

The wood rats are represented in the Pacific States by four species, some of which are somewhat difficult to distinguish from each other: the white-throated wood rat (*Neotoma albigula*), the desert wood rat or pack rat (*Neotoma lepida*, fig. 174), the dusky-footed wood rat (*Neotoma fuscipes*, fig. 171), and the bushy-tailed wood rat (*Neotoma cinerea*, fig. 173). Superficially they resemble the Old World rats (*Rattus*). The tail of the wood rat is covered with hairs long enough to obscure the scales beneath, whereas the scales on the Old World rat are conspicuous. The throat and breast of the wood rat are white; those of the Old World rat are ashy gray. The crowns of the molar teeth of the wood rat are flat (fig. 49); the molars of the Old World rat have three rows of tubercles (fig. 37).

Wood rats are mostly nocturnal. They live in a variety of habitats ranging from the hot dry desert to the humid forest. They make "houses" by piling up sticks, rocks, cacti, dried horse or cow manure, tin cans, camp knives and forks, and practically anything else they can carry (fig. 172). The dusky-footed wood rat's pile may be six feet high and may house many other species of animals. "Pack rat" is the name usually applied to the desert wood rat (*Neotoma lepida*). The desert wood rat was found to be the dominant species in a multispecies population of nocturnal rodents that was studied by MacMillen (1964b) in a semidesert area in the San Gabriel Mountains of southern California. During the dry rainless months this pack rat aggressively dominates the succulent prickly pear patches, with their water source. Its population alone does not decrease materially when

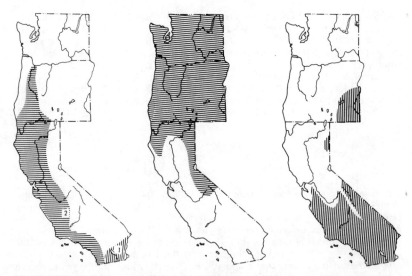

Map 69, left. (1) *Neotoma albigula*, (2) *Neotoma fuscipes*. **Map 70, center.** *Neotoma cinerea*. **Map 71, right.** *Neotoma lepida*.

Fig. 171. Dusky-footed wood rat (*Neotoma fuscipes*).

Fig. 172. House of dusky-footed wood rat.

Fig. 173. Bushy-tailed wood rat (*Neotoma cinerea*).

Fig. 174. Desert wood rat (*Neotoma lepida*).

the dry summer approaches as do the other rodent species (MacMillen, 1964b).

Wood rats feed chiefly on plant materials. The gestation period is reported to be between 23 and 38 days, depending on the species. The litter of three or four appears early in the spring. The eyes of the young are closed for 15 days. While the mother is in the nest, the young are usually fastened onto her teats, and if disturbed she drags them away still attached.

Wood rats have many enemies, including owls, foxes, coyotes, and large snakes. Although occasionally they live in buildings of man, they do very little damage except to steal grain and disturb the ranchers' sleep.

KEY TO THE MICROTINE MICE (Microtinae)

These rodents have long hairs on the anterior side of the ears, which tend to cover them. With the exception of the muskrat, the tail is never as long as the head and body. The crowns of the molars are prismatic, or made of alternating triangles and loops (figs. 42–48). The skull and dental features are necessary to identify certain species of microtines. The dental formula is 1-0-0-3/1-0-0-3.

1A. Tail not laterally compressed; hind foot less than 50 mm. 2
1B. Tail laterally compressed; hind foot more than 50 mm. Along rivers, marshes, and lakes in all three states; widely introduced.
    Ondatra zibethica, muskrat, p. 283, fig. 193.
2A. Upper incisors not grooved or equally bicolored longitudinally (yellow inside, white outside); tail longer than 5 mm. beyond the extended hind legs 3
2B. Upper incisors slightly grooved, with inner half yellow, and outer half white; M^3 with four transverse plates, with re-entrant angles nearly crossing the tooth (fig. 48); tail scarcely longer than extended hind legs. Bogs in the Cascade range and extreme northeastern Washington.
    Synaptomys borealis, northern bog vole, p. 275.
3A. Tail usually longer than 10 mm. beyond the extended hind legs. Not living among sagebrush or in desert areas 4
3B. Tail usually less than 10 mm. beyond the extended hind legs. Living in the desert areas, often above 2,000 feet elevation, usually among sagebrush in eastern California, Oregon, and Washington.
    Lagurus curtatus, sagebrush vole, p. 275, fig. 181.
4A. M^3 with four projections on the lingual side (figs. 42, 45) 5
4B. M^3 with three projections on the lingual side (figs. 46, 47) 12
5A. Posterior edge of palate a transverse shelf or a posteriorly projecting spine; angle between the last two projections on the lingual side of M^3 may be deeper than wide; M^3 without a posteriorly projecting "heel" (fig. 45); cheek teeth rooted 11
5B. Posterior edge of the palate not a transverse shelf; palate with many small holes; angle between the last two projections on the lingual side of M^3 wider than deep; M^3 often with a pronounced "heel" posteriorly (fig. 42); cheek teeth not rooted 6
6A. Hind foot 26 mm. or less; six plantar tubercles 7
6B. Hind foot usually more than 26 mm.; five plantar tubercles (see fig. 177); incisive foramen strongly constricted posteriorly (fig. 176). Generally in the Canadian or Alpine zone along cold-water streams and marshes in the Cascades and Blue Mountains of Oregon and Washington.
    Microtus richardsoni, water rat, p. 283, fig. 186.
7A. Tail usually less than 50 per cent of head and body length 8
7B. Tail usually more than 50 per cent of head and body length and more or less bicolored; incisive foramen is narrower posteriorly but is not abruptly constricted (fig. 176). Sea level to 8,000 feet in northern and eastern California, but including the San Bernardino Mountains, and over most of Oregon and Washington.
    Microtus longicaudus, long-tailed meadow mouse, p. 279, fig. 192.
8A. Anterior part of the incisive foramen clearly wider than the posterior part (fig. 176) 9
8B. Incisive foramen nearly parallel with the posterior half, usually slightly wider than the anterior half (fig. 176). Lowlands in grassy places over most of California and western Oregon in the Sonoran life zones.
    Microtus californicus, California meadow mouse, p. 281, fig. 191.

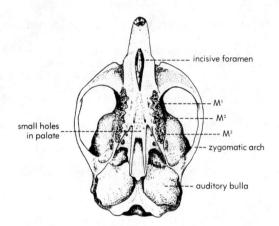

Fig. 175. *Microtus* skull showing features on the ventral surface.

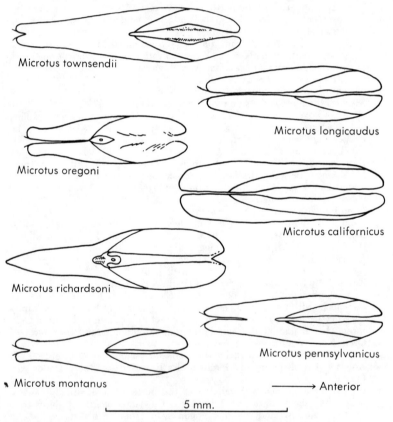

Fig. 176. Incisive foramina in *Microtus*.

9A. M² without a rounded posterior loop on the lingual side; four loops in all (fig. 44) 10

9B. M² with a rounded posterior loop on the lingual side (fig. 43); five loops in all; dark brown dorsally, including tops of hind feet; tail weakly bicolored. Marshes and meadows in northeastern Washington.
Microtus pennsylvanicus, meadow mouse, p. 281, fig. 188.

10A. Ears nearly concealed, with no ear patch of black fur; tail more or less bicolored and usually less than one-third of the head and body length; incisive foramen 4.5–5 mm. in length (fig. 176). Usually in wet meadows of Upper Sonoran, Transition, and Canadian life zones in Oregon, the eastern half of Washington, and the northern half of California, but sometimes spreading into sagebrush areas.
Microtus montanus, montane meadow mouse, p. 283, fig. 189.

10B. Ears prominent, frequently nearly surrounded by a black patch of fur; tail weakly bicolored and more than one-third of the head and body length; incisive foramen about 6 mm. in length (fig. 176). Humid Transition Life Zone and grasslands west of the Cascade crest in Washington, Oregon, and northwestern California.
Microtus townsendii, Townsend meadow mouse, p. 281, fig. 190.

11A. A band of dorsal reddish fur mixed with black hairs, rather clearly separated from the grayish sides; posterior edge of palate is truncate (fig. 179). Northeastern Oregon and all of Washington in chaparral and forest clearings.
Clethrionomys gapperi, Gapper red-backed mouse, p. 277, fig. 183.

11B. No band of dorsal reddish fur mixed with black hairs; posterior edge of palate with a posteriorly directed spine. Northwestern California and western Oregon in deep forests.
Clethrionomys occidentalis, western red-backed mouse, p. 279. fig. 182.

12A. Living in trees; tail more than 50 per cent of head and body length . 15

12B. Living on the ground; tail usually less than 50 per cent of head and body length 13

13A. Re-entrant angles on the cheek side of the M₁ half or less than half as deep as those on the lingual side; longest diameter of eye about 4 mm. . . 14

13B. Re-entrant angles on the cheek side of the M₁ almost as deep as those on the lingual side; longest diameter of the eye about 2 mm. Meadows from Humid Transition Zone into the Hudsonian Life Zone of northwestern California, western Oregon, and Washington.
Microtus oregoni, Oregon meadow mouse or creeping vole, p. 279, fig. 187.

14A. Tail less than 50 mm.; hind foot 16–18 mm. Grassy places in heather or under logs in the adjoining forests, mostly in the Canadian and Hudsonian life zones of northern California, Oregon, and Washington.
Phenacomys intermedius, heather vole, p. 275, fig. 184.

14B. Tail more than 50 mm.; hind foot 19–20 mm. Dense forests of spruce or fir in northwestern California and western Oregon (but rare) in the Transition and Canadian life zones, usually near water.
Phenacomys albipes, white-footed vole, p. 275.

15A. Yellowish red fur dorsally, nose of the same color (except the base of the vibrissae); brain case scarcely ridged. Northwestern California and western Oregon in fir trees.
Phenacomys longicaudus, red tree mouse, p. 277, fig. 185.

15B. Brownish fur dorsally, nose sooty; brain case strongly ridged. Northwestern Oregon in fir and hemlock trees.
Phenacomys silvicola, dusky tree mouse, p. 277.

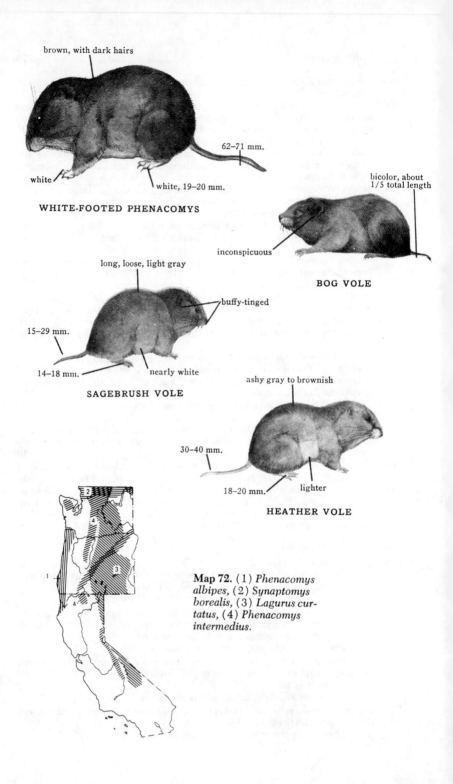

brown, with dark hairs

62–71 mm.

white

white, 19–20 mm.

WHITE-FOOTED PHENACOMYS

bicolor, about
1/5 total length

inconspicuous

BOG VOLE

long, loose, light gray

buffy-tinged

15–29 mm.

14–18 mm.

nearly white

SAGEBRUSH VOLE

ashy gray to brownish

30–40 mm.

18–20 mm.

lighter

HEATHER VOLE

Map 72. (1) *Phenacomys albipes*, (2) *Synaptomys borealis*, (3) *Lagurus curtatus*, (4) *Phenacomys intermedius*.

* White-footed vole (*Phenacomys albipes*). Length 168–74 mm., about 6.5 inches; *tail 62–73 mm.; hind foot 18.5–20 mm.*; ear 10–12 mm.; skull about 23 mm. condylobasilar length; molars rooted, those on the lower jaw with the lingual re-entrant angles about two times deeper than the outer (cheek) ones; with pattern of the M³ about as shown in fig. 46; *tail sparsely haired, sharply bicolored, more than half as long as head and body; upper parts brown with dark hairs,* under parts washed with buffy. Dense forests of northwestern California and western Oregon in the Transition Life Zone (rare). P. 285, Map 72.

Northern bog vole (*Synaptomys borealis*). Length 118–35 mm.; tail bicolored, 19–27 mm., less than 20 per cent of total length; hind foot 16–22 mm.; small, inconspicuous ears, 12–13 mm.; upper parts varying from grizzled gray to brown; under parts lead-colored; skull 24–25´mm.; crown of M³ as shown in fig. 48; upper incisors grooved, with yellow on one side of the groove and white on the other. In grass-covered runways among herbs in cold, boggy mountain valleys, mostly Hudsonian Life Zone in northern Washington. P. 284, Map 72.

Sagebrush vole (*Lagurus curtatus*). Length 108–40 mm., about five inches; *tail 15–29 mm.; hind foot 14–18 mm.*; ear (crown) 9 mm.; skull 21–24.6 mm.; *tail scarcely or barely reaching beyond the ends of the extended hind legs;* auditory bullae extending posteriorly beyond the level of the occiput; crown of M³ similar to that shown in fig. 47; fur long and fine, light grayish above and almost white below. Sagebrush Scrub; Upper Sonoran and Transition life zones in northeastern California and eastern Oregon and Washington. P. 291, fig. 181, Map 72.

* Heather vole (*Phenacomys intermedius*). Length 126–66 mm., about 5.5 inches; tail 28–40 mm.; hind foot 18–21 mm.; ear, crown, 14–16.5 mm.; skull about 27 mm.; molars rooted, those on the lower jaw with the lingual re-entrant angles about twice as deep as those on the cheek side; crown pattern of the M³ about as shown in figs. 46 and 180; hind foot with five plantar tubercles (fig. 177); *tail less than half head and body length and somewhat bicolored; upper parts ashy gray, sometimes tinged with brown,* under parts grayish. Open grassy places and heather patches in the yellow pine, red fir, lodgepole, spruce, and hemlock forests north from Fresno County in the Sierra Nevada in California; Transition and Canadian zones, but mostly the Hudsonian Life Zone in California, through most of Oregon and Washington. P. 284, fig. 184, Map 72.

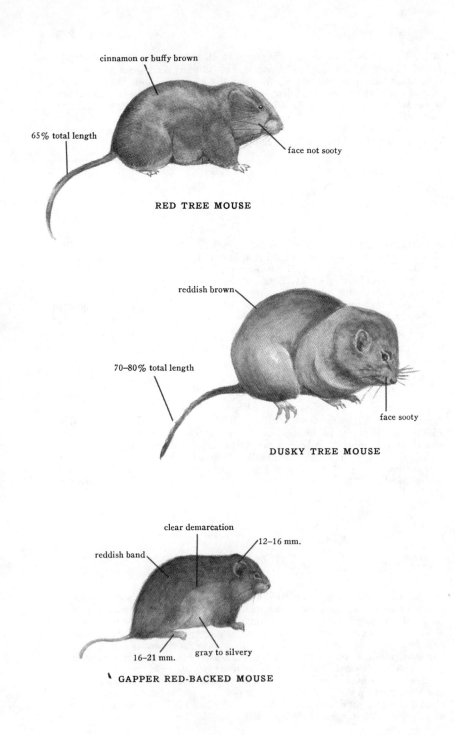

cinnamon or buffy brown

65% total length

face not sooty

RED TREE MOUSE

reddish brown

70–80% total length

face sooty

DUSKY TREE MOUSE

clear demarcation

12–16 mm.

reddish band

16–21 mm.

gray to silvery

GAPPER RED-BACKED MOUSE

❯Red tree mouse (*Phenacomys longicaudus*). Length 180–85 mm., about seven inches; *tail 73–80 mm.; hind foot 21–22.5 mm.;* ear 11 mm.; skull about 24.5 mm.; molars rooted, those on the lower jaw with the lingual re-entrant angles about two times deeper than the outer (cheek) ones; crown of M³ about as shown in fig. 46; ears nearly concealed in fur; *tail unicolored, hairy, and about 65 per cent total body length; light rust or cinnamon upper parts,* buffy white over lead-colored underfur below; lives largely in trees and constructs large nests far above the ground. Mixed Evergreen Forest in northwestern California and western Oregon in the Transition Life Zone. P. 287, Map 73.

Dusky tree mouse (*Phenacomys silvicola*). Length 171–205 mm.; tail 70–87 mm., well haired, blackish, and *between 70 and 80 per cent total length;* hind foot 21.5–23 mm.; ear 10 mm.; skull 26–28 mm.; molars rooted, those on the lower jaw with the lingual re-entrant angles about two times deeper than those on the outer (cheek) side; upper parts are *reddish brown,* under parts are whitish, more dusky. Large nests in the fir and hemlock forests of northwestern Oregon. (Some mammalogists believe this species to be a race of *Phenacomys longicaudus.*) P. 287, fig. 185, Map 73.

❮Gapper red-backed mouse (*Clethrionomys gapperi*). Length 138–62 mm.; tail 41–50 mm.; hind foot 16–21 mm.; ear 12–16 mm.; skull 21.0–24.3 mm.; rooted molars, those on lower jaw with re-entrant angles about the same depth on both sides; M³ pattern similar to that shown in fig. 45; palate extends back to level of the M³ (fig. 179); broad red dorsal area contrasting with gray or dusky sides and buffy white under parts; tail about half as long as head and body. Found north of the Columbia River in grassy meadows and rock slides and in chaparral in the Transition and Canadian life zones. P. 284, fig. 183, Map 74.

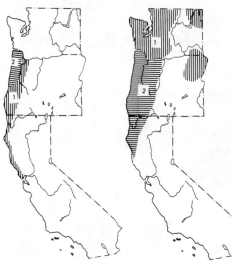

Map 73, left. (1) *Phenacomys longicaudus*, (2) *Phenacomys silvicola*. Map 74, right. (1) *Clethrionomys gapperi*, (2) *Clethrionomys occidentalis*.

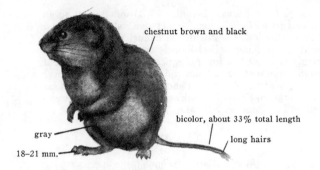

chestnut brown and black

bicolor, about 33% total length

long hairs

gray

18–21 mm.

WESTERN RED-BACKED MOUSE

not dark

reddish or grayish

50–93 mm.
bicolor

more than ⅓
total length

20–26 mm.

LONG-TAILED MEADOW MOUSE

hairs 3–5 mm.

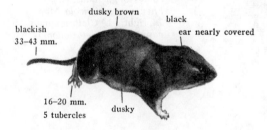

dusky brown

black

ear nearly covered

blackish
33–43 mm.

16–20 mm.
5 tubercles

dusky

OREGON MEADOW MOUSE

Western red-backed mouse (*Clethrionomys occidentalis*). Length 137–65 mm., about six inches; tail 45–56 mm.; hind foot 18–20.5 mm.; ear 10–12 mm.; skull 23–25 mm.; rooted molars, those on the lower jaw with re-entrant angles about the same depth on both sides; M³ pattern similar to that shown in fig. 45; end of palate posteriorly is a transverse shelf and extends back to level of the M³; chestnut brown, or brown mixed with considerable black above, gradually grading into sides and belly, which is buffy gray; tail about half as long as head and body, indistinctly bicolored. Found south of the Columbia River in Oregon and northwestern California, in deep woods of the Transition and Canadian life zones. P. 284, fig. 182, Map 74.

Long-tailed meadow mouse (*Microtus longicaudus*). Length 158–221 mm., about eight inches; tail 50–93 mm.; hind foot 20–26 mm.; ear 13–14 mm.; skull 25.6–30 mm. condylobasilar length; *tail usually more than one-third total length and more or less bicolored*; a dorsal band of reddish brown fur with grayish sides and bluish gray under parts; fur on nose and ears not darker; hairs on tip of tail 3–5 mm.; *incisive foramen narrowing gradually posteriorly but not to a point, 1 × 5.5 mm.* (fig. 176); molars without roots, M² with crown shaped as in fig. 44; two to four young. No clear-cut trails, among willows in the wet mountain meadows of the sagebrush, yellow pine, red fir, and Engelmann spruce, hemlock, and lodgepole forests; Transition and Canadian life zones in all three states. P. 291, fig. 192, Map 75.

Oregon meadow mouse (*Microtus oregoni*). *Length 130–56 mm., about 5.5 inches*; tail 33–43 mm.; *hind foot 16–20 mm.*; ear 9 mm.; skull 22–23 mm.; *incisive foramen relatively short and wide, dumbbell-shaped, 1 × 4 mm.* (fig. 176); molars without roots, upper molars with a crown pattern about as shown in fig. 178; five tubercles on the hind feet (similar to fig. 177); fur is short and dense, upper parts sooty gray to dark brown and black, belly dusky gray; ears scantily haired, black, and barely projecting from the fur; eyes noticeably small, 2–4 mm. in diameter; young appear in April and May. Tunnels in open grassy places and under dry logs, or in marshes and damp regions in redwood, fir, spruce, and hemlock forest; Transition into Hudsonian Life Zone. P. 289, fig. 187, Map 75.

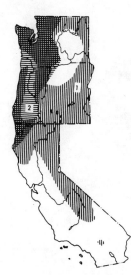

Map 75. (1) *Microtus longicaudus,* (2) *Microtus oregoni.*

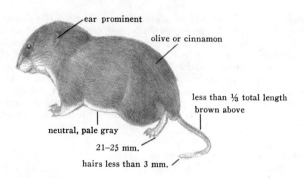

ear prominent

olive or cinnamon

less than ⅓ total length
brown above

neutral, pale gray

21–25 mm.

hairs less than 3 mm.

CALIFORNIA MEADOW MOUSE

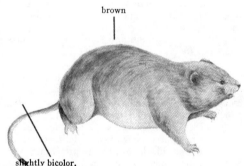

brown

slightly bicolor,
about 1/2 total length

TOWNSEND MEADOW MOUSE

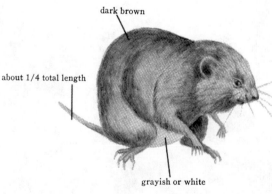

dark brown

about 1/4 total length

grayish or white

MEADOW MOUSE

California meadow mouse (*Microtus californicus*). Length 157–214 mm., about seven inches; tail 44–67 mm.; hind foot 21–25.5 mm.; ear 15 mm.; skull 26–29.5 mm.; *incisive foramen about as wide as or wider posteriorly than anteriorly,* 1.5 × 5 mm. (fig. 176); M³ pattern similar to that shown in fig. 42, and molars without roots; buffy brown or dark brown above, frequently with a reddish tinge on the middle of the back, under surface blue gray to white; *hairs on tip of tail less than 3 mm.;* ears project well above the fur. Upland meadows and grassy places in the Valley Grassland; Lower and Upper Sonoran life zones. P. 289, fig. 191, Map 76.

Townsend meadow mouse (*Microtus townsendii*). Length 170–225 mm.; tail slightly bicolored, 48–70 mm., about 40 to 50 per cent of head and body length; hind foot 20–26 mm.; ear 15–17 mm.; upper parts dark brownish; under parts dark grayish; skull 30–31 mm.; molars without roots; incisive foramen constricted (usually), about 5 mm. long (fig. 176); open grasslands in low country west of the Cascade Mountains in Oregon and Washington and in northwestern California. P. 289, fig. 190, Map 76.

Meadow mouse (*Microtus pennsylvanicus*). Length 165–76 mm.; tail comprises about one-fourth total length, 40–50 mm.; ear 14–15.3 mm.; upper parts dark brown, with under parts grayish or whitish fur; skull 25–27 mm., incisive foramen about 5 mm. in length (fig. 176); M² with a small posterior loop (fig. 43), five loops in all; molars without roots; palate with many small holes (fig. 178); hind foot 20–21 mm. Columbia Plateau in marshes and damp meadows, where it makes trails through dense vegetation. P. 289, fig. 188, Map 76.

Map 76. (1) *Microtus californicus,* (2) *Microtus townsendii,* (3) *Microtus pennsylvanicus,* (4) *Microtus richardsoni.*

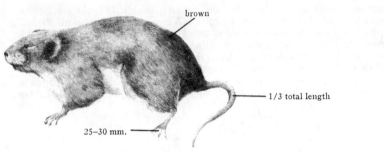

brown

1/3 total length

25–30 mm.

WATER RAT

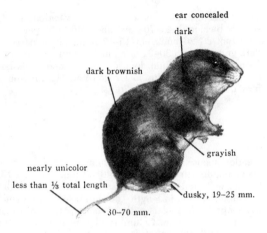

ear concealed

dark

dark brownish

grayish

nearly unicolor

less than ⅓ total length

dusky, 19–25 mm.

30–70 mm.

MONTANE MEADOW MOUSE

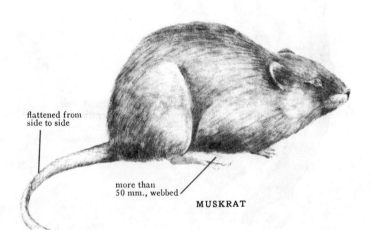

flattened from
side to side

more than
50 mm., webbed

MUSKRAT

Water rat (*Microtus richardsoni*). Length 198–261 mm., usually more than eight inches; tail about one-third total length, 69–92 mm.; hind foot 25–30 mm.; ear 15–20 mm.; skull 35–55 mm., foramen as in fig. 176; upper parts are dark brown to reddish brown; under parts are grayish brown; molars without roots, M³ pattern similar to that shown in fig. 42; two to 14 young; trails and burrows along alpine marshes and swift streams in the Cascade Mountains and in eastern Washington and Oregon in the Canadian and Hudsonian life zones. P. 287, fig. 186, Map 76.

Montane meadow mouse (*Microtus montanus*). Length, 145–90 mm., about 7 inches; tail, 30–70 mm.; hind foot, 18–25 mm.; ear (crown), 10–17 mm.; skull, about 28 mm.; *tail usually less than one-third the total length, nearly unicolored,* sometimes more or less bicolored, dark brown to buffy gray above, sometimes reddish-tinged, undersurface dark gray; *darker fur frequently showing on nose and ears; incisive foramen wedge-shaped coming almost to a point, posteriorly,* 1 × 4.5–5 mm. (fig. 176); posterior loop on lingual side of M² is open; molars without roots, M³ shaped as in fig. 42. Tunnels near springs and in wet grassy meadows of the yellow pine, red fir, Engelmann spruce, hemlock, and lodgepole forests where there is always green grass; Transition and Canadian life zones. (According to Murray Johnson (1963), the population in the Vancouver area, Washington, may prove to be a separate species. At present they are classified as *Microtus montanus canicaudus,* but nowhere does this population contact *montanus.*) P. 289, fig. 189, Map 77.

Muskrat (*Ondatra zibethica*). Length 435–620 mm., about 20 inches; tail scaly, sides flattened, 170–294 mm.; hind foot 62–88 mm.; ear, crown, 13–20 mm.; skull 46–54 mm., basilar length; dull rusty brown to dark brown all over, except that feet are darker and mouth region is lighter. Native along the Colorado River and along streams and lakes of eastern California; throughout most of the low country in Oregon and Washington; introduced widely in many other places, especially in the San Joaquin Valley, California. Generally found in cattail marshes or in the banks of slow-moving streams. P. 292, fig. 193, Map 78.

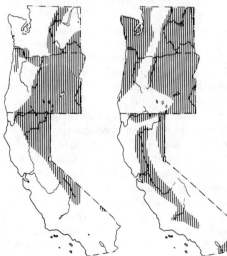

Map 77, left. *Microtus montanus.* **Map 78, right.** *Ondatra zibethica.*

Subfamily **Microtinae** (Microtine Mice)

The microtine mice, or voles, are characterized by a number of features, some or all of which apply to the various species. As a group, they are easily confused, so this special emphasis on biology and habitat for each species supplements the keys, brief descriptions, and figures.

Generally, the members of this subfamily have tails shorter than the head and body length; however, the muskrat (*Ondatra*) and the tree mice (*Phenacomys*) have tails half the total length or more. The ears of microtine mice are generally not as conspicuous as in other mice, largely because the long hairs on the sides of the head tend to cover them. All have flattened crowns on the molars, which have prisms of dentine surrounded by enamel. The re-entrant angles, which run more or less deeply into the sides of the molars, and the shape of the prisms on the crown are very useful in distinguishing the various genera (see figs. 42–48).

Sizes range from the gray sagebrush meadow mouse (*Lagurus curtatus*, fig. 181), scarcely five inches in length, to the muskrat (*Ondatra zibethica*, fig. 193), which may be over 15 inches long. There are six genera in this subfamily.

The most primitive of the microtines is the northern bog vole (*Synaptomys borealis*). It makes runways in the cold, boggy mountain meadows of northern Washington. Its short tail (20 per cent or less of its total length), inconspicuous ears, and grooved, or differentially colored, upper incisors are distinctive features, shared only by the sagebrush vole, which, however, inhabits dry areas. Little is known of the biology of the bog vole.

There are two species of red-backed mice. The Gapper red-backed mouse (*Clethrionomys gapperi*, fig. 183) is distinguished from its more southern relative, the western red-backed mouse (*Clethrionomys occidentalis*, fig. 182) and other similar mice by the red dorsal band, which is distinctly separated from the gray sides. The reddish back of the more southern species has many black hairs and is not distinctly separated from the color on the sides. The red-backed mice have rooted cheek teeth, and the re-entrant angles on the lingual side of the lower molars are about as deep as those on the cheek side. These red-backed mice live in deep forests under logs, but sometimes they are taken in wet meadows bordering forests, or are found in trees several feet off the ground.

Three to six are born in a nest made of lichens. Little is known about the general biology except that they feed on green vegetation.

The genus *Phenacomys* includes four species in this area, two of which live on the ground and two are arboreal. The heather vole (*Phenacomys intermedius*, fig. 184) is an alpine species and lives mostly in patches of heather (*Cassiope* and *Phyllodoce*) and huckleberry (*Vaccinium*), which grow in open places among the forests of lodgepole pine, white-barked pine, spruce, and hemlock. The tail, which is usually less than 40 mm. long, readily distinguishes the heather vole from the other three. The heather vole may be confused with certain species of *Microtus*, from which it can

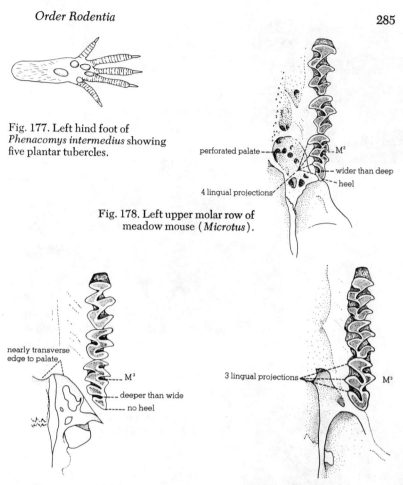

Fig. 177. Left hind foot of
Phenacomys intermedius showing
five plantar tubercles.

perforated palate

M³

wider than deep

heel

4 lingual projections

Fig. 178. Left upper molar row of
meadow mouse (*Microtus*).

nearly transverse
edge to palate

M³

deeper than wide

no heel

3 lingual projections

M³

Fig. 179. Left upper molar row of
the Gapper red-backed mouse
(*Clethrionomys gapperi*).

Fig. 180. Left upper molar row of
the heather vole (*Phenacomys
intermedius*).

be distinguished with certainty only by comparing dental features (figs.
178, 180). The *Phenacomys* have rooted molars. The molars on the lower
jaw have re-entrant angles on the lingual side twice as deep as those on
the cheek side. The heather vole builds large nests of soft, shredded blades
of snowgrass (*Juncoides*) and lichen in or under the snow. Summer nests
of dead grasses and mosses are made in underground burrows. It feeds on
bear grass (*Xerophyllum*), lousewort (*Pedicularis*), and huckleberry leaves.
Four young were found in one brood nest (Shaw, 1924).

The white-footed vole (*Phenacomys albipes*) is very rare in the forests
of northwestern Oregon and western Washington. Its longer tail (usually
over 60 mm.) and white feet distinguish it readily from the heather vole;

Fig. 181. Sagebrush meadow mouse (*Lagurus curtatus*).

Fig. 182. Western red-backed mouse (*Clethrionomys occidentalis*).

Fig. 183. Gapper red-backed mouse (*Clethrionomys gapperi*).

Fig. 184. Heather vole (*Phenacomys intermedius*).

Fig. 185. Red tree mouse (*Phenacomys longicaudus*). Photograph by
Alex Walker.

its dental features are different from the meadow mice. Practically nothing
is known of its biology.

The dusky tree mouse (*Phenacomys silvicola*, fig. 185) and the red tree
mouse (*Phenacomys longicaudus*) are distinguished by the dorsal brownish and reddish colorations, respectively. The dusky tree mouse also has a
dusky nose. Both live high in fir, spruce, or hemlock trees, where they make
large nests of cast-off resin ducts and mid-ribs of the needles, which they
use as food. The young in a litter range from one to three and are born between February and September after a gestation period of 28 days. This
period may be extended to 48 days by lactating females (Hamilton, 1962).
Such a long reproductive period, compared with other microtines of similar
size and considering the small litter size and slow development of the nursing young, is interpreted as a physiological adjustment to the difficulties of
converting energy that result from the diet of fir needles. Tree mice are
difficult to trap, apparently because they rarely come to the ground and
because they are not attracted by the rolled-oats baits that are most frequently used.

The seven species of meadow voles or meadow mice in the genus *Microtus* are sometimes difficult to distinguish externally from each other and
from other voles (*Phenacomys, Clethrionomys,* and *Lagurus*). They are
readily characterized, however, by dental features (figs. 42–48). All *Microtus* have rootless molars, and most species have four well-defined projections on the lingual side of the last upper molar (fig. 42). The water rat
(*Microtus richardsoni*, fig. 186) of the Cascade Mountains and the Oregon
meadow mouse (*Microtus oregoni*, fig. 187) have five plantar tubercles.

Fig. 186. Water rat
(*Microtus richardsoni*).

Fig. 187. Oregon meadow
mouse (*Microtus oregoni*).

Fig. 188. Meadow mouse
(*Microtus pennsylvanicus*).

Fig. 189. Montane meadow
mouse (*Microtus montanus*).

All other species have six tubercles. The water vole is strictly an alpine animal living around streams, marshes, and damp meadows. It feeds on blueberries (*Vaccinium*), avalanche lilies, asters, potentillas, and clover. It builds nests under the snow. A litter consists of two to seven young, born as late as September.

The Oregon meadow mouse occupies about all conceivable "mouse" habitats (Dalquest, 1948). It constructs tiny tunnels near grass roots and seldom ventures outside. It feeds on grasses and other green plants. The nest is a ball of dried grass sometimes placed in log cavities. A litter contains three to five, usually born in April or May. Unlike other species of *Microtus*, the creeping meadow mouse has only three well-defined projections on the lingual side of the upper molars, in this respect resembling the species of *Phenacomys* (fig. 46).

The meadow mouse (*Microtus pennsylvanicus*, fig. 188) appears only in northern Washington. It can readily be distinguished from other mice by the little posterior loop on the middle upper molar, M^2 (fig. 43).

The montane meadow mouse (*Microtus montanus*, fig. 189) has six tubercles on each hind foot. Its bicolored tail is less than 2.5 times the length of the hind foot. Where it occurs with the Townsend meadow mouse (*Microtus townsendii*, fig. 190) it may be tentatively identified by its shorter hind foot, which is less than 23.7 mm., and its grayish upper parts. The incisive foramina are also very different (see fig. 176). Both cut tunnels through the grass and make nests of dead grass under the ground and under the snow. Succulent stems and leaves of forbs (not grasses) are the chief food (Johnson, 1963). Throughout most of their range, the longer days and abundance of green food speed up the reproductive activity and rate of growth in litters born in the spring, compared with those born in the drier seasons with shorter days (Pinter, 1963). The litter size usually ranges from five to eight young for each species. Hawks, owls, weasels, and snakes are the chief enemies.

The California meadow mouse (*Microtus californicus*, fig. 191) inhabits the lowlands of California and southwestern Oregon, where its range overlaps that of the long-tailed meadow mouse (*Microtus longicaudus*, fig. 192). It can be distinguished by its short tail, which is less than one-third the total length. If it were not for the fact that they usually occupy different ranges, it would be difficult to distinguish the California meadow mouse, the montane meadow mouse, and the Townsend meadow mouse without comparison of the incisive foramina (fig. 176).

The population of *Microtus californicus* varies cyclically in the San Francisco Bay region, building up to a peak every three or four years and then declining rapidly. Pearson (1963) presents convincing evidence that this decline is largely caused by predators, which actually reduce the population and do not merely take off the surplus as seems to be the case in many other predator–prey relations.

The gestation period is three weeks, and breeding is throughout the year. The litters average 4.2 and range from one to nine young. Within fif-

Fig. 190. Townsend meadow mouse (*Microtus townsendii*).

Fig. 191. California meadow mouse (*Microtus californicus*).

teen hours after the young are born, ovulation and breeding may occur again. The young are weaned after two weeks. Thus a population of meadow mice may increase very rapidly. Lidicker and Anderson (1962) studied them as they became established in a 47-acre island in the San Francisco Bay. They invaded the entire island during the first growing season and fully exploited it during the second summer. Hawks, owls, weasels, and snakes are the chief enemies. This species may become an agricultural pest, especially in orchards and vineyards.

The long-tailed meadow mouse (*Microtus longicaudus*) is readily distinguished from most other microtine mice with which it may be associated by its bicolored long tail, which is over one-third (nearly one-half) its total length. The size and shape of its incisive foramen are also useful in identifying this species (fig. 176). These mice live in stream-side brush and do not make tunnels through the grass as do most of the other species. Breeding extends over the year, with litters ranging from two to eight young. The nest is made of plant fibers underground and in or under logs. Hawks, owls, weasels, snakes, and herons are the chief enemies. The long-tailed meadow mouse ranges above the agricultural zone in most places, and damage is relatively slight compared with the California meadow mouse of the lowlands.

All meadow mice swim well, using the hind feet for propulsion while the front feet are folded under the body and the tail trails behind. They have been observed to submerge for 20 seconds and to swim under water up to 20 feet (Fisler, 1961).

The sagebrush meadow mouse (*Lagurus curtatus*) occurs not only in the sagebrush regions of all three states but also in the bunch grass in eastern Washington. Its short tail, which is scarcely longer than the hind foot, distinguishes this species from all other microtines except the bog vole (*Synaptomys borealis*), which lives in very wet areas. There are six plantar tubercles in adults. The molars of both species also differ (figs. 47, 48). The sagebrush vole feeds on nearly anything that is green (James and Booth, 1954) and does not need water to drink. This rodent is frequently found in colonies, which probably represent families. The burrows are four to 18 inches deep and are cleaner than those of most rodents. The nest is made of sagebrush bark or grass stems. Like other meadow mice, they are active at all hours of the day and night. Mating usually takes place within 24 hours after parturition. Litters range from one to 11, averaging 5.2. The majority of females mate after they are two months old, and the period of gestation is about 25 days. The sagebrush vole is known to harbor fleas that may carry sylvatic plague, which can be transmitted to man. Agriculturally this species is of little, if any, importance.

Why are some of these mice so difficult to distinguish externally when they may belong in different genera? An explanation may be that many of the same factors act in natural selection on these unrelated animals with similar habitats, producing similarities in appearance as a result of parallel

Fig. 192. Long-tailed meadow mouse (*Microtus longicaudus*).

evolution (*parallelism*) or perhaps by the actual converging of the outward features (*convergence*). Thus certain species of *Microtus, Phenacomys, Clethrionomys,* and *Lagurus* may have similar external characteristics, yet their skeletal and dental features betray their real relationship. Another reason for external similarity may be that these genera are only recently diverging from a common ancestor.

The ranges of the meadow mice or voles have been widely studied. The California meadow mouse is known to have a small home range (Pearson, 1960a). Brant (1962) considered that the best estimate of the average maximum distance between points of capture for these voles was about 60 feet. Thus, this species is ideal for field experiments on homing ability. Some have found their way back to the home range when released 600 feet away. Intraspecific social factors are said to be the main reason for leaving the areas where they were released, but whether they reach the home range by navigation or random wandering, or both, is not known (Fisler, 1962).

Muskrat (*Ondatra zibethica*), fig. 193.

One sometimes sees a ratlike animal about as bulky as a half-grown house cat in a stream or pond. When it crawls out on the muddy bank, its rich brownish fur and long scaly tail, flat on the sides, serve to identify it. The muskrat gets its name from two musk glands that lie on either side of the lower abdomen. The musk is secreted through the reproductive organs, and in both sexes the glands are most highly developed close to breeding time. The muskrat is not likely to be confused with any other mammal. The smaller Norway rat, which swims readily, is grayish, with a round tail. The much larger beaver, introduced from the Rocky Mountain region but native also in parts of the Pacific States, is also aquatic but has a large tail, flat on the top and bottom.

The muskrat is seldom found far from water. When it is searching for new feeding grounds, it may wander considerable distances, but the ideal habitats are ponds, reservoirs, and irrigation canals that have plenty of rushes and cattails. However, a trout stream with no cattails or rushes often is heavily populated with them.

Like the beaver, the muskrat may make a house in the water, with the door submerged. The house is generally constructed of cattails, rushes, and other aquatic herbaceous plants. The enclosed nest is made of finely shredded leaves. Unlike the beaver, it does not build dams across streams, cut down trees, or dig long canals away from its pond. The muskrats along the Colorado River in California live in holes in the levees and banks, dug with the entrances under water.

In addition to tules, rushes, cattails, and other water-growing plants, muskrats eat bulbs and grasses. Captive animals are especially fond of carrots. They occasionally eat animal food, such as mussels, tadpoles, and snails. Sometimes muskrats form a raft several feet across, from water plants, on which they rest while eating. Such large floating masses are occasionally seen in ponds and lakes.

The muskrat is an important fur-bearing mammal. In the United States muskrat fur yields trappers about $30 million a year. Many sloughs and ponds, if stocked and properly managed, can be developed into a profitable business. The fur itself is of average durability and is frequently sold as "Hudson seal" after the longer guard hairs have been removed to expose the fine, soft underfur. The flesh is edible and in some Southern states is

Fig. 193. Muskrat (*Ondatra zibethica*).

Fig. 194. Tracks of muskrat, about half actual size.

sold as marsh hare. Muskrats do considerable damage when they dig holes in the levees of ponds or irrigation ditches. Not infrequently, however, pocket gophers are the real culprits. Many wildlife refuges are stocked with muskrats for the purpose of keeping tules and other water plants under control. Generally the habitat does not infringe on man's interests.

The hind foot of a muskrat is much larger than the forefoot, a fact that aids in identifying the tracks (fig. 194).

Besides man, the probable enemies of the muskrat are dogs, coyotes, minks, horned owls, trematodes, and roundworms. Although these predators and parasites take a great toll, they do not seem to reduce the muskrat population seriously. The mink is probably the chief predator of the muskrat where the two are found together. Errington (1963) believes that the mink removes only the excess population, and the physically disabled, the young without established home ranges, and animals forced out by floods or droughts are doubtless the ones most often killed by predators.

There are from three to nine young in a litter. Along the Colorado River in California, muskrats breed all year, although most of the young are born between February and November. The muskrat does not hibernate but is active under the ice in winter. Its thick underfur keeps the cold away from the skin, thus conserving body heat.

There is one species of muskrat native to the Pacific States, found along the lower Colorado River and in northeastern California and over most of Washington and Oregon except the high mountains (Map 78). Muskrats have been introduced from many different areas, mostly for fur raising. Many of these have obtained their freedom and become established in nature. The wisdom of thus introducing an animal into a locality beyond its natural range is questionable, especially where it can do damage.

There are geographic races that differ considerably in appearance. One of these subspecies is the Nevada muskrat, a dark, thick-coated animal that inhabits the streams, lakes, and ponds of eastern California. Another subspecies is the Colorado River muskrat, a pale-colored animal found along the Colorado River in California and the irrigation systems leading from it. Including the introduced animals, muskrats are found in all the life zones up into the Canadian and are especially common along the rivers, ponds, and lakes in the San Joaquin Valley of California.

Family **Muridae** (Old World Rats and Mice)

Dental Formula 1-0-0-3/1-0-0-3

This exotic family is worldwide in distribution. The tails are scantily haired and long. The molar teeth have three rows of tubercles running down them (figs. 36, 37), and the palate extends far posterior to the level of the last molar. Three introduced species—the Norway rat (*Rattus norvegicus*), the black rat (*Rattus rattus*), and the house mouse (*Mus musculus*)—will be treated rather fully because of their economic and medical importance.

KEY TO THE OLD WORLD RATS AND MICE (Muridae)

These rats and mice have all been introduced from the Old World. Their tails are noticeably scaly. They have three rows of cusps on the molars (figs. 36, 37) instead of the two found in New World mice and rats (figs. 35, 42). The dental formula is 1-0-0-3/1-0-0-3. There are no range maps.

1A. Total length more than 250 mm.; M^1 shorter than the combined lengths of M^2 and M^3 2
1B. Total length less than 250 mm.; M^1 longer than the combined lengths of M^2 and M^3. In all three states usually not far from human habitation.
   Mus musculus, house mouse, p. 297, fig. 196.
2A. Tail shorter than the head and body; parietal length along the temporal ridge is not less than the distance between the temporal ridges. Near human habitation in all three states.
   Rattus norvegicus, Norway rat, p. 297, fig. 195.
2B. Tail longer than the head and body; parietal length along the temporal ridges is less than the distance between the temporal ridges. Near human habitation in all three states.
   Rattus rattus, Black rat or roof rat, p. 297.

Fig. 195. Norway rat (*Rattus norvegicus*).

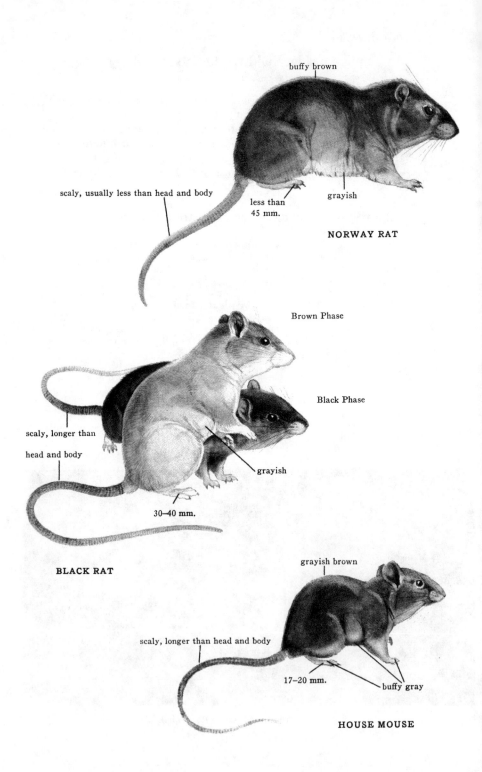

buffy brown

scaly, usually less than head and body

less than
45 mm.

grayish

NORWAY RAT

Brown Phase

Black Phase

scaly, longer than

head and body

grayish

30–40 mm.

BLACK RAT

grayish brown

scaly, longer than head and body

17–20 mm.

buffy gray

HOUSE MOUSE

Norway rat (*Rattus norvegicus*). Length 320–455 mm., about 16 inches; *tail less than head and body length, 120–210 mm.*, about 25 scales to the inch; hind foot 30–45 mm.; *molars with three rows of cusps*, not flat on the grinding surface (fig. 37); ears and tail nearly naked, scales clearly showing on the tail; buffy brown or rusty gray above, dirty white below. All three states, around cities, dwellings, and garbage dumps; introduced from the Old World into all three states. No range map is included. P. 298, fig. 195.

Black rat (*Rattus rattus*). Length 325–435 mm., about 16 inches; *tail longer than the head and body, 213–50 mm.*, with more than 25 scales to the inches; hind foot 30–39 mm.; skull 40–45 mm. total length; *molars with three rows of cusps*, not flat on the grinding surface (fig. 37); ears and tail nearly naked, scales showing on tail; *two color phases*: one is black above, with tail, ears, and under parts sooty; another is brown above, with white or yellowish below (the black phase is frequently referred to as the "black rat" and the brown phase as the "roof rat," "brown rat," and "Alexandrine rat"). Near habitations along the coast, in the interior valleys, and in the foothills of the Sierra Nevada; introduced from the Old World into all three states. P. 299, no map.

House mouse (*Mus musculus*). Length 150–80 mm., about seven inches long; *tail 70–98 mm., scantily haired* (scales showing clearly); hind foot 17–20 mm.; skull 20.5–22.5 mm.; *molars with three rows of cusps* (fig. 36); incisors not grooved; palate extending far behind the level of the last molar; grayish brown or buffy brown above; *buffy gray (never white) below*. About human habitations but also in the fields; introduced from the Old World into all three states. P. 299, fig. 196, no map.

Norway Rat (*Rattus norvegicus*), fig. 195

Probably no other mammal in the world has profited as much from civilization as the Norway rat. It is thought to be native to western China, from which it gradually worked its way westward to Europe, and then by ship to England and America. It swims icy rivers without hesitation and has made long migrations from the Old World to reach its new homes. In the Pacific States, however, it is apparently unable to protect itself in the wilds and so is generally restricted to cities, towns, and rural dwellings where there is protection.

Norway rats were introduced into the American Colonies at the time of the Revolution. Since then they have spread over the entire country, except for the arid desert regions. Rubbish and garbage dumps and even sewage-disposal systems are infested with them. The Norway rat is a good digger and a superb gnawer. Unless buildings are made of stone, brick, or concrete, it has no difficulty getting between the walls or under the floors, even of modern wooden structures. The four incisor teeth, continually worn by gnawing, are extremely efficient and may show a combined growth of 20 inches a year. It is a good climber and is frequently observed walking on telephone cables and electric wires far above the pavement.

Superficially the Norway rat resembles both the hispid cotton rat of the Colorado River Valley and the wood rats, which are widely distributed. The adult Norway rat is easily distinguished from the hispid cotton rat by its ashy gray under parts and nearly naked ears, which stand out clearly from the coarse hairs on the head. The cotton rat is whitish beneath, and during the winter is covered with long grizzly fur on its head and ears (fig. 170). The adult Norway rat is distinguishable from the wood rats (*Neotoma*) by its grayish instead of whitish feet and under parts. The scaly tail of the Norway rat is less than head and body length and is distinctly ringed. The scales on the tails of the wood rats are usually somewhat obscured by hairs. The molar teeth of the Norway rat have three distinct rows of tubercles running along them, whereas the wood rats have two (figs. 37, 49, 50).

Norway rats cost man thousands of dollars annually in his efforts with steel and stone to keep them out of the walls of buildings, besides the loss of stored grains and other goods, and the loss from fires caused by their gnawing the insulation off electric wires. Most serious, however, are the diseases passed to man. Norway rats harbor fleas, which carry the bacillus that causes bubonic plague, the black death. In the past, this dread disease has been brought to West Coast seaports by rats going from ship to wharf. Trichinosis is also passed from these rats to man.

The Norway rat is one of the most prolific mammals, with litters of eight to 12 at intervals throughout the year. When this rat invades rural areas, it is easily captured by owls, hawks, foxes, and weasels. A bulletin put out by the U.S. Fish and Wildlife Service, Washington, D.C., gives the most effective means of controlling Old World rats.

Black Rat (*Rattus rattus*)

This introduced species is represented by two color phases called the black rat and the roof rat. These may be distinguished from the heavier Norway rat by their weight (half a pound), slender body, and larger ears. (The Norway rat weighs from one to one and one-half pounds.) They also have tails longer than the combined head and body length, whereas the tail of a Norway rat will not reach to the end of its nose. There are about 25 scales to the inch on the tail of a Norway rat and more than this on the tail of the black rat or roof rat. The black rat lives along seaports and adjacent towns. It is frequently found along stream courses away from buildings. It is readily distinguished from other rats by its black pelage. The coloration of the roof rat resembles that of the Norway rat. The longer tail, however, readily distinguishes it from its larger relative. The roof rat lives along the coast, in the interior valleys, and even in the lower parts of the mountains.

House Mouse (*Mus musculus*), fig. 196

The house mouse was brought to America without doubt in storage boxes and barrels by early settlers. Today, except in isolated places, there is scarcely a warehouse that is not infested with this destructive little rodent, which has also spread to fields. On many occasions this mouse has been taken in traps set in weed patches along ditches or beside highways far from human habitation. In some places it appears to have driven out the native species of mice.

The house mouse superficially resembles native mice but may easily be distinguished by external appearance and certain dental characteristics.

Fig. 196. House mouse (*Mus musculus*).

The two groups of mice most likely to be confused with the house mouse are the white-footed mice and the harvest mice. The house mouse has buffy brown upper parts, which grade imperceptibly into gray—never white —under parts. The outer surfaces of the upper incisor teeth are flat and have no longitudinal grooves. When viewed from the side, each incisor has a distinct notch directly behind the cutting edge. The grinding surfaces of the molar teeth have three rows of tubercles, or bumps, along them. Both groups of native mice have molar teeth with flat surfaces or with two rows of tubercles; in addition, the harvest mice have front upper incisors with definite longitudinal grooves (fig. 160). The white-footed mice usually have white under parts as well as white feet.

House mice are omnivorous, eating seeds, grains, fruit, vegetables, cheese, and meat.

Individual house mice have been known to "sing" and are said to be able to trill and to run up all of the notes in an octave. They have many enemies besides man and house cats. The more important ones are owls, hawks, snakes, foxes, weasels, skunks, and raccoons. Most of these are relatively ineffective so long as the mice remain in buildings but serve admirably to keep their numbers reduced in the field. Barn owls and screech owls, however, frequently live in haylofts and other places where mice are numerous. Ranchers should encourage their presence here, where they are frequently more efficient than cats—as well as less destructive to songbirds.

House mice are very prolific, with as many as five litters of four to eight blind young a year. The nests consist of cotton, wool, rags, paper, or any other soft material, located in woodpiles, within walls, in dresser drawers, among discarded magazines or in upholstered furniture.

The house mouse, because of its smaller size, is a pest that in some respects is even harder to control than the Norway rat. Inside boxes, crates, and sacks it is frequently brought into otherwise rodent-proof structures where ideal conditions for rapid multiplication prevail.

Family **Zapodidae** (Jumping Mice)

Dental Formula 1-0-1-3/1-0-0-3

These long-tailed mice move by jumping. The skulls have large oval ant-orbital foramina and the zygomatic plate is nearly horizontal. The upper incisors are grooved.

The genus *Zapus* is the only representative of this family in the Pacific States. The species may be distinguished from other mice by their long tails and strong, well-developed hind legs, which are well adapted for making long leaps. There are four grinding teeth on each side of the head on the upper jaw; the first of these, however, is very small and easily overlooked.

The two groups of mice in the Pacific States without external cheek pouches and with grooved upper incisors are the jumping mice and the harvest mice. The former have tails much longer than the head and body;

the latter have tails about the same length as the head and body. The jumping mice hibernate, unlike most other mice.

KEY TO THE JUMPING MICE (Zapodidae)

The mice belonging to this family have tails about one and a half times the length of the head and body. The darker fur on the back is usually clearly demarcated from that on the yellowish sides. They have no external cheek pouches, but unlike other mice without external cheek pouches, they have four upper cheek teeth on each side of the jaw. The dental formula is 1-0-1-3/1-0-0-3.

1A. Western halves of Washington and Oregon and the coastal region of northern California. Upper premolar .50–.55 mm. in diameter, with a dark crescentic fold; baculum with a spadelike tip. Transition and Canadian life zones in moist undergrowth of shrubs, ferns, or weeds.
   Zapus trinotatus, Pacific jumping mouse, p. 303, fig. 198.
1B. Eastern halves of Washington and Oregon and the mountains of the northern half of California. Upper premolar .70–.75 mm. in diameter, without crescentic fold; no spadelike tip on the baculum. Transition and Canadian life zones in wet meadows.
   Zapus princeps, western jumping mouse, p. 303, fig. 197.

Fig. 197. Western jumping mouse (*Zapus princeps*).

Fig. 198. Pacific jumping mouse (*Zapus trinotatus*).

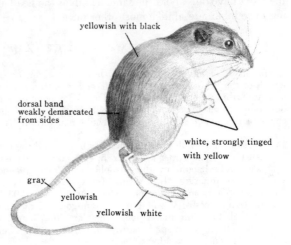

yellowish with black

dorsal band
weakly demarcated
from sides

white, strongly tinged
with yellow

gray

yellowish

yellowish white

WESTERN JUMPING MOUSE

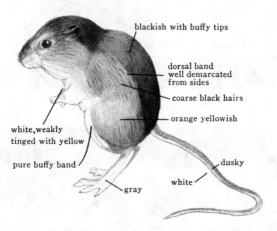

blackish with buffy tips

dorsal band
well demarcated
from sides

coarse black hairs

orange yellowish

white, weakly
tinged with yellow

pure buffy band

dusky

white

gray

PACIFIC JUMPING MOUSE

Zapus Dental Formula 1-0-1-3/1-0-0-3

Western jumping mouse (*Zapus princeps*). Length 215–55 mm., about 9.5 inches; tail 121–55 mm.; hind foot 30–37 mm.; skull 24.7–25.4 mm.; upper incisors grooved; four upper cheek teeth on each side, upper premolar small, .50– .55 mm. in diameter; baculum length .5 mm. or more, not spade-shaped at tip; *dark dorsal band not sharply demarcated from the sides*; sides of dull olive or lemon yellow with black hairs; *under parts pure white*; distinct narrow band of pure yellow between the belly and the sides; *ear conspicuously bordered with yellow*. Grassy meadows and aspen thickets along streams in eastern parts of all three states; Transition and Canadian life zones. P. 304, fig. 197, Map 79.

Pacific jumping mouse (*Zapus trinotatus*). Length 211–42 mm., about nine inches; tail 112–55 mm.; hind foot 30–36 mm.; skull 23.9–25 mm.; upper incisors grooved; four upper cheek teeth on each side, upper premolar .70–.75 mm. in diameter; baculum spade-shaped at tip; buffy-tipped dusky fur dorsally; sides orange yellow, with about as many black hairs as buffy; distinct line of pure buffy hairs between the sides and the belly; *under parts white, faintly tinged with yellow; tail grayish above, gradually changing to pure white below*. Chiefly meadows in the forests of redwood, fir, spruce, and hemlock. Transition Life Zone in the western half of Washington and Oregon and in northwestern California. P. 304, fig. 198, Map 79.

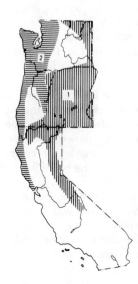

Map 79. (1) *Zapus princeps,* (2) *Zapus trinotatus.*

Pacific Jumping Mouse (*Zapus trinotatus*), fig. 198

If a person walks through a wet meadow at the edge of a grove of red-woods in northwestern California, he may be startled when a small mouse with a very long tail catapults from beneath his feet to safety five or six feet away. This is the Pacific jumping mouse. Like most other forms of jumping mice, it prefers grassy wet places in the Transition and Canadian life zones.

It has long hind legs, which contrast strikingly with the small, weak front legs. In some respects jumping mice resemble kangaroo rats and kangaroo mice in habits and appearance, but differ in the lack of fur-lined cheek pouches and by their preference for, or nearness to, moist habitats instead of arid places. They are excellent swimmers. The grooved upper incisor teeth, similar to those of a harvest mouse (fig. 160), distinguish a jumping mouse from any other similar small rodent without external cheek pouches except a harvest mouse. A jumping mouse may be distinguished from a harvest mouse by its shape, its smaller ears, and the length of its tail. The ears of a jumping mouse project only slightly beyond the fur, whereas those of a harvest mouse are large and conspicuous. The tail of a jumping mouse is close to 60 per cent of the total length; that of a harvest mouse is nearer 50 per cent of the total length. The long tail plays an important part in its method of locomotion and in preserving balance. Animals with broken or amputated tails turn somersaults when they land after a jump.

Jumping mice are not common, but locally they may be more abundant than trapping results would indicate. Bailey (1936), writing about the jumping mouse, describes it as making little piles of grass stems in meadows where it lives. These grass stems are cut three or four inches long, which help to distinguish them from much shorter similar cuttings of meadow mice. Other jumping mice may have similar habits which should help in locating their feeding grounds. The food of jumping mice consists almost entirely of seeds of wild grasses. They may, however, be attracted to a trap with prepared bait such as rolled oats. Nests of jumping mice are made mostly of very fine grasses and other vegetation. In summer the nests are frequently found on the surface of the ground. A litter consists of four to six young.

Little is known of the winter life of the Pacific jumping mouse, but presumably it hibernates in underground nests during the coldest weather. One captured in Humboldt County, California, became cold and inactive in foggy weather, and to all outward appearances was hibernating.

The only other species of the genus living in the Pacific States is the western jumping mouse (*Zapus princeps*). The two differ in the size of the premolar teeth and their bacula.

These mice are far too scarce to be of any serious economic importance. Their habits are such that they interfere little with man's interests. Their natural enemies are hawks, owls, weasels, skunks, and coyotes. So long as these are not seriously reduced, jumping mice will probably never increase in numbers sufficiently to become a nuisance anywhere.

Suborder HYSTRICOMORPHA

Family **Erethizontidae** (American Porcupines)

Dental Formula 1-0-1-3/1-0-1-3

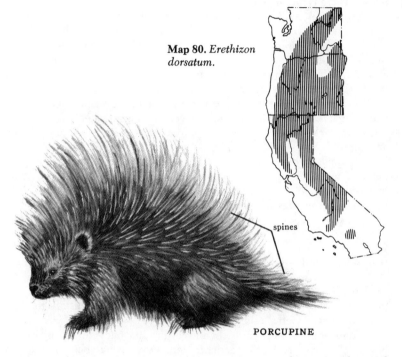

Map 80. *Erethizon dorsatum.*

spines

PORCUPINE

Porcupine (*Erethizon dorsatum*). Length 680–860 mm., about 28 inches; tail 175–300 mm.; hind foot 95–124 mm.; ear about 27 mm.; skull 90–110 mm.; yellowish to blackish above, with *stiff quills and spines* especially on rump and tail; weight up to 33 pounds. Chiefly in areas of coniferous trees, north from the San Bernardino and Tehachapi mountains and Marin County in California, through Oregon and Washington in the less humid Transition and Canadian life zones. Fig. 199, Map 80.

Porcupine (*Erethizon dorsatum*)

The porcupine (*Erethizon dorsatum*, fig. 199) is the only native representative in the United States belonging to this family, which in turn is our only native family of the suborder Hystricomorpha. The porcupine is largely arboreal and seems to have come from South America, where there are many other hystricomorph species. Like the other representatives of the suborder, it has very large antorbital canals through which run not only nerves and blood vessels, but a part of the jaw muscle as well. The dorsal side of the body and the tail are covered with long, sharp spines. The porcupine does not hibernate.

The introduced nutria (*Myocastor coypu*) is the only other hystricomorph rodent to be found in the wild state among the fauna of the Pacific States. There is no range map for the nutria.

Whether a porcupine is slow-moving and clumsy solely because of its extremely effective defensive armament is a matter for speculation. It can hardly be mistaken for any other native mammal. The porcupine is larger than a good-sized house cat; it may reach a weight of nearly 40 pounds, although half that amount is more nearly the average. Next to the beaver, it is our largest native rodent.

The long, stiff spines, which reach their greatest development on the tail and rump, are modified hairs. They are very loosely attached, and the sharp tips have back-slanting microscopic barbs that penetrate an animal's skin and continue to work in deeper. Most wild animals have no way of removing the quills, which may eventually penetrate a vital organ and cause death. The danger of stumbling over a porcupine at night on a trail is not inconsiderable. When a full-grown porcupine is attacked, it lowers its head between its front legs and erects the long spines all over its back. When the attacker approaches too close, it slaps violently with its spiny tail, driving dozens of quills into the enemy. Generally one slap is sufficient to discourage further aggression. However, 70 quills were once removed from a bulldog that insisted on finishing a fight which nearly cost the dog its eyesight and its life. After a severe fight, the quills become loosened and are thrown off the tail as it is slapped about—this is probably the basis for stories about the porcupine "throwing its quills." Such aimlessly thrown quills are too light to penetrate the victim's skin.

In summer porcupines eat herbs and shrubs. In winter and during periods of drought they feed on the tender underbark of young yellow pines, junipers, white firs, red firs, larch, and other trees, which they sometimes girdle and kill. However, there is some reason to believe that porcupines do far less damage to lumber interests than is generally supposed, because the trees they kill are young and most of them would die as the forest matures. Porcupines are excellent climbers, descending a tree backwards. They have been known to swim to get food.

Porcupines rest in the dense foliage of a particular tree or in a cave near the feeding grounds. There one can find hundreds of their oval-shaped brownish pellets. These droppings are the size of the last joint of one's little finger and are composed of plant materials resembling pressed sawdust (p. 466). When the rodents feed on herbaceous food in the spring or summer, the pellets resemble sheep or deer feces.

About camps porcupines frequently make themselves a nuisance by gnawing leather boots, saddles, ax handles, and even gunstocks, presumably

Fig. 199. Porcupine (*Erethizon dorsatum*).

because of the salty perspiration. They are also fond of sweet potatoes, mesquite beans, apples, and other fruits.

There are authentic reports that mountain lions, bobcats, fishers, and wolverines prey on porcupines. Quills are frequently found in the bodies of these animals, and occasionally the remains of a porcupine have been found after one of these predators has fed on it. One theory advanced on the achievement of this difficult feat is that, after bringing the porcupine to bay on a snowbank, the fisher might burrow under the snow and attack the vulnerable spineless belly, avoiding the tail, which thrashes harmlessly about on the snow. Fishers have been introduced from Canada into certain forests in Washington and Oregon for the purpose of controlling the porcupine population. Parasites must also cause considerable harm to the porcupine. Dozens of large roundworms were once found in the stomach and intestines of a large animal.

Very little is known about the breeding habits of the porcupine. The young are probably born in cavities under large rockslides or other similarly protected places. One, or possibly two, young seem to compose the average-sized litter, which comes in May or June. The young are large, are remarkably active, and have well-developed coats of hair and even some spines when they are born. Seven months was the gestation period for two females bred in captivity.

When there is specific evidence of porcupine damage to orchards or timbered areas, the animal should be controlled. However, some states protect porcupines, in spite of opposition from lumbering interests, since a person lost in the woods can kill one easily when in need of food. The flesh is edible, having a distinct resinous flavor.

There is one species of porcupine in the Pacific States. It ranges through all the zones, apparently without regard to life-zone boundaries, up into the Hudsonian Life Zone. The porcupine is rarely reported in the humid forests west of the Cascade Mountains. It is, however, to be found on isolated desert mountains far out on the Mojave Desert in California. Interestingly, too, it is the only species of a South American type of rodent to be listed in our native mammalian fauna of the Recent epoch. It is actually more closely related to the guinea pig (*Cavia*), capybara (*Hydrochoerus*), and the fine-furred chinchilla (*Chinchilla*) than to any of our native rodents.

Family **Capromyidae** (Nutria)

Dental Formula 1-0-1-3/1-0-1-3

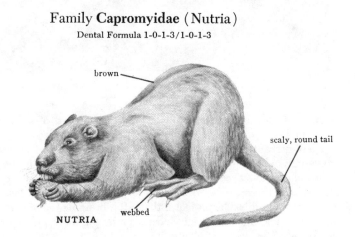

Nutria (*Myocastor coypu*). Dental formula 1-0-1-3/1-0-1-3. Length of head and body 500–630 mm.; tail round, scaly, and about 70 per cent of head and body length, or about 420 mm.; hind foot about 140 mm.; glossy dark yellowish brown or chestnut, dorsally; incisors deep orange red; cheek teeth with deep inner and outer re-entrant folds surrounded by enamel. Introduced into all three states in marshy areas. (There is no range map or photograph for the nutria.)

Nutria (*Myocaster coypu*)

The South American nutria or coypu has been introduced widely in the Pacific States on fur farms, and now can be found in a feral state in many places.

The nutria is larger than a muskrat but not as large as a beaver, from which it is easily distinguished by its round scaly tail. It has beaver-like habits, and may weigh up to 25 pounds. Its general coloration is brownish, which results from the pigment in the silky underfur showing through the long, coarse, clear guard hairs. The outer surface of the upper incisors is orange-colored and there are two enamel folds on each side of the upper molars. Although the nutria was introduced earlier, in the first part of the 1950's promoters of nutria fur imported thousands of animals, which they sold at prices up to $950 a pair. They agreed to buy back the offspring for $380 a pair as long as a market existed for breeding stock. The market soon became saturated, and no demand for the pelts developed. Thousands of nutria farmers were caught with substantial investments. This situation led to illegal release of large numbers of animals, which established themselves along the waterways of the Pacific States.

The nutria has a voracious appetite and eats all kinds of marsh vegetation as well as clover, alfalfa, carrots, and corn. As it spreads into agricultural land, it digs large burrows in the dikes and banks of irrigation canals and thus becomes a serious pest.

In the State of California, the Department of Agriculture is responsible for controlling the nutria. It issues permits to breeders and is responsible for eliminating the wild nutria.

Since 1948 wild nutria have been trapped in Los Angeles, San Diego, Merced, El Dorado, Lake, and Tulare counties in California. They have been taken in Oregon in all the counties west of the Cascade range and in Klamath, Union, and Malheur counties east of these mountains.

The Oregon Game Commission is concerned about its becoming established because of the potential damage to agriculture and to the native wildlife. Trappers in Oregon reported catching 38 nutrias in the 1958–59 season, but in the winter of 1961–62 the catch jumped to 492, with no more intensive trapping. The fur was worth only 57 cents a pelt and few trappers bothered to skin their catch.

The Department of Game in Washington reports that a colony of nutria has become established in King County. The animals were introduced in the late thirties.

The nutria may well serve as an example for other states to consider future protection from introduced fauna, which may become expensive nuisances, if not indeed dangerous pests.

10. Order Cetacea

The mammals of the order Cetacea are mostly marine, although some live in rivers, and some species are the largest animals in the world. They have fishlike bodies, with the forelimbs modified as flippers and the powerful tail provided with horizontal flukes. The hind limbs are not visible externally. There is scarcely any evidence of hair after birth. The young are nourished with milk, which may contain 21 to 35 per cent fat. The nostrils or nostril through which the animal breathes is on the top of the head and is called the "blowhole." Fat, or blubber, often several inches thick, aids in maintaining body temperature in icy waters. The large size of many whales also enables them to live in cold waters (see surface-volume relationships, p. 93).

The order is subdivided into two groups, the toothed whales (Odontoceti) and the baleen whales (Mysticeti). The toothed whales include the families Ziphiidae, Physeteridae, and Delphinidae, all of which have jaws with one or more pairs of teeth; they prey on large fishes, seals, and other whales. The baleen, or whalebone, whales off the Pacific States include the families Eschrichtidae, Balaenopteridae, and Balaenidae. All are toothless after birth and feed on small marine creatures. There is no key for Cetacea.

Whaling was formerly a very important industry, pursued mostly in the Northern Hemisphere. The old whaling vessels roamed the seas hunting the whale as a source of oil for lamps, spermaceti for candles, and whalebone for bustles, corsets, and ruffs. The nineteenth century saw only one interruption in whaling, in 1849, when the ships made anchor in San Francisco and other West Coast ports while the crews looked for gold. This tying up of hundreds of ships for indefinite periods greatly affected the economy. In 1900 whalebone sold for five dollars a pound, and a large bowhead whale would yield up to 3,000 pounds. The most valuable of all whale products, however, then and now, was ambergris, a soft grayish material rarely found in the digestive tract of occasional whales, used as a basis for the finest perfumes.

Until recently there was a whaling station in the outskirts of Eureka, California; Hedgpeth (1962) reports one still operating in San Francisco Bay at Point San Pablo, where hump-backed, fin-backed, Sei, and sperm whales are processed, mostly for pet food. Just off the coast near Eureka there is an excellent old whaling ground, in a region of cold summer climate where several large rivers enter the ocean. Possibly the food supply is increased where fresh and salt water mix, just as there are usually more numerous and varied fauna where one land biotic community meets another.

Today whaling is still an important industry, but the methods, the scene, and the uses for the products have changed. The steam whaling ship, the harpoon gun, and the factory ship of the twentieth century are a far cry from the old whaleboat that pursued Moby Dick with hand-hurled harpoons a hundred years ago. Today over 90 per cent of the whales are killed in southern seas. Huge cranes haul the big mammals aboard factory ships, where they are cut up by machinery and processed. Glycerine, pet food, margarine, meat, fertilizer, and soap are the products.

Many important studies center about the factory ships, where biologists make anatomical studies as the immense carcasses are flensed, or stripped, and cut up. Here they have the opportunity to observe hundreds of whales in their natural environment. Marked darts shot into the thick blubber enable them to obtain records of travel, growth, and age, as well as threatened depletion of the different species from hunting. Only with such detailed information can intelligent international agreements be formulated and diminishing species conserved.

Suborder ODONTOCETI

(Toothed Whales)

These whales are born with a range of a few to many calcified teeth. They have no baleen. There is a single external nostril near the top of the head. The flipper has five phalanges, the first and fifth usually being poorly developed. Three families are represented off the coast of the Pacific States: Ziphiidae, Physeteridae, and Delphinidae.

Family **Ziphiidae** (Beaked Whales)

These long-snouted whales are usually less than 30 feet long, with a sickle-shaped dorsal fin about two-thirds of the distance back from the anterior end. There is one large tooth (rarely two) in each side of the lower jaw.

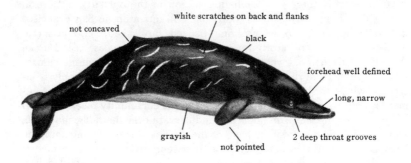

not concaved — white scratches on back and flanks — black — forehead well defined — long, narrow — grayish — not pointed — 2 deep throat grooves

BAIRD BEAKED WHALE

large tusk — throat groove

STEJNEGER   BEAKED WHALE

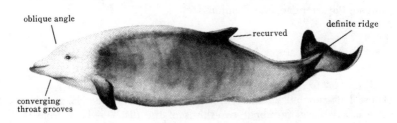

oblique angle — recurved — definite ridge — converging throat grooves

GOOSE-BEAKED WHALE

Berardius, dorsal fin straight along posterior border

Baird beaked whale (*Berardius bairdii*). Length, to 40 feet; black on the back with *dark grayish or whitish under parts; dorsal fin not concaved on its posterior margin, about two-thirds of the way back from the snout; long narrow snout; one or two teeth on each side of lower jaw in males* (buried in the gums in females), the anterior one nearly four inches long and the posterior one slightly more than two inches long; V-shaped groove beneath the chin. Rare.

Mesoplodon, mouth reaches to the level of the eye

Stejneger beaked whale (*Mesoplodon stejnegeri*). Length, to about 20 feet; *small recurved dorsal fin about two-thirds of the way back from the snout; two grooves on the throat converging toward the chin; in males, one large tooth on each side of the lower jaw,* up to eight inches long, laterally compressed; females essentially toothless. North Pacific Ocean; *very rare.* Six specimens from the California coast have recently been separated as a distinct species, *Mesoplodon carlhubbsi,* on the basis of skull characters (Moore, 1963). Externally, the anterior edge of the tooth in male *M. stejnegeri* rises in a straight line from gum to apex, while in male *M. carlhubbsi* there is a distinct convex curve between gum and apex. Other external differences unknown. One specimen of *M. carlhubbsi* was almost black, with a whitish beak and forehead and white streaks and blotches over the body (probably scars); another was blackish, with whitish under parts and beak, and lacked streaks. Roest (1964) reported the first known female of *M. stejnegeri* found along the central California coast.

Ziphius, mouth reaches less than half way to the level of the eye

Goose-beaked whale (*Ziphius cavirostris*). Length, to 28 feet; dorsal fin about two-thirds of the way back from the snout, *followed by a definite ridge to the tail;* color is variable; some have anterior end creamy white with posterior parts black, others are purplish above with sides spotted and white on the belly, and others leaden gray above with no white; throat grooves converge toward the chin; in the males *one tooth over two inches long projects forward in the anterior end of each side of lower jaw;* the females are generally toothless or with two very small teeth (up to 40 vestigial teeth may be embedded in the gums without sockets). Frequently travel in gams of 40 or more; rare off the California coast from San Diego to Humboldt County.

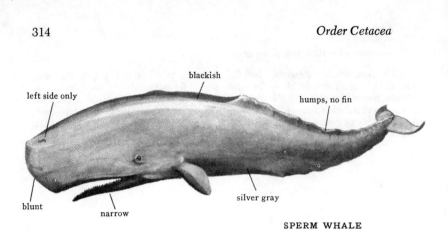

left side only

blackish

humps, no fin

silver gray

blunt

narrow

SPERM WHALE

Physeter, blunt snout

Sperm whale (*Physeter catodon*). Length, to 65 feet (males), 30 feet (females); dark bluish gray all over but sometimes with white on belly and lower jaw; 20–25 large teeth (up to eight inches long) on each side of lower jaw, with none or a few vestigial teeth on upper jaw; *head about one-third body length* and from side view almost square; no dorsal fin, but there is a row of humps on the posterior half; flippers small; spout goes diagonally forward; cephalopods are the chief food. The females give birth in tropical waters, but the males are in Arctic or Antarctic waters each summer. As many as 58 of these whales were once found beached in the Gulf of California (Cockrum, 1956). One was recently found along the central California coast (Roest, 1964). P. 315.

recurved

conic

PYGMY SPERM WHALE

Kogia, conical snout

Pygmy sperm whale (*Kogia breviceps*). Length eight to 13 feet; back is blackish and sides are grayish; nine to 15 needle-like teeth only on the lower jaw; *the narrow jaw does not reach to the end of the protruding, bulbous, and bluntly conic snout*; the nostril is to the left of the midline of the body. It has a small sickle-shaped dorsal fin and small flippers. Recently this rare whale was recorded for the fifth time along the central California coast (Roest, 1962). P. 316.

Family **Physeteridae** (Sperm Whales)

There is a spermaceti organ in the asymmetrical skull; there are many conical mandibular teeth but none in the upper jaw; there is no dorsal fin; there are two species; the larger sperm whale or cachalot may reach 65 feet in length; the smaller pygmy sperm whale is usually less than 13 feet; the nasal aperture is to the left of the midline of the body.

Sperm Whale (*Physeter catodon*)

The largest of the group of toothed whales is the famous sperm whale, which is caught off the coast of the Pacific States. The male is nearly twice the size of the cow and measures up to 65 feet in length. It is the most pugnacious of all the whales sought by the whaler, and in the early days of whaling many a boat was "stove in" and its crew lost after a big bull was wounded by harpoons. It is dark bluish gray and frequently has many long white scars about the head from battling the giant squid. The most striking feature about the sperm whale, however, is the enormous blunt head with the relatively small lower jaw that does not reach to the end of the snout. The lower jaw has 20 to 30 powerful teeth, which fit into sockets in the upper jaw, which has no teeth. Instead of a dorsal fin there is a series of humps that begin behind the middle of the back and extend nearly to the flukes. The flippers are relatively small, and the skull is asymmetrical. The single blowhole is forward; this is useful in tentative identification. Located in the large head is a reservoir somewhat to the right side of the canal that leads from the blowhole to the lungs. This reservoir is filled with an oily substance called *spermaceti*. The spermaceti organ is believed to be concerned with water pressure and may close the canal to the lungs during deep dives. A dive may last 20 to 30 minutes, or longer. As evidence of the depths to which whales go, a sperm whale once became entangled in a cable lying on the ocean bottom 3,240 feet deep, off the coast of northern South America. This depth would subject the whale's body to a pressure of 1,400 pounds per square inch. According to Dr. Remington Kellogg, mammalogist with the U.S. National Museum, the cows live largely in tropical waters with their calves, but the adult bulls travel in summer to the cold waters of the Arctic and Antarctic regions. The calves are 13 to 14 feet long at birth and are weaned after they are six months old. While suckling her calf the cow floats on her side and allows the young one to nurse and to breathe at the same time. Sperm whales are known to live eight to nine years. They feed chiefly on octopus and squid, but sharks and other fish are also eaten. A large one may require a ton of food a day.

The species has long been sought by whalers not only for the large quantities of valuable oil and spermaceti it produces, but also for the precious ambergris. This singular substance may possibly form as a concretion around the horny beaks of squid in the whale's intestines. Ambergris is lighter than water and has been found floating or cast upon the shore. Formerly it was used as medicine but today it forms the basis of the finest perfumes.

Pygmy Sperm Whale (*Kogia breviceps*)

Another kind of sperm whale, reported by the Scripps Institution of Oceanography at La Jolla, California, is the much smaller pygmy sperm whale. This toothed whale is small and has from nine to 15 pairs of teeth on the lower jaw only. It is black on the back and gray on the belly. It is only about eight to 13 feet long and is therefore smaller than some of the dolphins. It has a spermaceti reservoir but lacks the blunt nose of its larger relative. It too feeds on squid, in both the Atlantic and Pacific oceans. Little more is known about its way of life. It was formerly assigned to a separate family, Kogiidae, but is now (Walker, 1964) considered a species of Physeteridae.

Family **Delphinidae**

Tail with a notch posteriorly; sickle-shaped flippers;
well-developed dorsal fin (except in Lissodelphis)

These whales are usually less than 30 feet in length. The numerous teeth are conical and are usually present in both upper and lower jaws. There are 12 genera including the 13 species on the coast of the Pacific States.

Gill Bottle-Nosed Dolphin (Porpoise) (*Tursiops gillii*)

Frequently seen sporting in the surf along the coast of southern California is the bottle-nosed dolphin, or cowfish. The species is ten to 12 feet long. The back is bluish gray and the belly is white clear to the anus. The head and snout are dark, but both the upper lip and lower jaw are whitish. The lower jaw is slightly longer than the upper and each bears 20 to 26 pairs of teeth. The breeding season appears to be spring and early summer. Studies on pregnancy, birth, and behavior of the newborn Atlantic bottle-nosed dolphin (*Tursiops truncatus*) at the Aquaria at Marineland, Florida, indicate the period of gestation to be 12 to 13 months. This is an unusually long pregnancy for a carnivorous mammal. However, unlike the young mountain lion or wolf, the bottle-nosed dolphin must follow its mother from the time of birth, as do the young of hoofed mammals, which also have long pregnancies. Hence, the young bottle-nosed dolphin is quite well developed and swims readily immediately after birth. It is born tail first, and with a quick about-face movement the mother breaks the umbilical cord as the young floats to the surface for air. It has a large head, no teeth, and vibrissae on its snout. An hour or so later, when it finds the nipple, the mother's abdominal muscles force the milk into its mouth as she slowly glides through the water on her side. Nursing is only a matter of seconds. During the first month the infant stays close to its mother and to another dolphin that helps protect it from sharks. If it wanders too far, the mother calls it back by whistling. The young bottle-nosed dolphin sleeps under her tail flukes—both rising slowly to the surface every 30 to 40 seconds for air. Like many other young mammals, the youngsters are very playful and can be taught many things, such as retrieving objects thrown far out into the water. This species seems unable to breed until four years old; how long the animals live is not known. There is some evidence that a family consists of one adult male, three to five females, and young that are one or two years old.

The food of the bottle-nosed dolphin consists of several kinds of shoal fish; in the Gulf of Mexico it consumes large quantities of shrimp. Sometimes large schools of several hundred are seen from shipboard, making spectacular leaps of 15 to 20 feet out of the water. Because they have small commercial value compared with larger whales, they have not been studied sufficiently.

Offshore two other even more active species, often seen in schools of thousands, are the common dolphin (*Delphinus delphis*) and the beautiful Pacific white-sided dolphin (*Lagenorhynchus obliquidens*). The former is marked with black, yellow, and white and has a well-marked black V, margined with white, between the snout and the forehead. Its beak is about six inches long. The latter species is strikingly marked with black and yellow, but has a shorter beak and lacks the V-shaped mark on the snout.

Other small cetaceans occasionally seen from ships along the California coast and in San Francisco Bay are the Dall porpoise (*Phocoenoides dalli*) and the harbor porpoise (*Phocaena phocoena*). The black body with white sides of the Dall porpoise is about five to six feet long. Its flippers are small compared with other small cetaceans. It is said to feed almost entirely on

Fig. 200. Pacific blackfish (*Globicephala scammonii*).

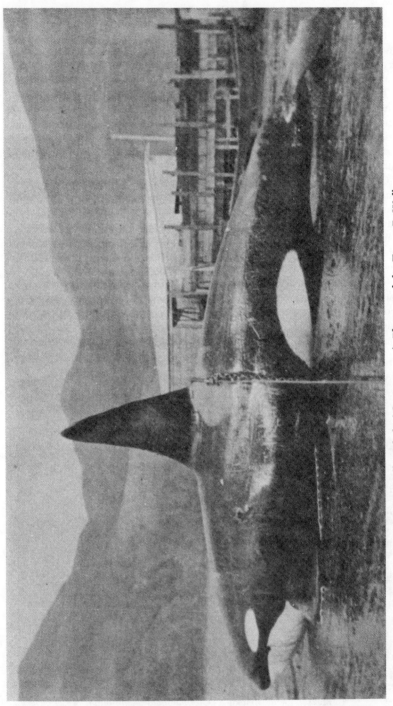

Fig. 201. Killer whale (*Orcinus orca*). Photograph by Ernest P. Walker.

squid. The harbor porpoise has a blackish back and a white belly. It has a blunt snout and a triangular fin. Fish comprise most of its food, but crustaceans and squid are also eaten.

Belonging to the same family as the dolphins and porpoises is the much larger killer whale (*Orcinus orca,* see fig. 201). This is the arch-predator of all the oceans and large seas of the world. The tall black dorsal fin, sometimes up to six feet in length in the bulls, the strikingly marked black-and-white body, the bluntly rounded snout, and jaws with many large conical teeth characterize these 20- to 30-foot monsters. Killer whales frequently hunt in packs or pods and can kill the largest baleen whales as a pack of wolves might attack and kill a bison. They frequently hunt aquatic birds, seals, and porpoises, which they swallow whole. Sometimes they force their prey into the sea by breaking up ice floes from beneath. They do considerable damage to the northern fur seals, especially the pups as they are learning to swim. Twenty-four seals were once found in the stomach of one killer whale.

Dolphins and porpoises (Delphinidae) have long won the attention of man not only because of their superb aquatic maneuvers in marineland circuses but in the solicitous care they give wounded and very young animals (Lilly, 1961). "Midwife" dolphins have been observed to assist a newly born dolphin to the surface of the water for its first breath of air and to help the mother protect the young from sharks for weeks later.

The way a dolphin locates food and communicates with others of its kind has recently attracted the attention of scientists. There is considerable evidence that a dolphin follows a school of fish, or even its own group, by the sense of taste, somewhat as a hound tracks by scent. The olfactory bulb is practically lacking in the brain of the dolphin, but numerous papillae all the way around the tongue apparently greatly increase the sense of taste. Perhaps one day man will train dolphins to hunt down schools of fish in the same way he now uses dogs to pursue game.

Considerable experimentation has been carried out with the Atlantic bottle-nosed dolphin (*Tursiops truncatus*), a close relative of the Gill bottle-nosed dolphin (*Tursiops gillii*) of the Pacific Coast.* These remarkable animals actually communicate with one another by means of grunts, whistles, clicks, pings, and other sonic and ultrasonic noises. According to the reactions of the animals, some of these sounds have been interpreted as "distress," "attention," and "irritation" (Lilly and Miller, 1961). Experiments show that dolphins avoid swimming into objects, and also locate prey, not by sight but by sonar similar to the echolocation of flying bats (see p. 109). The "pings" can also discriminate fish of different sizes at a distance (Kellogg, 1962). Whales probably have similar sound perception. Sonar may account for the simultaneous surfacing and diving of large schools. Still unexplained, however, is the occasional beaching of schools of whales, which are stranded and smother when the tide goes out.

---

* Walker (1964) lists only *Tursiops truncatus* and *T. aduncus* for this genus.

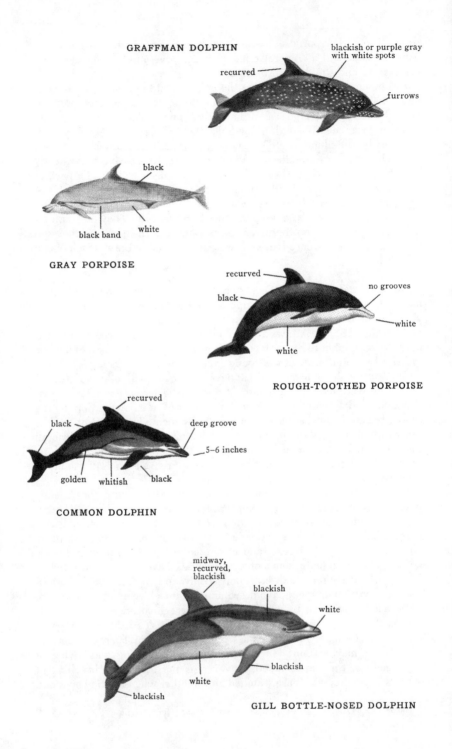

GRAFFMAN DOLPHIN

recurved

blackish or purple gray
with white spots

furrows

black

white

black band

white

GRAY PORPOISE

recurved

black

no grooves

white

white

ROUGH-TOOTHED PORPOISE

recurved

black

deep groove

5–6 inches

golden

whitish

black

COMMON DOLPHIN

midway,
recurved,
blackish

blackish

white

blackish

white

blackish

GILL BOTTLE-NOSED DOLPHIN

Stenella, nearly 100 teeth on the lower jaw; mandibular symphysis less than one-fifth the length of the ramus

Graffman dolphin (*Stenella graffmani*). Length, to eight feet; *white spots on purplish gray upper parts are conspicuous at close range; long beak distinctly marked off from forehead by transverse furrows;* teeth 43–47 in each tooth row, about 5 mm. in diameter, with rough furrowed crowns. Frequently stays close to ships for hours.

Gray porpoise (*Stenella styx*). Length, to eight feet; black above, white below; *narrow black bands extend in from the eye to the base of the flipper and from the eye to the anus.* Teeth 44 to 50 in each tooth row. Known to occur from ten miles south of the mouth of the Columbia River north to the Bering Sea.

Steno, 20 to 27 large teeth with rough crowns in each tooth row

Rough-toothed porpoise (*Steno bredanensis*). Length about eight feet; blackish above, sometimes with spots or blotches, and white below; *long white slender beak* with no transverse grooves between beak and forehead; beak laterally compressed; teeth have fine vertical wrinkles that give them a rough appearance. Rare.

Delphinus, 40 to 60 teeth in each tooth row; black ring encircles eye

Common dolphin (*Delphinus delphis*). Length, to seven feet; blackish tinged with greenish on the back, whitish on the belly and throat; *the golden stripes along the flanks and a saddle-like sway between the dorsal fin and the flukes are distinctive; beak five to six inches long, set off from forehead with a deep V-groove;* 40–60 pairs of small conical teeth in each jaw. Very common on open sea, often in schools of hundreds or thousands. P. 317.

Tursiops, 20 to 26 teeth in each tooth row

Bottle-nosed dolphin (*Tursiops gillii*), sometimes called "cowfish" or "common porpoise." Length, to 12 feet; purplish gray dorsally, *white on the belly to the anus,* but black from there to flukes; flukes and flippers pigmented, *white on upper lip,* and V-shaped dark streak on the side of the head; beak about three inches long. Teeth, 20–26 visible pairs on each jaw, each tooth about 5 mm. in diameter; one specimen had 24 teeth above and 23 below on each side. It is reported north to San Francisco Bay. P. 316.

no fin

black

short

white

NORTHERN RIGHT WHALE DOLPHIN

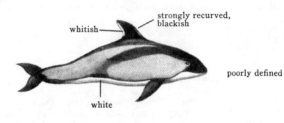

whitish

strongly recurved,
blackish

poorly defined

white

PACIFIC WHITE-SIDED DOLPHIN

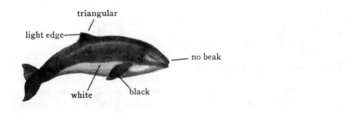

triangular

light edge

no beak

white

black

HARBOR PORPOISE

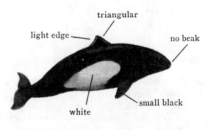

triangular

light edge

no beak

small black

white

DALL PORPOISE

Lissodelphis, 44 to 47 teeth in each tooth row; no dorsal fin

Northern right whale dolphin (*Lissodelphis borealis*). Length, to eight feet; *jet black back and sides contrast with the pure white narrow stripe on belly; no dorsal fin; beak not well differentiated from the forehead;* teeth small, sharp-pointed, with 44 pairs in the upper jaw and 47 pairs in the lower. Generally far from shore. Rare.

Lagenorhynchus, 22 to 45 teeth in each tooth row

Pacific white-sided dolphin (*Lagenorhynchus obliquidens*). Length, to ten feet; *beak poorly defined, about two inches long,* separated from the forehead by a cross groove; greenish black on upper parts, with gray stripes on the sides, and *a white belly; dorsal fin whitish on the strongly concaved hind edge;* prominent dorsal and ventral ridges on the posterior part of the body; 22–45 pairs of teeth, each about 5 mm. in diameter in each jaw; common offshore, frequently in large schools. P. 317.

Phocaena, 23 to 27 teeth in each tooth row; teeth spadelike

Harbor porpoise (*Phocaena phocoena*). Length, to six feet; blackish or brownish dorsally, *black on back of flippers and flukes, white on belly; beakless; triangular dorsal fin;* teeth, 23–27 pairs on each jaw; a sluggish inhabitant of bays. Common in San Francisco Bay, south at least to Pismo Beach in California, but replaced by the bottle-nosed dolphin in southern Californa. P. 317.

Phocoenoides, 23 to 27 teeth in each tooth row

Dall porpoise (*Phocoenoides dalli*). Length, to seven feet; *no beak; triangular dorsal fin* 6.5 inches high; greenish black to jet-black flippers; flukes 18 inches wide; flukes and back with a large area of shining white on the middle of the sides; 23–27 pairs of very small, pointed teeth on each jaw. Travels at high speed in small groups, usually well offshore. P. 317.

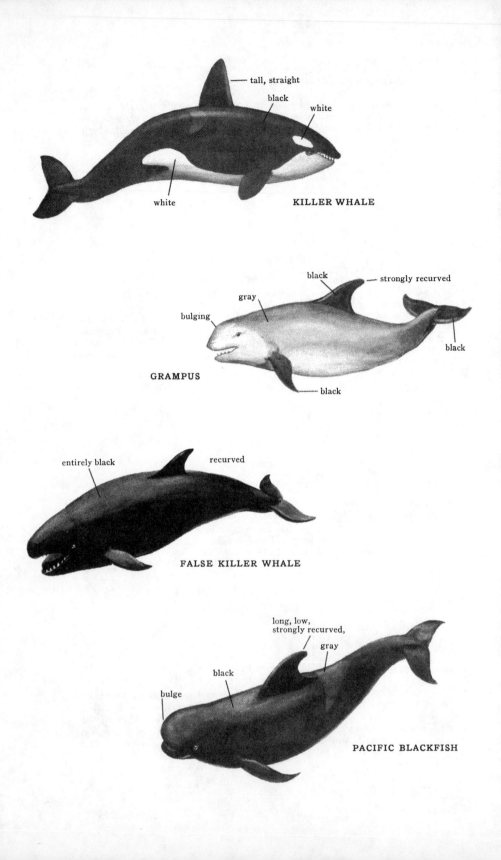

tall, straight

black

white

white

KILLER WHALE

black

strongly recurved

gray

bulging

black

GRAMPUS

black

entirely black

recurved

FALSE KILLER WHALE

long, low,
strongly recurved,

gray

black

bulge

PACIFIC BLACKFISH

Orcinus, ten to 13 recurved teeth in each tooth row

Killer whale (*Orcinus orca*). Length, to 30 feet; black upper parts, *also a white patch behind and above the eye, grayish behind the dorsal fin,* and white patches high upon the sides; the males have *a very high, nearly straight dorsal fin occasionally six feet long, higher than its basal length*; blunt snout; hunts in packs. Fig. 201. P. 319.

Grampus, three to seven teeth in each mandibular ramus

Grampus (*Grampus griseus*), also known as Risso's dolphin. Length, to 13 feet; *blunt nose*; gray body with *flippers and flukes black; lighter gray or white on ventral surface*; strongly recurved dorsal fin high and narrow at midlength of body; *white streaks and spots probably represent old scars; forehead very prominent*; teeth, three to seven pairs usually in the lower jaw only. Rare, apparently occurring singly.

Pseudorca, eight to 12 teeth in each tooth row

False killer whale (*Pseudorca crassidens*). Length, about 18 feet; *black all over* with star-shaped scars on sides and head; *recurved fin near midlength*; flippers about one-tenth body length; eight to 12 pairs of strong teeth on each jaw. Sometimes seen in great gams or pods of a hundred or more.

Globicephala, ten to 12 teeth in each tooth row

Pacific blackfish (*Globicephala scammonii*), also called pilot whale. Length, to 18 feet; *black except for narrow ventral white stripe and gray saddle* just behind dorsal fin; long low recurved dorsal fin closer to head than to the flukes; *forehead bulging over the short beak*; about ten to 12 pairs of teeth toward the front of each jaw, each tooth about one-half inch in diameter. Frequently seen well offshore in schools of five to 50; feeds largely on squid (fig. 200).

Suborder MYSTICETI
(Whalebone Whales)

The baleen whales are large and may reach a length of 100 feet or more. They have no functional teeth. They feed largely on small species of invertebrates. The water is strained through plates of horny baleen (whalebone), which hang down from the roof of the mouth. There are two nostrils (blowholes) on the top of the head. Three families are represented off the coast of the Pacific States. These are Eschrichtidae, Balaenopteridae, and Balaenidae.

Interest has long been centered on whether whales drink seawater. Certainly the cetaceans off the coast along the Pacific States have little or no contact with fresh water, although in some parts of the world some of them live in rivers. Most cetaceans (and also pinnipeds) obtain the necessary water by eating fish which have a high water and low salt content. Such food, however, is high in protein and requires considerable water to rid the body of the urea that forms as protein is used. Baleen whales, which feed mostly on marine invertebrates, take up much more salt than do the cetaceans that feed on fish, because the invertebrates are nearly in osmotic equilibrium with seawater. Samples from the kidneys of baleen whales show the urine to be much more concentrated than seawater; thus they readily excrete the excess salt from the food—and from the seawater if swallowed. Water is conserved in the females, since even the milk contains a smaller percentage; whale milk may be over one-third fat, compared with cow's milk, which is rarely as much as 5 per cent fat. Consequently, whales (and pinnipeds), by excreting concentrated urine, gain more water from their food than they excrete in the urea and excess salts. There may be special glands for the excretion of salt similar to those possessed by some birds, although no marine mammal is known to drink saltwater. Further study is needed on this subject.

Family **Eschrichtidae** (Gray Whales)

The gray whale measures up to 55 feet long. There is no dorsal fin but low round humps in the rear portion of the back. Throat grooves are present. There is a single genus, consisting of one species.

Gray Whale (*Eschrichtius glaucus,* formerly *Rhachianectes glaucus*), fig. 202

Each winter in December and January there is a southward movement of gray whales as they skirt the coastline on their long trip from the North Pacific and Arctic oceans to the breeding lagoons along western Baja California and off southern Sonora and Sinaloa, Mexico. In recent years the Institution of Oceanography at La Jolla, California, has contributed much to our knowledge of this interesting species of whale. It ranges from 30 to 50

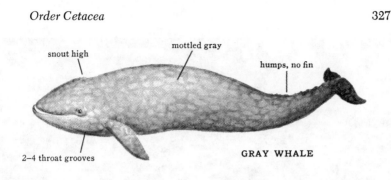

snout high

mottled gray

humps, no fin

2–4 throat grooves

GRAY WHALE

Eschrichtius, monotypic genus

Gray whale (*Eschrichtius glaucus,* formerly *Rhachianectes glaucus*). Length, 32–50 feet; weight 20–35 tons; slight humps but *no dorsal fin*; two to four throat grooves; blackish mottled with white patches; baleen short and yellow; *mottled gray or blackish*; peduncle of flukes slender, without prominent keel above and below; mouth bisecting head, the snout high and rigid; spout vertical and spreading. Shore-frequenting species. P. 326, fig. 202.

feet in length and may weigh up to 35 tons. There are generally so many barnacles and whitish scars on the older mammals that the original blackish slate color is nearly obscured. There are two to four short furrows on the throat, and there is no dorsal fin as in the true rorqual (family Balaenopteridae). The thick yellowish blades of whalebone are less than 20 inches long. Unlike other large whales, the gray whale has been known to live after being stranded until the tide returned to float it. These whales travel at a rate of six to seven miles an hour. They surface every three to seven minutes and blow three or four spouts of warm moist air some 20 feet high. The herds, gams, or pods are rarely seen and are widely spaced. A whole gam has been observed to surface and then submerge at nearly the same time, and there is reason to believe that some kind of communication exists among the members. Future research may reveal a new kind of sonar such as that employed by the bats and toothed whales.

The gray whale gives birth only once in two years. Therefore, since only about half the females breed each season, the most commonly observed group of gray whales is one female and two males (Gilmore, 1958).

After a gestation period of 12 months, the female gives birth in the breeding lagoon to a single calf 14 to 17 feet long and weighing up to 1,500 pounds. The cow probably nurses the young by lying on her side, as other whales do. The calf nurses for five months, and the cow protects it assiduously. Sometime between the middle of March and the middle of May the gam starts the long trip back to Arctic waters. Meanwhile the rest of the females have been bred, and will give birth the following winter (Gilmore, 1956).

In the southern breeding lagoons of Baja California, the gray whales feed on sardines. Here they may number up to 4,400 each winter. In the cold Arctic waters they are said to feed on krill, which in this case is composed of amphipod crustaceans.

Fig. 202. Gray whale (*Eschrichtius glaucus*) and calf. Courtesy of Dr. Carl L. Hubbs, Scripps Institution of Oceanography.

Early one April a few miles south of Carmel, California, in a deep protected cove, a large gray whale was observed close to the shore floating on its side and almost covered with seaweed. It appeared to be quite dead until it slowly raised one flipper straight up into the air. Then a pair of flukes surfaced near its head—probably the "dead" cow suckling her calf. After a few moments the big animal righted itself, blew a short spout, and slowly sank. Both whales soon surfaced and, swimming close together, spouted simultaneously. After describing a close circle, as though orienting themselves, they swam straight north, diving, surfacing, and spouting in unison. The Arctic Ocean, 6,000 miles away, was their goal, one of the longest migrations of any mammal.

Formerly the gray whales also lived in the Atlantic, but they were apparently exterminated there before definite records were kept. Records of a hundred years ago show that one thousand a day passed San Diego, California, during the southward migration. Then came the uncontrolled slaughter by West Coast whalers, one of whom, Captain C. M. Scammon, contributed much to our knowledge of the cetaceans. After a few seasons of butchery on the open sea and in breeding lagoons, the gray whale was seen no more. Then some years ago, Dr. Roy Chapman Andrews discovered it making regular migrations along the coast of Korea. More recently, it has again become common off the California coast. Present estimates are of an annual migration of 3,000 whales. They are protected by the International Whaling Agreement of 1937. It is hoped that Mexico will make a reserve of their breeding grounds and that they will continue to increase until the "one thousand a day" return. With intelligent harvesting, the future of the gray whale could be secure.

Family **Balaenopteridae**

Dorsal fin present; up to 105 feet long;
numerous sheets of whalebone

These are the fin-backed whales or rorquals, a term that applies to species of *Balaenoptera* and *Sibbaldus*. This family includes the largest whales, which may be up to 105 feet in length. The head is small, compared with other whales. A dorsal fin is always present, usually far posterior. The baleen plates are relatively short. Throat grooves are present. There are three genera and five species in the waters off the Pacific States.

Blue Whale (*Sibbaldus musculus*)

The blue whale is a true rorqual. It is the largest animal that ever lived. In summer these large cetaceans are found near the packs of polar ice in both ends of the world. Occasionally they occur off the West Coast. In one season three females were reported from the Antarctic region that exceeded 100 feet in length. In 1948 a female that measured 89 feet was killed and weighed piece by piece on a Japanese factory ship in the Antarctic. Its weight was 300,707 pounds, or over 150 tons. More than a ton of krill (mostly crustaceans) has been found in the stomach of one of these whales.

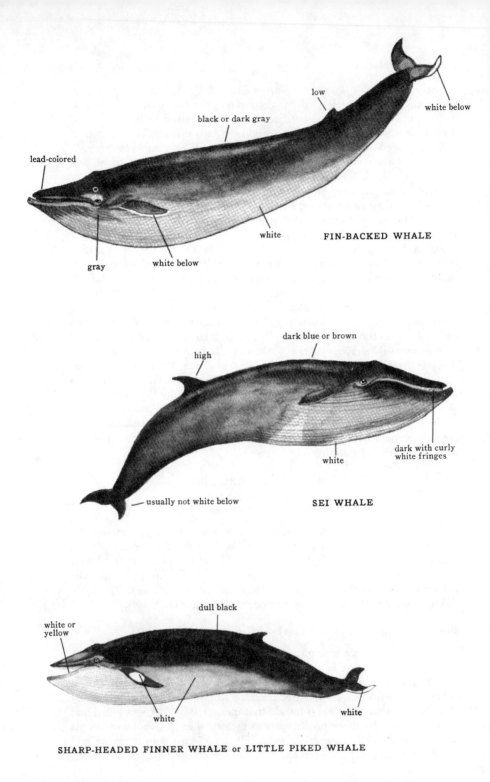

FIN-BACKED WHALE

low

black or dark gray

white below

lead-colored

gray

white below

white

SEI WHALE

dark blue or brown

high

dark with curly white fringes

white

usually not white below

SHARP-HEADED FINNER WHALE or LITTLE PIKED WHALE

dull black

white or yellow

white

white

Balaenoptera, length, up to 80 feet; blackish dorsally with some white on flanks

Fin-backed whale (*Balaenoptera physalus*). Length, to 80 feet; head is V-shaped, flat on top; a rorqual that is black or brownish gray above and *white below, including lower surface of tail and flukes*; lower right jaw is without color (asymmetrical pigmentation on head); *baleen is purple and white or lead-colored, two to three feet long; dorsal fin small and well behind middle of body*; very swift; spout, an inverted cone accompanied by a whistle; when "sounding," arches back slightly but does not expose flukes. Probably the commonest whale seen in summer off the Pacific coast.

Sei whale (*Balaenoptera borealis*). Length, to 60 feet; *a rorqual with grooves not reaching the chin*; pigmentation on head symmetrical; *baleen is mostly black*, with curly white "hairs" on the inner surface; *ventral side of flukes not white*; dark blue or brownish above and a little white on the belly; *dorsal fin about two-thirds back*, hooked; spout cone-shaped, accompanied by a whistle.

Sharp-headed finner whale (*Balaenoptera acutorostrata*), also called little piked whale. Length, to 33 feet; smallest of the rorquals; *throat grooves not reaching navel; white band on outer surface of flipper; underflukes white; yellowish white or pure white baleen, about ten inches long*, is distinctive; dorsal fin prominent, concaved posterior edge; spout poorly defined. Recently reported stranded along the central California coast (Roest, 1962).

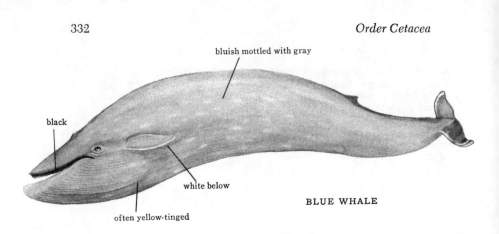

bluish mottled with gray

black

white below

often yellow-tinged

BLUE WHALE

Sibbaldus, length, 100 feet or more; bluish dorsally, yellowish to white ventrally

Blue whale (*Sibbaldus musculus*). Length, to 105 feet; largest animal that ever lived; *a rorqual with an all-over bluish cast, often with grayish patches on the back and sides; underside of flipper white;* dorsal fin very small and far back; *ventral grooves extending more than halfway to the tail;* baleen black, up to three feet long; diatoms may cause "sulfur bottom" beneath; spout high and columnar. P. 329.

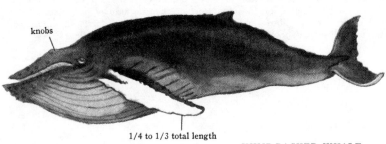

knobs

1/4 to 1/3 total length

HUMP-BACKED WHALE

Megaptera, length, to 54 feet, dorsum black, white below

Hump-backed whale (*Megaptera novaeangliae*). Length, to 54 feet; baleen about three feet long, nearly black; similar to a fin-backed whale but with a stockier build and with *huge flippers one-fourth to one-third total length;* prominent bumps on head; black with varying amounts of white ventrally and beneath the flippers and the flukes; low triangular dorsal fin about two-thirds back; *rows of conspicuous knobs* associated with bristles on the snout and along the edges of the lower jaw; often "breeches" (leaps clear of the water); "lobtails" by beating the water with its powerful flukes; sometimes strikes the water with a loud slap of its flippers; spout is a low broad jet of vapor accompanied by a puff; arches back strongly and exposes flukes when going into a deep dive; commonest whale off the Washington coast.

Family **Balaenidae** (Right Whales)

Length, up to 70 feet; large head with bow-shaped mouth

Right whales may be up to 70 feet in length, with a head nearly one-fourth of the total length. There is no dorsal fin, nor are there throat grooves present. The baleen is up to eight feet long. There is a single genus with one species living off the coast of the Pacific States. It is rare.

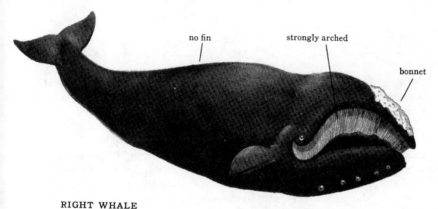

no fin   strongly arched   bonnet

RIGHT WHALE

Eubalaena, blackish except for white bellies in some individuals; horny bonnet; baleen eight feet long

Right whale (*Eubalaena sieboldii*). Length 45–70 feet; a baleen whale with *no dorsal fin or throat grooves; dorsal contour of head and mouth very strongly arched upward;* horny excrescence or "bonnet" on front portion of upper jaw harbors parasitic crustaceans; *whalebone about eight feet long, blackish;* V-shaped spout. It was the "right" whale to harpoon because it did not sink when killed.[4] One was reported off California in 1924 and another in 1955.

11. Order Carnivora, Suborder Fissipedia

The order Carnivora is composed of the flesh-eating mammals, of great diversity in habits and appearance. There are two suborders, the Fissipedia, or land-living species, and the Pinnipedia, which are mostly marine.

The suborder Fissipedia ranges in size from tiny weasels to huge bears. The "divided" foot, which may have only four toes, the long, pointed canine teeth, and the three incisors on both sides of both jaws constitute perhaps the most characteristic features of the suborder Fissipedia. Except for the bears, the line of upper cheek teeth bends at the junction of the molars and premolars. Many carnivores, such as the species of cats, have sharp retractile claws; others, like the skunks, possess anal scent glands. Some representatives of the suborder are aquatic, some are arboreal, and others are cursorial, or adapted to running. The young are altricial at birth. There are six families and several genera and species in the Pacific States.

Certain species of fissiped carnivores become fat in summer and autumn. In winter these species (the black bear and the striped skunk) in cold regions may remain in their dens for weeks at a time without eating or drinking. Such "winter sleep" (or dormant condition) should not be confused with hypothermy or true hibernation (or torpid condition), in which the body temperature approaches the ambient temperature and the rates of breathing and heart beat are greatly reduced. Animals in winter sleep are easily awakened; those that hibernate, undergoing hypothermy, become active only after several minutes or hours. Probably no carnivore undergoes hypothermy. Most species are predaceous, but some feed largely on plants.

In general, carnivores are valuable fur bearers and act as a control on many detrimental rodents. The part carnivores play in the functioning of a biotic community is well known to scientists but poorly understood by many others. Because individual carnivores do damage occasionally, predator control organizations often try to eliminate all predators, with the result that the plant-eating mammals become much more of a liability. Except where they are actually detrimental to man's interests, carnivores should be protected by law because of their importance in the biotic community.

KEY TO THE FISSIPED CARNIVORES
Land-living carnivores

1A. Tail as long as or longer than hind foot; less than 100 pounds . . . 3
1B. Tail shorter than hind foot (may appear absent); foot plantigrade with five toes; more than 100 pounds 2
2A. Claws of forefeet usually less than 2.5 inches (63 mm.) long; no large hump over the shoulders. Mountains (except in deserts); chiefly in the coniferous forests of the Transition and Canadian life zones.
Euarctos americanus, black bear, p. 351, fig. 212.
2B. Claws on forefeet usually longer than 2.5 inches (63 mm.); large humps over the shoulders. Rare or nearly extinct in northwestern Washington.
Ursus, sp., grizzly bear, p. 351.
3A. Dog- or fox-like; 42 teeth 4
3B. Not dog- or fox-like; less than 42 teeth 9
4A. Hind foot more than 150 mm.; skull more than 160 mm. 5
4B. Hind foot less than 150 mm.; skull less than 160 mm. 6
5A. Hind foot usually less than 250 mm.; skull length usually less than 250 mm. Widely distributed in all life zones in all three states.
Canis latrans, coyote, p. 341, fig. 205.
5B. Hind foot usually more than 250 mm.; skull length usually in excess of 250 mm. Rare in the Sierra Nevada, with occasional records in Washington near the Canadian border.
Canis lupus, wolf, p. 341, fig. 206.
6A. With a band of coarse black hairs running dorsally down to the black tip of the tail; tail triangular in cross section; gray dorsally 7
6B. Without a band running dorsally on the tail; tail round in cross section 8
7A. Tail more than 12 inches (300 mm.) in length; living on the mainland. Mostly in the Foothill Woodland throughout California to northwestern Oregon.
Urocyon cinereoargenteus, gray fox, p. 339, fig. 209.
7B. Tail 12 inches or less in length; living on the islands off the California coast.
Urocyon littoralis, island fox, p. 341, fig. 210.
8A. Tail usually white-tipped; red, black, or silver fur dorsally; feet blackish; skull length more than 130 mm. Mostly in Cascade Mountains and Sierra Nevada, but introduced in the lowlands of western Oregon, Washington. It occurs also in the Sacramento Valley, California.
Vulpes fulva, red fox, p. 339, fig. 207.
8B. Tail usually black-tipped, gray dorsally; skull length less than 130 mm. Mostly in dry desert areas in California; some may still remain in southeastern Oregon.
Vulpes macrotis, kit fox, p. 339, fig. 208.
9A. Tail with alternating light and dark bands; tail always much longer than hind foot 10
9B. Tail without alternating light and dark bands, or if bands are present, then with white spot on back side of a black ear; ear tufts of long hair . . 11
10A. Dark bands complete all around the tail; skull over 100 mm. in length; palate extending posteriorly behind the last molar more than its width. Mostly along streams and lakes through all biotic communities and life zones up through the Canadian in all three states.
Procyon lotor, raccoon, p. 356, fig. 215.

10B. Dark bands not complete on the under side of the tail; skull less than 100 mm.; palate not extending behind the last molar more than its width. Rocky and brushy places south from southwestern Oregon through California; not found on the floor of the central valleys, but ranges up to the Canadian Life Zone.

     Bassariscus astutus, ringtail, p. 356, fig. 216.

11A. Catlike; 30 teeth or less; digitigrade with fully retractile claws . . . 12
11B. Not catlike; 32 teeth or more; plantigrade or without fully retractile claws   15
12A. Tail longer than hind foot; ears not tufted 13
12B. Tail about the length of hind foot; ears frequently terminated with tufts of long hair   14
13A. Length 24–32 inches; lower elevations in all three states; feral.

     Felis cattus, house cat.

13B. Length six to eight feet. Throughout all the states except the deserts, chiefly in the Upper Sonoran and Transition life zones but also in the Canadian Life Zone in places.

     Felis concolor, mountain lion, p. 389, fig. 234.

14A. Hind foot less than 190 mm.; tail barred dorsally. Throughout all three states in nearly all communities and life zones.

     Lynx rufus, bobcat, p. 389, fig. 236.

14B. Hind foot more than 190 mm.; tail not barred dorsally. Wilder parts of the mountains of northeastern Washington.

     Lynx canadensis, Canadian lynx, p. 389, fig. 235.

15A. Teeth 38; living in high mountains or in extensive coniferous forests . 16
15B. Teeth less than 38 18
16A. Size of house cat or less, 12 pounds or less; sagittal crest not projecting 10 mm. or more behind the rest of the skull 17
16B. Size of small bear (20–40 pounds); sagittal crest projecting 10 mm. or more behind the skull; shaggy pelage blackish dorsally with two broad yellowish or tan bands low along the sides. Rare; in the Transition, Canadian, and Hudsonian life zones in the Sierra Nevada, northern Coast Range, and Cascade Range, but none in Oregon for many years.

     Gulo luscus, wolverine, p. 365, fig. 225.

17A. Yellowish brown dorsally, yellowish orange on throat and chest; skull length 95 mm. or less; length of M^1 less than 11 mm. Lodgepole, Red Fir, Douglas Fir, hemlock, and spruce forests of the Transition, Canadian, and Hudsonian life zones of all three states.

     Martes americana, marten, p. 263, fig. 218.

17B. Dark brown to blackish with "frosted" hairs dorsally; white spots on throat and breast; skull more than 95 mm.; length of M^1 more than 11 mm. Lodgepole, Red Fir, Yellow Pine, Douglas Fir forests, chiefly in the Transition and Canadian life zones of all three states.

     Martes pennanti, fisher, p. 363, fig. 219.

18A. Not living in the ocean 19
18B. Living in the ocean off the coast of central California; toes webbed; two lower incisors on each half of the jaw.

     Enhydra lutris, sea otter, p. 368, fig. 232.

19A. Dorsally shining black with white stripes; or brown, grizzly gray, or pure white; without webs between all toes; 34 teeth 20
19B. Dorsally brownish with fully webbed toes on all four feet; body tapers gradually into thick, long tail; 36 teeth. Along streams and lakes in Washington, Oregon, northern half of California, and along the Colorado River, sometimes locally in salt water.

     Lutra canadensis, river otter, p. 368, fig. 231.

20A. Black with white spots or stripes 21
20B. Brown, grizzly gray, or white, but never black with white spots or
stripes 22
21A. Black with white spots and four short white stripes. Rocky and brushy habitats nearly throughout all three states in the Sonoran, Canadian, and Transition life zones.
Spilogale putorius (formerly *Spilogale gracilis*), spotted skunk,
p. 367, fig. 228.
21B. Black with two white stripes running down the back. Weedy and brushy habitats nearly throughout all the states in the Sonoran and Transition life zones.
Mephitis mephitis, striped skunk, p. 367, fig. 229.
22A. Clear brown or pure white dorsally, never grayish or yellowish brown; without black and white stripes on the head; last upper molar wider than long (*Mustela*) 23
22B. Grizzly grayish or yellowish-brown dorsally with a median longitudinal white stripe on the head; last upper molar triangular and slightly longer than wide. Nearly all communities and life zones throughout all three states except the western parts of Washington and Oregon.
Taxidea taxus, badger, p. 367, fig. 226.
23A. Belly and throat white or yellowish; frequently, but not always, with a white spot or other white markings on the face; except for a black-tipped tail, the animal may be pure white in winter 24
23B. Belly and throat brownish; sometimes with white spots on the throat and in the inguinal region; no white on the face. Along streams, lakes, and fish-supporting waters through all life zones to the Canadian in Washington, Oregon, and northern California.
Mustela vison, mink, p. 363, fig. 222.
24A. Tail usually less than 45 per cent of the head and body length; nearly pure white ventrally; postglenoid length more than 47 per cent of the condylobasal length. Red Fir, Douglas Fir, Lodgepole, Redwood, and Subalpine forests in the Canadian and Hudsonian zones in northern California, Oregon, and Washington.
Mustela erminea, ermine, p. 365, fig. 221.
24B. Tail usually more than 45 per cent of the head and body length; more or less yellowish ventrally; postglenoid length less than 47 per cent of the condylobasal length. Nearly all life zones in all three states except southeastern Caifornia.
Mustela frenata, long-tailed weasel, p. 365, fig. 220.

Family **Canidae** (Foxes, Wolves, and Coyotes)
Dental Formula 3-1-4-2/3-1-4-3

The members of the dog family have long legs adapted to running (cursorial). They have nonretractile claws and walk on their toes (digitigrade). All have bushy tails. They have well-developed carnassial cheek teeth. The cheek tooth row behind the incisor arches outward strongly at the molars. There are six species in the Pacific States. See key, p. 335.

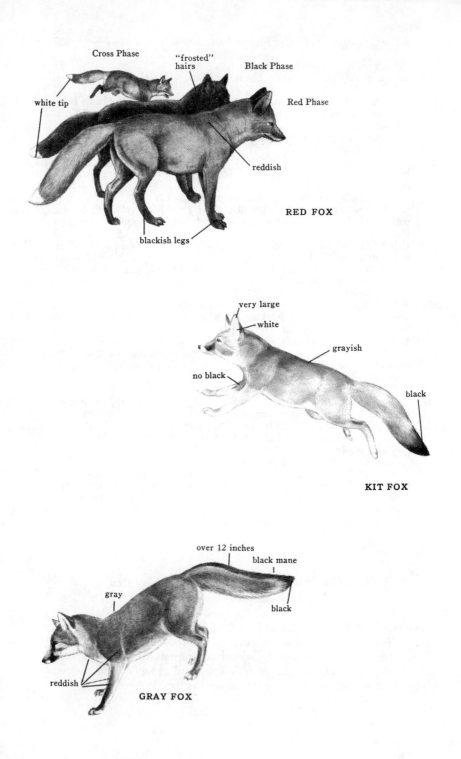

Cross Phase

"frosted" hairs

Black Phase

Red Phase

white tip

reddish

blackish legs

RED FOX

very large

white

grayish

no black

black

KIT FOX

over 12 inches

black mane

gray

black

reddish

GRAY FOX

Red fox (*Vulpes fulva*). Length 900–1000 mm., about 36–40 inches; tail thick, cylindrical, *always more or less white-tipped*, 305–400 mm.; hind foot 132–70 mm.; ear, notch, 85–107 mm.; skull 137–51 mm.; with V-shaped temporal ridges; *several color phases: red phase is rich, rusty red dorsally, with backs of ears and front of legs blackish*; whitish below; *black phase is blackish all over*, sometimes with silvery hairs; *cross phase is similar to the red phase but darker and duller*, with a definite *darker band on the back and across the shoulders*. Native in the high Sierra Nevada and north from California across Oregon and Washington; mostly in the Red Fir, Lodgepole, and Subalpine forests, but also in the Alpine Fell-fields, where they feed on montane meadow mice and white-tailed hares; chiefly Canadian and Hudsonian life zones. It is now widely and firmly established in parts of the Sacramento Valley, California, and in many counties in northwestern Oregon, the latter being the result of introduction from the southern United States. Its origin in the Sacramento Valley is unknown. P. 347, fig. 207, Map 81.

Kit fox (*Vulpes macrotis*). Length 600–840 mm., about 30 inches; *tail 225–323 mm., with a tip of black hairs*; hind foot 108–37 mm.; ear, crown, large, 78–94 mm.; skull 105–22 mm.; with V-shaped temporal ridges; gray with some rusty above, whitish below and *inside the ears*. In the Mojave and Colorado deserts and along the west side of the San Joaquin Valley in California, and possibly in southeastern Oregon; Sagebrush Scrub, Shadscale Scrub, Creosote Bush Scrub, Joshua Tree Woodland, Alkali Sink, and Valley Grassland; mostly Lower Sonoran Life Zone. P. 348, fig. 208, Map 82.

Gray fox (*Urocyon cinereoargenteus*). Length 880–1080 mm., about three feet; *tail 280–440 mm., about 15 inches, with a black "mane" running down the dorsal side to the black tip*; hind foot 100–150 mm.; ear, crown, 60–100 mm.; skull 110–31 mm., *with lyre-* or U-shaped temporal ridges; blackish gray above with rusty and white below. Practically throughout California and the western half of Oregon in the Sagebrush belt and communities mostly below the Yellow Pine Forest; chiefly Upper Sonoran and Transition life zones. P. 349, fig. 209, Map 83.

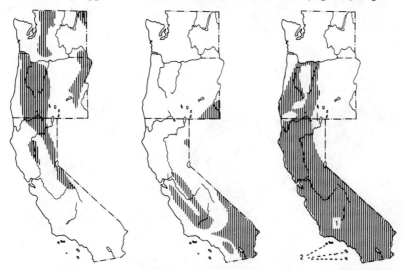

Map 81, left. *Vulpes fulva.* **Map 82, center.** *Vulpes macrotis.* **Map 83, right.** (1) *Urocyon cinereoargenteus*, (2) *Urocyon littoralis.*

grayish

reddish

less than 12 inches

black mane

ISLAND FOX

broad head

short

held high
when running

WOLF

long pointed

held low
when running

COYOTE

Canidae (Dog Family), Dental Formula 3-1-4-2/3-1-4-3

Island fox (*Urocyon littoralis*). Length 590–785 mm., about 28 inches; *tail 110–290 mm., 6–10 inches, with black dorsal "mane" ending in a black tip*; hind foot 100–157 mm.; ear 60–70 mm.; skull 96–106 mm.; gray with rusty and white below. On the islands off the southern California coast; brushy and rocky places, from which to forage along the seacoast. P. 349, fig. 210, Map 83.

Wolf (*Canis lupus*). Length 1000–2000 mm.; tail 350–500 mm.; hind foot 220–310 mm.; about 4.5 feet; tail black-tipped, bushy, about 12 inches; *weight 60–100 pounds* (about twice as much as a coyote); anteroposterior diameter of canine at gum level 12 mm. or more; last upper premolar about 25 mm. In Washington and Sierra Nevada of California, very rare. P. 342, fig. 206, Map 84.

Broad head, Short, rounded ears

Coyote (*Canis latrans*). Length 980–1320 mm., about three feet (desert subspecies) to four feet long (mountain subspecies); tail 290–400 mm.; *hind foot 165–225 mm.; ear, crown, 100–155 mm.*; skull 170–213 mm.; anteroposterior diameter of canine at gum level 11 mm. or less; last upper premolar (carnassial) 20 mm. or less; small to large collie-dog size; ears erect; buffy gray and black, or reddish above, lighter below; *tail dark-tipped*. In nearly all communities and life zones in all three states. P. 344, fig. 205, Map 85.

long pointed ears.

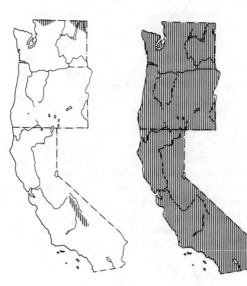

Map 84, left. *Canis lupus.*
Map 85, right. *Canis latrans.*

Wolf (*Canis lupus*), fig. 206

Until recently it seemed that this species—like the grizzly bear—was extinct. Every year there are reports of wolves, but these animals have usually proved to be the large subspecies of coyote that lives in the mountains or in the Great Basin region. However, reports continue to come from persons who know the difference between coyotes and wolves, and these cannot be dismissed lightly. Early in the spring of 1962 the California Fish and Game officials asked me to come to their headquarters in Fresno and identify an animal that had been killed near Woodlake, at the western edge of Sequoia National Park. The animal was a wolf. All the measurements, especially the diameter of the canine alveolus (the socket of the tooth), its total length, and the width of the rhinarium (the hairless area at the tip of the snout), were far greater than those of any coyote on record. The long, coarse gray fur and the short, erect ears on the broad skull were unlike those of any known dog. Wolves have more massive heads and relatively shorter ears and tails than coyotes (fig. 205). The specimen was frozen and sent to the Museum of Vertebrate Zoology at the University of California in Berkeley, where the skin and skeleton were prepared. Dr. Seth Benson, Curator of Mammals, verified the identification.

Wolves have not been common, at least for the last 60 years, in the Pacific States. In Washington they had largely disappeared before 1920. There are authentic records of two wolves, one taken in the Olympic Peninsula and the other in the northeastern part of the state, where it may have strayed from Canada. The last record of a wolf killed in Oregon was made by one of the Biological Survey predatory animal hunters on the Sycan Marsh, east of Fort Klamath, in 1927. California museums had no authentic record of a wolf until 1922, when one was trapped in the Providence Mountains in eastern San Bernardino County. Another was trapped in Lassen County in 1924. These two specimens appear to be the only wolves in California until the Woodlake specimen in 1962. The first two California specimens seem to be a type of plains wolf, probably stragglers from Nevada. The Woodlake specimen is the first authentic wolf record west of the Sierra Nevada in over 125 years. Doubtless others have been killed, but specimens are needed for positive identification and record.

It seems likely that a few wolves remain in the high central Sierra Nevada or even in the northern Cascade Mountains, and that in hard, cold winters one may occasionally venture to lower elevations for food. Trappers and others who know coyotes and wolves report that a few wolves still roam the wild Kern Plateau region of the southern Sierra Nevada. Whether they are the original race or have been introduced is yet to be determined. A statistical study of the Woodlake specimen at the Museum indicates that it has a close affinity with the wolves of northeastern Asia. The possibility of introduction cannot be ruled out. A number of roadside "zoos" and private parties are known to keep wolves, which may have escaped or been released. An animal suspected of being a wolf should be reported to the au-

Fig. 203. Tracks of the gray fox, nearly actual size.

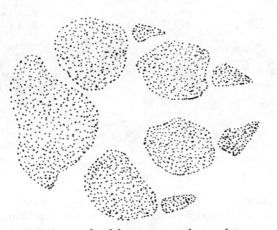

Fig. 204. Tracks of the coyote, nearly actual size.

thorities, and the skull from a kill should be saved. It is only by comparing details of the teeth and skull that a wolf can with certainty be distinguished from a large dog or coyote.

A wolf may be distinguished from a coyote by the position of the tail when running. The tail is held straight out behind or raised high over the back, whereas the coyote's tail is usually held lower than the body. The wolf is nearly twice as large as the coyote and has much smaller ears in proportion to the large broad head. The fur of a wolf is long and coarse. In general the coloration is grayish and resembles that of a coyote, but the under parts are less white and the legs and feet are less contrastingly reddish. Some specimens are nearly white. The skull of a full-grown wolf is readily distinguished from that of a coyote; it is rarely less than 200 mm. in length, whereas the coyote's skull is rarely over 200 mm. The anteroposterior diameter of the upper canine at the gumline of a wolf is 12 mm. or more at the base, whereas that of a coyote does not exceed 11 mm. The length of the upper carnassial (Pm^4) of a wolf is about 25 mm.; that of a coyote is

Fig. 205. Coyote (*Canis latrans*).

about 20 mm. It is easy to confuse a wolf with certain large dogs, which have smaller teeth although the skull is the same size. Serological tests indicate that dogs are more closely related to coyotes than to wolves.

The wolf feeds on ground squirrels, rabbits, and hares, but it may also prey on the larger hoofed mammals such as deer, elk, bighorn, and mountain goats. It has been persecuted for centuries because it attacks man's domestic animals, and occasionally even man himself. Wolves frequently hunt in packs.

Wolves breed in February or March, and a litter of about seven pups is born 63 days later.

Today, only a few untouched areas remain that are large enough for the wolf. Even these "detrimental" predators should be preserved before it is too late.

Coyote (*Canis latrans*), fig. 205

Except for the rare wolf, the coyote is the largest native member of the dog family found wild in the Pacific States. Because of its grayish or tawny color it is sometimes known locally as a gray wolf, especially the large subspecies which lives in the mountains and in the lava-bed regions. The true wolves, however, are much larger and sturdier. The track of a coyote (fig.

204) resembles that of a dog so closely that even expert trappers find it difficult to distinguish. It is readily distinguished from that of the mountain lion (fig. 233) and the bobcat, however, by the shape of the pad and the absence of claw marks.

The coyote and its relatives have been severely persecuted with guns, traps, and poison. Nevertheless, it seems to be holding its own in many places, which speaks well for the adaptiveness of so large an animal. Where sheep are raised, the coyote must be controlled. Too frequently this control is attempted by promiscuously scattering poison bait, which kills not only fine hunting dogs but also foxes, skunks, raccoons, badgers, and other beneficial predators that restrict the rodent population. Coyotes sometimes kill fawns, but rarely quail or other game birds. Their chief food includes rabbits, hares, ground squirrels, gophers, meadow mice, kangaroo rats, and even insects. Coyotes may occasionally attack newborn calves, but, in spite of this, many cattlemen do not allow coyotes killed on their ranches because of the good they do in removing the much more destructive grass-eating rodents.

The fur of coyotes living in the mountains is longer and thicker, and hence more valuable, than that of coyotes living in the valleys or deserts. Many trappers make their living from the prime winter pelts. Consequently, if coyotes must be removed from an area, winter is the time to do it.

Fig. 206. Captive wolf (*Canis lupus*).

Fig. 209. Gray fox (*Urocyon cinereoargenteus*).

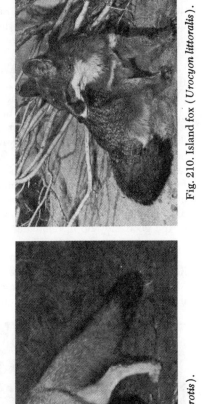

Fig. 210. Island fox (*Urocyon littoralis*).

Fig. 207. Red fox (*Vulpes fulva*).

Fig. 208. Kit fox (*Vulpes macrotis*).

Coyotes generally make their dens in natural crevices and caves, but they sometimes enlarge a burrow dug by a Beechey ground squirrel or a badger. They live in every life zone in the Pacific States.

An average litter consists of six or seven pups, although as many as 11 have been observed. These are born in the early spring. Perhaps the only important enemy of the coyote is man. A few young pups are killed by eagles and porcupines, and others die from parasitic worms.

The mountain, valley, and desert subspecies of the coyote show considerable variation in size and coloration and were formerly known as separate species.*

Red Fox (*Vulpes fulva*), fig. 207

Persons who go into the high Sierra Nevada or Cascade Mountains may be fortunate enough to see a red fox. It is much more common, however, in northwestern Oregon and Washington, having been introduced there from the eastern United States. The yellowish red fur and very bushy, cylindrical, white-tipped tail, along with the blackish legs, clearly distinguish the red fox from the gray-colored coyote of the same region and from the gray fox, which normally lives in the brushy foothills at much lower elevations, especially in California. In size the red fox is between these two species. The red fox is peculiar in that it exhibits color phases—red, cross, silver, and black—which grade imperceptibly into one another. The cross phase has a band of darker fur running down the back and across the shoulders, roughly forming a cross; otherwise, its fur is yellowish red. Some trappers estimate that half to three-fourths of the red foxes in the Sierra Nevada are of the cross phase, while less than 5 per cent are silver, and about 1 per cent are black. In the Cascade Mountains, however, it has been estimated that 48 per cent are of the black or silver phase. The pelts of all of these color phases are highly prized in the fur trade. Red fox fur is very durable.

The red fox feeds on marmots, ground squirrels, mice, wood rats, pikas, hares, and possibly several species of mountain birds and even grasshoppers and berries. Among its enemies are bobcats, mountain coyotes, and golden eagles. Some mammalogists believe that sheep-grazing in high mountain meadows reduces the productivity of the red fox by reducing vegetation, thus indirectly affecting its rodent food supply.

This species of fox probably does not dig a den, like its desert-living relative, the kit fox, but uses the natural labyrinths in the great rock slides which are so plentiful in its native habitat.

While the red fox is normally an alpine animal found in the high mountains, chiefly of the Cascades and Sierra Nevada, in the Canadian and Hudsonian life zones, colonies of them are reported in California at lower levels. The Zoology Department of the University of California at Davis has skins of animals from the Sacramento Valley which do not appear to be different

---

* Some zoologists (Storer and Usinger, 1963) give different species names to the mountain coyote (*Canis latrans*) and the valley coyote (*Canis ochropus*).

from those of the midwestern United States. Early settlers in the Valley did not mention the red fox, so it seems likely that it was introduced.

Since the range of the red fox in the California mountains is far above the regions normally inhabited by man, it rarely conflicts with his interests. In Washington, however, the introduced animals are numerous enough to harm game birds and are considered predators. The red fox is a prized and valuable fur bearer, and where it is not doing harm it should be protected in national parks and other wildlife areas. The red fox mates in January or February, and four to five pups are born 49 to 55 days later.

The tracks of a red fox closely resemble those of the gray fox (fig. 203). They are smaller than coyote tracks and have a different shape. There is one recognized species in the Pacific States.

Kit Fox (*Vulpes macrotis*), fig. 208

Campers in the Mojave and Colorado deserts are frequently astonished to see a small gray-colored fox with large ears and a black-tipped tail come within the campfire circle to pick up food. This kit fox is readily distinguished from the gray fox, which has a dark band of stiff hairs along the upper side of the tail. Kit foxes are frequently seen in the daytime on the desert, and not infrequently their dead bodies are seen along the roadside, where, in spite of their incredible bursts of speed, they have failed to dodge passing cars. As a general rule, the kit fox spends the heat of the day in a burrow in the soft, sandy earth. The burrow is about nine inches in diameter and is round, in contrast with that of a badger, which is more elliptical.

The track of a kit fox resembles that of a gray fox (fig. 203), although it is smaller. Its food consists chiefly of desert rodents, lagomorphs, and insects. It may take a big desert kangaroo rat out of a live trap, and occasionally it takes poultry. The fur, although not nearly so valuable as that of the red fox, brings enough to make it well worth the time of desert trappers. In the San Joaquin Valley of California, the kit fox is the chief predator in limiting the high rodent population on grazing land. Killing of these animals should be controlled, since they are far more beneficial than harmful. Poisoned-meat bait, which kills many of them, should be outlawed except under most unusual circumstances, since too many carnivores other than those for which the bait is intended fall victim. As a result, the rodent population increases alarmingly, becoming a serious threat to human health, to grazing, and to agricultural interests.

It is estimated that there is one adult pair of kit foxes for each 3.5 square miles of desert. The foxes are monogamous for at least a year. Young kit foxes are born in the burrow early in February or March. Four or five pups constitute an average-sized litter, although as many as seven are known.

There is one species of kit fox in the Pacific States. It lives in the Inyo region, the Mojave Desert, the Colorado Desert, and in the southern half of the San Joaquin Valley, in the Lower Sonoran Life Zone of California and southeastern Oregon.

Gray Fox (*Urocyon cinereoargenteus*), fig. 209

Throughout the chaparral-covered foothills of the three states one may occasionally see an animal resembling a small shepherd dog. This is the gray fox. Its general steel gray coloration, with varying amounts of yellowish red fur along the sides and on the legs, and, above all, the darker hairs that run down the back and become conspicuous along the top of the tail distinguish the gray fox from any other animal in the same habitat. The coyote and the kit fox both lack these external features. The track of a gray fox (fig. 203) is similar to that of a small dog but narrower.

The food of the gray fox consists of gophers, rabbits, white-footed mice, wood rats, and probably several species of birds. Included also is a considerable amount of vegetable material, such as the berries of manzanitas and toyons.

Dens are frequently found under large rocks or in crevices in cliffs. The young are born in early spring; four pups seem to be the average for a litter, although seven have been recorded.

Unlike other members of the dog family, the gray fox readily climbs leaning trees, or even vertical ones when the limbs fork near the ground.

Gray foxes are afflicted with many diseases and parasitic worms, which also affect dogs. Its chief enemies are eagles, dogs, and man. Although of fairly large size, gray foxes are timid creatures and readily retire even when smaller animals threaten them. Large raccoons have been seen to drive gray foxes from their food.

It has been estimated that there are as many as four gray foxes per square mile in certain favored areas of chaparral. Poison bait, placed for coyotes, kills many of these fine animals, which feed chiefly on detrimental rodents.

The gray fox is found on the mainland of California and Oregon, chiefly in the Upper Sonoran Life Zone. The Townsend, California, and Arizona gray foxes are geographic variations of this single species.

The island fox (*Urocyon littoralis*), the other species of this genus, lives on the islands that lie off the coast of California. Every island has a different subspecies of this fox.

Family **Ursidae** (Bears)

The bear family, Ursidae, is now probably represented by only a single species in the Pacific States, the black bear. The grizzly bear became extinct over most of its former range in the Pacific States about 1925, and in the rest of the Northwest more recently (Dalquest, 1948). However, a few may still remain in Washington. All bears have plantigrade feet and rudimentary tails. The molar teeth have blunt cusps and are not as sharp as in most other carnivores. The upper molars and premolars form straight lines behind the canine teeth.

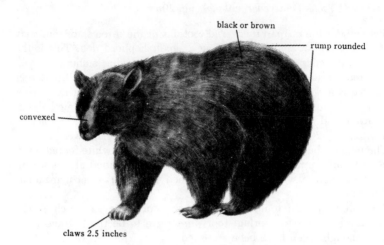

black or brown

rump rounded

convexed

claws 2.5 inches

BLACK BEAR

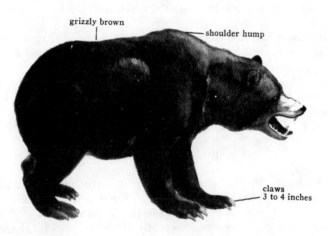

grizzly brown

shoulder hump

claws
3 to 4 inches

GRIZZLY BEAR

Black bear (*Euarctos americanus*). Length up to five feet; 40 inches high at the shoulder; *tail six inches or less*; hind foot up to nine inches; front claws about 2.5 inches; skull about 300 mm.; *cinnamon brown to black all over; no large shoulder hump or "dish" face as found in grizzly bears; brown face; sloping rump.* Native in the forested mountain regions of all three states and reported by Roest (1963) from the southern Coast Ranges of northern San Luis Obispo County, California; chiefly in Yellow Pine, Douglas Fir, Red Fir, Lodgepole, and Redwood forests, Transition and Canadian life zones. P. 352, fig. 212, Map 86.

last molar ∠1"

Grizzly bear (*Ursus chelan*). Length four to six feet or larger, and 3–3.5 feet high at the shoulders; *claws on forefeet, three to four inches long; a pronounced hump over the shoulders;* hairs yellowish brown but frequently tipped with white to give grizzly appearance. The grizzly bear is nearly extinct in the Pacific States. In California, most recent evidence of one was in the 1920's; in Oregon, about 1933; and in Washington, estimates from the Game Department are of about ten in the remote mountains. P. 354, Map 86.

last molar ∠1"

Map 86. (1) *Euarctos americanus*, (2) *Ursus chelan*.

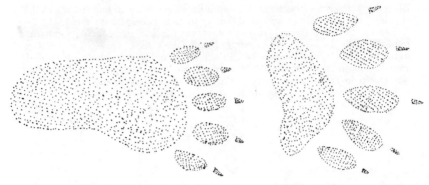

Fig. 211. Tracks of a black bear, about one-third actual size.

Black Bear (*Euarctos americanus*), fig. 212

The black bear is the largest carnivore (except for the grizzly) in the Pacific States. The so-called brown or cinnamon bear is only a different color phase of the black bear. The color phases range from light brown (cinnamon) to nearly solid black, the former in most localities being more numerous. Indeed, a female black animal may have both brown and black cubs.

It seems unnecessary to describe, even superficially, so large (sometimes the weight is as much as 500 pounds) and well known an animal as the black bear. Perhaps no wild mammal could be recognized more quickly by the novice. Protection in our national parks has done much to introduce this relatively shy animal to an interested public. So accustomed has it become to people and so willing to eat garbage, or camp supplies when they are not properly looked after, that it presents serious problems to park authorities.

Although a carnivore by structure, the black bear is largely a vegetable feeder, eating especially roots, fruits, nuts, and grasses. An examination of the droppings indicates that it also eats many insects, fish, and small rodents. It rarely preys on other large mammals, although an occasional individual kills pigs, sheep, or fawns.

Since black bears live mostly in the Transition and Canadian life zones of the mountains, they are subject to low temperatures and food shortages when the snow lies deep on the ground. As fall approaches, the black bear becomes very fat, and the stomach becomes shrunken and half rigid. In this condition, the bear retires to a hollow log or cave and becomes dormant, but does not truly hibernate. It is capable of being roused to action if sufficiently disturbed. It becomes dormant irrespective of the daily temperature if it has sufficient fat. If it is not fat, the animal may remain active during the winter. The black bear frequently emerges from its den in very good condition, but the fat is soon lost when it is forced to resort to an early spring grass diet before the fattening foods are available.

Usually two very small cubs are born, although one and three are fre-

Fig. 212. Black bear (*Euarctos americanus*).

quently seen; four and rarely even five are recorded. These are born in the winter den, where they remain for about three months before they follow the mother about. The following autumn the cubs will den with the mother until spring, after which she forces them to shift for themselves. The female bear breeds only in alternate years. A black bear with cubs is dangerous and should never be approached closely. Bears should never be fed from the hand. They are powerful animals that can readily send a person to the hospital with bad scratches and bites when food is withheld or after the supply has been exhausted.

The sense of sight is poor in the black bear, but the senses of smell and hearing are very keen. Except for man with his traps, dogs, and guns, the black bear has few enemies. True, it has been observed to withdraw from its food at the approach of a striped skunk or wolverine. However, an excellent sense of hearing and a great delicacy of smell help it avoid most dangers.

Partially protected by game laws and totally protected in the national parks, the black bear's future seems assured, and it is not likely to go the way of the unfortunate grizzly bear.

So-called "bear trees" are frequently found near bear trails, showing where the huge animals rear up on their hind legs and scratch the bark as high as they can reach. Bears sometimes scratch and chew the trail signs and other wooden structures made by man until they fall apart.

The large five-toed tracks of a black bear (fig. 211) could hardly be mistaken for those of any other mammal. The tracks of the rare wolverine may show five toes, but its foot pads are entirely different. The tracks of a mountain lion (fig. 233) are four-toed and much smaller than a bear's, because a bear is plantigrade and walks with its heel on the ground.

Grizzly Bear (*Ursus chelan*)

The largest carnivore in North America is the grizzly bear. Certainly in size and power the grizzly has no match on the continent, except man with his high-powered rifle. Dr. C. Hart Merriam (1918), who was an authority on grizzly bears, described no fewer than eight species in the Pacific States.* However, if these bears were living today, they would probably be considered subspecies of a single species. Now they are nearly extinct. In California, the last grizzly was killed at Horse Corral Meadows in the mountains of Tulare County in 1922. Another bear may have lived in Sequoia National Park until about 1925. In Oregon, the grizzly seems to have disappeared about 1933 when one was reported on the Willamette River by the Forest Service. Dalquest (1948) reported the grizzly bear extinct over most of Washington, stating that "a few may remain in the remote part of the northern Cascades." The Game Department of Wash-

---

* The eight species were *U. magister, U. tularensis, U. henshawi, U. californicus, U. mendocinensis, U. colusus, U. klamathensis,* and *U. chelan.*

ington estimated in 1961 that there were about ten of them still living in the remote mountains.

Extinct! A zoologist must write this word remorsefully after the name of a vertebrate species. Many people are distressed when any large creature is killed, but the death of an individual is nothing compared with the extermination of a species. Species are foundation planks of the universe, into which ages of evolutionary processing have gone. It is a sad commentary on our civilization that in our "progress" we have failed to provide sanctuary for these great bears—a symbol of the wilderness and a source of enjoyment and study for future generations. Any bear thought to be a grizzly, or any material thought to be connected with a grizzly, should be referred to Dr. Tracy I. Storer, an authority at the University of California at Davis.

Family **Procyonidae** (Raccoons)

Members of this family have plantigrade feet, and their teeth lack the carnassial characteristics of most other carnivorous mammals. They usually have more or less ringed tails. The raccoon and the ringtail are the only representatives of the family in the Pacific States, although the long-snouted, long-tailed coati of Latin America may occasionally cross the Mexican and Arizona borders into southern California. The coati is not included here.

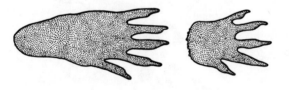

Fig. 213. Tracks of a raccoon, about half actual size.

Fig. 214. Tracks of a ringtail, nearly actual size.

RACCOON

Procyonidae Dental Formula 3-1-4-2/3-1-4-2

Raccoon (*Procyon lotor*). Length 640–940 mm., about 32 inches; tail *generally with six black rings that are complete on the under side,* 190–340 mm.; hind foot 83–130 mm.; ear 45–65 mm.; skull 99–135 mm.; grayish brown tipped with black above, light gray below; *a black mask across the face.* All over the three states except the deserts and not in the mountains above the Canadian Life Zone; chiefly along streams, marshes, and ponds. P. 357, fig. 215, Map 87.

RINGTAIL

Ringtail (*Bassariscus astutus*). Length 615–810 mm., about 28 inches; tail *generally with eight black rings incomplete on the under side,* 310–438 mm.; hind foot 57–73 mm.; ear, crown, 40–47 mm.; skull, condylobasal length, 74–80 mm.; brown shaded with black on the back, whitish below; *a narrow black circle around each eye surrounded by a wider white area.* California and southwest Oregon, except the central valleys, the deserts, and the northeastern part of California; rocky and brushy places frequently near streams; Upper Sonoran to the lower parts of the Canadian life zones. P. 359, fig. 216, Map 88.

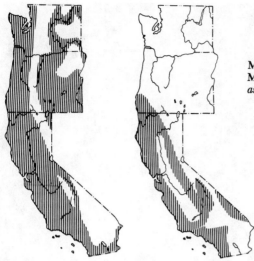

Map 87, left. *Procyon lotor.*
Map 88, right. *Bassariscus astutus.*

Raccoon (*Procyon lotor*), fig. 215

The raccoon is widely distributed in the Pacific States, usually along water courses or lakes. It is a heavily built animal nearly two feet long, weighing ten to 15 pounds, and rarely as much as 29 pounds. The general coloration of a coon is gray, with a black "mask" across the eyes and alternate black and gray stripes that extend entirely around the tail.

The ringtail is the only other mammal in the United States with a similarly ringed tail, but the rings are incomplete on the under side. Coons are common even in regions where they are seldom seen. Great numbers of their baby-like tracks are often seen in the mud of irrigation ditches and on dusty roads. They range through all the life zones up to the Hudsonian and live in holes in trees, under rocks, or even in thick tule patches if a supply of food is close at hand. In cold weather they may den up but do not hibernate. Coons frequently call to each other with a long, mournful *who-oo-oo-oo*, particularly on rainy nights in autumn. They have very good eyesight and will invariably see a dog long before being seen by it. They are more fearful of dogs than of human beings.

The raccoon is probably the most omnivorous native carnivore in the area, with the possible exception of the black bear. Its meals have been known to include crayfish, fish, turtles, frogs, small mammals, birds, eggs, insects, corn, melons, acorns, berries, grapes, and figs. Figs are especially prized after they have fallen and are partially dried. Well-beaten coon trails leading to fig trees are commonly seen during the early autumn months in the Sacramento Valley in California. The pulp of a watermelon is sometimes entirely removed and eaten without making a hole larger than a sil-

Fig. 215. Raccoon (*Procyon lotor*).

ver dollar in the rind. Raccoons occasionally become too numerous locally; in such cases they may have to be removed so as not to become a detriment to the farmer. They should be taken in winter when the fur is thickest (prime), since summer-killed animals are generally worthless. However, continued persecution is in no way justified.

Of all the species of fur bearers in California, the raccoon is fourth in numbers caught. It is hunted with dogs for sport and for the meat. In winter it is also caught for the pelt. In the winter of 1959–60, trappers took 1,370 pelts, with an average price of only $1.56 each.

Raccoons are very curious animals, liking to handle everything, especially food, with their sensitive hands. This characteristic often leads to their capture, when the trapper covers the trigger of the trap with tinfoil or other shiny metal.

The gestation period is 63 days. The young are born between December and April, there being from two to seven in a litter. When taken quite young, coons are said to make good pets. This, however, is contrary to the experience of many people, unless "good pets" include those that can never be safely handled without heavy gloves.

Raccoons are fond of water, and although they may wander far from it while hunting, most of their life is spent near streams, lakes, or marshes. Adult raccoons frequently wash their food before eating it.

Like a bear, a raccoon walks with its heel on the ground and makes a fairly large track (fig. 213), which is not likely to be mistaken for that of any other native mammal.

There is one species of raccoon, but this has recognized geographic variations.

Ringtail (*Bassariscus astutus*), fig. 216

In the Upper Sonoran Life Zone of California and southern Oregon, and sometimes in the higher mountains, lives the ringtail, or cacomistle. A beautiful animal, slightly larger than a gray squirrel, it is related to the raccoon, but is smaller, has a longer tail in proportion to the body, and has black rings around the tail which do not meet on the under side. Besides these easily observed structural features, its face is more foxlike and the dentition is different. The ringtail is seldom seen, though it may be common, because it generally inhabits brushy, rocky slopes and is strictly nocturnal. It may come out in the daytime when frightened from its nest, however. There is reason to believe it is active chiefly in the middle of the night, well after dusk and long before dawn. Photographic records of night ani-

Fig. 216. Ringtail (*Bassariscus astutus*).

mals at bait show the ringtail invariably coming after the gray foxes, raccoons, and striped skunks have had their fill and departed.

The food of the ringtail consists chiefly of small rodents such as the white-footed mouse and the wood rat, both of which are common in the chaparral regions of the foothills. Brush-dwelling small birds are sometimes eaten, and on occasion the fruit of the manzanita, cascara, and madrone. A captive animal refused to eat any of these foods but would venture from its nest even in daylight to lick honey from the end of a stick. On several occasions ringtails have been known to enter inhabited cabins to catch mice. One occupied cabin in the foothills of the Sierra Nevada has had ringtails in the attic for the past 20 years. A pair has been seen to leave the attic nest nightly about ten or eleven o'clock and move slowly toward a brush-covered hillside. When hunting in the shadows, the ringtails moved quietly and swiftly. In open moonlight places, however, where a horned owl or other predator might attack it, the long ringed tail was arched over the back toward the head as the animal bounced from rock to rock in a most conspicuous manner. It thus appeared much larger than when hunting in the thick brush.

The northern Sacramento Valley in California has many caves under projecting layers of lava rock, well protected from rain. The dusty floors are covered with tracks of mice and wood rats and, invariably, ringtails (fig. 214). The ringtail generally spends the day in a permanent den, which may be in a hollow tree, a rock pile, or a crevice in a cliff. Three or four young, born in May or June, compose a litter. It is a month before the eyes and ears are fully open.

Ringtails are trapped for their fur and they destroy harmful rodents; hence they should be protected. There is one species of ringtail in the Pacific States.

Family **Mustelidae** (Weasels, Minks, Martens, Fishers, Wolverines, Badgers, Otters, and Skunks)

The family Mustelidae includes a somewhat heterogeneous group of carnivores. Those of the Pacific States include the marten, fisher, ermine, long-tailed weasel, mink, wolverine, badger, spotted skunk, striped skunk, river otter, and sea otter. They have in common short legs with five toes on each foot, fur of fine quality which is often very valuable, and scent glands which are frequently highly developed. The rostrum is short. There is one molar tooth on each side of the upper jaw and two molars on each side of the lower jaw. The number of premolar teeth varies with the different species. Only mustelid mammals have this combination of features. The pictorial key and the key to the fissipid carnivores help to identify the species in the Pacific States. See key, p. 335.

Fig. 217. Track pattern of
a marten in the snow.

Fig. 218. Marten (*Martes
americana*). Photograph
by Ed Cesar.

Fig. 219. Fisher (*Martes pennanti*).

light brown

yellowish orange

MARTEN

"frosted" fur

blackish brown

whitish spots

FISHER

brown

dark brown

whitish spots

brown

MINK

Martes Dental Formula 3-1-4-1/3-1-4-2

Marten (*Martes americana*). Length 540–730 mm., about 26 inches; tail 180–240 mm.; hind foot 70–95 mm.; ear, crown, 26–45 mm.; skull 72–83.6 mm.; *light golden brown* above, with feet and tip of tail blackish; *yellowish or orange on throat and chest*; tail bushy and round. From Sierra Nevada and north Coast Ranges in California across Oregon and Washington. Yellow Pine, Red Fir, Lodgepole, Subalpine, and Redwood forests; Transition to Hudsonian life zones. P. 369, fig. 218, Map 89.

Fisher (*Martes pennanti*). Length 830–1033 mm., about 36 inches; tail 340–422 mm.; hind foot 90–128 mm.; ear, crown, 35–50 mm.; skull 98–125 mm.; *dark brown with head and shoulders grayish*; blackish legs and tail; *irregular white spots on the lower surface*. North from the Sierra Nevada and north Coast Ranges in California across Oregon and Washington. Upper Yellow Pine, Red Fir, and Lodgepole forests; chiefly Canadian Life Zone, but ranging up and down into the next zones also. P. 371, fig. 219, Map 90.

Mustela Dental Formula 3-1-3-1/3-1-3-2

Mink (*Mustela vison*). Length 447–720 mm., 20–30 inches; tail 150–90 mm.; hind foot 58–74 mm.; skull about 70 mm.; males weigh about three pounds, or nearly twice as much as the females; toes webbed at their bases; *ear low (about 13 mm. notch), scarcely projecting above fur; brown to dark brown all over, darkest on last half of tail*; sometimes with irregular white spots on chin and belly. Widely distributed north of San Francisco Bay, Fresno and Inyo counties, California, and over Oregon and Washington, along fish-supporting marshes, lakes, and streams from the Lower Sonoran to the Canadian Life Zone. P. 374, fig. 222, Map 91.

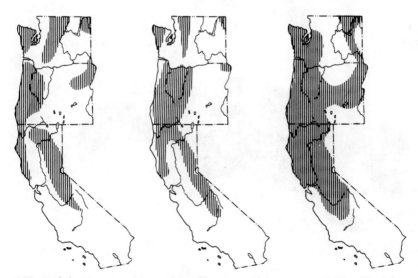

Map 89, left. *Martes americana.* **Map 90, center.** *Martes pennanti.* **Map 91, right.** *Mustela vison.*

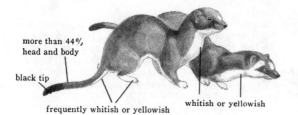

more than 44%
head and body

black tip

frequently whitish or yellowish

whitish or yellowish

LONG-TAILED WEASEL

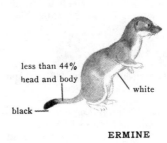

less than 44%
head and body

white

black

ERMINE

brownish band

claws
white

WOLVERINE

Long-tailed weasel (*Mustela frenata*). Length 311–545 mm., about 16 inches; *tail more than 44 per cent of head and body length,* 113–65 mm.; hind foot 35–47 mm.; ear, crown, 13 mm.; skull about 50 mm., its postglenoid length is less than 47 per cent of its condylobasal length; summer, *uniform brown above and yellowish white below*; winter, may be *pure white; basal part of undertail frequently whitish or yellowish; black tip to tail at all times*; some individuals have a white spot only between the eyes and the nose, and others have a large white spot also in front of each ear. (The two figures in the drawing represent two of several subspecies.) Throughout Pacific States; Lower Sonoran into the Hudsonian Life Zone. P. 372, fig. 220, Map 92.

Ermine (*Mustela erminea*). Length 190–340 mm., about eight inches; *tail less than 44 per cent of the head and body length,* 42–59 mm.; hind foot 23–44 mm.; skull about 34 mm., postglenoid length more than 47 per cent of its condylobasal length; summer, *brown above and white below, including inside of the legs, but not the under side of the tail.* Some ermines may have *pure white* only on the throat and inguinal regions; winter, may have pure white fur all over, *except tip of tail,* which is always black. High mountains from Tulare County north to the Trinity and Salmon River mountains of California, and most of Oregon and Washington; Red Fir, Lodgepole, and Subalpine forests; Canadian and Hudsonian life zones. P. 373, fig. 221, Map 93.

Wolverine (*Gulo luscus*). Dental Formula 3-1-4-1/3-1-4-2. Length 850–1125 mm., about three feet long; tail 190–260 mm.; hind foot 161–92 mm.; ear, crown, 50–55 mm.; skull 140–65 mm.; stout-bodied with a "humped" back; dark brown or blackish, with two wide brownish or yellowish bands that *start on the head, running down the sides, to the top of the base of the tail*; claws pearly white. At present rarely in the high Sierra Nevada of California and in the high mountains of Oregon and Washington; chiefly in the Subalpine Forest and the Alpine Fellfields; Hudsonian and Alpine-Arctic life zones. P. 375, fig. 225, Map 94.

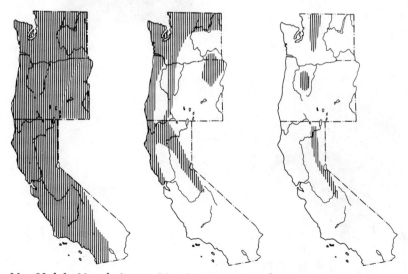

Map 92, left. *Mustela frenata.* **Map 93, center.** *Mustela erminea.* **Map 94, right.** *Gulo luscus.*

single stripe

white markings

long claws

BADGER

white at base
of hairs

STRIPED SKUNK

white stripes

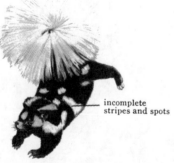

incomplete
stripes and spots

SPOTTED SKUNK

Badger (*Taxidea taxus*). Dental Formula 3-1-3-1/3-1-3-2. Length 545–871 mm., from 20 to 24 inches; tail 90–150 mm.; hind foot 90–125 mm.; skull 108–132 mm., brownish gray above, *with black and white markings on the head; a white stripe running from the nose nearly to the middle of the back; feet black; long foreclaws.* Practically all over three states except the humid coastal belt, from sea level to alpine meadows, from dry deserts to dense Red Fir Forest; Lower Sonoran to Hudsonian Life Zone. P. 377, fig. 226, Map 95.

Striped skunk (*Mephitis mephitis*). Dental Formula 3-1-3-1/3-1-3-2. Length 600–800 mm., about two feet; tail 185–390 mm.; hind foot 65–88 mm.; skull 69–87 mm.; *pure black with two pure white stripes starting on top of the head and running down the back and onto the tail; tail hairs white at base.* Throughout all three states, except in the hottest and driest parts of the deserts and the high mountains; generally near streams; from the Lower Sonoran up into the Canadian Life Zone. P. 381, fig. 229, Map 96.

Spotted skunk (*Spilogale putorius*). Dental Formula 3-1-3-1/3-1-3-2. Length 345–473 mm., about 13 inches; tail 126–78 mm.; *hind foot* 39–55 mm.; skull 51–62 mm.; *black and white stripes and spots that run forward onto the sides of the head; tail white-tipped with one or two white spots at its base.* Throughout all three states except hottest parts of the deserts; in rocky, brushy places; Lower Sonoran into the Transition Life Zone. P. 379, fig. 228, Map 97.

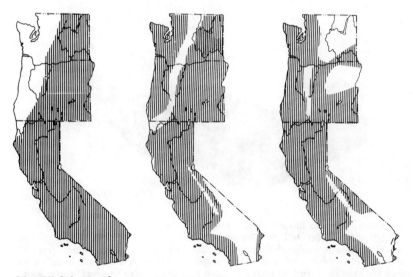

Map 95, left. *Taxidea taxus.* **Map 96, center.** *Mephitis mephitis.* **Map 97, right.** *Spilogale putorius.*

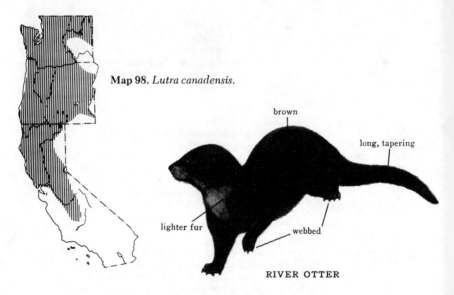

Map 98. *Lutra canadensis.*

RIVER OTTER

River otter (*Lutra canadensis*). Dental Formula 3-1-4-1/3-1-3-2. Length 890–1300 mm., about four feet; tail 300–500 mm.; hind foot 100–146 mm.; skull 104–13 mm.; *a long slender cylindrical neck nearly as wide as head; body with long, gradually tapering tail;* all feet fully webbed; *dark brown with light throat;* very small ears. Washington, Oregon, and most of California, along rivers, marshes, and lakes. P. 383, fig. 231, Map 98.

SEA OTTER

Sea otter (*Enhydra lutris*). Dental Formula 3-1-3-1/2-1-3-2. Length 760–1810 mm., *four to six feet;* tail 260–360 mm.; hind foot 150–220 mm.; weight, males, 60–80 pounds, females, 35–60 pounds; skull 130–40 mm.; *dark brown "frosted" above; feet webbed and hind limbs flattened to form flippers;* tail little longer than the extended legs. At present known to occur off San Mateo County, south to the Santa Barbara Islands, California, and north to Washington, among the kelp beds. (No range map.) Rare. P. 384, fig. 232.

Marten (*Martes americana*), fig. 218

If one wishes to see a marten in its native environment, the best opportunities would be far away from the haunts of man. Indeed, human ways and marten ways do not seem to be at all compatible. Deep coniferous forests or large rockslides in high mountains are the best places to look for this beautiful fur bearer. It is about the size of a gray squirrel and has rich yellowish brown fur, a bushy cylindrical tail, and large catlike ears. These easily observed features, and the orange yellowish fur on the throat and chest, distinguish the creature from other native mammals.

The marten can climb a tree as well as a squirrel, for which it is sometimes mistaken. In fact, the marten should be thought of as an arboreal mustelid. It is frequently seen by hikers in the back country in broad daylight. In some cases it has approached within a few feet of a person to secure choice food. The animal may rob a lunch box or a fish basket if it is neglected for only a few minutes. A marten was once coaxed with canned sardines to within five feet of a camera.

The marten preys on the Douglas squirrel, the northern flying squirrel, and the western red-backed mouse; perhaps also the snowshoe hare, the pika, and a variety of small rodents. In an examination of some 500 marten scats, or droppings, in the Grand Teton National Park in Wyoming, Murie (1961) found that voles were the flesh eaten most and Oregon grape, blueberry, and rhamnus berries the plants eaten most. In winter the marten searches rock taluses for food.

The animal is one of our most valuable fur bearers; since it is easily trapped, it is now fully protected in California by law until its population builds up. In 1952–53, before the season was closed on martens, the average price per skin of the 38 pelts taken was $14.16. The marten is still legally trapped in Washington and Oregon, where in 1961 a pelt brought up to $35.00. Because it lives in dense forests, and mostly in isolated areas, it does little if any harm to man's interests.

The gestation period appears to be nine months, apparently because of delayed implantation or delayed development of the fertilized egg. Martens breed in midsummer, but there are no recognizable embryos in females taken in early winter. At the U. S. Fish and Wildlife Experimental Fur Farm, this long gestation period was shortened by subjecting a pregnant female to exposures of artificial light. The female does not breed until she is two years old. The young are born in April and number up to five in a litter. The only two marten dens seen by the author were in the Mount Lassen region. One was 60 feet up in a dead hollow tree, the other in a rocky bank. The latter was occupied continually for six years.

In traveling, the animals leave a distinctive trail with tracks in pairs—one behind the other—or in groups of four (fig. 217). A marten may travel up to 15 miles in a single night searching for food.

Most of the martens in the Pacific States live in the mountains and thick forests of the Canadian and Hudsonian life zones. There is one species of marten.

Fig. 220. Long-tailed weasel (*Mustela frenata*).

Fig. 221. Ermine (*Mustela erminea*). Photograph by Alex Walker.

Fig. 222. Mink (*Mustela vison*). Photograph by Ed Cesar.

Fisher (*Martes pennanti*), fig. 219

Another valuable fur-bearing mammal in the Pacific States that is becoming very rare is the fisher. This large, weasel-like animal may still be seen in the Sierra Nevada region between Yosemite and Sequoia national parks and in the Trinity Mountains of California. The chances of seeing one of these beautiful animals in the woods, however, are slight; very few mammalogists have been so fortunate.

An adult male fisher is slightly over three feet long and weighs about ten pounds. The female, which is half as large, has finer, more valuable fur. Frequently, the pelt is brownish gray above, with dark brown or black on legs, feet, tail, and belly. However, some fishers are nearly black or very dark in overall coloration. Irregular blotches of white are sometimes found between the front legs, but more frequently these white areas are larger between the hind legs. The brown bushy tail is about three-fourths the length of the body. The claws and teeth are sharp and, being white, contrast strikingly with the dark fur.

The fisher has doubtless been misnamed, for all evidence points toward mammals and birds as its chief food—porcupines, squirrels, wood rats, mice, marmots, mountain beavers, quail, and grouse. It seems to have mastered the difficult technique of preying on porcupines. Hardly a fisher is caught that does not have quills in its skin, and, strangely enough, these do not seem to fester or otherwise harm the fisher.

Fishers do little if any harm to domestic animals. They occupy the more unsettled areas in the forests somewhat lower in altitude than those occupied by the marten and the wolverine. In 1961, Oregon began transporting fishers from Canada and releasing them in the wilds of Klamath and Wallowa counties as part of a program for porcupine control. Twenty-four animals have been released and it is hoped they will increase and spread. The nest is usually in an inaccessible tree hole, but may be in a rock slide if there are no trees.

A prime pelt has sold for as much as $100, although $50 is more common. This high value has decimated the population. There is a closed season on fishers in all three states. No native mammal, even if harmful, should be permitted to become extinct.

Although fishers may have as many as five young in a litter, two is the usual number. Breeding records of those kept in captivity in Canada indicate the period of gestation to be between 338 and 358 days. This long period probably represents delayed implantation of the fertilized eggs or delayed development, as in the marten. The one to four young are born in late March or early April. Although blind and helpless at first, they are hunting with the mother after three months. Fishers have few enemies except man, but are reported to have been killed by mountain lions. They live largely within the Canadian and Upper Transition life zones in heavy timber; since many timber areas have been cut, it seems likely that the fisher's range is becoming seriously limited.

The tracks are five-toed and—like those of the marten—occur in twos, with one track directly behind the other, or they may be grouped in fours (fig. 217).

The fisher has been successfully raised in captivity, where its ration of lean meat and mash is the same as that for minks.

The fisher is a solitary animal, controlling a large territory of ten square miles, from which it excludes other fishers except during breeding periods. Hence the population probably never was large.

There is one species of fisher in the Pacific States. It ranges from the southern Sierra Nevada in California north through the forested areas of Oregon and Washington.

Long-tailed Weasel (*Mustela frenata*), fig. 220

The long-tailed weasel can readily be distinguished from the mink, marten, or ermine by its size and by the contrasting colors of the back and belly. It is half as large as the mink and marten but twice the size of the ermine. Its tail is almost half the length of the head and body (Hall, 1951). Its long, slender body is covered with soft short fur, brownish dorsally and yellowish or whitish on the ventral surface. In certain localities in winter, the animal sheds its brown summer coat and becomes pure white, except for the black-tipped tail. In the Sierra Nevada and east of the Cascade mountains the animal molts to white fur in winter; west of these mountains the winter molt is brown, like the summer pelage. It is active through the entire winter.

The weasel is very commonly observed hunting in the daytime and is known to be active also at night. It is extremely quick, and the slender body is admirably adapted to climbing trees, squirming through rock piles, brush, or thick growth in search of food, which consists largely of small rodents and, sometimes, rabbits and birds. It frequently runs through the burrows of mountain beavers and pocket gophers.

A long-tailed weasel built its nest and reared four young under the floor of a tent one summer within 20 feet of a nest of the russet-backed thrush. Both the parents and young ones were seen to sniff about the nest when it was occupied by the young birds, but they never harmed it, probably because there was an abundance of meadow mice close by. White-crowned sparrows of the Sierra Nevada have been observed to mob a weasel that is hunting in the vicinity. One young long-tailed weasel killed and partially ate its brother rather than eat freshly cracked hen's eggs that were placed in the cage for them. Along with various kinds of mice and pocket gophers, a mole's mummified body was found by a weasel's nest. It kills its prey by biting through the skull into the base of the brain case. A weasel will eat 40 per cent of its body weight every day. It has powerful scent glands.

Although the fur of a long-tailed weasel may become pure white during the winter and is popularly called "ermine," it is not very valuable. Occasionally weasels are reported to do harm, especially to young chickens or turkeys; however, such forays are unusual, and the damage reported is often caused by a larger predator. Weasels probably are beneficial, especially in protecting young orchards from meadow mice and pocket gophers.

The tracks of a long-tailed weasel resemble those of a small mink (fig. 223), generally with but four toe prints. The little toe seldom shows in the track.

Mating occurs in July or August; the single litter consists of six to nine young, born in the spring after a gestation period averaging 279 days (Wright, 1948). This long gestation period is the result of delayed implantation of the blastocysts, which reach the uterus two weeks after mating but are not attached to its wall until nearly four weeks before parturition. The young are two-thirds grown and are out of the nest by the middle of June. They stay near the home den for a week or two, even after they are able to go with the mother on mouse hunts. In captivity they reach maximum growth in approximately 80 days.

Ermine (*Mustela erminea*), fig. 221

A pair of white-crowned sparrows chirp excitedly about a clump of willows near the edge of a mountain lake just below timber line in the high Sierra Nevada. Suddenly a small, slender mammal appears and lopes to safety in a rock pile. There is a glimpse of an incredibly short tail, rich brown fur on the back, a tiny white spot on the nose, and pure white under parts, usually including whitish feet. It is the ermine, which is sometimes called the short-tailed weasel, the smallest true carnivore in the Pacific States. It resembles the long-tailed weasel, except for the tail and body size. The tail of an ermine is one-fourth of its entire length and has no white beneath; that of the long-tailed weasel is more nearly one-third of its total length and is frequently whitish or yellowish near the base on the under side.

The ermine is found chiefly in the Canadian Life Zone or higher, and so seldom conflicts with man. It ranges at least from Kings Canyon National Park in California north through Oregon and Washington.

The ermine resembles the long-tailed weasel in its food habits. It prefers small rodents to birds, fish, or insects. It has been observed to bring to its den as many as four short-tailed mice, probably meadow mice or phenacomys, in a single day. In a period of 37 days one female brought to her den 78 mice, 27 pocket gophers, 34 chipmunks, three wood rats, and four ground squirrels. The ermine hunts in the day as well as at night. There are occasionally several hours of inactivity, apparently for sleeping. It is a powerful animal for its size and hunts over a considerable territory. An ermine was observed to run, without a stop, to its den nearly 300 yards away, carrying a large white-footed mouse nearly as heavy as itself.

Although white-crowned sparrows, juncoes, rosy finches, and Clarke nutcrackers become excited and scold an ermine every time they catch sight of one, there is no evidence that it ever attacks them. In summer, at least, its food is made up almost entirely of small rodents.

Ermine dens are located under the spreading roots of large trees and under large rocks. The entrance need not be larger than an inch in diameter. It may be a hole in an exposed hollow root or may be dug in the earth. Very little is known about the breeding habits of the ermine. The young are born in April and May. As many as 13 compose a litter, although the average is four. It is known that in the high Sierra Nevada the young are not yet large enough to leave the den by the first of August.

The ermine usually sheds its brown fur late in the autumn and becomes pure white during the winter months, except for a black-tipped tail. In the woods of the Northwest, however, where little or no snow falls, it does not always change color when it molts. West of the Cascade Mountains in Washington the ermine's winter fur is only slightly paler brown than its summer pelage. East of the Cascades it normally becomes pure white.

The tracks of the ermine resemble those of the larger long-tailed weasel and the still larger mink (fig. 223). The animal has five toes on each foot, but in shallow tracks only four of these show.

This agile predator has few enemies, except possibly the horned owl or the marten. A severe winter with insufficient food is doubtless the worst enemy it experiences. The fur has little value, and, since many ermines live well above the regular lines of the trapper, few of them are taken.

There is one other species of weasel in the Pacific States, the larger long-tailed weasel, which might be confused with the ermine.

Mink (*Mustela vison*), fig. 222

Anyone who spends a great deal of time along mountain streams or around the cattail marshes of lowland lakes and ponds may occasionally see a mink. The semiaquatic animal is nearly as long as a house cat but is much more slender. It may weigh up to three pounds. Its brown fur is among the most beautiful and durable—and therefore probably the most sought after—of any of our native fur bearers. Like its smaller relative, the long-tailed weasel, the mink has relatively short legs, a long neck, and a tail less than half the length of its body. Along the ventral surface are irregular small white areas that vary in size and position. Minks have powerful scent glands.

Although the mink is partially aquatic in habits and can readily catch

Fig. 223. Tracks of a large mink, nearly actual size.

fast-swimming fish, it is sometimes found at a considerable distance from water. Generally it is nocturnal, although it is frequently seen in the daytime. A mink has five toes on each foot; the track usually shows only four, but occasionally the small toe also shows in deep mud (fig. 223).

In addition to various species of fish, frog, and crayfish, the mink eats mice, muskrats, rabbits, and many kinds of birds, particularly crippled water birds. One time an old mink with teeth nearly worn to the gum was caught; it had entered a chicken coop the night before and killed six hens but had eaten only a small part of one. In winter, minks sometimes cache considerable numbers of coots, ducks, and muskrats, the latter being a favorite food. They usually pluck a bird before eating it. Frequently they catch crayfish on the bottom of a stream, and they eat meadow mice, dead birds, and dead fish washed up by the ocean.

Because of its great value as fur bearer and predator, the mink should be protected all year round. If local damage is done by raiding a chicken house or fish hatchery, the animal should be trapped live and sold to a fur breeder or transported where it will do no damage.

An average of five, and as many as ten, young are known to occur in a single litter, once a year. The period of gestation varies from 38 to 85 days, depending on the time the animal was bred. This variability—as in the marten and the fisher—may perhaps also be explained by the delayed development of the fertilized egg.

The home range of a male mink may be more than 1,100 acres. However, Errington (1963) found about 30 minks living in a 935-acre marsh in Iowa, where there were 9,000 muskrats.

Besides man and the great horned owl, the mink has few enemies. Sometimes it becomes infected with worm parasites, such as trematodes and nematodes, which may eventually cause death.

Since the price of the fur is relatively high, mink ranching is profitable in cold mountainous parts of the West, several ranches having over 500 animals. Some of the largest mink ranches are near the coast, where the cool weather results in beautiful coats of rich brown fur. Certain valuable mutations such as platinum have been developed and are now being successfully grown on ranches. The genetic formulas for the various genotypes are well known to mink breeders.

There is one species of native mink. It ranges through all the life zones up to the Hudsonian.

Wolverine (*Gulo luscus*), fig. 225

The second largest member of the weasel family is the wolverine. Its powerful, squat body, which is about a yard long, somewhat resembles that of a badger. It is, however, much larger, weighing 20 to 35 pounds.

The back, belly, feet, and muzzle vary in color from brown to nearly black. Across its forehead is a grayish area, and along each side of the body is a broad yellowish gray or brownish gray band that ends on the

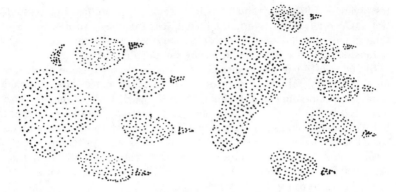

Fig. 224. Tracks of a wolverine, about half size.

top of the base of the tail. The wolverine is now very rare, and records indicate that it was never common.

One summer morning in 1953, a party from the National Audubon Camp at Norden, California, saw a wolverine at Squaw Valley. It was walking slowly about large boulders under which lived yellow-bellied marmots. When alarmed, the animal loped off toward the rock-covered mountains somewhat in the manner of a weasel or an otter. Its tracks and scat were later located on a hillside near the meadow. That part of the Sierra Nevada was regularly visited by groups from the camp, but this was the first wolverine seen over a period of six years. Since then, others have been reported from the High Sierra.

There is considerable evidence based on reliable observation that the wolverine is not aggressive, but when attacked, or to protect its young, it will fight so ferociously that even the black bear and the mountain lion hesitate to attack it.

In and near Sequoia and Yosemite national parks in California, wolverines have been seen in broad daylight and sometimes at surprisingly close range. The tracks may be mistaken for those of wolf, coyote, or mountain lion unless the mark of the fifth toe shows or the imprint of the foot is carefully examined (fig. 224).

The wolverine probably eats many small animals, including porcupines, and feeds on the carcasses of much larger animals. Since its home is at timber line, it probably does not prey on domestic animals. It is reputed to follow the trapper over his line and to eat either the bait or the catch. On occasion it breaks into cabins to get at food stores and even tears up valuable furs. However, wolverines are very scarce and damage is negligible. Their limited numbers make them relatively unimportant as fur bearers. It is claimed that the fur is ideal for parkas because frost from the breath will not adhere to it; because of the relatively erect position of the guard hairs, compared with the fur of other animals, it will not freeze

Fig. 225. Wolverine (*Gulo luscus*).

or mat so readily. The wolverine is now completely protected by law in California.

From one to four young, born from April to June, are in a litter. The den is probably in a rock crevice or beneath talus.

There is one species, located in northern Washington (a recent record [1965] is from Three-fingered Jack Mountain in Oregon) and south along the Sierra Nevada to Walker Pass in Kern County, California, chiefly in the Canadian and Hudsonian life zones, where it is still occasionally reported.

Badger (*Taxidea taxus*), fig. 226

Sometimes in high mountain meadows or in the rolling foothills bordering valleys one sees a low, squat animal about the size of a raccoon, trotting with a wobbling gait. The grizzly-gray back and short, bushy tail are characteristic of the badger. The most striking features, however, are black-and-white markings on the face and the very long front claws. A single median white line extends from the nose over the forehead to the neck. On either side and running parallel are dark bands extending laterally past the eyes. Below and behind the eye is another white band, flanked by still another black one, making the markings of the face quite unlike those of any other native mammal. When seen at a distance in a mountain meadow, a badger may be confused with a yellow-bellied marmot, which is nearly the same size; the badger, however, runs with a steady trotting or gliding motion, and the marmot runs with a loping gallop.

Fig. 226. Badger (*Taxidea taxus*).

The badger is superbly equipped to dig out its food, which consists of ground squirrels, rats, mice, gophers, and chipmunks. The presence of a badger is suggested by large, freshly dug, elliptical burrows eight or more inches in diameter around the dens of ground squirrels—its chief food—or chipmunks. Here it lies in wait. The tracks are distinctive (fig. 227). The very long front claws show in all but the shallowest tracks.

The badger seems to be active at all times of the day but especially during the late afternoon. Although it may prefer more friable soils for its fossorial forays, the hard-baked earth in the middle of an unpaved road is no obstacle if a ground squirrel or gopher is the reward. The badger is a powerful animal for its size, and it is doubtful if any animal smaller than a mountain lion, or any but the largest dog, could subdue it.

The fur is of little value, seldom bringing more than a dollar. The occasional damage caused by the badger—a horse can break a leg in a badger hole—is more than offset by the good it does in greatly reducing the harmful rodent population.

Before the white man came, badgers had few enemies and easily maintained themselves even with a low reproduction rate. Now with much of their rodent food eliminated by cultivation and large-scale poisoning campaigns, the badgers are rapidly decreasing in number.

Fig. 227. Tracks of a badger, about half size.

The male badger is a solitary animal; the female alone raises the family. The young are born in the spring; as many as five have been observed in one litter, although two are perhaps more usual. When taken young enough, they make interesting pets, although they can never be given complete freedom, especially if there is a lawn or garden nearby.

Like many other species of mustelids, the badgers possess scent glands similar to those of the skunk, but they are inoffensive since they do not spray the scent.

There is one species of badger. It ranges widely, from the Lower Sonoran into the Canadian Life Zone.

Spotted Skunk (*Spilogale putorius*), fig. 228°

"Well, I've seen lots of skunks, but never have I seen one stand on his hands and act like a clown by holding a white parasol over himself when he is all ready to spray you." These were the words of a woman who was watching at close range for the first time the peculiar behavior of a spotted skunk. To anyone whose acquaintance with skunks is limited to the larger striped skunk, the little spotted one is most surprising. It is about the size of a half-grown kitten and has many stripes and spots which readily distinguish it from the striped skunk. Any skunk with a white stripe which starts behind each eye and below the ear on the side of the head is a spotted skunk.

Spotted skunks are much more active and agile than their larger relatives and are more weasel-like in appearance. Like them, however, the animal is quite capable of defending itself with powerful scent glands at the base of its tail. When surprised away from its den or other cover, it assumes various attitudes of defense. The tail may be brought up over the back and pointed toward its head in such a way that the stiffly erect hairs of the white tip form a beautiful rosette, from under which the little animal watches every move of its enemy. Besides presenting this display of warning blacks and whites, the skunk occasionally strikes the ground audibly with its front feet. If these warnings fail and the intruder comes closer, the little skunk may stand on its forefeet and extend its hind legs and tail as high in the air as possible. This peculiar behavior is often referred to as the handstand. It is assumed when the spotted skunk is closely pressed by

° Formerly *Spilogale gracilis*. See Van Gelder (1959).

Fig. 229. Striped skunk (*Mephitis mephitis*).

Fig. 228. Spotted skunk (*Spilogale putorius*).

dogs or men. In this position the long white hairs of the tail are spread widely and conspicuously between the body of the skunk and the attacker. A bite into this part of the tail would not seriously injure the skunk, but the attacker would get his mouth, nose, and eyes filled with the powerful scent, which causes violent nausea and temporary blindness. Striped skunks are also said to handstand.

When the spotted skunk hunts at night, its white-tipped tail sways from side to side with the regularity of a metronome. Frequently it stops to rout out a beetle or grasshopper. If something startles the creature, it bobs along with the conspicuous white-tipped tail waving a warning. Insects, rodents, small birds, and possibly bird eggs constitute most of its food. It also eats table scraps and often becomes quite tame when its confidence has been gained by regular feeding.

The spotted skunk lives under old buildings with low floors or in burrows formerly used by ground squirrels or in rockslides. Because of its nocturnal habits it is seldom seen. The animal is regarded as beneficial because of the large number of harmful insects and rodents it eats. The fur has little value.

There is evidence that the gestation period may be as long as 120 days. A litter consists of six young, born in early spring. The spotted skunk is erroneously known as civet cat, polecat, and phobia skunk. The last name is applied because the animal's bite is supposed to cause hydrophobia. However, the skunk is probably no more dangerous in this respect than any other wild creature.

The track resembles that of the striped skunk (fig. 230), except for its smaller size. The spotted skunk ranges widely over the three states, but its distribution is somewhat local. There is one species in the West, found in all the life zones up to the Canadian.

Striped Skunk (*Mephitis mephitis*), fig. 229

If there is one of the smaller wild mammals that enjoys almost complete immunity from attack, it must be the striped skunk. About the size of a large house cat, with a very bushy tail, general all-over black coloration, and two white stripes extending from the neck to the tail, the striped skunk is widely known and would readily be recognized by reputation alone. In the eastern United States it sometimes lacks the full-length white stripes and has only one slender white stripe from the nose to the back of the neck, where it widens to a large white spot. Such "black skunks" are not found among the western animals.

The striped skunk possesses powerful scent glands near the base of the tail, which are encased in muscles that are voluntarily controlled. It will not discharge its scent unless provoked, and then only as a last resort. When the animal is brought to bay, it strikes the ground audibly with its forefeet and even makes short rushes before actually using its potent weapon. Finally it backs up to the enemy with its tail erect and discharges the scent in fine yellow droplets accurately toward the tormentor, to a dis-

Fig. 230. Tracks of a striped skunk, about actual size.

tance of 25 feet. The acrid scent is sprayed into the air through small ducts that open just inside the anus; it can be detected from a considerable distance when the wind is right.

Although striped skunks sometimes get into chicken coops and do considerable damage, such depredations are uncommon; more often they feed on grasshoppers, grubs, beetles, and many other harmful insects in the warmer months of the year and where winters are not too severe. They also eat meadow mice and other rodents that are detrimental to the farmer. The good that striped skunks do far overbalances the infrequent harm. Along the coast where there are sand dunes covered with sufficient plant growth to make the digging of burrows easy but safe, there are frequently many striped skunks. These animals hunt along the beaches at night, eating dead animals brought in by the sea and digging the sand crabs out of the soft sand. Most of the animals live in logged-over areas, weed-grown fields, and streamside thickets where food is abundant.

The striped skunk has durable fur. It is sometimes used for food, and the gall bladder is said to be used in special Chinese medicines. These skunks live in holes in the earth, frequently dug by other animals, under old buildings, and in rock piles. During extremely cold weather they sleep for weeks at a time, but apparently do not truly hibernate. As many as ten young have been observed in a litter, though six is the usual number.

The striped skunk has few enemies except man and large dogs, although horned owls have been known to eat them. Their powerful defense protects them from most enemies. It is said that other animals avoid the striped skunk whenever possible. However, late one summer night a large striped skunk was eating some bait left for the purpose of obtaining pictures of a gray fox. A fox approached, whereupon the skunk struck the ground with its forefeet and spread its tail threateningly. The fox continued to approach, the skunk did not use its scent, and the two ate the bait together. This may have been an unusual case, but it seems to indicate that the striped skunk will not use its scent defensively unless its life is threatened.

When the ducts from the scent glands in a young animal have been properly removed by a veterinarian, the striped skunk makes an excellent pet. It is as playful and as clean as an ordinary house cat.

The tracks are distinctive, showing rather long claws on the forefeet and shorter ones on the hind feet (fig. 230). In this respect they resemble the tracks of a badger but are somewhat smaller. There is one species of striped skunk, widely distributed over the Pacific States; it ranges through all the life zones up to the Canadian.

River Otter (*Lutra canadensis*), fig. 231

Fortunate is the person who has seen a long, graceful river otter swimming beneath the clear surface of a quiet pool in a mountain stream or lake. The sleek body is about three feet long, with a thick tapering tail, a long, round head with prominent whiskers, small ears and short legs with all four feet fully webbed. These features adapt the river otter to aquatic life better than any other mustelid except the rare sea otter. Some river otters have taken up a marine existence around the San Juan Islands in Puget Sound.

Although the river otter is generally thought of as nocturnal, it is frequently seen hunting for food or playing on its slides in the daytime. The slide, on the bank of a stream or lake, is a foot wide and may be more than 25 feet long. Sometimes it is made in the snow. The otter climbs up and slides down—much like a boy at a favorite swimming hole—with forelimbs dangling loosely at the sides. The hind legs give an occasional push. Most wild river otters are seen when hunting fish, frogs, turtles, crayfish, insects, or, on occasion, young birds. They can remain submerged for a considerable time and are said to be fast enough to catch trout, for which reason fishermen dislike them. However, most of the fish caught by otters are not of game quality but are "rough" fish that actually eat trout eggs or otherwise discourage the presence of game fish. Otters are not known to catch salmon. In captivity they cannot be kept in good health when fed on fish alone. Today there are so few river otters along mountain trout streams and other watercourses that any damage they do must be insignificant compared to that of man-made practices such as drainage, irrigation, power projects, and pollution, which annually take an alarming toll of fish.

The river otter has a short, thick pelt of soft, brown, very durable fur, which makes it one of the most valuable fur bearers in the country. For this reason, if for no other, it should be encouraged to increase in numbers wherever its conflict with man's interest is not too great. In California it is protected by law and may not be killed at any time. The river otter has few enemies except man and possibly certain parasitic worms.

River otters are known to travel within a year 50 to 60 miles along streams, and sometimes when mating they may go considerable distances overland. Most of their travel is at night. Along streams and lakes frequented by river otters are "haul-out" places, where they roll about on the grass to dry. They frequently leave "signs," feces or scent from the anal glands, on a wisp of grass. Apparently they do not dig burrows, but enlarge those of other animals, in brush piles or in the tules, as much as half a mile from water.

Fig. 231. River otter (*Lutra canadensis*).

The time of mating is not known in the West, but in the Midwest it takes place in midsummer, and the young cubs are born from nine and a half months to over a year later. There are from two to four cubs in a litter. They are born toothless and blind, and are quite helpless for six weeks. They then become very playful, and after a short time the mother coaxes them into the water, where she teaches them to catch and hold food. The female will not tolerate the presence of the male near the young until they are six months old. Otters are known to live 14 years.

The Hoopa and Klamath Indians of northwestern California use the river otter skin in their ceremonial brush dances. The tracks of a river otter can hardly be mistaken for those of any other mammal. All five of the short, clawed toes show in the track, with the webs between the toes clearly indicated. The track of the heavy tail may also show in the snow or in deep mud.

There is one species of river otter. It ranges through all the life zones up to the Canadian. The rare sea otter that occurs off the California coast belongs to a different genus.

Sea Otter (*Enhydra lutris*), fig. 232

As a heavy sea churns against the rugged Carmel coast of California, the observer may see, riding the great waves far below, objects resembling the floating bladders of kelp. A closer look with a good pair of binoculars reveals a sight that few mammalogists have ever seen—a herd of sea otters.

Fig. 232. Sea otter (*Enhydra lutris*).

This mammal played a most important part in the exploration and settlement of the West Coast by the Russians, who came for its fur. After a period of 170 years of exploitation, the sea otter has come back from near extinction off the California coast. Once again the world's rarest and most valuable fur-bearing animal is seen sporting about in the waters off the rocky shores. Twenty-five years of government protection of this rare species has doubled the population, until in 1938 a herd numbering almost a hundred was discovered south of Carmel.

The sea otter is between five and six feet long, with broad flipper-like hind feet. The pelt varies from nearly black to dark brown and is sprinkled with long silvery white hairs. The head and shoulders of some specimens are quite gray, but this coloration does not seem to be correlated with age. The inch-long, dense fur traps a blanket of air when the animal submerges, thus insulating it from the cold water. If the fur becomes coated with slime from fish or oil from passing ships, it no longer acts as an insulating mechanism, and the otter becomes chilled and dies (Kenyon, 1963).

Along the California coast sea otters probably never come ashore. They are most often seen floating on their backs, sometimes with the feet and tail sticking straight up out of the water, or swimming among the floating kelp. They scratch a great deal, apparently to dislodge external parasites. Frequently they wrap strands of kelp about themselves or fold their forefeet over it to prevent drifting ashore as they sleep on their backs. The entire herd rests often, especially after a period of rough water. While feeding, the herd scatters and each animal searches for its own food by diving from 10 to 120 feet (Kenyon, 1963). All four limbs are frequently extended high into the air for long periods of time. Often this position is maintained by taking one of the toes of a hind foot in its mouth as it bobs about on the swells. Scientists speculate that this extension of the limbs into the air and sunlight may be concerned with acquiring vitamins, or that it may serve as thermoregulation.

While eating, the sea otter floats on its back, using the chest as a table. Between mouthfuls an abalone may be held close to the chest as the animal rolls over and over in the water. All evidence indicates that the sea otter off the California coast feeds largely on sea urchins, while mollusks and fish are of less importance. One has been observed to break the shell of a sea urchin against a rock held on its chest. An adult may eat one-fourth of its weight daily (Kenyon, 1963).

Rough water seems to act as a stimulus for mating; on calm days there is very little sexual activity in the herd. Courtship may be initiated by either sex. Normally one pup is born, but two have been reported. The pup, born at any season, is given constant attention for a year (Kenyon, 1963). As the female swims or floats on her back or side, the pup rides or is pulled along with its head under her foreleg. The mother, when hunting on the bottom for food, returns to the pup, as it floats among the big bladders of kelp, each time she comes to the surface. The male shows no interest. The young sea otter is called a pup as long as it has woolly, yellow-brown hair; after it loses this pelage it is called a cub until it becomes an adult.

A species of Acanthocephalia is known to parasitize the intestines of the sea otter. Killer whales are natural predators of the sea otter, but in spite of government protection irresponsible lawbreakers with high-powered rifles are still its worst enemies. It is hoped that the number of sea otters will increase and that they will begin to appear at other places in their former range. Sea otters have been seen off Año Nuevo Island, off the coast of San Mateo County (Orr and Poulter, 1964) and Sonoma County, California, and along the Oregon coast (Bailey, 1936). By 1963 the range appeared to be from Washington south to the Santa Barbara Islands in California (Boolootian, 1961).

Family **Felidae** (Cats)

Members of the cat family have sharp, fleshcutting cheek teeth; those of the Pacific States also have retractile claws. Today there are three native cats in the area: the mountain lion, the bobcat, and the Canadian lynx. There is little doubt that the Mexican jaguar ranged at least as far north as the Tehachapi Mountains in Kern County, California, a century ago, but it will not be included, nor will the domestic cat, which may be turning wild in the Sacramento Valley, California, and possibly also in other places in the Pacific States.

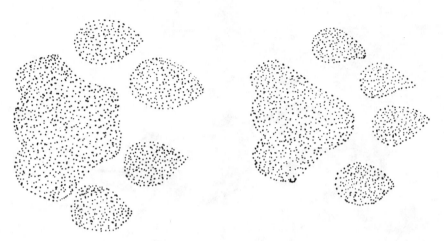

Fig. 233. Mountain lion tracks, nearly half size.

Fig. 234. Mountain lion (*Felis concolor*).

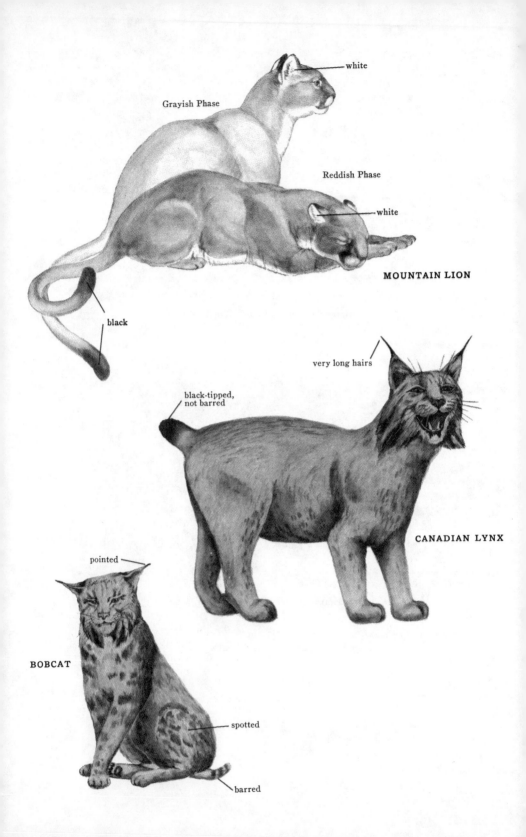

Mountain lion (*Felis concolor*). Dental Formula 3-1-3-1/3-1-2-1. Length 1500–2700 mm., about six to eight feet; tail 530–785 mm., 2–2.7 feet; hind foot 220–92 mm., 9.5–11 inches; skull 170–237 mm.; *tail dark-tipped; two color phases: red phase,* ochraceous tawny above, white below, and inside the ears; *gray phase,* dusky gray above, white below, and inside the ears. Cubs spotted with black. Practically throughout all three states including the Colorado River bottom, but not found on the floor of the central valleys or in the Colorado and Mojave deserts in California. Upper Sonoran and Transition life zones chiefly. P. 390, fig. 234, Map 99.

Lynx Dental Formula 3-1-2-1/3-1-2-1

Canadian lynx (*Lynx canadensis*). Length 825–950 mm.; tail 95–125 mm.; hind foot 200–250 mm.; skull 120–36 mm.; pelage soft, gray with slightly yellowish tone; ear and tail are black-tipped; under parts gray with indistinct black spots; summer pelage with a reddish tone, ears with tufts of long hairs. Northern Washington in forested areas in the higher mountains. P. 390, fig. 235, Map 100.

Bobcat (*Lynx rufus*). Length 710–900 mm., about 30 inches; *tail 120–210 mm., with one or more transverse dark dorsal bars before the dark tip;* hind foot 138–85 mm.; ear, crown, 52–90 mm.; skull 113–35 mm.; *tufted ears; more or less spotted all over.* Throughout most of Washington, Oregon, and California in nearly all communities and life zones. P. 391, fig. 236, Map 101.

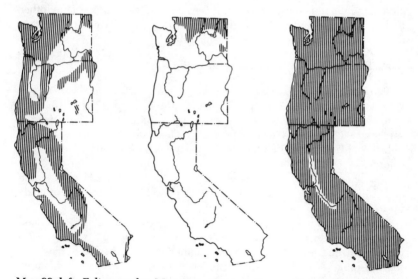

Map 99, left. *Felis concolor.* **Map 100, center.** *Lynx canadensis.* **Map 101, right.** *Lynx rufus.*

Mountain Lion (*Felis concolor*), fig. 234

Many people who have spent their lives in the coniferous forests and chaparral-covered foothills where mountain lions are relatively common have never seen one of these big cats. Certainly, no other wild animal could be mistaken for the mountain lion—or cougar, puma, or panther, as it is frequently called—unless it is the spotted jaguar, which may cross the Mexican border into southern California. Adult mountain lions range from six to eight feet in length, including the long tail, and closely resemble big, tawny house cats. They occur in two color phases, one grayish brown and the other reddish brown, but there may be intermediates between the two. The young kittens are spotted and have rings around their tails. The skin of the mountain lion is of little value, owing to the quantity of guard hairs, except as a trophy. The track (fig. 233) is large, and the pad has a characteristic three-lobed appearance at the rear, which is absent in that of dogs and coyotes (fig. 204).

The cubs most frequently arrive in April, although they may be born in any month. A litter contains two or three young—probably never more than four. The den is generally in a cave or crevice of a big rockslide at the base of a rocky cliff and is often quite accessible.

The chief food of the mountain lion is deer, and it is popularly supposed to kill and eat a deer a week. However, no more than 50 per cent of the food of an adult is deer, the rest being smaller animals such as skunks, porcupines, and dogs.

The worst enemy of the mountain lion is man, with his dogs; rarely is it killed by others. There are a few authentic cases of a mountain lion's attacking human beings. However, it seems to prefer venison to any other flesh. Except for "killers," or old animals incapable of catching deer, it seldom attacks livestock if deer are plentiful.

Canadian Lynx (*Lynx canadensis*), fig. 235

The short, black-tipped tail and the long, pointed dark-edged ears tipped with long black hairs readily distinguish the Canadian lynx from the smaller bobcat or wildcat. It may weigh up to 28 pounds. The pelage is soft gray with a yellowish wash dorsally. The under parts are gray with indistinct black spots. In summer the pelage is shorter and is reddish in color.

Mating occurs in January or February, and the young are born in March or April, after at least a 60-day gestation period. The litter may include up to four kittens.

The Canadian lynx ranges widely over the forested areas of Canada and comes south into the Pacific States only in the higher parts of the Cascades, the Blue Mountains, and the mountains of northeastern Washington. Its range largely corresponds to that of the red fox in Washington, where it feeds on rodents, birds, and especially the snowshoe hare, its prin-

Fig. 235. Canadian lynx (*Lynx canadensis*).

cipal food in winter. In Canada the lynx population follows the rhythmic rise and fall of the snowshoe hare population.

In Washington, the animal is classified as a fur bearer, and a few dozen pelts are taken annually. Large skins may bring $60. The lynx rarely becomes a problem to ranchers or farmers because it prefers the more remote and isolated regions.

Bobcat (*Lynx rufus*), fig. 236

The large catlike animal lying in a clearing or sunning itself on a rock on chaparral-covered slopes is probably a bobcat, or wildcat, especially if it has long legs, a short tail, and sharp-pointed ears. The gray or reddish fur, spotted with brown or black, a tail barred with black, and a weight of 15 to 20 pounds clearly distinguish the bobcat from the larger Canadian lynx, which it superficially resembles. The bobcat is found throughout the Pacific States in practically every habitat and life zone, from below sea level in Death Valley to the Hudsonian Life Zone at timberline. Many statements about its habits are not verified by careful study. Sportsmen, generally, are of the opinion that the bobcat preys extensively on quail and other game birds. Yet examination of the stomachs of hundreds of hunted (not trapped) bobcats indicates a very small percentage of any kind of birds. Mostly found are detrimental and disease-carrying ground

Fig. 236. Bobcat (*Lynx rufus*).

squirrels, pocket gophers, meadow mice, white-footed mice, brush rabbits, cottontails, hares, and wood rats. Some deer, particularly small ones or those weakened by hunger, are killed in the winter.

Stomach records of trapped specimens are of little value unless the bait used by the trapper is known, since traps are frequently baited with wings, heads, and viscera of game birds. The few quail a bobcat is able to catch are likely to be the cripples, weaklings, or those having coccidiosis—a disease that may decimate an entire covey. In catching such diseased birds the bobcat is a preserver rather than a destroyer of game. Those who contend that the bobcat is threatening extinction to certain game birds must realize that the quail and the bobcat have lived together successfully for thousands of years.

The track of a bobcat is larger than that of a house cat but much smaller than that of a Canadian lynx or mountain lion (fig. 233), which it re-sembles in shape.

The bobcat prefers rocky, brushy country for hunting and raising its young. The den may be a protected cavity or cave among the rocks. The young are born any time in the spring and summer months, but probably in April. Three kittens are an average litter.

The pelt is soft, with very few harsh hairs. It is not valuable, yet it brings enough to make trapping worth while. Bobcats are wastefully killed by the poisoned-meat pellets that are scattered about during coyote and "vermin" drives. Many fur bearers and rodent destroyers are left to rot during these disgraceful campaigns.

There is one species of bobcat, which is found in all three states.

12. Order Carnivora, Suborder Pinnipedia

This suborder of Carnivora has the limbs modified as flippers; the species off the Pacific Coast are almost entirely marine. Unlike carnivores which may have four digits, pinnipeds always have five toes on each limb; the first toe on the front foot and the first and fifth digits on the hind foot are usually longer than the rest and are clawless. The tail is very short or obsolete. The incisors are *always* fewer than three on each side of the lower jaw. The cheek teeth are conical or with sharp crowns and are similar in appearance. They are sometimes variable in number.

The body of pinnipeds is covered with a thick layer of fat, which may amount to one-fourth of the weight. This blubber provides buoyancy and padding, as well as reserve energy during lactation and long fasts, and is only moderately effective as an insulator. According to Scheffer (1958), the basal metabolic rate, so important in maintaining body heat, is higher than in other similar-sized animals.

The osmotic pressures of the blood and urine in the harbor seal are only slightly greater than in man (Scheffer, 1958). The manner in which pinnipeds obtain water and keep the salt content of their bodies at the proper level is apparently the same as in the Cetacea (see p. 326). They get ample water from their food alone to keep the blood more dilute than seawater. The urine can be more concentrated than seawater.

Four species of pinnipeds live compatibly, and often are closely contiguous, on Año Nuevo Island off the central California coast: the harbor seal, the elephant seal, the California sea lion, and the Steller sea lion, along with an occasional Alaska, or northern, fur seal. Such fighting as does occur is mostly within a given species rather than between members of different species (Orr, 1963b). Pinnipeds are polygamous: in the otariid family, one bull mates with 15 to 40 females, depending on the species; in the phocid family the number is smaller.

The gestation period of eight to 12 months after coitus is long in relation to other similar-sized mammals. Delayed implantation is probably the rule in most pinnipeds. Usually there is a single pup, precocial at birth. Pinniped milk, like whale milk, is very rich, being 42 per cent fat.

Natural enemies are large sharks and killer whales. Of the three living families, two are represented on the Pacific Coast. There is no range map.

KEY TO THE PINNIPED CARNIVORES
Marine-living carnivores (except sea otter)

1A. External ears present; postorbital process present (Otariidae) . . . 2
1B. No external ears; no postorbital process (Phocidae) 5
2A. Body longer than 210 cm. (male) and 150 cm. (female); coarse hair . 3
2B. Body shorter than 210 cm. (male) and 150 cm. (female); soft underfur
. . . . 4
3A. Body longer than 245 cm. (male) and 200 cm. (female); forehead sloping
in male; wide space between upper molar and posterior premolar. Along
the coast, at least to San Nicolas Island, California.
Eumetopias jubata, Steller sea lion, p. 397, fig. 239.
3B. Body shorter than 245 cm. (male) and 180 cm. (female); forehead bulging in male; no wide space in the upper cheek teeth row. Along the coast
of all three states.
Zalophus californianus, California sea lion, p. 397, fig. 240.
4A. Upper profile of skull gradually sloping. Rare; coastal islands off southern
California.
Arctocephalus townsendi, southern fur seal, p. 397, fig. 238.
4B. Upper profile of skull nearly flat in female; bulging only in male. Migrating
off coast of Washington, Oregon, and northern California.
Callorhinus ursinus, northern fur seal, p. 397, fig. 237.
5A. Body longer than 200 cm.; body grayish or tan; 30 teeth. Islands off southern California coast and north to British Columbia.
Mirounga angustirostris, northern elephant seal, p. 399, fig. 242.
5B. Body shorter than 200 cm.; body spotted, ringed, or blotched; 34 teeth.
Along the coasts of all three states 6
Phoca vitulina, harbor seal, p. 399, fig. 241.
6A. Variable dark spots on a gray to white background; posterior margin of
palate is V-shaped. Common along the coasts of all three states.
6B. Yellowish bands around the neck, over the shoulder, and around the rump;
34 teeth; posterior margin of palate broadly U-shaped, sometimes nearly
straight across. Very rare wanderer off the coast of the Pacific States.
Histriophoca fasciata, ribbon seal, p. 399.

Family **Otariidae** (Eared Seals and Sea Lions)

These pinnipeds have small external ears, and their hind flippers (legs)
can be brought up alongside the body. The skull has postorbital processes.
The first and second upper incisors are small, but the third is large and
like a canine in form. There are four species in the coastal waters off the
Pacific States, some of which have regular migrations.

The northern fur seal (*Callorhinus*) breeds on the Pribilof Islands in the
Bering Sea off Alaska. It spends months on the open ocean before it returns to its birthplace the following year. This migration may be 10,000
kilometers or more, but what guides these animals, sometimes in weeks
of dense fog, is not known. It is a fertile field for investigation. Even sea
lions on the California coast move north in winter (Scheffer, 1958).

Recent investigations reveal that sea lions orient themselves, with respect to food at least, by means of very effective echolocation similar to
that used by bats and porpoises (Poulter, 1963a, b).

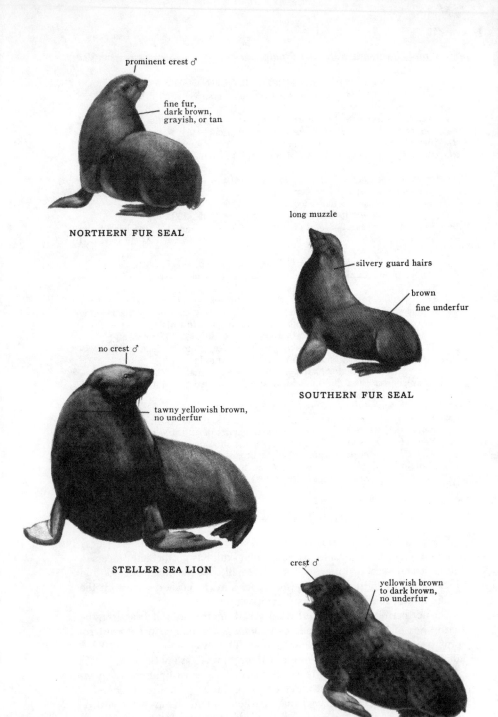

prominent crest ♂

fine fur,
dark brown,
grayish, or tan

NORTHERN FUR SEAL

long muzzle

silvery guard hairs

brown

fine underfur

SOUTHERN FUR SEAL

no crest ♂

tawny yellowish brown,
no underfur

STELLER SEA LION

crest ♂

yellowish brown
to dark brown,
no underfur

CALIFORNIA SEA LION

Northern fur seal (*Callorhinus ursinus*). Dental Formula 3-1-4-2/2-1-4-1. Length, male, up to eight feet, female, up to five feet; male may weigh 700 pounds, female, 130 pounds; *male is dark brown*, female and young are more grayish; *fine underfur* beneath the guard hairs; male has short muzzle and a *prominent crest on the forehead*; skull of male 220–75 mm., female 170–200 mm.; interorbital breadth of skull about 20 per cent of the condylobasal length. Mostly 10–50 miles off the coast of California, Oregon, and Washington in the open ocean in winter. P. 401, fig. 237.

Southern fur seal (*Arctocephalus townsendi*). Dental Formula 3-1-4-2/2-1-4-1. Length, male, up to six feet; *thick brown underfur, which anteriorly is covered with silvery guard hairs; long pointed muzzle with the nose to occiput line concaved*; skull, condylobasal length, male, 235–55 mm., female, 200–220 mm.; interorbital less than 15 per cent of the skull length; sockets of the last upper molar well behind the level of the opening formed by the zygomatic arch; cheek teeth widely spaced. San Nicolas Island (possibly other islands nearby); rare. P. 402, fig. 238.

Steller sea lion (*Eumetopias jubata*). Dental Formula 3-1-4-1/2-1-4-1. Length, male, up to 13 feet, female, up to nine feet; old bull may weigh 2,000 pounds, and the female half as much; adult *tawny or yellowish brown,* pup dark brown; *no underfur; bull without crest on the forehead*; tiny external pointed ears about 75 mm.; hind flippers can be brought up alongside the body; *last upper molar far behind the other cheek teeth* and located at about the level of the posterior end of the opening formed by the zygomatic arch. Remote rocky places all along the coast north from the Channel Islands, but mostly north of San Francisco; breeding on the Farallons and Año Nuevo Island, off Central California. P. 402, fig. 239.

California sea lion (*Zalophus californianus*). Dental Formula 3-1-4-2/2-1-4-1 or 3-1-4-1/2-1-4-1. Length, male, up to eight feet, female, up to six feet; weight of male up to 1,000 pounds, and female up to 600 pounds; male dark brown (nearly black), female often light brown or tan; no underfur; *adult male with protruding crest on the forehead*; tiny external ears about 60 mm. long; hind flippers can be brought up alongside the body; *last upper molar spaced about the same as the other cheek teeth* and anterior to the level of the opening formed by the zygomatic arch. Breeding from the Channel Islands off California south along the Mexican coast; occurring in rocky places and on islands all along the coast south of Vancouver Island (in winter), but mostly south of the Golden Gate, California. P. 404, fig. 240.

HARBOR SEAL

grayish, yellow blotches
no underfur

always extended behind

RIBBON SEAL

yellowish bands

yellow bands

NORTHERN ELEPHANT SEAL (male)

tan, grayish,
or brown

proboscis

always extended behind

Phoca and *Histriophoca* Dental Formula 3-1-4-1/2-1-4-1 (see p. 485).

Harbor seal (*Phoca vitulina*). Length about six feet; weight up to 300 pounds; grayish with white spots, or yellowish with blotches of blackish or grayish; no underfur; no external ears; hind flippers cannot be brought up alongside the body. Mostly in harbors and bays along the coast. P. 405, fig. 241.

Ribbon seal (*Histriophoca fasciata*). Length of male about six feet, female about five feet; weight up to 200 pounds; male is dark brown with wide bands of yellow around the neck, over the shoulder, and around the body at the level of the rump; female is grayish, with only a faint indication of bands. Posterior margin of the palate is broadly U-shaped; Dr. Aryan Roest identified one at Morro Bay, California, the only record on the coast of the Pacific States. It is found occasionally away from the northwestern Bering Sea. P. 406.

Northern elephant seal (*Mirounga angustirostris*). Dental Formula 2-1-4-1/ 1-1-4-1. Length, old male, up to 14–16 feet, occasionally 17 feet; female, 7 to 11 feet; weight of male, up to 5,000 pounds; *dark grayish*, but just before molting the hairs apparently turn brown or tan; *no underfur*; outer epidermis sloughs off during the molt; *adult male has inflatable proboscis*; no external ears; no spots except for old scars; hind legs cannot be brought up alongside the body; two upper and one lower incisor on each side of jaws. Anywhere offshore but most likely on the islands off the southern California coast. Known to breed on the Farallon Islands, California. P. 407, fig. 242.

Fig. 237. A family of northern fur seals (*Callorhinus ursinus*). Photograph by Dr. Victor B. Scheffer, U.S. Fish and Wildlife Service.

Fig. 238. Southern fur seal (*Arctocephalus townsendi*). Photograph by Dr. George A. Bartholomew.

Northern Fur Seal (*Callorhinus ursinus*), fig. 237, and
Southern Fur Seal (*Arctocephalus townsendi*),* fig. 238

In the open ocean ten to 50 miles off the California coast in winter, one may see a small group of northern fur seals. Usually such a group consists of adult females and young animals; the old males generally stay in more northern waters. Sometimes they approach within a few feet of a boat or ship and tread water in order to get a better look. Not infrequently one is seen resting on the surface of the ocean, with its flippers, which are relatively longer than those of the sea lion, arched up over its back or belly, probably to provide shade and to act as thermoregulators (Bartholomew and Wilke, 1956). The thick fur prevents effective heat loss, and the function of heat control is largely taken care of by the large, black, naked flippers, which are equipped with sweat glands. While the seal is on land, heat loss is facilitated by fanning the flippers about, but in cold water heat loss is reduced by holding the flippers out of the water, especially while resting. Thermoregulation by the flippers is much less important in those pinnipeds with no fur that live in warmer waters.

Drs. Kenyon and Scheffer (1953), biologists of the U. S. Fish and Wildlife Service, state that the belligerent fur seal bulls end their long trek to the Pribilof Islands early in June. Each bull establishes himself as lord of a small territory, usually less than 40 feet in diameter, and by the middle of June a harem of about 40 cows has arrived. Territoriality is expressed only by the bull fur seal, and his territory is established in the rookery of his birth (Kenyon, 1960). The female returns year after year to her birthplace. Young fur seals will return to their birthplace even when removed by man. This is thought to be an inherited survival factor related to nursing.

The harem is zealously guarded by the old monarch. Other bulls are savagely driven off in bloody and sometimes mortal combat. For nearly two months the male maintains his station and neither drinks nor eats. A 600-pound bull may lose one-third of his weight during the breeding season. Within a few hours to two weeks of the arrival of the cows, the single pup is born and the cows are bred again. The gestation period is a year. The cow is much smaller than the bull, weighing 60 to 100 pounds. The cow may be gone a week or more at a time, sometimes traveling 100 miles for food. When she returns, the pup gorges on as much as a gallon of the rich milk; then the mother goes off again. The cow does not teach the pup to swim. Instead it ventures into the water on its own accord after it is a few weeks old.

Killer whales and large sharks take many of the young seals, but a nematode worm is the greatest enemy. Twenty per cent of the pups may die of worm infections each season, and natural mortality during the first years may be as high as 70 per cent.

* Referred to as *Arctocephalus philippii* by some zoologists.

Northern fur seals travel 6,000 miles round trip during the winter migration; except for man and possibly some of the larger whales, they are the most widely traveled of all mammals. As a result of tagging experiments, it is now known that northern fur seals born on the Pribilof Islands may migrate down the Asiatic coast as well as the North American coast.

Seals eat squid and many kinds of fish of little commercial value. They have taken fish off hooks 180 feet below the surface.

At one time the northern fur seal was near extinction because of uncontrolled hunting. Protection by international treaties came just in time to save the species. Today the herds are models of the way protection and conservation pay off. Knowledge of the seal's life history and ecology has enabled scientists to determine how many males can be taken each year without endangering the future of the herds. The nonbreeding males congregate in herds by themselves. It is from the three-year-olds in these groups that the harvest of furs is taken. The harvest yields 65,000 pelts annually, with a value of six million dollars—already many times the price originally paid for Alaska. The fur is very dense and is covered with coarse guard hairs, which are removed in processing.

A related species is the southern fur seal (*Arctocephalus townsendi*), which lives much farther south. Before the sealers of the nineteenth century nearly exterminated it, this fur seal was common on the Farallon Islands and south along the Mexican coast. Apparently the tendency of this species to stay in caves during the daytime saved the colonies from extinction (Walker, 1964). Then for a quarter of a century there was no authenticated record of one until a lone male was found living on San Nicolas Island by Dr. George A. Bartholomew of the University of California, Los Angeles. In 1954 Dr. Carl Hubbs of the Scripps Institution of Oceanography in La Jolla found 14 of these rare seals on Guadalupe Island, and in 1956 Dr. Raymond Gilmore of the same institution found 92 seals there. Bartholomew and Hubbs (1960) report counts of up to 107 of these mammals.

Steller Sea Lion (*Eumetopias jubata*), fig. 239

When visitors at the Cliff House in San Francisco train their binoculars on the famous Seal Rocks by the Golden Gate, they may see the great tawny yellowish brown body of a bull Steller sea lion weaving its way to a position above the pounding sea. A large bull may weigh a ton, which is at least twice the weight of the smaller California sea lion bull more frequently seen farther south. The range of the Steller sea lion is from the Channel Islands off the southern California coast north to the Bering Sea. Although these majestic marine mammals most frequently occupy remote rocky coasts well away from civilization, they can frequently be observed in large numbers at the Sea Lion Caves on the coast of Oregon and on Año Nuevo Island off the central California coast. Occasionally they swim far up rivers. Scheffer (1958) reports one captured in a pasture nearly 75 miles inland near Oregon City.

Fig. 239. Steller sea lion (male) (*Eumetopias jubata*).

During the breeding season the dominant old bulls gather harems of cows, which they protect by loud vocal challenges and actual combat. The cow is a fourth the size of the bull. A year after mating, the cow gives birth to a single dark brown pup weighing 40 pounds. It plays and learns to swim in the shallow tidepools well above the surf. After three months of nursing, the pup can swim well enough to catch fish.

This species, along with the California sea lion, has been accused by fishermen of robbing their lines and tearing the seines and other gear. The charge has not been proved satisfactorily to many scientists. Sea lions dive down to 600 feet for food. Squid and herring have been found in their stomachs. Laws protecting Steller sea lions in Alaskan waters have been suspended except around one large refuge. According to Karl W. Kenyon of the U. S. Fish and Wildlife Service, there are about 50,000 of the animals along Alaskan and Canadian shores. In 1938 about 2,000 lived on the Channel Islands off California, but these had declined to about 50 by 1960 (Bartholomew and Boolootian, 1960). The cause of the decline, in the opinion of these authors, was the substantial increase since 1955° in the ocean temperature off the coast of California. The Channel Islands are at the southern limit of the range of the Steller sea lions, so probably they

° California Cooperative Oceanic Fisheries Investigations Progress Report, 1956–58 (Marine Research Committee, Sacramento), 856 pp.

became a zone of physiological stress for these large mammals or for some of their important food species. It is to be hoped that other refuges can soon be established where the Steller sea lions are free from persecution. The intangible value of our wildlife cannot be measured in dollars and cents.

California Sea Lion (*Zalophus californianus*), fig. 240

The barking of a California sea lion along the rocky coast will long be remembered by anyone who has heard it. The animal weaves and crawls awkwardly about on the slippery rocks, but is extremely graceful even in the heaviest seas. The pelage is highly variable in color; some animals are light tan, others are whitish about the muzzle, but most are dark brown. These sea lions have small ears and, like the fur seals, have hind flippers that rotate and can be brought up alongside the body. This enables them to climb upon rocks well above the level of the sea to rest and sun themselves. They swim very rapidly underwater by simultaneous backward strokes of the strong front flippers, while the hind flippers act more or less as a rudder. The bulls weigh 500 to 1000 pounds, and are much larger than the females, or cows. During the breeding season the dominant bulls gather harems of several cows, which they protect aggressively. The ratio

Fig. 240. California sea lion bulls (*Zalophus californianus*).

of males to females on the Channel Islands appears to be one to ten (Bartholomew and Boolootian, 1960). They mate between May and August, and a year later one pup is born.

Killer whales and, above all, men are the worst enemies. Thousands of sea lions have been ruthlessly slaughtered because they are supposedly detrimental to fishing interests. Research on the food habits, however, does not bear out this indictment, and all that can be said against them is they do some damage to nets and other fishing gear. They eat largely noncommercial fish, mollusks, and crustaceans. Problems of water for the body and salt elimination are probably similar to those described for the cetaceans (p. 326).

The California sea lion breeds from the Channel Islands south, or, according to Scheffer (1958), south from Piedras Blancas (just south of Monterey), California. It ranges along the coast from central Mexico to Vancouver Island. The first week of August finds thousands of them back on Año Nuevo Island off the central California coast. Thus, except in summer, the range of the California sea lion, a temperate to tropical species, widely overlaps that of the much larger Steller sea lion, a subarctic to temperate species which inhabits the area from Bering Sea south to the Channel Islands. There were about 13,000 California sea lions living on the Channel Islands in 1960 (Bartholomew and Boolootian, 1960). The males and females show different patterns of movement along the California coast. The males move north in winter and are regularly found in the Barkley Sound area on southern Vancouver Island, British Columbia.

Family **Phocidae** (Hair Seals or Earless Seals)

These seals have no external ears, and their hind flippers cannot be brought up alongside the body. The fur is stiff, with no woolly underfur in the adults. There are no postorbital processes on the skull. The molars and premolars are not distinguishable in adult seals; hence the number of postcanine teeth is important in using the key. The incisors have pointed crowns and are simple.

Harbor Seal (*Phoca vitulina*), fig. 241

The harbor seal or hair seal is found along the coast of the Pacific States, especially in protected harbors and bays. A herd may often be seen, according to Hedgpeth (1962), just north of the east approach to the San Francisco Bay Bridge, where a large sandbar is exposed at low tide. Protection from the sea does not seem necessary, however, because considerable numbers are found on San Nicolas Island, the outermost of the continental islands off the California coast, which has no bays or harbors. Occasionally they have been known to ascend rivers for many miles.

The harbor seal is up to six feet long. It is earless, and its pelage is covered with whitish spots with gray centers. It has lost the soft underfur, and only coarse outer hairs remain.

Fig. 241. Harbor seals (*Phoca vitulina*).

The fixed position of the hind flippers behind the body makes it impossible for the harbor seal to climb on high rocks, as do sea lions. On land the seals employ an undulatory motion that gives them the appearance of giant caterpillars. In the water they propel themselves by lateral undulations of the tail and hind flippers, with the foreflippers giving an occasional guiding stroke.

Harbor seals feed on fish, mollusks, and crustaceans. They do not form harems but are polygamous. Mating takes place in September, and the single pup, with dark pelage, is born in early spring. The prenatal pelage of the pup of the harbor seal and certain others seals is white and is usually shed in the uterus before birth. This fact acquired meaning when it became known that these seals invaded temperate regions after geologic ages of giving birth on ice and snow, where pups with white pelage were favored by selection (Scheffer, 1958).

Ribbon Seal (*Histriophoca fasciata*)

The strikingly marked ribbon seal is the rarest of all the pinnipeds on the coast of the Pacific States. It was thought to be limited to its range north of the Aleutian Islands, until, in November 1962, one was lassoed by a cowboy and pulled ashore near Morro Bay, California. It was identified by Dr.

Aryan Roest of the California State Polytechnic College, and appears to be the first and only record of the species in this part of the world. The captive ate live anchovies.

The yellowish bands that circle the neck and run over the shoulders and around the waist of the brown male are only faintly discernible on the yellow or gray female. Even in the far North this seal is not common. A few are killed by Eskimos on the icepacks in winter and on the open ocean in spring and fall. The skin of the ribbon seal is frequently tanned and used as a waterproof bag on boat or dogsled trips.

Like the harbor seal, this species cannot bring its hind flippers alongside the body and cannot climb far above the water level. Practically nothing is known of its biology.

Northern Elephant Seal (*Mirounga angustirostris*), fig. 242

Off the coast of southern California and Mexico are several small islands that have been the breeding places for centuries of this largest of the pinnipeds, the northern elephant seal. Like so many other large mammals, it was hunted almost to extinction by sealers in the nineteenth century. Dr. George A. Bartholomew (1952) of the University of California, Los Angeles, has made special studies of the social and reproductive behavior of this large seal, which has staged such a miraculous return. The northern elephant seal is largely confined to subtropical and other warm waters. The rookeries formerly ranged from Baja California to a point north of San Francisco until the seals were decimated and reduced to one small herd on Guadalupe Island off the coast of Mexico. Now there are good-sized colonies on some of the other islands besides Guadalupe Island, and the seals have strayed as far north as southeastern Alaska. A population in excess of 15,000 now lives off the coast of California (Bartholomew and Hubbs, 1960), small numbers being on Año Nuevo Island north of Monterey Bay and the Farallon Islands west of San Francisco Bay (Radford, Orr, and Hubbs, 1965).

The large gray or tan bull northern elephant seal is sometimes over 17 feet in length, and weighs an estimated 5,000 pounds. The female is much smaller. When the elephant seal molts, the epidermis peels off along with the hair.

The species has no external ears. The hind flippers, though useless on land, are powerful swimming appendages. The most remarkable feature is the proboscis of the adult male, which appears to be a secondary sex organ used solely for territorial defense in the breeding season. When relaxed, the proboscis is nearly a foot long and hangs over the mouth. When the adult bull prepares to sound his challenge, however, the organ is inflated; it quivers and bends down, to lie against the roof of the open mouth and pharynx. Sound is produced not by the vocal chords but by short bursts of snorts. These can be heard long distances as they are amplified by the

Fig. 242. Northern elephant seal (*Mirounga angustirostris*).

mouth and pharynx, which also act as resonators. The nasal excretion is under study as a possible means of salt elimination.

During the breeding season, the most powerful bulls maintain not so much a harem as a dominant position among a group of gregarious females by means of the greatly amplified snorts, and by actual combat when necessary. There are only half as many males as females on the breeding grounds, yet only one bull in seven does most of the mating.

Although they swim easily and gracefully, northern elephant seals have an undulatory motion on land and drag their hind flippers. This slow progression limits the size of territory the dominant male can command effectively. Such an area usually contains a dozen cows, compared with the larger area covered by the more active bull northern fur seal, which averages 40 cows. During the breeding season the cows leave the pups temporarily in order to get food. When they return, the pups take so much milk they resemble fur-covered balloons. The pups are occasionally crushed to death by the heavy bodies of the old bulls, which entirely ignore their presence. The dominant bulls seem to fast the entire breeding season, from December through March. The food is known to include dogfish shark, ratfish, and squid. The large "night eyes," capable of greatly enlarged pupils, is one indication that these seals feed at depths greater than 300 feet.

A single pup is born, and there is some evidence that the females do not breed every year. Large sharks and killer whales are probably the main enemies, being surpassed only by man, and possibly by certain parasites.

At sea the northern elephant seal is probably solitary, but on the beaches it becomes highly gregarious, even in the nonbreeding season.

The seals haul themselves out on beaches that are only a few feet above the surf. Frequently California sea lions romp over their huge bodies or even go to sleep on them, thus obtaining warmth on cold days. None of this seems to disturb the elephant seals. A huge bull may open its eyes to watch a person standing less than ten feet away, but it usually soon goes to sleep again if the person stands quietly.

13. Order Perissodactyla

The hoofed animals that belong to the order Perissodactyla have the main axis of the foot directly over the middle or third digit, which is always the largest of the toes (mesaxonic). The astragalus has a pulley-like articulation with the tibia, but its other end is distinctly flattened. The femur has a third trochanter, not present in Artiodactyla. The cheek teeth are nearly all molariform, with complexed crowns. They may be hypsodont or lophodont and bunodont. The last molar is commonly bilobed. There is one family (Equidae), represented in the Pacific States by an introduced established species of wild horse (*Equus caballus*) and the wild burro (*Equus asinus*). There is no evidence that the African zebras, escaped from the Hearst Ranch in San Luis Obispo County, California, are going to establish themselves, and they will not be considered part of the fauna.

See Chapter 14 for key to the hoofed animals, Perissodactyla and Artiodactyla.

Family **Equidae** (Horses, Burros, Zebras)

Wild Burro (*Equus asinus*)

Many native mammals are adapted to live in the hottest and driest of all North American deserts—Death Valley. However, the largest one living in the great sink is a foreigner from Africa—the wild burro. The sandblasting gales, the record high temperatures, the perennial drought, salty or even poisonous water, all spelled death for many a gold explorer, but not for his liberated burro. Long ages of evolution in the Sudan and Ethiopia prepared the burro for the climate and terrain of Death Valley. Survival in its African home meant competing with many other large hoofed species in eating the wiry twigs of desert plants, finding scarce water holes, and escaping lions. In Death Valley the mesquite, a new experience, was splendid food. The burro, with its seemingly inherited "know-how," found water holes in the mountains. The only hoofed com-

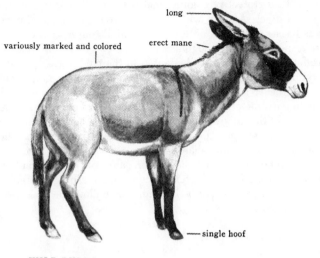

long

variously marked and colored

erect mane

single hoof

WILD BURRO

Wild burro (*Equus asinus*). Dental Formula 3-1-3-3/3-1-3-3. About four feet high at the shoulders; very large ears; *erect mane on neck; single hoof on each foot*. Well established in Death Valley, California, and in the surrounding mountains; native of northeast Africa. P. 410.

petitor was the mountain sheep at the water holes. Thus, without much competition for food and water, with practically no predators except man, and probably with very few, if any, of its native African parasites, the burro is doing well—too well for the native mountain sheep, which dislikes drinking the water after it has been roiled by herds of long-eared asses.

The burro is about four and a half feet tall at the shoulders, has very long ears, a short mane running down the back of the neck, and a scantily haired tail with a definite tassel on the end. The general coloration in Africa is a creamy or bluish gray. There is usually a well-developed dark stripe that runs across the shoulders. The under parts, throat, and muzzle are whitish, and frequently there is considerable white on the legs, with more or less indistinct dark zebra-like stripes running across the outer sides of the legs and feet. Some of the wild animals in Death Valley may be mules, since they occasionally show horse characteristics, such as different color, heavily haired tail, and smaller ears. Some are much larger than the typical burros described here and show variation in markings from the wild type.

The animals are very shy, and even on the great alluvial fans amid sparse vegetation their protective coloring makes them difficult to see as long as they remain quiet. Anyone who has ever had experience with domestic burros as beasts of burden on a desert or high-country pack trip has the greatest respect for their toughness and ability to live on what the land has to offer. They seem as well adapted to the cold, bleak, granite slopes above timberline, cropping the short sparse bunches of grass among the rocks, as to the lava-strewn mountains of the deserts. Horses and mules would soon perish in either place if left to their own devices. Although not native, the wild burros are now doubtless more numerous than certain native species, for example, the wolverine in the Sierra Nevada. The burro is now a part of our mammalian fauna.

There is some reason to believe there are still some essentially wild horses (*Equus caballus*) in eastern Oregon and Washington, but since direct recent evidence seems to be lacking, they will not be included as part of the present fauna.

14. Order Artiodactyla

The hoofed animals that belong to the order Artiodactyla have the main axis of the foot directly between the third and fourth digits (paraxonic). The astragalus has both ends rounded. The femur is without a third trochanter. The premolars are usually simpler than the molars, and the last molar is usually three-lobed. There are four families of artiodactyls established wild in the Pacific States. These are the introduced pigs (Suidae) and three native families: deer (Cervidae), pronghorns (Antilocapridae), and sheep, goats, and bison (Bovidae). The pigs are not cud-chewing; they have well-developed upper incisors and canines, and simple stomachs. The other three families are cud-chewing (ruminants); they have no upper incisors, and canines are usually lacking except in the elk (*Cervus*) and the American woodland caribou (*Rangifer*). The members of these three families have complex four-chambered stomachs, which hydrolyze cellulose and other plant carbohydrates. Such a digestive apparatus enables the animals to browse or graze steadily and then retire away from predators as well as the midday heat for the more time-consuming cud-chewing and digestion.

KEY TO THE HOOFED ANIMALS
(Perissodactyla and Artiodactyla)

These animals are the large hoofed species, some of which have been introduced into the Pacific States. The dental formulas vary from species to species.

1A. With two or more toes on each foot 2
1B. With one toe on each foot.
　　Equus asinus, wild burro, introduced, p. 411.
2A. Upper incisors absent; horns or antlers, at least in the males . . . 3
2B. Upper incisors present; tusklike canine teeth.
　　Sus scrofa, wild boar, introduced, p. 416.
3A. Without two white bands crossing the throat 4
3B. With two white bands crossing the throat; no dewclaws; no metatarsal glands.
　　Antilocapra americana, pronghorn, p. 437, fig. 254.

Fig. 243. Canadian elk (*Cervus canadensis*).

4A. With branched antlers, at least in the males; lachrymal bones not in contact with nasal bones 5

4B. With permanent unbranched horns in both sexes; lachrymal bones in contact with nasal bones 11

5A. Antlers distally flattened 6

5B. Antlers distally cylindrical 7

6A. Antlers may be in both sexes and asymmetrical, one with a large forward-projecting brow tine, the other with a small one; no dewlap.
Rangifer tarandus caribou, American woodland caribou, p. 421.

6B. Antlers symmetrical and in males only; dewlap present.
Alces alces, moose, p. 421, figs. 251, 252.

7A. With a neck mane of longer hairs; over 450 pounds 8

7B. Without a neck mane; less than 450 pounds 9

8A. San Joaquin Valley and Inyo and Colusa counties, Cailfornia.
Cervus nannodes, tule elk, p. 419.

8B. Northwestern California; Oregon and Washington.
Cervus canadensis, Canadian elk, p. 419, fig. 243.

9A. Antlers over the crown branching dichotomously (fig. 245); tail with some black hairs 10

9B. Antlers directed forward, with spikes originating from one main beam (fig. 245); no black hair on top of the long oval- or triangular-shaped tail, which is white below.
Odocoileus virginianus, white-tailed deer, p. 423, fig. 250.

10A. Tail round and short with a black tip (sometimes with a black stripe running from the rump to the tip) (fig. 245); white rump patch extending onto the rump above the base of the tail; metatarsal gland usually more than three inches long.
Odocoileus hemionus (except subspecies *columbianus*),
mule deer, p. 423, fig. 246.

10B. Tail flat, black on the upper surface and white on the edges and under side; white rump patch not extending onto the rump above the base of the tail (fig. 245); metatarsal gland usually less than three inches long.
Odocoileus hemionus columbianus, black-tailed deer, p. 423,
fig. 247.

11A. Not one color, black or dark brown; less than 500 pounds 12

11B. Black or dark brown all over; over 500 pounds. Now confined to a few ranches.
Bison bison, bison, p. 439.

12A. Elsewhere than Catalina Island and San Luis Obispo County, California 13

12B. Catalina Island or San Luis Obispo County, California, *feral* . . . 14

13A. Long white wool; black saber-like horns in both sexes.
Oreamnos americanus, mountain goat, p. 439, fig. 257.

13B. Gray or brown short hairs; large spiraled horns in males, curved in females.
Ovis canadensis, mountain sheep or bighorn, p. 437, figs. 258, 259.

14A. San Luis Obispo County, California; brown; long hairs on throat and fore-parts; large curved horns.
Ammotragus lervia, Barbary sheep, introduced, p. 439.

14B. Catalina Island, California; varicolored; horns spiraled.
Capra hircus, goat, introduced, p. 439.

Family **Suidae** (Pigs)

Pigs have simple stomachs and do not chew the cud. The canine teeth may grow to form tusks, and upper incisors are always present. The cheek teeth are bunodont with low crowns, and are usually distinguishable as molars and premolars. The main metacarpal and metatarsal bones are distinct and do not fuse.

bristly hairs   hairy   naked   tusk

WILD BOAR

Wild boar (*Sus scrofa*). Dental Formula 3-1-4-3/3-1-4-3. Length about five feet, and between two and three feet high at the shoulders; weight, up to 600 pounds or more; *canine tusks; bristly hairs, hairy ears; naked snout.* Introduced, or reverted to wild condition from domestic stock; reported in Monterey, San Luis Obispo, and Butte counties, California, and possibly in other places.

Wild Boar (*Sus scrofa*)

Not infrequently as one wanders over the oak-covered hills in Butte County or along the more isolated slopes of chaparral in San Luis Obispo or Monterey County, one may come upon several yards of freshly broken turf. Anyone who has ever seen domestic pigs rooting for bulbs, roots, and mushrooms will recognize the work as that of a member of the pig family. The only native member of this family in the United States is the collared peccary (*Pecari angulatus*), which is fairly common in southern Texas, New Mexico, and Arizona but does not range into the Pacific States. The wild boar, undoubtedly an ancestor of our domestic swine, originally ranged over Europe, North Africa, and parts of western and central Asia. Wild boar hunting used to be a favorite sport. In Germany in the seventeenth century a prince is reported to have killed 30,000 wild pigs over a period of some 40 years. Remains of wild pigs are frequently found in peat moss and in the moors of the British Isles, and even today they are reported in Germany around the Black Forest area.

The gestation period is four months, and the sow has six to 12 young per litter. The young of the original wild pigs have longitudinal stripes, which are rarely seen in domestic swine but are occasionally seen in those that have reverted to the wild condition. Sight is poorly developed, but hearing is acute. The sense of smell is extremely well developed, enabling the animal to detect enemies and to find underground food. The wild boar is the only "split-hoofed" animal in the fauna of the Pacific States that has a single stomach and does not chew the cud. Its chief enemy is man, although mountain lions, coyotes, bobcats, and golden eagles may take a few of the young. It is doubtless the most dangerous of our wild mammals when wounded, cornered, or accompanied by young.

The purebred wild boar is about three feet high and is covered with stiff bristly hairs, which are mostly blackish brown, mixed with some yellow. A band of longer hairs runs down the back. The ears, which are held erect, are heavily haired. These features, along with the naked fleshy snout, the canine tusks which emerge from the mouth, and the short tail, distinguish this animal from any other western mammal.

Like most other animals in this order, the wild boar has four hoof-covered toes on each foot, two of which are smaller ones higher up on the foot, which may or may not reach the ground. In contrast, the collared peccary has three toes on each hind foot.

Family **Cervidae** (Elk, Moose, Caribou, and Deer)

The males of this family have antlers that grow on skin-covered pedicles and are shed each year. The females of the caribou (*Rangifer*) of Arctic North America and of the reindeer (*Rangifer*) of Siberia and northern Europe may also have antlers. Dewclaws, vestigial digits not reaching to the ground, are always present. Members of Cervidae are browsers and have no upper incisor teeth. The lower canines are incisor-like. The cheek teeth are selenodont and may be high-crowned. The animals have a complex stomach and chew the cud. The bones of the metacarpals and metatarsals are fused to form a cannon bone, which supports the leg from the hock joint to the fetlock. There is no gall bladder. The lachrymal bones do not touch the nasals. Most of the species are polygamous.

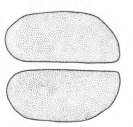

Fig. 244. Elk track, about one-third actual size.

unbranched **tines**

bez tine

beam

brown tine

grizzly brown

tawny

throat mane

CANADIAN ELK

CANADIAN ELK (cow)

unbranched

brow and bez tines

buffy gray

white

mane

TULE ELK

Cervus Dental Formula 0-1-3-3/3-1-3-3

Canadian elk (Wapiti) (*Cervus canadensis*). Length about eight feet; large massive antlers in males only, with well-developed brow and bez tines (fig. 243); *face blackish, with long hairs along the neck, forming a dark brown mane on the throat; grayish brown on back and sides, with a tawny patch on the rump; canine teeth in the upper jaw.* In Washington and Oregon two subspecies inhabit the Canadian and Transition life zones, especially in summer: the Roosevelt elk (*C.c. roosevelti*) is west of the Cascades and south into Del Norte and Humboldt counties in northwestern California; the Rocky Mountain elk (*C.c. nelsoni*) is mostly east of the Cascades in Washington and Oregon and introduced in other localities. P. 424, fig. 243, Map 102.

Tule elk (*Cervus nannodes*). Length about seven feet; antlers of male with brow and bez tines; long hairs on the neck forming *grizzled grayish brown throat mane; buffy gray on back, with a tawny rump patch; canine teeth in the upper jaw.* Now limited to a small area near Tupman, Kern County, California; successfully introduced into Owens Valley, Inyo County, and into Cache Creek, Colusa County, California; inhabits marshes, river bottoms, and open plains in Valley Grassland and now Sagebrush Scrub; Lower and Upper Sonoran life zones in California. Map 102.

Map 102. (1) *Cervus canadensis nelsoni* and *Cervus canadensis roosevelti*, (2) *Cervus nannodes*, (3) *Rangifer tarandus caribou.*

MOOSE (cow)

flattened

bell

MOOSE (bull)

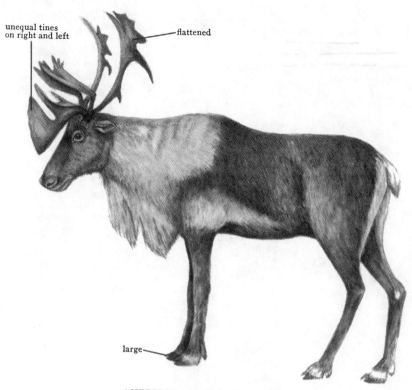

unequal tines
on right and left

flattened

large

AMERICAN WOODLAND CARIBOU

Moose (*Alces alces*). Dental Formula 0-0-3-3/3-1-3-3. Length ranges up to ten feet; palmate antlers, in bull only (fig. 252); dewlap; black to brown dorsally, with white "stockings" on legs. No known population in the Pacific States, although occasional wanderers from Canada are reported in eastern Washington. Generally near rivers or lakes. P. 430, figs. 251, 252 (no range map).

American woodland caribou (*Rangifer tarandus caribou*). Dental formula 0-1-3-3/3-1-3-3. Length ranges up to eight feet; antlers semipalmate distally, may be present in both sexes; pelage varies from nearly white to dark brownish, with white neck or throat fringe; small white rump patch. Feeds on grasses, sedges, and tree lichens. Population about 50 in northeastern Washington. P. 432, fig. 253, Map 102.

beam

branched tines

no brow or bez tines

more or less white

small

3–5 inches long

MULE DEER—Doe

MULE DEER

tines unbranched

beam

no brow or bez tines

large
white below

about 1
inch long

WHITE-TAILED DEER —Doe

WHITE-TAILED DEER

Odocoileus Dental Formula 0-0-3-3/3-1-3-3

Mule deer (*Odocoileus hemionus*). Length ranges from four feet to nearly six feet, depending on the subspecies; *antlers of male dichotomously branched* (i.e., not single tines issuing from one main beam) (fig. 245); *no brow or bez tines*, but frequently there is a spike or snag near the base on the inside; *no upper canine teeth; metatarsal gland, three to five inches long* (fig. 245); in summer, yellow or reddish brown, and in winter bluish gray; young fawns spotted; rump patch white, but size varies with subspecies; tail varies from white with black tip to entirely black dorsally (fig. 245). The so-called black-tailed deer (*O.h. columbianus*) is the subspecies, readily distinguishable by the black dorsal surface of the tail. It is found in the central California Coast Ranges, north through Oregon and Washington, west of the Cascades. Five other subspecies of mule deer (see Map 103) occupy the rest of California and east of the Cascades in Oregon and Washington. The black-tailed subspecies intergrades with some of the others in central and northeastern California and up through central Oregon and Washington. Lower Sonoran Zone into the Hudsonian Life Zone in summer; in winter mostly below the Transition Life Zone; chiefly a forest-edge species living in brushy places rather than in dense forests. P. 425, figs. 246–48, Map 103.

White-tailed deer (*Odocoileus virginianus*). Length about five feet; *tines of antlers originating from a single main beam* (fig. 245); no brow or bez tines, but there is a snag or spike on the inside near the base; tail triangular, brownish dorsally (outside) and pure white beneath; metatarsal gland about one inch long; in summer, upper parts bright chestnut, and in winter, grayish; tail carried conspicuously erect while running. Rare in northeastern California; mostly restricted to the lower Columbia River (*O.v. leucurus,* Columbia white-tailed deer) and to northeastern Washington (*O.v. ochrourus,* Pend Oreille white-tailed deer). It inhabits dense forest and brushy areas, including the low marshy flood plains of the Columbia River, and along the Umpqua River in southwestern Oregon. P. 429, fig. 250, Map 104.

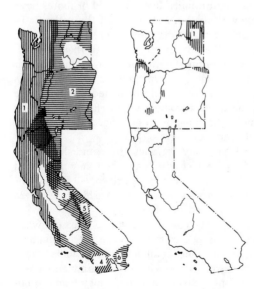

Map 103, left. (1) *Odocoileus hemionus columbianus,* (2) *Odocoileus hemionus hemionus,* (3) *Odocoileus hemionus californicus,* (4) *Odocoileus hemionus fulginata,* (5) *Odocoileus hemionus inyoensis,* (6) *Odocoileus hemionus eremicus.* **Map 104, right.** (1) *Odocoileus virginianus ochrourus,* (2) *Odocoileus virginianus leucurus.*

Canadian Elk (Wapiti) (*Cervus canadensis*), fig. 243, and
Tule Elk (*Cervus nannodes*)

There is nothing in nature that will thrill a seasoned naturalist more than the bugling of a Canadian elk. Fancy yourself early in October seated on a fallen redwood in a forest of northern California or in a meadow sur-, rounded by alpine firs farther north in Washington. The sun is setting, and no sound breaks the stillness except an occasional rustle of a shrew-mole hunting in the dead leaves. Then, from the mountainside comes a long, high-pitched call somewhat reminiscent of a siren but with a bell-like quality. It is answered by another far away. If you are near a meadow, you may then have a ringside seat at a great prizefight between two powerful bull elk.

The bull closely guards his herd of perhaps a dozen cows with yearling calves. He chases back into the herd a cow that strays too far, just as a sheep dog brings back a wandering ewe. He does not permit the two- or three-year-old bulls to approach his harem too closely; when he starts after them they go crashing off through the woods at full speed.

But if the big bull is challenged by another of the same size and age, a fierce fight results. The antagonists rush at each other with their formidable antlers. The fight may last for a few minutes or for several hours, until one has had enough and goes off into the woods, leaving the other in charge of the harem. The fight may end in a death stab for one of the bulls; it may end with death by starvation and thirst for both if the antlers become interlocked. Cows, too, occasionally fight among themselves by rearing on their hind legs and striking with their sharp forehoofs.

There are certain areas in the range where during the rutting season, according to Graf (1956), the mature bulls—five years old or more—have "signposts," which they scrape with the bur at the base of the antler, indicating a territory into which other males may not enter. The cows and calves at any season tend to nose the post or scrape it with their incisors.

A Canadian elk may possibly be confused with a deer; however, its much larger size, the heavily maned neck, and the larger antlers, with the points coming from a single beam (not dichotomously branched), differentiate it from the mule deer, whose antlers dichotomously fork (fig. 245). An elk may weigh up to 1,000 pounds. The track of an elk (fig. 244) resembles that of a calf rather than that of a deer (fig. 249).

Canadian elk browse leaves from many deciduous trees and shrubs, but they also graze in meadows. They conflict with man when they invade his fields and gardens. Most of them have now been driven out of regions where there is agriculture, except in parts of eastern Washington, where they are fenced out of fields or confined in refuges.

The gestation period is 255 days. The cow is at least two years old when she gives birth, in the spring, to a single calf. Twins are not uncommon, and there are rarely triplets. Like the young of all deer in the Pacific States, elk calves are spotted and remain so until the winter hairs grow out. There are scarcely any enemies left except the mountain lion, which would probably not attack a full-grown elk. Coyotes will occasionally attack a calf. The Canadian elk has been widely introduced in many counties in Washington.

There are two subspecies of Canadian elk; the brown Olympic or Roosevelt elk (*C.c. roosevelti*) lives in the humid forests of all three states, and the lighter-colored Rocky Mountain elk (*C.c. nelsoni*) lives in the forests mostly east of the Cascades crest.

Another species, the tule elk (*Cervus nannodes*), formerly ranged from Kern County north to Butte County, California. Today it is fenced in on an 1,100-acre reserve near Tupman in Kern County, to prevent damage to farms. This species has been transplanted to Cache Creek, Colusa County, and to Owens Valley, Inyo County, California, where it is becoming well established. Efforts are under way to establish a special reserve near Independence, which are meeting opposition from ranchers, who complain of damage to forage and fences. People interested in protecting the elk would like to see all livestock removed from the area and an elk reserve created there. It is to be hoped that by the creation of this reserve the tule elk will not, like the grizzly bear, become extinct.

The Canadian elk lives chiefly in the Transition and Canadian life zones, but the tule elk ranges through the Upper and Lower Sonoran zones. Map 102 shows the present ranges of the two species.

Mule deer (*Odocoileus hemionus*), figs. 246, 247

No native mammal inspires so much interest as the mule deer. In the national parks it is often fed at very close range, which is a dangerous practice even with the "tamest" deer. Moreover, this unnatural feeding causes stomach disorders and tends to concentrate the animals in too small an area, thus encouraging parasites and other diseases. Not infrequently such deer have to be killed to protect the rest of the herd.

Six subspecies of mule deer live in the Pacific States. Their ranges are shown in Map 103. The "granite" bucks of the Sierra Nevada of California and the larger "lava" bucks of northeastern California and eastern Oregon and Washington can be identified in the field by most hunters. The black-tailed deer (*O.h. columbianus*) is by far the best known and most easily identified of all the subspecies. It ranges from central California in the coastal mountains up through Oregon and Washington, mostly west of the summit of the Cascade Mountains. Most subspecies of mule deer have short tails, round in cross section, which are white nearly all around, with a black tip. The tail of the black-tailed subspecies appears more flattened and is black or dark brown on the outside (dorsal) surface. The white rump patch on all the other mule deer goes over the base of the tail onto the rump. In the black-tailed deer, it is smaller, does not go onto the rump above the tail, and is limited to the insides of the legs (fig. 245). All of the subspecies have dichotomously branched antlers, which readily distinguish them from the white-tailed deer (*Odocoileus virginianus*), in which the prongs come from a single beam (fig. 245).

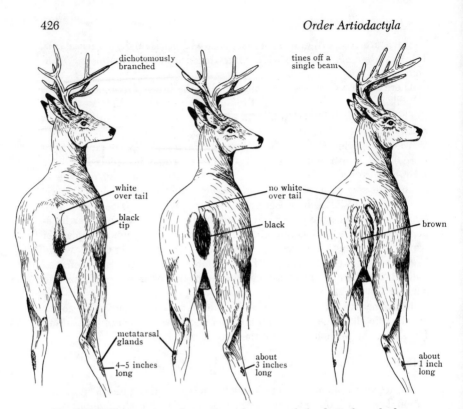

Fig. 245. Differences in antlers, tails, and metatarsal glands. Left, mule deer. Center, black-tailed deer. Right, white-tailed deer.

Mule deer vary considerably in size. The black-tailed deer of the San Juan Islands and other islands of Puget Sound are smaller and darker than those on the mainland. The bucks of these "jackrabbit deer" weigh about 100 pounds—small compared with the large "lava" bucks (*O.h. hemionus*), which may weigh 400 pounds. The males shed their antlers annually. Mule deer lose theirs in January, and a new set starts growing in early spring. These are covered with a soft mosslike skin called velvet. The velvet is supplied with nerves and blood vessels, which provide the growing antlers with food and oxygen (fig. 246). As the antlers harden, the blood supply is gradually shut off; the velvet dries up and is rubbed off early in the autumn. The polished antlers are ready for combat with other males when the buck begins to assemble its harem in October. The number of points on the antlers does not indicate the age of the buck, although up to a certain age older bucks usually have more points.

Although the black-tailed deer temporarily form large feeding bands, they are not herd animals. There are sometimes small family and buck groups; the does establish activity centers in their territories which they protect from other females, especially while the fawns are young. No such territorial centers are known for the bucks (Dasmann and Taber, 1956).

Fig. 246. Mule deer buck (*Odocoileus hemionus californicus*).

Fig. 247. Black-tailed deer (*Odocoileus hemionus columbianus*).

Fig. 248. Mule deer fawn (*Odocoileus hemionus*).

The black-tailed deer lives most of its life in the area where it was born. Other mule deer migrate 50 miles or more from their summer range in the high country to the lowlands, where breeding begins as early as October. Females over one year old are gathered in harems and are bred. The gestation period ranges from 195 to 212 days. Young does usually have a single fawn, weighing 16 to 18 pounds; older does frequently have twins, or even triplets. Most of the fawns are born by late June. They are spotted for about three and a half months, and seem to have little or no odor at first (fig. 248). Hunting dogs have been seen to pass close to where a fawn is hidden without detecting it. The fawn begins foraging after the first week, but nurses heavily for at least two months.

In summer, the mule deer on the west slope of the Sierra Nevada have a home range of half a mile to three-quarters of a mile in diameter; in winter, adequate food, water, cover, and bedding places are located in a range half as large (Leopold *et al.*, 1951).

The black-tailed deer not infrequently lives in dense forests of fir, hemlock, and cedar. The other subspecies of mule deer inhabit more open forests in the less humid regions of the Pacific States.

The black-tailed deer readily *intergrades* with other mule deer, indicating that they are subspecies rather than separate species. Intergradation results in specimens that may show characteristics of both subspecies. Such zones of intergradation occur in northern and central California and continue through Oregon and Washington.

Like other deer, the mule deer are browsers. An abundance of grass does not necessarily mean good deer country, although the animals are fond of

Fig. 249. Deer track, about
one-third actual size.

clover and alfalfa. The primary browse is huckleberry, salal, blackberry, bitterbrush, and snowbrush. Burning over the stable vegetation results in second growth that is rich in protein, especially in the coastal forests and chaparral. Over two pounds of food and two to three quarts of water are taken daily per hundredweight. Salt or mineral licks are frequently visited by deer. They will drink muddy water in the basins nearby instead of clear water in a stream a few feet away.

The mule deer is the most important big game of the Pacific States. All three states now consider the deer population a renewable natural resource, and hundreds of thousands of dollars are spent each autumn by deer hunters. The annual deer kill is aimed at keeping the population within the food supply of its natural habitat and thus preventing damage to orchards, gardens, and agricultural crops. A sound research program is necessary in order to determine the size and sex of the surplus population before each hunting season.

Next to man, the mountain lion is the chief enemy of the mule deer. It has been estimated that these big cats kill 50 deer in the course of a year, which is enough to increase the desire of hunters to exterminate them. This may be in line with most effective deer control. However, in the national parks and in wildlife areas, where deer are not hunted, mountain lions are a necessary control on the population, and their presence should be encouraged. Mountain lions *do not* exterminate deer—the two were in balance long before man began his management programs.

Coyotes probably have little effect in reducing the deer population. Anyone who has seen a doe defend her fawn from a large dog can imagine the vigorous attack launched by a deer on a coyote, with the result that the coyote would look elsewhere for food that was easier to take.

The tracks of the deer, unlike those of the sheep, have pointed toes (fig. 249).

White-tailed Deer (*Odocoileus virginianus*), fig. 250

Any deer with a large, conspicuous white tail held erect as it dashes away is almost certain to be a white-tailed deer. Although once this species ranged over most of Washington and Oregon, it is at present much more limited. There are two subspecies of white-tailed deer in the Pacific States. The Pend Oreille, or Idaho white-tailed deer, is found principally in the northeastern corner of Washington, and the Columbia River white-tailed deer occurs along the lower Columbia River in both Oregon and Washington.

Fig. 250. White-tailed deer bucks (*Odocoileus virginianus*).

The smaller ears, larger tail, smaller metatarsal gland, and the antlers with prongs coming from a single beam readily distinguish the white-tailed deer from the black-tailed and Rocky Mountain subspecies of mule deer that also occupy a part of its range (fig. 245). Dorsally (outside) the tail of a white-tailed deer is the same color as the back; it is never black as in the black-tailed deer.

The habitat of the white-tailed deer is different from that of the mule deer. Along the lower Columbia River it lives in the low, damp, marshy islands and flood plains (Dalquest, 1948). In northeastern Washington it is also found in larch and cottonwood forests as well as the denser types of forest. In late evening or early morning it has been seen to mix with the cattle in the damp meadows of Pend Oreille County in Washington. The main concentration of white-tailed deer in Oregon is along the Umpqua River in the southwestern part of the state, where it frequents oak and other hardwood scrub forests (Mace, 1962). Rarely is it found in the open forests occupied by mule deer. The white-tailed deer is more cunning and shy, as well as far less numerous, than the larger mule deer. The kill of mule deer in Washington was over 60,000 in 1961, compared with 11,000 white-tails.

Moose (*Alces alces*), figs. 251, 252

The moose occasionally wanders into Washington from Canada. There was once a report of it, though unconfirmed, in the Blue Mountains of southeastern Washington.

The moose is the largest member of the deer family and is easily distin-

Fig. 251. Cow moose (*Alces alces*).

Fig. 252. Bull moose (*Alces alces*).

guished from the elk, caribou, and smaller species by its long "white stocking" legs, shoulders noticeably higher than the hips, and heavy thick muzzle. The dewlap, a hanging fold of skin under the neck, is prominent. The bull is further characterized by large palmate antlers.

It mostly inhabits willow swamps, where it wades in the water, browsing on the vegetation. It may plunge its head in to the ears, sometimes completely submerging in deep water for several seconds, before floating to the surface with a mouthful of food.

While land is still obtainable in northern Washington, it would be highly desirable to establish a moose and caribou reserve.

American Woodland Caribou (*Rangifer tarandus caribou*), fig. 253

The American woodland caribou differs from all other members of the deer family in the Pacific States in that 60 to 70 per cent of the females bear antlers (Banfield, 1961). Another difference is that the antlers are asymmetrical: one of the brow tines is well developed, whereas the other is abortive. They are semipalmate and branch far out toward the tips (fig. 253). The antlers of the bulls are shed in December or January, but those of the cows do not drop off until spring.

The woodland caribou is mostly dark chocolate-colored, with a small white rump patch. It is white or grayish around the neck and immediately above the hoofs. The broad spreading hoofs with sharp cuplike edges are adapted to walking and running rapidly over mud and snow. A bull weighs up to 400 pounds.

In summer the cows, calves, and yearlings form small groups, while the bulls either remain solitary or form small bands of their own. In winter they all band together in a large herd. Over most of their range the Ameri-

Fig. 253. American woodland caribou (*Rangifer tarandus*). Bull with one antler shed, and cow. Photograph by Kyle M. Walker.

can woodland caribou live in dense birch, alder, or coniferous forests, but occasionally they come into the open to drink, to wallow in the mud of bogs and swales, or just to stand in the sunshine. Woodland caribou feed on tree and shrub foliage, arboreal lichens, grasses, and mosses. A single calf is born, sometimes showing very faint spots. Occasionally there may be twins.

The American tundra caribou, which form great herds farther north, and the Old World reindeer have been placed in the species *tarandus* by Banfield (1961), who revised the genus and made the caribou in eastern Washington the subspecies *Rangifer tarandus caribou* (Gmelin).

The species is protected by law, but they are occasionally mistaken for deer and are killed by hunters. In 1962 there was still a small herd of perhaps 50 American woodland caribou in an area of virgin timber 20 miles long and 10 miles wide in northeastern Washington. Plans of the U. S. Forest Service call for continued cutting of this timber, with the inevitable result that the population will be gradually reduced. It is hoped that a reserve can be established before the caribou becomes extinct in Washington.

Family **Antilocapridae**

The pronghorn is the only living representative of this family. It is the only hoofed animal that sheds its horns annually from a bony core. The horn has a prong, which projects forward from the main stem, unlike that of true antelopes, bison, and mountain sheep. There are two white bands across the throat, and there is no dewclaw. The pronghorn has a complex stomach and is a cud chewer; there are no upper incisor teeth. The lachrymal bones do not touch the nasal bones. This family is an old one in North America, and representative antilocaprids are found in fossil records as far back as the Miocene period.

Pronghorn (*Antilocapra americana*), fig. 254

The pronghorn stands about three feet high at the shoulders and may be mistaken by the inexperienced for a deer. However, the pronghorn prefers open country to brushy or forested areas. Both male and female have horns, not antlers, which are shed off a bony core in November or December. The core remains and is soon covered with hairy skin. The new horn forms at the tip and grows downward. Each horn bears one branch, a little prong which projects forward, from which the animal gets its name.

The rump of the pronghorn has a conspicuous patch of long, coarse white hair, which stands up when the animal is frightened. This "flashing" of the rump patch enables the herd to keep together when running, especially at night. The pronghorn, unlike the deer, has no metatarsal gland between the heel and the toes. The tracks are similar to deer tracks, but the tips of the toes are spread farther apart (fig. 255). When alarmed or curious, the creature gives a peculiar whistle best described as *whe-oo*.

Fig. 254. Pronghorn buck (*Antilocapra americana*).

Its food consists chiefly of sagebrush and various grasses and desert plants. The pronghorn is a nuisance to stockmen when it descends on alfalfa fields without regard for anything but the highest and tightest fences. There is much unoccupied suitable range in southeastern Oregon.

Mating takes place in October; two fawns, rarely spotted, are born in May or June after a gestation period of 230–40 days. They scarcely exceed a hare in size. Although pronghorns have been estimated to run 38 miles an hour, which makes them the swiftest North American mammals, they have many enemies; besides men, wolves and coyotes prey on them, and golden eagles may occasionally catch the fawns.

The best place to see pronghorns is in the northeastern sagebrush areas of California, or in eastern Oregon, where they still live in sizable herds. They were introduced into the Yakima Valley by the Washington Department of Game, and in 1961 Washington had a herd of 125. Back in 1954 there was an isolated report of two seen in western Fresno County, California. The pronghorns live mostly in the Lower and Upper Sonoran life zones.

Fig. 255. Pronghorn track, about one-third actual size.

Fig. 256. Mountain goat track, about one-third actual size.

Family **Bovidae** (Cattle, Sheep, Old World Antelopes, and Goats)

These mammals are usually of large size. Their horns are not shed and may be present in both sexes. There are no upper incisors; the stomach is complex, and all are cud chewers. The lower canine is spatulate and looks like an incisor. The main metarsal and metacarpal bones are fused into a cannon bone. The lachrymal bones touch the nasal bones. This family provides meat, milk, leather, and wool, and serves as beast of burden in many parts of the world.

Fig. 257. Mountain goat (*Oreamnos americanus*).

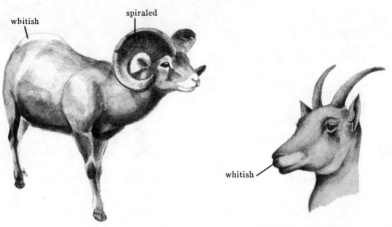

whitish · spiraled

whitish

MOUNTAIN SHEEP

MOUNTAIN SHEEP (female)

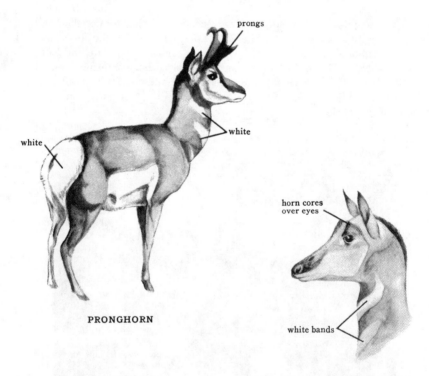

prongs

white

white

horn cores
over eyes

PRONGHORN

white bands

PRONGHORN (female)

Mountain sheep or bighorn (*Ovis canadensis*). Dental Formula 0-0-3-3/3-1-3-3. Length up to four feet; *large, thick, curved horns in male,* female horns slender and falcate; horns are never shed; grayish brown to ash gray; belly and rump patch white. In California, mostly in desert ranges in the Colorado and Mojave deserts; also in the San Bernardino and San Gabriel mountains and the Sierra Nevada north from Olanche Peak, Tulare County, to Mammoth Pass, Mono County. Rare in Oregon and in the northern Cascades of Washington. P. 440, figs. 258, 259, Map 105.

Pronghorn (*Antilocapra americana*). Dental Formula 0-0-3-3/3-1-3-3. Length nearly five feet; *males have true horns up to 20 inches long, with prongs directed forward;* females have prongless horns up to three inches long; the sheath of the horn is shed annually, but the core, which is directly over the orbit, remains; there are no dewclaws; yellowish brown above, white below; two throat bands and rump patch pure white. Native in northeastern California and eastern Oregon, but introduced in central Washington in 1938. P. 433, fig. 254, Map 105.

Map 105. (1) *Ovis canadensis,* (2) *Antilocapra americana,* (3) *Oreamnos americanus.*

black

long white wool

MOUNTAIN GOAT

hump   shaggy

BISON

horns twisted and flattened

pendulant ears

WILD GOAT

long wool

BARBARY SHEEP

Mountain goat (*Oreamnos americanus*). Dental Formula 0-0-3-3/3-1-3-3. Length up to six feet; black saber-like permanent horns in both sexes; long white hairs and woolly underfur over the entire body except the face; throughout the Cascade Mountains and near Sullivan Lake in Pend Oreille County, Washington. Introduced in 1950 into Chief Joseph Mountains of northeastern Oregon, and perhaps other places in Oregon. P. 440, fig. 257, Map 105.

Bison (*Bison bison*). Dental Formula 0-0-3-3/3-1-3-3. Height five to six feet; weight, up to 2,000 pounds; *cattle-like*; dark brown massive head with large hump over the shoulders in males. Bison have been liberated by private interests in the Umtanum district in Yakima and Kittitas counties, Washington, where they are used as beef cattle. There is a small herd on a large ranch near Fresno, California, and perhaps other introductions. (There is no range map.)

Wild goat (*Capra hircus*). Dental Formula 0-0-3-3/3-1-4-3. Length about four to five feet; tail four to six inches; height 30–40 inches; *horns flattened from side to side*, curved backward or *spirally twisted*; variously colored; many breeds. Native in countries around the Red Sea. (Should not be confused with the mountain goat, *Oreamnos americanus*, which is native in the Rocky Mountains and the Cascade Mountains.) Introduced wild on Catalina Island as a potential game animal; reverted to the wild on the mainland from domestic flocks. It occurs in various localities, especially in the more inaccessible parts of the Coast Ranges in Santa Barbara, Ventura, San Luis Obispo, and Monterey counties, California. (No range map.)

Barbary sheep or aoudad (*Ammotragus lervia*). Dental Formula 0-0-3-3/3-1-3-3: Length about four feet, height about three feet; masses of long, pale reddish yellow hair on the throat, chest, and forelimbs. A native of the Atlas Mountains of northern Africa, this species may have established itself from the Hearst Ranch in the mountains of San Luis Obispo County; it may also occur in San Benito County, California. (No range map.)

Mountain Goat (*Oreamnos americanus*), fig. 257

A band of mountain goats working its way across a steep rocky slope in the Cascade or Olympic Mountains of Washington is an impressive sight. The mountain goat is smaller than a deer. The long, soft white wool, longer on the neck, chin, and forelegs, the black saber-like horns, and the black hoofs give it a distinctive appearance. The nearest relatives of the mountain goat are certain Old World antelope of Europe and Asia, with horns similar to those of sheep and cattle. The two toes have large hoofs with soft pads, which help in climbing about the rocky ledges. The hoofs have large dewclaws, or vestigial digits not reaching to the ground. Mountain goat tracks (fig. 256) are about the size of deer tracks (fig. 249), but the toes are wider apart.

Although the mountain goat is frequently seen far above timberline, it is also readily found in spruce and hemlock forests, and at even lower elevations in winter. It seeks the protection of trees in cold rainy weather, for although the long shaggy wool is excellent protection against dry cold, it seems ineffective in wet weather. Mountain goats feed, mostly in early morning and late evening, on boreal grasses, forbs, shrubs, and lichens. They have been seen to select a few stalks from a bunch. The adults have a low grunt, and the kids have a squeaky bleat. They readily detect moving objects, although their vision is not as keen as a deer's, nor are hearing and smell particularly well developed.

Goats breed after two years. The period of gestation is reported to vary from 147 to 178 days. Single births are the rule, although twins are not unusual. The kids have a pure white woolly coat and stand about a foot high. The average mountain goat weighs 150 pounds, although 300 pounds is not unknown.

Although golden eagles and large mammals may take a few kids, the steep rocky slopes and cliffs protect the mountain goat from all enemies except man with his long-range rifle. In Washington, the hunting season on mountain goats was completely closed from 1925 to 1948, at which time the herds had increased to a number that permitted restricted hunting. By 1960 the number was estimated at 6,000, and in 18 different areas 800 hunting permits were issued. About 40 per cent of the permit holders were successful. Biologists keep the herds under study, which should assure a continuing population level from year to year. In Oregon, mountain goats were introduced into Wallowa County in 1950 by the Game Commission.

Mountain Sheep or Bighorn (*Ovis canadensis*), figs. 258, 259

The mountain sheep, or bighorn, is the size of a small deer. The horns of the adult male are massive spirals, but those of the ewes rarely form a half-circle. Some zoologists have suggested that the horns may have a thermoregulatory function, since they are proportionately larger on sheep in

Fig. 258. Mountain sheep ewes (*Ovis canadensis*).

the hot dry desert mountains than on those in the north. As yet no evidence supports the suggestion.

The color of the mountain sheep ranges from dark yellowish to grayish brown, with the abdomen, insides of the legs, and rump being nearly pure white. Vision and hearing are acute. Bighorn prefer rough country where visibility is good and there is little competition from other grazing animals.

There are four or possibly five races of mountain sheep that range from Canada to Mexico, mostly along the eastern parts of all three states. The original band of about 20 bighorn near the Canadian border in Okanogan County, Washington, was increased in 1961 by 12 introduced sheep, and the next year the Game Department planned to release 55 in the southeastern part of the state.

Sizable herds are frequently seen on Mount San Gorgonio and San Antonio in southern California. Contrary to popular opinion, most of the mountain sheep are now to be found in the desert ranges surrounding Death Valley or in southern California in the Little San Bernardino, Santa Rosa, San Jacinto, and other desert ranges. There are from 600 to 900 desert bighorn in Death Valley. It is estimated that Inyo County contains 40 per cent of the mountain sheep in California.

In the desert mountains, mostly at elevations up to 4,000 feet, live scat-

Fig. 259. Mountain sheep ram (*Ovis canadensis*).

tered bands totaling at least 1,500 sheep. In contrast to those in the Sierra Nevada and other high ranges, these bighorn live most of the year close to the desert floor, ascending the mountains only as summer progresses, following the retreat of good foraging conditions on the lower desert slopes. After the winter rains, the sheep return in early spring to the lower canyons, which are covered with wild flowers (Goodman, 1962). Here the lambs are born.

These desert-dwelling bighorn may be able to survive long periods of drought without free water, as do many smaller desert animals. This hypothesis is based on the fact that mountain sheep have been found at least 20 miles from known water. However, this is discounted by those who maintain that there is a constant need for water, depending on the weather conditions and the nature of the forage, and that the sheep must remain close to permanent water holes. Some people claim that the wild burros muddy the desert water holes and thus cause the mountain sheep to leave the area. Evidence for this is not lacking (Welles, 1960). However, these water holes are small rocky basins incapable of staying roiled for long, so

Fig. 260. Mountain sheep track,
about one-third actual size.

the wild burros may not be so important a factor in reducing the range of the bighorn as was formerly supposed.

Much less numerous are the bighorn of the larger races found in the Sierra Nevada. Formerly on the lava plateaus of eastern Oregon and Washington, they were reintroduced in the Steen Mountains of Lake and Harney counties in southeastern Oregon. According to Jones (1950), about 400 mountain sheep were believed to be in the Sierra Nevada. The severe winter storms keep them from ranging very far west of the Sierra crest. East of the Sierra they usually do not range far above the valley floor in winter.

Mountain sheep tracks can be distinguished from mule deer tracks because the tips of the toes are not closer together than their bases (fig. 260). The mountain sheep has shorter legs than the mule deer; the interval between its tracks averages 16 inches, whereas that for the mule deer averages 18 inches. The droppings also differ. Those of the sheep have a tailed chocolate-drop form, and those of the mule deer tend to be longer and rounded at both ends (p. 464).

Most of the year the adult rams move in bands separated from the ewes, younger rams, and lambs. During the breeding season, however, they have terrific fights, which follow a definite pattern. Two rams stand close together, with the head near the other's tail. The aggressor kicks rapidly and viciously upward with its forefeet at the other's genitals. Sometimes they lunge at each other and crash head-on. These collisions can be heard a long distance in the mountains.

The mating season starts in the middle of November and lasts well into December. The gestation period is 180 days. Probably the worst enemy of the bighorn is the weather—a severe winter may decimate that year's lambs. Golden eagles may take a few lambs. Mountain lions, coyotes, and the rare wolverines are not important predators.

An epidemic of scabies contracted from domestic sheep caused great diminution a number of years ago. Bighorn have few parasites, external or internal. Overgrazing of their winter range by domestic stock and deer may cause some hardship. Mule deer have been observed to withdraw when mountain sheep approached a feeding area. Sedge, grasses, and small alpine forbs constitute the chief food.

The mountain sheep is a nervous creature and needs an ample amount of wild area not encroached upon by roads, ski lifts, and improved trails.

Appendixes

A. Collecting and Preparing Specimens for Study

Study of mammals is greatly facilitated by access to skins, skulls, and even skeletons, and one learns much in the course of preparing specimens. Many problems can be solved in no other way than by making up study skins. The number of small animals taken by collectors is insignificant compared with the number that lose their lives to predators, parasites, disease, and pesticides. Animals that are run over, or killed or trapped by hunters, are a source of specimens, which will provide data for future problems.

A collection of mammal skins is also an excellent means of stimulating the interest of children and adults alike. A well-displayed collection of skins in national and state parks, representing the small mammals found there, is of great educational value to visitors who see a live animal and want to know what it is.

Most of the small mammals that are collected for specimens are trapped in an ordinary snap-type mouse or rat trap. Pocket gophers, moles, and larger mammals require other kinds of traps. Perhaps the best pocket gopher trap is the Macabee trap, which is set in the underground runways. This trap is also useful set upside down in mole runways.

Before setting a trap for a certain species, the collector should learn all he can about it—where it is likely to be found, what it eats, and what its habits are—in order to increase his chance of success. In snap traps several kinds of bait may be used. Many small mammals like rolled oats, bacon rind, cheese, and butter. Most traps are made with a place for bait on the trigger, but this procedure frequently breaks the skull and the value of the specimen is correspondingly reduced. The bait should be placed between the trigger and the spring. This will bring the animal far enough into the trap so that its skull will not be crushed when the trap is sprung. Many small mammals will not come to bait, so the trap can be effectively set across the runway.

If a number of traps are set, the location should be marked with a piece of white cloth tied to a bush or weed. Traps should be run as early as possible in the day, in order to save the specimens from being eaten by ants. It is likewise necessary to collect the catch early if the weather is warm, for if the sun should strike the trapped animal, the fur may "slip" and the skin be ruined. Traps left set during the day should be visited in the evening before dark. If live traps are set, they should be visited frequently to

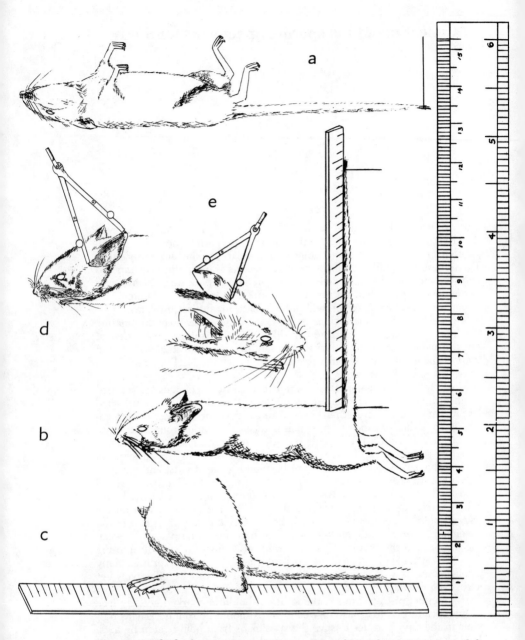

Fig. A1. Method of measuring specimens. Use ruler with centimeters on left (smallest divisions are millimeters) and inches on right. (a) Total length, from tip of nose to tip of tail vertebrae (not hairs). (b) Length of tail, from where it joins back (sacral vertebrae) to tip of tail vertebrae. (c) Length of hind foot, from heel to end of longest claw. (d) Ear from notch. (e) Ear from crown.

avoid unnecessary suffering or death by starvation, which quickly over-takes many small animals when caught. An abundance of bait placed in live traps will save many small species from freezing on a cold night. Young, Sullivan, Sherman, and Havahart live traps are highly recommended for cottontails and larger mammals; animals captured in these traps are rarely injured. A live trap designed by the author (1949a) is excellent for pocket gophers.

After a dead animal has been brought into camp or laboratory, it should be prepared as a specimen study skin. The following procedure has many variations but will be found satisfactory for a person just learning the technique.

MATERIALS NEEDED

scissors (two pairs)
scalpel
tweezers
wire cutters
needle (curved taxidermist's needle is best)
white thread (No. 50)
powdered arsenic and powdered alum mixed half and half (kept in a tight jar), or borax
small brush

hydrogen peroxide
cornmeal
absorbent cotton
cotton batting
annealed wire of different sizes for tails and legs
pins
tag labels
India ink
pen
rule (preferably metric)

PROCEDURE

Measurements. The specimen must be accurately measured *before* it is skinned, because the skinning, stuffing, and drying frequently distort the different parts of the body. These measurements consist of total length, length of tail, length of hind foot, and length of ear measured from notch or crown (fig. A1). The measurements, usually made in millimeters (25 millimeters approximately equal one inch), are recorded on the tag label of the specimen in that order. Thus the label of a specimen might read: 234-92-31-18. This means that before being skinned the specimen measured 234 mm., the tail 92 mm., the hind foot 31 mm., and the ear from notch 18 mm. Sometimes it is desirable to give the ear measurements both *from notch* and *from crown*, in which case the label would read 234-92-31-e^n18-e^c16. When there is no indication of how the ear was measured, it is understood to be *from notch*.

Skinning. A pocket gopher is a good animal for a beginner to use for his first specimen, because it is easily obtained, the skin is tough, and yet the animal is large enough to be handled easily. Proceed as follows:

Lay the animal on its back. With the scissors or scalpel, barely slit through the skin beginning just in front of the anus and running up the belly about one and a half inches (the length depends on the size of the animal). With the fingers or the dull end of the scalpel, separate the skin on each side of the slit from the abdominal wall (fig. A2). *Use plenty of cornmeal to absorb the body fluids and keep the fur dry.*

After loosening the skin from the thighs, push the knee joints up through the incision and cut. Then separate the skin still further from the sides of the abdomen and the sides of the thighs by cutting any flesh that adheres

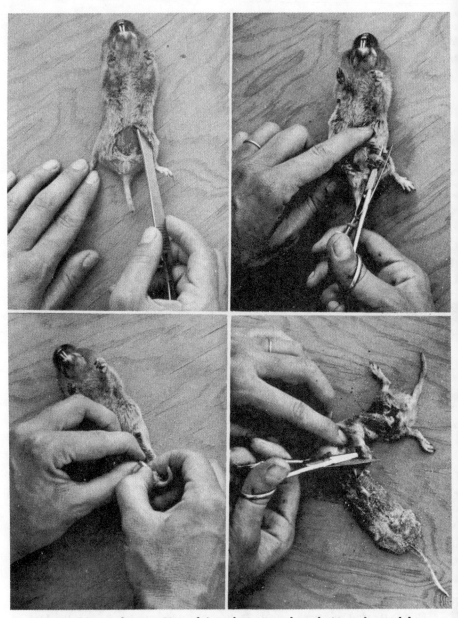

Fig. A2. Steps in skinning. *Upper left:* make incision through skin on lower abdomen and loosen skin around body. *Upper right:* cut hind leg at knee joint. *Lower left:* pull tail vertebrae out of tail skin. *Lower right:* cut forelimb at elbow.

to the skin. (Use cornmeal freely.) Then cut the skin loose from the ends of the intestine and the genitalia so that it is free from all of the posterior end of the body except the tail.

Remove the skin carefully up the tail from the base a little way. Then with the index finger, the middle finger, and the thumb tightly pinched around the tail vertebrae behind the skin, slip the skin off the tail. With a few animals such as skunks and muskrats, it may be necessary to split the under side of the tail in order to remove the tail vertebrae. The skin may now be pulled inside out over the body toward the anterior end. Cut all skin muscles and fat so that they remain on the carcass rather than on the skin. (Use plenty of cornmeal.) When the front legs are reached, sever the joints at the elbows.

Proceed to work the skin over the head until the bases of the ears and the eyes are visible (fig. A3). With a fine pair of scissors cut the cartilage at the base of the ears. Cut the skin around the eyes and mouth *as close to the skull as possible*. Remove the skin to the tip of the nose and, along with the skin, cut off *only* the cartilaginous tip.

Pull off all of the flesh and fat and draw the skin down over each leg to the ankle or wrist. Cut the tendons at the ankle or wrist and remove the muscles from the bone. Cut a small wire (No. 20 or 24) about an inch longer than the bone and insert it alongside the bone under the skin into the heel of the foot.

Brush arsenic-alum mixture or borax on the bone. These materials prevent insects from eating the dried skins. With fine sheets or fibers of absorbent cotton, wrap the bone and the wire, thus making an artificial leg to fill the skin.

Cut a wire of smaller diameter than the tail but about one inch longer and make an artificial tailbone by twirling absorbent cotton fibers *tightly* on it. Dust the artificial tailbone in the arsenic-alum mixture or with borax and insert it into the tail (fig. A4). With a brush, also dust all of the flesh side of the skin with the mixture. Close the mouth by sewing a few stitches across it.

Turn the skin right side out and make a "body" of cotton batting by rolling the cotton between the hands, until it is slightly larger and slightly longer than the carcass. Grasp it with the tweezers in such a way that the cotton will be carried into the nose of the skin. Work the rest of it into the skin. It may be necessary to add more cotton over the hips if they are too flat.

Divide the posterior end of the cotton body and insert the free end of the wrapped tail wire in it. Stuff all of the body into the skin. Sew up the incision, always inserting the needle through the flesh side of the skin.

Pin the specimen out on a drying board with the soles of all the feet down and the tail and nose held close to the board with pins. The skin is now left to dry, away from intense light or insects.

The sex of the animal is determined by examining the carcass. Look for the uterus and ovaries (female) or for the penis and testes (male). These are sometimes difficult to find in immature small mammals.

Remove the head from the carcass and boil it, for only a minute or two for a mouse-sized mammal, in water to which a little hydrogen peroxide has been added in order to bleach the skull. After it is boiled, pull the lower

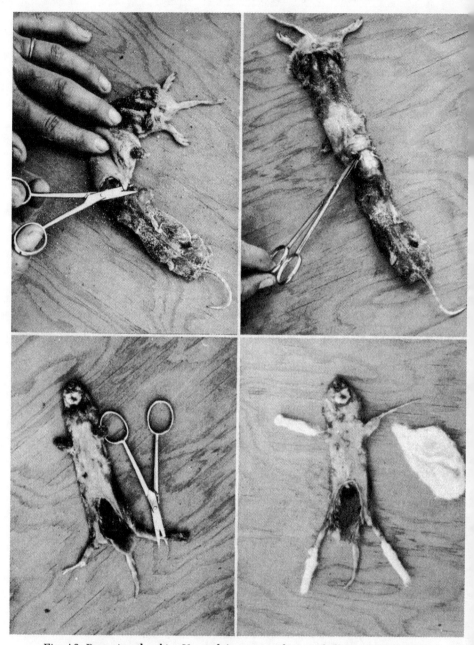

Fig. A3. Preparing the skin. *Upper left:* cut ear close to skull. *Upper right:* cut eyelids close to skull. *Lower left:* cut tendons in heel to remove muscle from bone. The muscle has been removed from the hind leg on the left side of this picture. *Lower right:* wire leg bones and wrap with absorbent cotton. Upper right leg is wired but not wrapped.

jaw straight down, breaking the muscles, until it is free from the skull. Pick the flesh carefully off the skull and the lower jaw; then wash the brain out through the *foramen magnum* (the large opening at the base of the skull). The brain is easily removed by alternately stirring it with a tooth-pick or leaf stem, then by shaking the skull back and forth rapidly under running water. A more effective way to clean skulls is to use dermestid beetles, found under desiccated carcasses lying beside the road. Placed in a tight can or box containing the skull, they clean off the dried flesh, leav-ing even the most delicate bones intact. These beetles should never be kept near the stored skins.

After the skin and the skull have been prepared, the final step is making the tag label. The skulls of most small mammals can be preserved by plac-ing them in small glass vials with cotton at top and bottom. The skull should be numbered with India ink and the same number placed on the tag, which is attached to the right hind leg of the skin. The symbol indicating the sex should also be placed on the skull and on the tag: male ♂ and female ♀. Other items that must go on the tag are *locality, measurements, date,* and the *collector's name.* The scientific name, if it is known, should also be in-cluded. Other items—life zone, altitude, habitat, and number of embryos—are sometimes included if the collector thinks them significant.

The finished specimen skin and skull may then be stored for future ref-erence in a dark insect-proof box. Although the skins are treated to prevent the dermestid beetles and moths from attacking them, the case in which they are kept should be fumigated every few months with carbon bisul-phide or other fumigant that will *kill* insects.

Specimens that are carefully prepared and cared for will keep for years and possibly for centuries. Every well-kept collection, no matter how small, may prove to contain valuable scientific data.

After the skinning and mounting have been completed, the collector should thoroughly wash his hands if arsenic was used. If considerable skin-ning is to be done, it is well to use a 5 per cent iron-dialyzed Merck liquid to prevent the skin from cracking under the fingernails and becoming in-fected.

Do not expect the first skin to look professional. As with most techniques, only practice makes perfect. Three well-made study skins, properly labeled, are shown in fig. A5.

Preparing skins of fur-bearing mammals for the market involves differ-ent techniques, depending on the kind of mammal. Most skins prepared for the market fall into two types: *cased skinning,* used for muskrat, mink, skunk, otter, fox, coyote, and sometimes raccoon; and *open skinning,* used for raccoon, bobcat, beaver, and bear (fig. A6).

In *cased skinning* the incisions are made along the inside of each hind leg from the toe to the anus and from the anus along the underside to the tip of the tail. The skin is removed, as already described. Next, it is pulled over a drying board with the flesh side out and tacked. It is then allowed to dry in a cool place. Modifications of this technique are made for various mammals. The tail of a muskrat, for example, is never skinned but is cut off. The toes of a skunk are left on the carcass, but the toes of a mink, marten, or silver fox are left on the pelt.

In *open skinning* the incisions are made from the tip of the chin along the belly to the tip of the tail, then along the inside of the legs from wrist

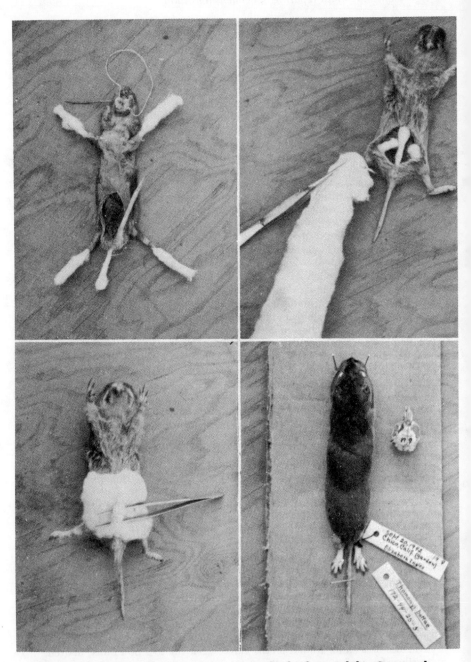

Fig. A4. Stuffing the skin. *Upper left:* insert artificial tail into tail skin. Sew mouth shut. *Upper right:* turn skin right side out, ready for cotton body. *Lower left:* insert free end of tail wire into the split cotton body. *Lower right:* pin out completed skin to dry. Clean and number skull. Add identifying tag (unattached tag merely shows information on opposite side).

to wrist and ankle to ankle. After the skin is removed, it is slightly stretched and tacked on a flat surface to dry. Beaver skins are stretched on a round hoop.

Fur-bearing mammals should never be trapped or killed for their pelts until they are fully *prime*. Prime furs, those in which the new fur hairs have become fully grown, have the highest value. When the new fur hairs start, they are deep in the skin and highly pigmented. As they develop, they move to the outer edge of the skin and become more erect, and the pigment leaves the root, migrating out the medulla of the hair toward its tip (fig. A7). The flesh side of a prime skin is clear; that of an unprime skin is dark or bluish because the undeveloped fur hairs are still highly pigmented. On a prime skin the fur stands up, but on an unprime skin the fur is flat. Most mammals of the Pacific States are fully prime only during the winter months.

Many accounts of rodent and lagomorph species call attention to the fact that individuals may be carriers of plague, tularemia, and relapsing fever.

Tularemia has been isolated from the following rodents and lagomorphs:
  Beechey ground squirrel (*Otospermophilus beecheyi*)
  California meadow mouse (*Microtus californicus*)
  deer mouse (*Peromyscus maniculatas*)
  dusky-footed wood rat (*Neotoma fuscipes*)
  Norway rat (*Rattus norvegicus*)
  black-tailed hare (*Lepus californicus*)

Relapsing fever has at present been isolated only from:
  chipmunk (*Eutamias*, species not known)
  Douglas squirrel (*Tamiasciurus douglasii*)

Plague has been found in the following rodents and lagomorphs:
  Beechey ground squirrel (*Otospermophilus beecheyi*)
  Belding ground squirrel (*Citellus beldingi*)
  Townsend ground squirrel (*Citellus townsendii*)
  Sierra Nevada golden-mantled ground squirrel (*Callospermophilus lateralis*
  rock squirrel (*Otospermophilus variegatus*)
  chipmunk (*Eutamias*, species not known)
  Douglas squirrel (*Tamiasciurus douglasii*)
  northern flying squirrel (*Glaucomys sabrinus*)
  yellow-bellied marmot (*Marmota flaviventris*)
  bushy-tailed wood rat (*Neotoma cinerea*)
  dusky-footed wood rat (*Neotoma fuscipes*)
  desert wood rat (*Neotoma lepida*)
  pinyon mouse (*Peromyscus truei*)
  California meadow mouse (*Microtus californicus*)
  northern grasshopper mouse (*Onychomys leucogaster*)
  Botta pocket gopher (*Thomomys bottae*)
  Ord kangaroo rat (*Dipodomys ordii*)
  Nuttall cottontail (*Sylvilagus nuttallii*)
  cottontail (*Sylvilagus*, species not known)
  black-tailed hare (*Lepus californicus*)

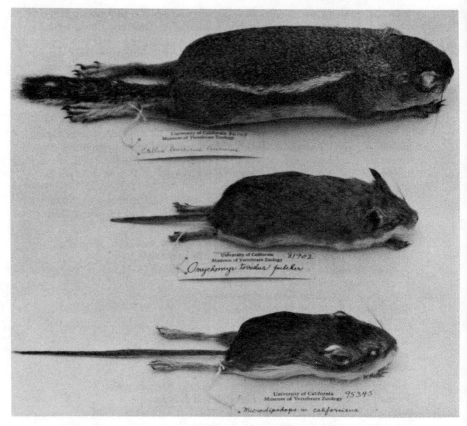

Fig. A5. Three well-made specimen skins. *Top:* antelope ground squirrel (*Citellus leucurus*). *Center:* southern grasshopper mouse (*Onychomys torridus*). *Bottom:* dark kangaroo mouse (*Microdipodops megacephalus*).

Dr. Robert Holdenried, U.S. Public Health Service, has provided the names of mammals known to harbor these diseases in the western United States and has made suggestions for handling and skinning them.

In collecting dead or live rodents and lagomorphs from traps, use gloves or forceps to place them in a paper sack, and fold it tightly at the top. Place the sack in a tight container with enough chloroform or formalin to kill the fleas and other ectoparasites. When skinning, *use rubber gloves,* which, before removing, should be dipped in a warm solution of Lysol or formalin (3 or 4 per cent). Sterilize all instruments used in skinning. *Never handle a dead or sick rodent*—it may have died or be dying of the plague. Many diseases are transmitted to man by bites. These should be carefully cleansed with a warm antiseptic solution and painted with iodine. It must be remembered that, although a rodent may appear to be quite healthy, the fleas on its body and its body fluids may be capable of infecting man.

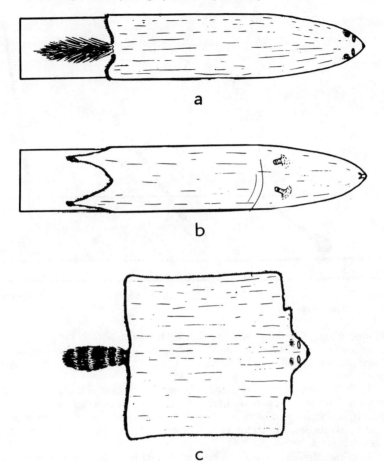

a

b

c

Fig. A6. Two methods of skinning and stretching. (a,b) Mink (one-fifth actual size), dorsal and ventral views of cased method. (c) Raccoon (one-tenth actual size), open method.

TECHNIQUE FOR PREPARING AND PRESERVING
BACULA

The skin and the skull are most useful in the study of mammals, but the *baculum* or penial bone (*os penis*) is becoming increasingly important. A method of collecting and preserving these bones is herewith described.

The baculum in small mammals may be removed by first grasping the end of the penis with tweezers and extending it out of the terminal skin. The proximal limits of the bone can be easily ascertained with the point of a pair of scissors, and the penis removed with the bone intact by cutting

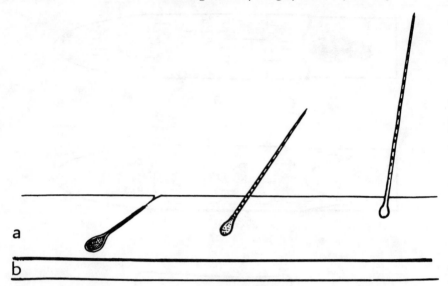

Fig. A7. Diagram of skin showing development of a fur hair. (a) Skin layers. (b) Muscle layers.

behind it. The baculum with its adhering tissues may then be wrapped in a piece of paper with pertinent information such as locality, date, measurements of the animal, and breeding condition. In larger animals, the baculum may be removed as the animal is skinned.

In the laboratory, the baculum is placed in a solution of 2 per cent potassium hydroxide for a period of two hours to two days to soften the adhering tissues. Care must be taken, especially with rice rats, voles, cotton rats, and muskrats, lest the baculum remain too long in the solution and cartilage processes dissolve.

Adhering tissues are ready to be removed with scalpel and forceps when the *glans penis* is transparent and soft. Extreme care must be taken at this step, since many bacula are delicate and fragile. Measurements of the baculum may be taken at this time with calipers or micrometer. These would include total length, dorsal-ventral and lateral widths of base, and dorsal-ventral and lateral widths of shaft midway between ends.

Individual bacula can be dried and stored in vials with labels. They can also be stored as a wet mount, stained or unstained, in glycerin, or they can be imbedded with labels showing data in individual blocks of casting plastic. Staining can be done in Haines solution (2,000 cc. of 2 per cent potassium hydroxide to .1 gram of Alizarin Red S).

B. Scats

Another kind of information which the serious student of mammals will find very useful is concerned with scats or fecal droppings. Because most mammals are timid or are nocturnal in their behavior, their presence is often determined by scats, tracks, or other signs, which a naturalist learns to recognize and to look for in likely places.

The scats shown here were drawn by Mrs. Mary V. Hood, a naturalist living in Los Angeles, California, who has made a specialty of this feature. By comparing samples found in the field with the drawings, the student should have little difficulty in identifying the scats of most of the genera (but not always the species) of common mammals.

Of course, only a few representative samples are shown. Under natural conditions, scats show considerable variation. If the scats to be identified resemble most closely the deer mouse drawing, the student may reasonably call them the scats of *Peromyscus*, but not *Peromyscus maniculatus*, especially if other species also occur in the same range. On the other hand, if the scats resemble those of a black bear, porcupine, or pika, the student can be quite sure about the proper species, since there is only one species of these genera in the Pacific States.

In identifying scats, careful consideration should be given to the place found. One would not normally expect to find the scats of a mammal far from its natural habitat. Thus, little round pellets found on a rock in the Foothill Woodland could not be expected to be those of a pika because it does not live there, but similar pellets in the Alpine Fell-fields of the high Sierra could fairly safely be identified as such.

When scats can be *positively* identified, they should be kept for future comparison. Perhaps the best way to preserve scats is to dry them thoroughly and place them in small plastic boxes. Moth balls or other dry preservatives may be added to prevent the growth of mildew and other fungi.

Good photographs of scats showing the proper reduction or enlargement in size are very useful. Such photographs should be made of scats of wild animals or of those *only recently captured* in order to avoid photographing abnormal specimens.

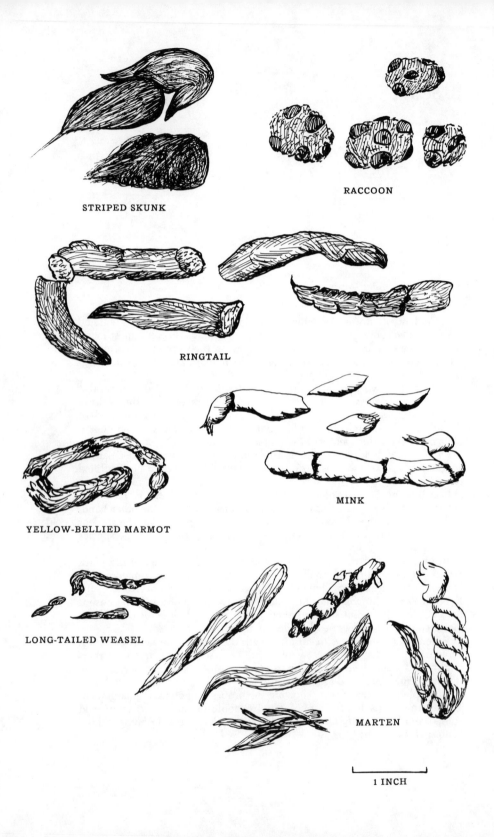

STRIPED SKUNK

RACCOON

RINGTAIL

MINK

YELLOW-BELLIED MARMOT

LONG-TAILED WEASEL

MARTEN

1 INCH

Scats of Smaller Carnivores and Marmot

Striped skunk (*Mephitis mephitis*). Found along weedy ditches or at the edge of alfalfa fields, where the animal searches for insects. The scats often show the hard indigestible parts of insects and the hairs of animals it has eaten.

Raccoon (*Procyon lotor*). Deposited on streamside rocks or logs, in the animal's search for food. The scats may contain fish scales, crayfish (appendages partially digested), manzanita berries, watermelon seeds, and fig seeds.

Ringtail (*Bassariscus astutus*). Found in caves or under rock ledges, especially in chaparral-covered places.

Mink (*Mustela vison*). Found on boulders or logs beside streams or lakes. Sometimes the droppings contain fish scales and feathers of water birds.

Yellow-bellied marmot (*Marmota flaviventris*). Found on large flat rocks used as lookouts. The droppings frequently show indigestible plant fibers.

Long-tailed weasel (*Mustela frenata*). Found on boulders, logs, or near the underground den. The scats usually contain short hairs of small rodents.

Marten (*Martes americana*). The twisted appearance seems characteristic. The scats are light brown to black in color and are found on large rockslides near the den.

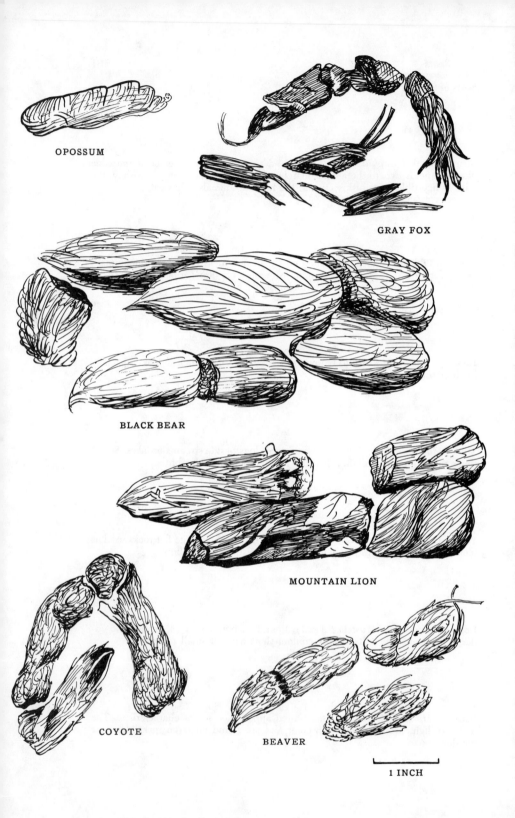

OPOSSUM

GRAY FOX

BLACK BEAR

MOUNTAIN LION

COYOTE

BEAVER

1 INCH

Scats of Opossum, Larger Carnivores, and Beaver

Opossum (*Didelphis marsupialis*). These relatively long, convoluted scats are found near the den, which may be in a hollow log or rock pile.

Gray fox (*Urocyon cinereoargenteus*). Found along trails in chaparral-covered places. Often the scats contain hair and blades of grass.

Black bear (*Euarctos americanus*). In early spring the scats contain considerable grass; later in summer they contain manzanita berry hulls and parts of ants, mice, and other animals. Frequently they consist of undigested parts of only one kind of food.

Mountain lion (*Felis concolor*). These large scats can only be confused with a bear's, but will contain hair and very rarely grass. The lion tends to deposit them at "scrapes" along its runways, where it has scraped the leaves and grass into a little pile over the dung.

Coyote (*Canis latrans*). Sometimes black and shiny, with bits of bone, beetles, ants, and fur. They are very similar to scats of a large dog.

Beaver (*Castor canadensis*). Composed largely of wood and woody fibers, they are found on beaver dams and along well-worn trails.

CANADIAN ELK

PRONGHORN

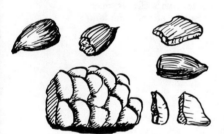

MOUNTAIN SHEEP

DOMESTIC SHEEP

1 INCH

MULE DEER

Scats of Hoofed Mammals

Canadian elk (*Cervus canadensis*). Scats of the calf are bullet-shaped; those of the adult are acorn-shaped and are much larger than those of a deer, sheep, or hare.

Pronghorn (*Antilocapra americana*). The pellets are frequently "caked" but occur also as flattened individual pieces. Found among the sagebrush and rabbit brush of northeastern California.

Domestic sheep (*Ovis aries*). The pellets are pointed, and sometimes "caked." They are not as long as those of mountain sheep, but are *probably not distinguishable* from those of mule deer.

Mountain sheep (bighorn) (*Ovis canadensis*). The pellets are long and usually pointed, being much longer than those of deer or domestic sheep.

Mule deer (*Odocoileus hemionus*). The different sizes may represent different ages. The large "caked" droppings are popularly supposed to be those of bucks. Deer feces *can probably not be distinguished* from those of domestic sheep. They are not as long and bullet-shaped as those of mountain sheep.

PIKA

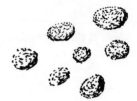

BRUSH RABBIT

WHITE-TAILED HARE

BLACK-TAILED HARE

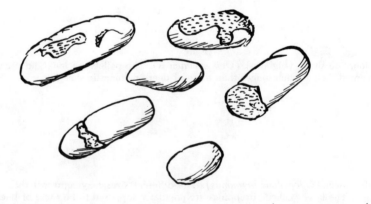

PORCUPINE

1 INCH

Fibrous Pellet-like Scats

Pika (*Ochotona princeps*). The tiny pellets are found in incredible numbers in the high mountains beneath rock talus, where the pika spends the winter.

Brush rabbit (*Sylvilagus bachmani*). Deposited in little piles consisting of several pellets. Occasionally the scats are found singly.

White-tailed hare (*Lepus townsendii*). The large round droppings are common in meadows in the high mountains, such as Tuolumne Meadows in Yosemite National Park. The scats contain much undigested grass, and pellets may be eaten when food is scarce.

Black-tailed hare (*Lepus californicus*). The relatively large pellets contain considerable fibrous material. Pellets may be passed in a partially digested condition and then eaten.

Porcupine (*Erethizon dorsatum*). Scats in winter resemble brown pressed sawdust and in summer are black. They are like deer scats except that both ends are rounded (one end is pointed in deer scats). Found in large numbers beneath branches of large coniferous trees.

CALIFORNIA
LEAF-NOSED BAT

MOUNTAIN
POCKET GOPHER

MONTANE MEADOW MOUSE

PALLID BAT

HEATHER VOLE

ANTELOPE GROUND SQUIRREL

DEER MOUSE

LODGEPOLE CHIPMUNK

BUSHY-TAILED WOOD RAT

DUSKY-FOOTED WOOD RAT

SIERRA NEVADA GOLDEN-MANTLED
GROUND SQUIRREL

1 INCH

BELDING GROUND SQUIRREL

Scats of Small Mammals

California leaf-nosed bat (*Macrotus californicus*). Obtained from a captured specimen. Scats would presumably be found beneath roost.

Mountain pocket gopher (*Thomomys monticola*). Seldom seen above ground, except where the nest is in the snow, in which case hundreds of pellets may be scattered over a few square feet. Scats of other species may be slightly larger.

Montane meadow mouse (*Microtus montanus*). Most frequently found along runways cut through the grass. The dung, similar for all species, is sometimes dark green.

Pallid bat (*Antrozous pallidus*). Found under roosts in old buildings and caves.

Heather vole (*Phenacomys intermedius*). The tiny scats are found in piles a few inches from the winter nests. They resemble porcupine scats except for size.

Antelope ground squirrel (*Ammospermophilus leucurus*). Most commonly seen near its burrow in the desert.

Deer mouse (*Peromyscus maniculatus*). The small oblong pellets, sometimes with two or three attached, are found in mountain cabins and near the dens of this most ubiquitous of all wild mice.

Lodgepole chipmunk (*Eutamias speciosus*). The pellets, often twisted like the marten's, are found about feeding areas or along runways on top of fallen logs.

Bushy-tailed wood rat (*Neotoma cinerea*). Found in stables, woodsheds, and under rock ledges in the higher mountains.

Dusky-footed wood rat (*Neotoma fuscipes*). The dung, found in great quantities in the large nests, is excellent garden fertilizer and is gathered and sold commercially. The scats doubtless resemble those of other wood rats.

Sierra Nevada golden-mantled ground squirrel (*Callospermophilus lateralis*). The droppings are frequently found on logs, rocks, and other lookouts in the Yellow Pine, Red Fir, and Lodgepole forests.

Belding ground squirrel (*Citellus beldingi*). Found on or near the mounds used as lookouts.

C. Pronunciation of Some Mammalian Genera

Following is a list of generic names that are frequently mispronounced. The pronunciation of these names as given in *Webster's New International Dictionary*, Second Edition, follows. In the Third Edition the pronunciation is the same.

āle, ădd, ăccount, ärm, àsk, ēve, ĕvent, ĕnd, silĕnt, makēr, īce, ĭll, charĭty, ōld, ôbey, ôrb, ŏdd, cŏnnect, cūbe, ûnite, ŭp, menü.

Antilocapra	ăn'tĭ·lô·kā'prà
Aplodontia	ăp'lô·dŏn'shĭ·à
Castor	kàs'tēr
Didelphis	dĭ·dĕl'fĭs
Dipodomys	dĭ·pŏd'ô·mĭs
Erethizon	ĕr'ê·thī'zŏn
Mephitis	mê·fī'tĭs
Microdipodops	mī'krô·dĭp'ô·dŏps
Mustela	mŭs·tē'là
Neotoma	nê·ŏt'ô·mà
Odocoileus	ō'dô·koi'lê·üs
Onychomys	ŏn'ĭ·kō'mĭs
Phenacomys	fê·năk'ô·mĭs
Procyon	prō'sĭ·ŏn
Reithrodontomys	rīth'rô·dŏnt'ô·mĭs
Sciurus	sī·û'rŭs
Spilogale	spī·lŏg'à·lē
Sylvilagus	sĭl·vĭ·lā'gŭs
Taxidea	tăks·ĭd'ê·à
Thomomys	thō'mô·mĭs
Urocyon	û·rŏs'ĭ·ŏn

D. Principles of Zoological Classification

All of the materials of science, and indeed the progress of civilization, have been constructed on some sort of orderly arrangement of subjects. We cannot properly write or speak about objects until they have been named and the names have been generally accepted, nor can we learn much about animals until we know their names and something about their evolutionary affinities to one another. The naming and arranging of animals to show their position in relation to each other is the job of the taxonomist. This is the work that must be done *first* in natural science, and it is primary knowledge a student must acquire if he is to progress in science. Anyone wishing to be a zoologist must learn to speak the language. One of the fundamental goals of modern biological research is concerned with the origin of species. Formerly the data bearing on this problem were largely structural or anatomical in nature, but today we find geneticists, ecologists, physiologists, mathematicians, and a host of experimental biologists contributing to the problem of how species arise, and hence indirectly to the orderly arrangement or classification of the species.

Thus, as more and more data are acquired, particularly about the morphology of an animal and perhaps in the future also about its physiology, ecology, and embryology, it may become necessary to revise its former systematic position. Some species might be split to form two or more species, or two or more species might be shown to be one and the same. Taxonomy, then, is not just a system of sorting and labeling specimens but also of keeping them properly arranged and named in the light of the most recent investigations. Chaos would soon result if this naming and arranging were done without strict adherence to some sort of rules.

In the case of animals the International Rules for Zoological Nomenclature is the accepted basis. These rules include the famous Law of Priority, which in essence says: *the valid name of a genus or species can only be that name under which it was first designated.* Such a system was first employed by Linnaeus in 1758. The tenth edition of *Systema Naturae* of the Swedish naturalist was the first to use the binomial system of naming species and hence is considered the starting point for the names of animals.

Thus, every species of animal is given a *scientific name* of two words, a generic Latin name spelled with a capital, and another Latin named spelled without a capital. Examples: *Homo sapiens* (man), *Procyon lotor* (raccoon), *Rattus norvegicus* (Norway rat). Subspecies or geographic races are trinomial, of which the first two apply to the species, and the last to the particular race, thus: *Thomomys bottae mewa* (digger pine Botta pocket gopher.

The theoretical obligatory hierarchy used in zoological classification follows: Phylum, Class, Order, Family, Genus, Species.

These groups may have many other "super," "infra," or "sub" groups intercollated among them to make a more complete and meaningful system. None of the groups can be absolutely defined, but the species, which theoretically is the basic unit, is most nearly definable in practice.

While no definition of a species has been made that will hold in all cases, the best one among higher vertebrates seems to be the concept of a "biological or genetic species." In it the general idea is that *a species is a group of interbreeding animals in nature with hereditary characteristics that can be passed on by highly fertile parents to successive generations.* In practice the genetic species cannot ordinarily be used because of the difficulty of getting breeding data. However, in the nature of the variations and their distinctions from other known populations, the morphologically based species are known to parallel closely those of the known genetic species and hence *are the ones* used in naming and classifying animals.

Thus, in practice, when the morphological or structural characteristics of one group *intergrade* with those of another, the two are considered subspecies or geographic races of the same species. Geographic races or subspecies are *allopatric,* or occupy different areas, whereas different species may be allopatric but may also occupy the same area at the same time and be *sympatric.* Different species do not normally interbreed to produce fertile offspring, whereas different subspecies do. Hence, two interbreeding subspecies are not likely to be found in the same home area, since the two would soon become one. Different species occupy different niches, but they may also satisfactorily occupy the same habitat at the same time.

The modern systematist is concerned with learning more about relationships and variations within populations. To accomplish these ends, he is now employing electrophoretic and serological methods and behavioral studies. Populations are being studied mathematically. His field work is today concerned also with behavior and adaptation.

E. Classification and Check List of Native and Introduced Species of Recent Mammals of the Pacific States

Class MAMMALIA, Subclass THERIA, Infraclass METATHERIA

Order MARSUPIALIA

Family **Didelphidae**—opossums
  Genus **Didelphis**
    D. marsupialis Linnaeus—common opossum

Class MAMMALIA, Subclass THERIA, Infraclass EUTHERIA

Order INSECTIVORA

Family **Soricidae**—shrews
  Genus **Sorex**
    S. cinereus Kerr—masked shrew
    S. lyelli Merriam—Mount Lyell shrew
    S. preblei Jackson—Malheur shrew
    S. merriami Dobson—Merriam shrew
    S. trowbridgii Baird—Trowbridge shrew
    S. vagrans Baird—vagrant shrew
    S. obscurus Merriam—dusky shrew
    S. pacificus Coues—Pacific shrew
    S. ornatus Merriam—ornate shrew
    S. willetti von Bloeker—Santa Catalina shrew
    S. trigonirostris Jackson—Ashland shrew
    S. sinuosus Grinnell—Suisun shrew

In general, this classification is arranged according to Miller and Kellogg (1955), modified where new species have been described or where populations previously considered species have been regrouped or given new names. Walker (1964) is being followed for certain ground squirrels and Cetacea and spelling of the group names above the species level. The vernacular names are those of widest use in the area, except for the Leporidae, which were suggested by Dr. J. Harold Sevaraid of Sacramento State College.

Genus **Sorex** (*Continued*)
   S. *tenellus* Merriam—Inyo shrew
   S. *palustris* Richardson—water shrew
   S. *bendirii* (Merriam)—marsh shrew

Genus **Microsorex**
   M. *hoyi* (Baird)—pigmy shrew
Genus **Notiosorex**
   N. *crawfordi* (Coues)—gray shrew

Family **Talpidae**—moles and shrew-moles
Genus **Neurotrichus**
   N. *gibbsii* (Baird)—shrew-mole
Genus **Scapanus**
   S. *townsendii* (Bachman)—Townsend mole
   S. *orarius* True—coast mole
   S. *latimanus* (Bachman)—broad-handed mole

Order **CHIROPTERA**

Family **Phyllostomatidae**—leaf-nosed bats
Genus **Macrotus**
   M. *californicus* Baird—California leaf-nosed bat
Genus **Choeronycteris**
   C. *mexicana* Tschudi—long-tongued bat

Family **Vespertilionidae**—evening bats
Genus **Myotis**
   M. *lucifugus* (LeConte)—little brown myotis
   M. *yumanensis* (H. Allen)—Yuma myotis
   M. *velifer* (J. A. Allen)—cave myotis
   M. *occultus* Hollister—Arizona myotis
   M. *keenii* (Merriam)—Keen myotis
   M. *evotis* (H. Allen)—long-eared myotis
   M. *thysanodes* Miller—fringed myotis
   M. *volans* (H. Allen)—hairy-winged myotis
   M. *californicus* (Audubon and Bachman)—California myotis
   M. *subulatus* (Say)—small-footed myotis
Genus **Lasionycteris**
   L. *noctivagans* (LeConte)—silvery-haired bat
Genus **Pipistrellus**
   P. *hesperus* (H. Allen)—western pipistrelle
Genus **Eptesicus**
   E. *fuscus* (Palisot de Beauvois)—big brown bat
Genus **Lasiurus**
   L. *borealis* (Müller)—red bat
   L. *cinereus* (Palisot de Beauvois)—hoary bat
   L. *ega* Gervais—western yellow bat

Genus **Euderma**
    E. maculata (J. A. Allen)—spotted bat
Genus **Plecotus**
    P. townsendii Cooper—lump-nosed bat
Genus **Antrozous**
    A. pallidus (LeConte)—pallid bat

Family **Molossidae**—free-tailed bats
Genus **Tadarida**
    T. brasiliensis (I. Geoffroy–Saint-Hilaire)—Brazilian free-tailed bat
    T. femorosacca (Merriam)—pocketed free-tailed bat
    T. molossa (Pallas)—big free-tailed bat
Genus **Eumops**
    E. perotis (Schinz)—western mastiff bat

Order **LAGOMORPHA**

Family **Ochotonidae**—pikas
Genus **Ochotona**
    O. princeps (Richardson)—pika

Family **Leporidae**—hares and rabbits
Genus **Lepus**
    L. townsendii Bachman—white-tailed hare
    L. americanus Erxleben—snowshoe hare
    L. californicus Gray—black-tailed hare
Genus **Oryctolagus**
    O. cuniculus (Linnaeus)—domestic rabbit
Genus **Sylvilagus**
    S. floridanus (J. A. Allen)—eastern cottontail
    S. nuttallii (Bachman)—Nuttall cottontail
    S. audubonii (Baird)—Audubon cottontail
    S. bachmani (Waterhouse)—brush rabbit
    S. idahoensis (Merriam)—pigmy rabbit

Order **RODENTIA,** Suborder **SCIUROMORPHA**

Family **Aplodontiidae**—mountain beavers
Genus **Aplodontia**
    A. rufa (Rafinesque)—mountain beaver

Family **Sciuridae,** Subfamily **Sciurinae**—squirrels
Genus **Marmota**
    M. monax (Linnaeus)—woodchuck
    M. flaviventris (Audubon and Bachman)—yellow-bellied marmot
    M. caligata (Eschscholtz)—hoary marmot
    M. olympus (Merriam)—olympic marmot

Genus **Citellus**
C. *townsendii* (Bachman)—Townsend ground squirrel
C. *washingtoni* A. H. Howell—Washington ground squirrel
C. *richardsonii* (Sabine)—Richardson ground squirrel
C. *beldingi* (Merriam)—Belding ground squirrel
C. *columbianus* (Ord)—Columbian ground squirrel
C. *mohavensis* (Merriam)—Mohave ground squirrel
C. *tereticaudus* (Baird)—round-tailed ground squirrel

Genus **Otospermophilus**
O. *variegatus* (Erxleben)—rock squirrel
O. *beecheyi* (Richardson)—Beechey ground squirrel

Genus **Ammospermophilus**
A. *leucurus* (Merriam)—antelope ground squirrel
A. *nelsoni* (Merriam)—San Joaquin antelope ground squirrel

Genus **Callospermophilus**
C. *lateralis* (Say)—Sierra Nevada golden-mantled ground squirrel
C. *saturatus* (Rhoads)—Cascades golden-mantled ground squirrel

Genus **Eutamias**
E. *alpinus* (Merriam)—alpine chipmunk
E. *minimus* (Bachman)—least chipmunk
E. *amoenus* (J. A. Allen)—yellow pine chipmunk
E. *panamintinus* (Merriam)—Panamint chipmunk
E. *umbrinus* (J. A. Allen)—Uinta chipmunk
E. *speciosus* (Merriam)—lodgepole chipmunk
E. *ruficaudus* A. H. Howell—red-tailed chipmunk
E. *townsendii* (Bachman)—Townsend chipmunk
E. *quadrimaculatus* (Gray)—long-eared chipmunk
E. *sonomae* Grinnell—Sonoma chipmunk
E. *merriami* (J. A. Allen)—Merriam chipmunk

Genus **Sciurus**
S. *carolinensis* Gmelin—eastern gray squirrel
S. *griseus* Ord—western gray squirrel
S. *niger* Linnaeus—fox squirrel

Genus **Tamiasciurus**
T. *hudsonicus* (Erxleben)—red squirrel
T. *douglasii* (Bachman)—Douglas squirrel

Family **Sciuridae**, Subfamily **Pteromyinae**—flying squirrels
Genus **Glaucomys**
G. *sabrinus* (Shaw)—northern flying squirrel

Family **Geomyidae**—pocket gophers
Genus **Thomomys**
T. *bottae* (Eydoux and Gervais)—Botta pocket gopher
T. *talpoides* (Richardson)—northern pocket gopher
T. *townsendii* (Bachman)—Townsend pocket gopher
T. *monticola* J. A. Allen—mountain pocket gopher
T. *mazama* Merriam—Mazama pocket gopher
T. *bulbivorus* (Richardson)—Camas pocket gopher

Family **Heteromyidae,** Subfamily **Perognathinae**—pocket mice
Genus **Perognathus**
P. *longimembris* (Coues)—little pocket mouse
P. *inornatus* Merriam—San Joaquin pocket mouse
P. *parvus* (Peale)—Great Basin pocket mouse
P. *xanthonotus* Grinnell—yellow-eared pocket mouse
P. *alticolus* Rhoads—white-eared pocket mouse
P. *formosus* Merriam—long-tailed pocket mouse
P. *baileyi* Merriam—Bailey pocket mouse
P. *penicillatus* Woodhouse—desert pocket mouse
P. *fallax* Merriam—San Diego pocket mouse
P. *californicus* Merriam—California pocket mouse
P. *spinatus* Merriam—spiny pocket mouse

Family **Heteromyidae,** Subfamily **Dipodomyinae**—kangaroo rats and kangaroo mice
Genus **Dipodomys**
D. *heermanni* LeConte—Heermann kangaroo rat
D. *panamintinus* (Merriam)—Panamint kangaroo rat
D. *stephensi* (Merriam)—Stephens kangaroo rat
D. *ingens* (Merriam)—giant kangaroo rat
D. *merriami* Mearns—Merriam kangaroo rat
D. *nitratoides* Merriam—San Joaquin kangaroo rat
D. *ordii* Woodhouse—Ord kangaroo rat
D. *agilis* Gambel—Pacific kangaroo rat
D. *venustus* (Merriam)—Santa Cruz kangaroo rat
D. *elephantinus* (Grinnell)—big-eared kangaroo rat
D. *microps* (Merriam)—Great Basin kangaroo rat
D. *deserti* Stephens—desert kangaroo rat

Genus **Microdipodops**
M. *megacephalus* Merriam—dark kangaroo mouse
M. *pallidus* Merriam—pallid kangaroo mouse

Family **Castoridae**—beavers
Genus **Castor**
C. *canadensis* Kuhl—beaver

Order **RODENTIA,** Suborder **MYOMORPHA**

Family **Cricetidae,** Subfamily **Cricetinae**—rats and mice
Genus **Reithrodontomys**
R. *megalotis* (Baird)—western harvest mouse
R. *raviventris* Dixon—salt marsh harvest mouse

Genus **Peromyscus**
P. *crinitus* (Merriam)—canyon mouse
P. *californicus* (Gambel)—California mouse

Genus **Peromyscus** (*Continued*)

 P. eremicus (Baird)—cactus mouse
 P. maniculatus (Wagner)—deer mouse
 P. oreas Bangs—forest deer mouse
 P. boylii (Baird)—brush mouse
 P. truei (Shufeldt)—pinyon mouse

Genus **Onychomys**

 O. leucogaster (Wied-Neuwied)—northern grasshopper mouse
 O. torridus (Coues)—southern grasshopper mouse

Genus **Sigmodon**

 S. hispidus Say and Ord—hispid cotton rat

Genus **Neotoma**

 N. albigula Hartley—white-throated wood rat
 N. lepida Thomas—desert wood rat
 N. fuscipes Baird—dusky-footed wood rat
 N. cinerea (Ord)—bushy-tailed wood rat

Family **Cricetidae**, Subfamily **Microtinae**—rats and mice

Genus **Synaptomys**

 S. borealis (Richardson)—northern bog vole

Genus **Clethrionomys**

 C. gapperi (Vigors)—Gapper red-backed mouse
 C. occidentalis (Merriam)—western red-backed mouse

Genus **Phenacomys**

 P. intermedius Merriam—heather vole
 P. albipes Merriam—white-footed vole
 P. longicaudus True—red tree mouse
 P. silvicola A. B. Howell—dusky tree mouse

Genus **Microtus**

 M. oregoni (Bachman)—Oregon meadow mouse or creeping vole
 M. richardsoni (De Kay)—water rat
 M. pennsylvanicus (Ord)—meadow mouse
 M. montanus (Peale)—montane meadow mouse
 M. californicus (Peale)—California meadow mouse
 M. townsendii (Bachman)—Townsend meadow mouse
 M. longicaudus (Merriam)—long-tailed meadow mouse

Genus **Lagurus**

 L. curtatus (Cope)—sagebrush meadow mouse

Genus **Ondatra**

 O. zibethica (Linnaeus)—muskrat

Family **Muridae**—Old World Rats and Mice

Genus **Rattus**

 R. norvegicus (Berkenhout)—Norway rat
 R. rattus (Linnaeus)—black rat

Genus **Mus**

 M. musculus Linnaeus—house mouse

Family **Zapodidae**—jumping mice
Genus **Zapus**
   Z. princeps J. A. Allen—western jumping mouse
   Z. trinotatus Rhoads—Pacific jumping mouse

Order **RODENTIA**, Suborder **HYSTRICOMORPHA**

Family **Erethizontidae**—American porcupines
Genus **Erethizon**
   E. dorsatum (Linnaeus)—porcupine

Family **Capromyidae**—nutria
Genus **Myocastor**
   M. coypu (Molina)—nutria

Order **CETACEA**, Suborder **ODONTOCETI**

Family **Ziphiidae**—beaked whales
Genus **Berardius**
   B. bairdii Stejneger—Baird beaked whale
Genus **Mesoplodon**
   M. stejnegeri True—Stejneger beaked whale
Genus **Ziphius**
   Z. cavirostris G. Cuvier—goose-beaked whale

Family **Physeteridae**—sperm whales
Genus **Physeter**
   P. catodon Linnaeus—sperm whale
Genus **Kogia**
   K. breviceps (Blainville)—pygmy sperm whale

Family **Delphinidae**—toothed whales
Genus **Stenella**
   S. graffmani (Lönnberg)—Graffman dolphin
   S. styx (Gray)—Gray porpoise
Genus **Steno**
   S. bredanensis (Lesson)—rough-toothed porpoise
Genus **Delphinus**
   D. delphis Linnaeus—common dolphin
Genus **Tursiops**
   T. gillii Dall—bottle-nosed dolphin
Genus **Lissodelphis**
   L. borealis (Peale)—northern right whale dolphin
Genus **Lagenorhynchus**
   L. obliquidens Gill—Pacific white-sided dolphin

Genus **Orcinus**
  O. orca (Linnaeus)—killer whale
Genus **Grampus**
  G. griseus (G. Cuvier)—grampus
Genus **Pseudorca**
  P. crassidens (Owen)—false killer whale
Genus **Globicephala**
  G. scammonii Cope—Pacific blackfish
Genus **Phocaena**
  P. phocoena (Linnaeus)—harbor porpoise
Genus **Phocoenoides**
  P. dalli (True)—Dall porpoise

Order **CETACEA**, Suborder **MYSTICETI**

Family **Eschrichtidae**—gray whales
Genus **Eschrichtius**
  E. glaucus (Cope)—gray whale

Family **Balaenopteridae**—fin-backed whales
Genus **Balaenoptera**
  B. physalus (Linnaeus)—fin-backed whale
  B. borealis Lesson—Sei whale
  B. acutorostrata Lacépède—sharp-headed finner whale
Genus **Sibbaldus**
  S. musculus (Linnaeus)—blue whale
Genus **Megaptera**
  M. novaeangliae (Borowski)—hump-backed whale

Family **Balaenidae**—right whales
 °Genus **Eubalaena**
  E. sieboldii (Gray)—right whale

Order **CARNIVORA**, Suborder **FISSIPEDIA**

Family **Canidae**—foxes, wolves, and coyotes
Genus **Canis**
  C. latrans Say—coyote
  C. lupus Linnaeus—wolf
Genus **Vulpes**
  V. fulva (Desmarest)—red fox
  V. macrotis Merriam—kit fox

° *Eubalaena sieboldii, E. glacialis,* and *E. australis* may be a single species (Walker, 1964).

Genus **Urocyon**
    U. cinereoargenteus (Schreber)—gray fox
    U. littoralis (Baird)—island fox

Family **Ursidae**—bears
  *Genus **Euarctos**
    E. americanus Pallas—black bear
  Genus **Ursus**
    U. chelan Merriam—grizzly bear

Family **Procyonidae**—raccoons
  Genus **Bassariscus**
    B. astutus (Lichtenstein)—ringtail
  Genus **Procyon**
    P. lotor (Linnaeus)—raccoon

Family **Mustelidae,** Subfamily **Mustelinae**—weasels, minks, martens, and fishers
  Genus **Martes**
    M. americana (Turton)—marten
    M. pennanti (Erxleben)—fisher
  Genus **Mustela**
    M. erminea Linnaeus—ermine
    M. frenata Lichtenstein—long-tailed weasel
    M. vison Schreber—mink

Family **Mustelidae,** Subfamily **Guloninae**—wolverines
  Genus **Gulo**
    G. luscus (Linnaeus)—wolverine

Family **Mustelidae,** Subfamily **Taxidiinae**—badgers
  Genus **Taxidea**
    T. taxus (Schreber)—badger

Family **Mustelidae,** Subfamily **Mephitinae**—skunks
  Genus **Spilogale**
    S. putorius (Linnaeus)—spotted skunk
  Genus **Mephitis**
    M. mephitis (Schreber)—striped skunk

Family **Mustelidae,** Subfamily **Lutrinae**—otters
  Genus **Lutra**
    L. canadensis (Schreber)—river otter

Family **Mustelidae,** Subfamily **Enhydrinae**—otters
  Genus **Enhydra**
    E. lutris (Linnaeus)—sea otter

---

* Some zoologists place the black bear in the genus *Ursus,* with Euarctos as a subgenus.

Family **Felidae**—cats

  Genus **Felis**
    F. concolor Linnaeus—mountain lion

  Genus **Lynx**
    L. canadensis Kerr—Canadian lynx
    L. rufus (Schreber)—bobcat

Order **CARNIVORA**, Suborder **PINNIPEDIA**

Family **Otariidae**—eared seals and sea lions

  Genus **Callorhinus**
    C. ursinus (Linnaeus)—northern fur seal

  Genus **Arctocephalus**
    °A. townsendi Merriam—southern fur seal

  Genus **Eumetopias**
    E. jubata (Schreber)—Steller sea lion

  Genus **Zalophus**
    Z. californianus (Lesson)—California sea lion

Family **Phocidae**—hair seals or earless seals

  Genus **Phoca**
    P. vitulina Linnaeus—harbor seal

  Genus **Histriophoca**
    H. fasciata (Zimmermann)—ribbon seal

  Genus **Mirounga**
    M. angustirostris (Gill)—northern elephant seal

Order **PERISSODACTYLA**

Family **Equidae**—horses, burros, zebras

  Genus **Equus**
    E. asinus Linnaeus—wild burro

Order **ARTIODACTYLA**, Suborder **SUIFORMES**

Family **Suidae**—pigs

  Genus **Sus**
    S. scrofa Linnaeus—wild boar

° This species is referred to as *Arctocephalus philippii* by Walker (1964).

Order **ARTIODACTYLA**, Suborder **RUMINANTIA**

Family **Cervidae**—elks, moose, caribou, and deer

Genus **Cervus**
    C. canadensis (Erxleben)—Canadian elk
    C. nannodes Merriam—tule elk
Genus **Odocoileus**
    O. hemionus (Rafinesque)—mule deer
    O. virginianus (Zimmermann)—white-tailed deer
Genus **Alces**
    A. alces (Linnaeus)—moose
Genus **Rangifer**
    R. tarandus (Linnaeus)—American woodland caribou

Family **Antilocapridae**—pronghorns

Genus **Antilocapra**
    A. americana (Ord)—pronghorn

Family **Bovidae,** Subfamily **Bovinae**—cattle

Genus **Bison**
    B. bison (Linnaeus)—bison

Family **Bovidae,** Subfamily **Caprinae**—sheep and goats

Genus **Oreamnos**
    O. americanus (Blainville)—mountain goat
Genus **Capra**
    C. hircus Linnaeus—goat
Genus **Ammotragus**
    A. lervia (Pallas)—Barbary sheep or aoudad
Genus **Ovis**
    O. canadensis Shaw—mountain sheep or bighorn

F. Dental Formulas of Genera

(except Order Cetacea)

Order MARSUPIALIA

Didelphis (common opossum),
5-1-3-4/4-1-3-4

Order INSECTIVORA

Sorex (shrew),
3-1-3-3/1-1-1-3
Microsorex (pigmy shrew),
3-1-3-3/1-1-1-3
Notiosorex (gray shrew),
3-1-1-3/2-0-1-3
Neurotrichus (shrew-mole),
3-1-2-3/3-1-2-3
Scapanus (mole),
3-1-4-3/3-1-4-3

Order CHIROPTERA

Macrotus (leaf-nosed bat),
2-1-2-3/2-1-3-3
Choeronycteris (long-tongued bat),
2-1-2-3/0-1-3-3
Myotis (myotis),
2-1-3-3/3-1-3-3
Lasionycteris (silvery-haired bat),
2-1-2-3/3-1-3-3
Pipistrellus (pipistrelle),
2-1-2-3/3-1-2-3
Eptesicus (brown bat),
2-1-1-3/3-1-2-3
Lasiurus (red, hoary, and yellow bats),
1-1-2-3/3-1-2-3
or 1-1-1-3/3-1-2-3
Euderma (spotted bat),
2-1-2-3/3-1-2-3
Plecotus (lump-nosed bat),
2-1-2-3/3-1-3-3

Antrozous (pallid bat),
1-1-1-3/2-1-2-3
Tadarida (free-tailed bats),
1-1-2-3/2-1-2-3
or 1-1-2-3/3-1-2-3
Eumops (mastiff bat),
1-1-2-3/2-1-2-3

Order LAGOMORPHA

Ochotona (pika),
2-0-3-2/1-0-2-3
or 2-0-2-3/1-0-2-3
Lepus (hare),
2-0-3-3/1-0-2-3
Oryctolagus (domestic rabbit),
2-0-3-3/1-0-2-3
Sylvilagus (cottontails and rabbits).
2-0-3-3/1-0-2-3

Order RODENTIA

Aplodontia (mountain beaver),
1-0-2-3/1-0-1-3
Marmota (woodchuck and marmot),
1-0-2-3/1-0-1-3
Citellus (ground squirrel),
1-0-2-3/1-0-1-3
Otospermophilus (rock squirrel and Beechey ground squirrel),
1-0-2-3/1-0-1-3
Ammospermophilus (antelope ground squirrel),
1-0-2-3/1-0-1-3
Callospermophilus (golden-mantled ground squirrel),
1-0-2-3/1-0-1-3

Eutamias (chipmunk),
1-0-2-3/1-0-1-3
Sciurus (gray squirrel and fox
squirrel),
1-0-2-3/1-0-1-3
or 1-0-1-3/1-0-1-3
Tamiasciurus (red squirrel and
Douglas squirrel),
1-0-2-3/1-0-1-3
or 1-0-1-3/1-0-1-3
Glaucomys (flying squirrel),
1-0-2-3/1-0-1-3
Thomomys (pocket gopher),
1-0-1-3/1-0-1-3
Perognathus (pocket mouse),
1-0-1-3/1-0-1-3
Dipodomys (kangaroo rat),
1-0-1-3/1-0-1-3
Microdipodops (kangaroo mouse),
1-0-1-3/1-0-1-3
Castor (beaver),
1-0-1-3/1-0-1-3
Reithrodontomys (harvest mouse),
1-0-0-3/1-0-0-3
Peromyscus (mouse),
1-0-0-3/1-0-0-3
Onychomys (grasshopper mouse),
1-0-0-3/1-0-0-3
Sigmodon (cotton rat),
1-0-0-3/1-0-0-3
Neotoma (wood rat),
1-0-0-3/1-0-0-3
Synaptomys (bog vole),
1-0-0-3/1-0-0-3
Clethrionomys (red-backed mouse),
1-0-0-3/1-0-0-3
Phenacomys (vole and tree mouse),
1-0-0-3/1-0-0-3
Microtus (meadow mouse),
1-0-0-3/1-0-0-3
Lagurus (sagebrush meadow mouse),
1-0-0-3/1-0-0-3
Ondatra (muskrat),
1-0-0-3/1-0-0-3
Rattus (rat),
1-0-0-3/1-0-0-3
Mus (house mouse),
1-0-0-3/1-0-0-3
Zapus (jumping mouse),
1-0-1-3/1-0-0-3
Erethizon (porcupine),
1-0-1-3/1-0-1-3
Myocastor (nutria),
1-0-1-3/1-0-1-3

Order CARNIVORA

Canis (coyote and wolf),
3-1-4-2/3-1-4-3
Vulpes (red fox and kit fox),
3-1-4-2/3-1-4-3
Urocyon (gray fox and island fox),
3-1-4-2/3-1-4-3
Euarctos (black bear),
3-1-4-2/3-1-4-3
Ursus (grizzly bear),
3-1-4-2/3-1-4-3
Bassariscus (ringtail),
3-1-4-2/3-1-4-2
Procyon (raccoon),
3-1-4-2/3-1-4-2
Martes (marten and fisher),
3-1-4-1/3-1-4-2
Mustela (ermine, weasel, and mink),
3-1-3-1/3-1-3-2
Gulo (wolverine),
3-1-4-1/3-1-4-2
Taxidea (badger),
3-1-3-1/3-1-3-2
Spilogale (spotted skunk),
3-1-3-1/3-1-3-2
Mephitis (striped skunk),
3-1-3-1/3-1-3-2
Lutra (river otter),
3-1-4-1/3-1-3-2
Enhydra (sea otter),
3-1-3-1/2-1-3-2
Felis (mountain lion),
3-1-3-1/3-1-2-1
Lynx (lynx and bobcat),
3-1-2-1/3-1-2-1
Callorhinus (northern fur seal),
3-1-4-2/2-1-4-1
Arctocephalus (southern fur seal),
3-1-4-2/2-1-4-1
Eumetopias (Steller sea lion),
3-1-4-1/2-1-4-1
Zalophus (California sea lion),
3-1-4-1/2-1-4-1
or 3-1-4-2/2-1-4-1
Phoca (harbor seal),
3-1-4-1/2-1-4-1°
Histriophoca (ribbon seal),
3-1-4-1/2-1-4-1°
Mirounga (elephant seal),
2-1-4-1/1-1-4-1°

° Because molars cannot be distinguished
from premolars in adult seals but the number of post-canine teeth is important in identification, these formulas may be written as
3-1-5/2-1-5 and 2-1-5/1-1-5.

Order PERISSODACTYLA

Equus (wild burro),
  3-1-3-3/3-1-3-3

Order ARTIODACTYLA

Sus (wild boar),
  3-1-4-3/3-1-4-3*
Cervus (elk),
  0-1-3-3/3-1-3-3
Odocoileus (deer),
  0-0-3-3/3-1-3-3
Alces (moose),
  0-0-3-3/3-1-3-3

Rangifer (caribou),
  0-0-3-3/3-1-3-3
Antilocapra (pronghorn),
  0-0-3-3/3-1-3-3
Bison (bison),
  0-0-3-3/3-1-3-3
Oreamnos (mountain goat),
  0-0-3-3/3-1-3-3
Capra (goat),
  0-0-3-3/3-1-4-3
Ammotragus (Barbary sheep),
  0-0-3-3/3-1-3-3
Ovis (mountain sheep),
  0-0-3-3/3-1-3-3

* Formula variable.

Selected Bibliography

Anthony, H. E. 1928. Field book of North American mammals. Putnam, New York, 674 pp., 48 plates.

Armstrong, F. H. 1962. Range extension of the Beechey ground squirrel. Murrelet (Seattle) 43(2):28.

Bailey, Vernon. 1936. The mammals and life zones of Oregon. North American Fauna No. 55, 416 pp.

Ball, Melvin. 1963. The feeding of the pallid bat. Ingles collection, Fresno State College, Fresno, Calif.

Banfield, A. W. F. 1961. A revision of the reindeer and caribou genus *Rangifer*. Nat. Mus. Canada Bull. No. 177, Biol. Series No. 66, 137 pp.

Bartholomew, George A. 1952. Reproductive and social behavior of the northern elephant seal. Univ. Calif. Pub. Zool. 47:369–472.

Bartholomew, George A., and Richard A. Boolootian. 1960. Numbers and population structure of the pinnipeds on the California Channel Islands. Jour. Mammal. 41(3):366–75.

Bartholomew, G. A., and T. Cade. 1957. Temperature regulation, hibernation, and aestivation in the little pocket mouse, *Perognathus longimembris*. Jour. Mammal. 38:60–72.

Bartholomew, George A., and Carl L. Hubbs. 1960. Population growth and seasonal movements of the northern elephant seal, *Mirounga angustirostris*. Extrait de Mammalia 24(3):313–24.

Bartholomew, George A., and Jack W. Hudson. 1960. Mammalian hibernation: Aestivation in the Mohave ground squirrel, *Citellus mohavensis*. Bull. Mus. Comp. Zool. 124:193–208.

———. 1961. Desert ground squirrels. Scientific Amer. 205(5):107–16.

Bartholomew, George A., and Richard E. MacMillen. 1961. Oxygen consumption, estivation, and hibernation in the kangaroo mouse, *Microdipodops pallidus*. Physiol. Zool. 34(3):177–83.

Bartholomew, George A., and Ford Wilkie. 1956. Body temperature in the northern fur seal, *Callorhinus ursinus*. Jour. Mammal. 37(3):327–37.

Blair, W. Frank, *et al.* 1957. Vertebrates of the United States. McGraw-Hill, New York, 819 pp.

Boolootian, Richard A. 1961. The distribution of the California sea otter. Calif. Fish and Game 47(3):287–92.

Brant, D. H. 1962. Measures of the movements and population densities of small rodents. Univ. Calif. Pub. Zool. 62:105–84.

Broadbooks, Harold E. 1958. Life history and ecology of the chipmunk, *Eutamias amoenus,* in eastern Washington. Misc. Pub. Mus. Zool. Univ. Mich. No. 103.

———. 1965. Ecology and distribution of the pikas of Washington and Alaska. Amer. Midl. Nat. **73**(2): 299–335.

Burt, William H. 1936. A study of the baculum in the genera *Perognathus* and *Dipodomys.* Jour. Mammal. **17**(2):145–56.

———. 1940. Territorial behavior and populations of some small mammals of southern Michigan. Misc. Pub. Mus. Zool. Univ. Mich. No. 45, 58 pp.

———. 1943. Territoriality and home range concepts applied to mammals. Jour. Mammal. **24**:346–52.

———. 1958. The history and affinities of the recent land mammals of western North America. Zoogeography, AAAS Pub. No. 51, pp. 131–54.

———. 1960. Bacula of North American mammals. Misc. Pub. Mus. Zool. Univ. Mich. No. 113.

Christian, John J. 1961. Phenomena associated with population density. Proc. Nat. Acad Sci. **47**(4):428–49.

Church, Ronald L. 1962. Pulmocutaneous water loss and response to water deprivation in the kangaroo rat, *Dipodomys venustus.* Paper given before the Western Society of Naturalists, San Jose, Calif.

Cockrum, E. Lendell. 1956. Sperm whales stranded on the beaches of the Gulf of California. Jour. Mammal. **37**(2):288.

———. 1962. Introduction to mammalogy. Ronald, New York, 455 pp.

Colbert, Edwin H. 1955. Evolution of the vertebrates. Wiley, New York, 479 pp.

Dalquest, Walter W. 1948. Mammals of Washington. Univ. Kans. Pub. Mus. Nat. Hist. No. 2, 444 pp., 140 figs.

Darlington, P. J., Jr. 1957. Zoogeography: The geographical distribution of animals. Wiley, New York, 675 pp.

Darwin, Charles. 1859. On the origin of species by means of natural selection or, the preservation of favored races in the struggle for life. J. Murray, London, 502 pp.

Dasmann, Raymond F., and William P. Dasmann. 1963. Mule deer in relation to a climatic gradient. Jour. Wildlife Mgmt. **27**(2):196–202.

Dasmann, Raymond F., and Richard D. Tabor. 1956. Behavior of Columbia black-tailed deer with reference to population ecology. Jour. Mammal. **37**(2):143–64.

Dasmann, William P. 1958. Big Game of California. Calif. Dept. of Fish and Game, 55 pp.

Daubenmire, Rexford F. 1952. Forest vegetation of northern Idaho and adjacent Washington, and its bearing on concepts of vegetation classification. Ecol. Monogr. **22**(4): 301–30.

Davis, David E., and Frank B. Golley. 1963. Principles in mammalogy. Reinhold, London, 355 pp.

Dice, Lee R. 1940. Speciation in *Peromyscus.* Amer. Naturalist **74**:289–98.

———. 1947. Effectiveness of selection by owls of deer mice (*Peromyscus maniculatus*) which contrast in color with their background. Contrib. Lab. Vert. Biol. Univ. Mich. No. 34, 20 pp.

Dice, Lee R., and Philip M. Blossom. 1937. Studies of mammalian ecology in southwestern North America with special attention to the colors of desert mammals. Carnegie Inst. Washington Pub. No. 485.

Errington, Paul L. 1963. The phenomenon of predation. Amer. Scientist 51(2):180–92.

Findley, J. S. 1955. Speciation in the wandering shrew. Univ. Kans. Pub. Mus. Nat. Hist. No. 9, 68 pp.

Fisler, George F. 1961. Behavior of salt marsh *Microtus* during winter high tides. Jour. Mammal. 42:261–71.

———. 1962. Homing in the California vole, *Microtus californicus*. Amer. Midl. Nat. 68(2):357–68.

Gilmore, Raymond M. 1956. The California gray whale. Zoonooz (San Diego), February.

———. 1958. The story of the gray whale. Privately printed, San Diego, Calif., 16 pp., 9 illus.

Golley, F. B. 1960. Energy dynamics of a food chain of an old-field community. Ecol. Monogr. 30:187–206.

Goodman, John. 1962. Desert mountain sheep. Ingles collection, Fresno State College, Fresno, California.

Graf, William. 1955. Cottontail rabbit introduction and distribution in western Oregon. Jour. Wildlife Mgmt. 19(2):184–88.

———. 1956. Territorialism in deer. Jour. Mammal. 37(2):165–70.

Griffin, Donald R. 1950. The navigation of bats. Scientific Amer. 183:52–55.

———. 1958. More about bat radar. Scientific Amer. 199:40–44.

———. 1959. Echoes of bats and men. Doubleday, Garden City, N.Y., 156 pp.

Grinnell, Allan, and Donald R. Griffin. 1958. Sensitivity of echolocation in bats. Biol. Bull. 144(1):10–22.

Grinnell, Joseph, *et al.* 1937. Fur-bearing mammals of California. 2 vols. Univ. Calif. Press, Berkeley, 777 pp., 13 plates, 345 figs.

Hall, E. Raymond. 1946. Mammals of Nevada. Univ. Calif. Press, Berkeley, 710 pp.

———. 1951. American weasels. Univ. Kans. Pub. Mus. Nat. Hist. No. 4, 466 pp.

Hall, E. Raymond, and Keith R. Kelson. 1959. The Mammals of North America. 2 vols. Ronald, New York, 1,083 pp.

Hall, E. Raymond, and J. M. Linsdale. 1929. Notes on the life history of the kangaroo mouse (*Microdipodops*). Jour. Mammal. 10:298–305.

Hall, Joseph G. 1960. Willow and aspen in the ecology of beaver on Sagehen Creek, California. Ecology 41(3):484–94.

Hamilton, W. J. 1939. American Mammals—their lives, habits, and economic relations. McGraw-Hill, New York, 434 pp., 92 figs.

Hamilton, William J., III. 1962. Reproductive adaptations of the red tree mouse. Jour. Mammal. 43(4):486–504.

Hansen, Charles Goodman. 1956. An ecological survey of the vertebrate animals on Steen's Mountain. Doctoral dissertation, Oregon State Library, Corvallis.

Hansen, Richard M., and Richard S. Miller. 1959. Observations on plural occupancy of pocket gophers' burrowing systems. Jour. Mammal. 40(4): 577–84.

Harris, Van T. 1952. An experimental study of the habitat selection by prairie and forest races of the deer mouse, *Peromyscus maniculatus.* Contrib. Lab. Vert. Biol. Univ. Mich. No. 56, 53 pp.

Hartmann, Carl G. 1952. Possums. Univ. Texas Press, Austin, 174 pp., many photographs.

Hawbecker, Albert C. 1944. The giant kangaroo rat and sheep forage. Jour. Wildlife Mgmt. **8**:161–65.

———. 1958. Survival and home range in the Nelson antelope ground squirrel. Jour. Mammal. **39**(2):207–15.

Hayne, D. W. 1949. Calculation of size of home range. Jour. Mammal. **30**:1–18.

Hedgpeth, Joel W. 1962. Introduction to seashore life of the San Francisco Bay Region and the coast of northern California. Univ. Calif. Press, Berkeley, 136 pp.

Herschkovitz, Philip. 1961. On the nomenclature of certain whales. Fieldiana Zool. **39**(49):547–65.

Hoffmeister, Donald F., and Woodrow W. Goodpaster. 1962. Life history of the desert shrew, *Notiosorex crawfordi*. Southwestern Nat. **7**(3–4): 236–52.

Hooper, Emmet T. 1952. A systematic review of the harvest mice (genus *Reithrodontomys*) of Latin America. Misc. Pub. Mus. Zool. Univ. Mich. No. 77, 255 pp., 9 plates.

Howard, Walter E., and Henry E. Childs, Jr. 1959. Ecology of pocket gophers with emphasis on *Thomomys bottae mewa*. Hilgardia **29**(7):277–358.

Ingles, Lloyd G. 1941. Natural history of the Audubon cottontail. Jour. Mammal. **22**(3):227–50.

———. 1949a. An improved live trap for pocket gophers. Murrelet (Seattle) **30**(3):55.

———. 1949b. Ground water and snow as factors affecting the seasonal distribution of pocket gophers, *Thomomys monticola*. Jour. Mammal. **30**(4):343–50.

———. 1952. The ecology of the mountain pocket gopher, *Thomomys monticola*. Ecology **33**(1):87–95.

———. 1960a. A quantitative study on the activity of the dusky shrew (*Sorex vagrans obscurus*). Ecology **41**:785–90.

———. 1960b. Tree climbing by mountain beavers. Jour. Mammal. **41**(1): 120–21.

———. 1961a. Home range and habitats of the wandering shrew. Jour. Mammal. **42**(4):455–62.

———. 1961b. Reingestion in the mountain beaver. Jour. Mammal. **42**(3): 411–12.

Jackson, Hartley H. T. 1961. Mammals of Wisconsin. Univ. Wis. Press, Madison, 504 pp.

James, William B., and Ernest S. Booth. 1954. Biology and life history of the sagebrush vole. Walla Walla Coll. Pub. Biol. Sciences No. 4, 21 pp.

Johnson, Donald R. 1963. Effect of habitat changes on the food habits of rodents. Paper given before the Society of Mammalogists, Albuquerque, N.M.

Johnson, Murray. 1963. Personal communication.

Johnson, Murray L., and Burton T. Ostenson. 1959. Comments on the nomenclature of some mammals of the Pacific northwest. Jour. Mammal. 40(4):571–77.

Jones, F. L. 1950. A survey of the Sierra Nevada bighorn. Sierra Club Bull. June, pp. 29–76, 12 figs.

Kellogg, Winthrop. 1962. Dolphins and hearing. Natural History 71(2): 31–38.

Kendeigh, S. C. 1961. Animal ecology. Prentice Hall, New York, 468 pp.

Kenyon, Karl W. 1960. Territorial behavior and homing in the Alaskan fur seal. Extrait de Mammalia 24(3):431–44.

———. 1963. Recovery of a fur bearer. Natural History 72(9):12–21.

Kenyon, Karl W., and Victor B. Scheffer. 1953. The seals, sea lions, and sea otters of the Pacific Coast. Wildlife Leaflet No. 344, U. S. Fish and Wildlife Service, 28 pp.

Krutzsch, Philip H., and A. H. Hughes. 1959. Hematological changes with torpor in the bat. Jour. Mammal. 40(4):547–54.

Leopold, A. Starker. 1959. Wildlife of Mexico. Univ. Calif. Press, Berkeley, 568 pp.

Leopold, A. Starker, Thane Riney, Randall McCain, and Lloyd Tevis, Jr. 1951. The jawbone deer herd. Game Bull. Calif. Dept. Nat. Resources, Dept. Fish and Game, San Francisco, No. 4, 139 pp., 56 figs.

Lidicker, W. Z., Jr., and P. K. Anderson. 1962. Colonization of an island by *Microtus californicus,* analysed on the basis of runway transects. Jour. Animal Ecology 31:503–17.

Lilly, John C. 1961. Man and dolphin. Doubleday, Garden City, N.Y.

Lilly, John C., and Alice Miller. 1961. Vocal exchanges between dolphins. Science 134:1873–76.

Lyman, Charles P. 1963. Hibernation in mammals and birds. Amer. Scientist 51(2):127–38.

McCulloch, C. Y., and J. M. Inglis. 1961. Breeding periods of the Ord kangaroo rat. Jour. Mammal. 42(3):337–44.

Mace, Robert U. 1962. Oregon's big game resources. Wildlife Bull No. 2, Oregon Game Commission, 33 pp.

MacMillen, Richard Edward. 1964a. Water economy and salt balance in the western harvest mouse, *Reithrodontomys megalotis.* Physiol. Zoology 37(1):45–56.

———. 1964b. Population ecology, water relations, and social behavior of a southern California semi-desert rodent fauna. Univ. Calif. Pub. Zool. 71:1–59, 4 plates.

Manville, Richard H. 1959. The Columbian ground squirrel in northwestern Montana. Jour. Mammal. 40(1):26–45.

Merriam, C. Hart. 1918. Review of the grizzly and brown bears of North America. North American Fauna No. 41, 136 pp.

Miller, Gerrit S., and Remington Kellogg. 1955. List of the North American Recent mammals. U. S. Nat. Mus. Pub. No. 205, 954 pp.

Moore, Joseph Curtis, and Eugenia Clark. 1963. Discovery of right whales in the Gulf of Mexico. Science 141:269.

Mossman, Archie S. 1955. Reproduction of the brush rabbit in California. Jour. Wildlife Mgmt. 19(2):177–84.

Munz, Philip A., and David D. Keck. 1949. California plant communities. El Aliso 2:87–105.

———. 1950. California plant communities. El Aliso 2:199–202.

Murie, Adolph. 1961. Some food habits of the marten. Jour. Mammal. 42(4):516–21.

Murray, Keith. 1954. Distribution of small mammals in California. Calif. Dept. Public Health, Bureau of Vector Control, Parts I and II (unpublished).

Nichters, Richard. 1957. The effect of variation in humidity and water intake on activity of *Dipodomys*. Jour. Mammal. 38(4):502–11.

Odum, Eugene P. 1953. Fundamentals of Ecology. Saunders, Philadelphia, 384 pp.

Orr, Robert T. 1950. Rarity of the deep. Pacific Discovery 3(6):13–15.

———. 1954. Natural history of the pallid bat, *Antrozous pallidus* (LeConte). Proc. Calif. Acad. Sci. 4(28):165–246.

———. 1963a. Another record for the Pacific bottlenose dolphin. Jour. Mammal. 44(3):424.

———. 1963b. Interspecific behavior in pinnipeds. Paper given before the Society of Mammalogists, Albuquerque, N.M.

Orr, Robert T., and Thomas C. Poulter. 1964. Northward movement of the California sea otter. Calif. Fish and Game 50(2):122–24.

Pearson, Oliver. 1953. Metabolism of hummingbirds. Scientific Amer. 188(1):69–72.

———. 1959. A traffic survey of *Microtus Reithrodontomys* runways. Jour. Mammal. 40(2):169–80.

———. 1960a. Habits of *Microtus californicus* revealed by automatic photographic recorders. Ecol. Monogr. 30:231–49.

———. 1960b. The oxygen consumption and bioenergetics of harvest mice. Physiol. Zool. 33(2):152–60.

———. 1963. Carnivore-mouse predation. Paper presented before the Society of Mammalogists, Albuquerque, N.M.

Pearson, Oliver P., Mary R. Koford, and Anita K. Pearson. 1952. Reproduction of the lump-nosed bat (*Corynorhinus rafinesqui*) in California. Jour. Mammal. 33(3):273–320.

Pedersen, R., and Jack Stout. 1963. Oregon sea otter sighting. Jour. Mammal. 44(3):415.

Pinter, Aelita J. 1963. Effects of nutrition and photoperiod on reproduction and growth in *Microtus montanus*. Paper given before the Society of Mammalogists, Albuquerque, N.M.

Poulter, Thomas C. 1963a. Sonar signals of the sea lion. Science 139:753–59.

———. 1963b. The sonar of the sea lion. IEEE Trans. Ultrasonic Engineering UE-10(3):109–11.

———. 1964. The use of active sonar by the California sea lion, *Zalophus californianus*. Submitted to Jour. Exper. Biol.

Radford, Keith W., Robert T. Orr, and Carl L. Hubbs. 1965. Reestablishment of the northern elephant seal (*Mirounga angustirostris*) off central California. Proc. Calif. Acad. Sci. (4th series) 31(22):601–12.

Reynolds, Hudson G. 1960. Life history notes on Merriam's kangaroo rat in southern Arizona. Jour. Mammal. 41(1):48–58.

Roest, Aryan. 1962. Marine mammal records from central California. Paper given before the Western Society of Naturalists, San Jose, Calif.

———. 1963. Bears in Coast Ranges. Ingles collection, Fresno State College, Fresno, Calif.

———. 1964. *Physeter* and *Mesoplodon* strandings on the central California coast. Jour. Mammal. **45**(1):129–36.

Rudd, Robert L. 1955. Population variation and hybridization in some California shrews. Systematic Zool. **4**:21–34.

Sanderson, Ivan T. 1955. Living mammals of the world. Hanover House, New York, 303 pp., 190 color photographs, many black-and-white photographs.

Scheffer, Victor B. 1958. Seals, sea lions, and walruses. Stanford Univ. Press, Stanford, Calif., 179 pp.

Schevill, W. E., W. A. Watkins, and C. Ray. 1963. Underwater sounds of pinnipeds. Science **141**:50–53.

Schmidt-Nielsen, Knut, and Bodil Schmidt-Nielsen. 1953. The desert rat. Scientific Amer. **189**(1):73–78.

Science and the citizen. 1964. (A monthly "department.") Scientific Amer. **211**(6):60–64.

Severaid, Joye Harold. 1950. The pigmy rabbit (*Sylvilagus idahoensis*) in Mono County, California. Jour. Mammal. **31**(1):1–4.

Seymour, George. 1960. Furbearers of California. California Dept. Fish and Game, 55 pp.

Shaw, William T. 1924. Alpine life of the heather vole (*Phenacomys olympicus*). Jour. Mammal. **5**(1):12–15, 4 plates.

———. 1925. Duration of the estivation and hibernation of the Columbian ground squirrel. Ecology **6**:75–85.

Sheppe, Walter, Jr. 1961. Systematic and ecological relations of *Peromyscus oreas* and *P. maniculatus*. Proc. Amer. Philosophical Soc. **105**(4):421–46.

Simpson, George Gaylord. 1945. The principles of classification and a classification of mammals. Amer. Mus. Nat. Hist. No. 85, 350 pp.

———. 1953. Evolution and Geography. Condon Lectures, Oregon State System of Higher Education, 64 pp.

Sorenson, M. W. 1962. Some aspects of water shrew behavior. Amer. Midl. Nat. **68**(2):445–62.

Stickel, L. F. 1954. A comparison of certain methods of measuring ranges of small mammals. Jour. Mammal. **35**:1–15.

Storer, Tracy, and Robert L. Usinger. 1963. Sierra Nevada natural history. Univ. Calif. Press, Berkeley, 374 pp., 65 plates.

Sumner, F. B. 1932. Genetic, distributional and evolutionary studies of the subspecies of deer mice (*Peromyscus*). Bibliographia Genetica (The Hague), **9**:1–106.

Sumner, Lowell, and Joseph S. Dixon. 1953. Birds and mammals of the Sierra Nevada. Univ. Calif. Press, Berkeley, 484 pp.

Sutton, Dallas A. 1962. Chromosomes of some Sciuridae. Paper given before the Western Society of Naturalists, San Jose, Calif.

———. 1963. Proposed revision of *Eutamias townsendii* subspecies. Paper given before the Western Society of Naturalists, Stockton, Calif.

Tamsitt, J. R. 1960. The chromosomes of the *Peromyscus truei* group of white-footed mice. Texas Jour. Science 12(3–4):152–57.

Taylor, Mary P. 1963. Morphology of the stomach of the grasshopper mouse. Paper given before the Society of Mammalogists, Albuquerque, N.M.

Troughton, Ellis. 1947. Furred animals of Australia. Scribner, New York, 374 pp., 25 plates.

Van Gelder, Richard George. 1959. Taxonomic revision of the spotted skunks, genus *Spilogale*. Bull. Am. Mus. Nat. Hist. 117(5):229–392.

Walker, Ernest P., Florence Warnick, Kenneth I. Lange, Howard E. Uible, Sybil E. Hamlet, Mary A. Davis, and Patricia F. Wright. 1964. Mammals of the world. 2 vols. Johns Hopkins, Baltimore. 1,500 pp., over 1,800 photographs. Bibliography, vol. 3, 769 pp.

Walker, Kenneth M. 1955. Distribution and taxonomy of the small pocket gophers of northwestern Oregon. Doctoral dissertation, Oregon State Univ., Corvallis.

Welles, Ralph. 1960. Progress report on the Death Valley Burro Survey. Desert Bighorn Council, Fourth Annual Meeting, Las Cruces, N.M.

Wick, William O. 1962. Mole and gopher control. Bull. 804, Coop. Extension Service, Oregon State Univ., Corvallis, 16 pp.

Wilke, F., and K. W. Wilke. 1954. Migration and food of the northern fur seal. Trans. 19th North Amer. Wildlife Conf., pp. 430–40.

Wright, Philip L. 1948. Breeding habits of captive long-tailed weasels (*Mustela frenata*). Amer. Midl. Nat. 39(2):338–44.

Wynn-Edwards, V. C. 1964. Population control in animals. Scientific Amer. 211(2):68–74.

———. 1965. Self-regulatory systems in populations of animals. Science 147(3665):1543–48.

Index

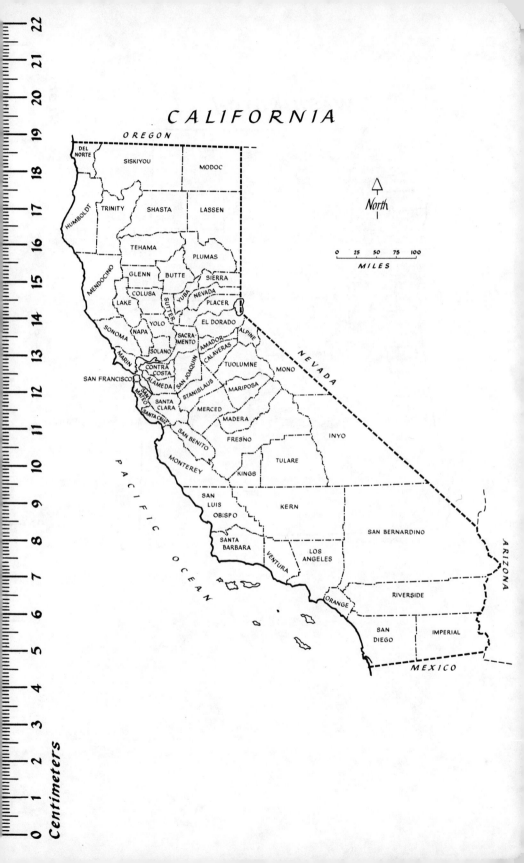

WASHINGTON

CANADA

WHATCOM

SAN
JUAN
ISLAND

SKAGIT

OKANOGAN

FERRY

PEND OREILLE

CLALLAM

SNOHOMISH

CHELAN

STEVENS

JEFFERSON

KITSAP

KING

DOUGLAS

LINCOLN

SPOKANE

IDAHO

GRAYS
HARBOR

MASON

THURS-
TON

PIERCE

KITTITAS

GRANT

ADAMS

WHITMAN

PACIFIC

LEWIS

YAKIMA

FRANKLIN

GAR-
FIELD

WAHKIAKUM

COWLITZ

BENTON

WALLA
WALLA

COLUMBIA

ASOTIN

CLARK

SKAMANIA

KLICKITAT

PACIFIC OCEAN

CLATSOP

COLUMBIA

WASH-
ING-
TON

MULTNOMAH

HOOD
RIV-
ER

SHERMAN

GILLIAM

UMATILLA

WALLOWA

TILLAMOOK

YAMHILL

CLACKAMAS

WASCO

MORROW

UNION

POLK

MARION

JEFFERSON

WHEELER

GRANT

BAKER

LINCOLN

BENTON

LINN

CROOK

LANE

DESCHUTES

COOS

DOUGLAS

LAKE

HARNEY

MALHEUR

CURRY

JOSEPHINE

JACKSON

KLAMATH

CALIFORNIA

NEVADA

OREGON